£10-95

A COUNTRY AT WAR 1939–1945

JENNIFER CRWYS-WILLIAMS

A COUNTRY AT WAR 1939–1945

THE MOOD OF A NATION

ASHANTI PUBLISHING
(PTY) LIMITED
P.O. Box 5091 Rivonia 2128

Published by Ashanti Publishing (Pty) Ltd
PO Box 5091
Rivonia 2128

ISBN 1 874800 49 9

First published 1992

End-paper photograph of our 'Lady in White', Perla Siedle Gibson. She sang the men and women out to war, and she sang them in as they returned.
Photograph of Miss Crwys-Williams by Andy Katz.

Book Design: Photoprints, Cape Town
Typeset by Photoprints
Printed by CTP Book Printers, Cape Town

BK3262

To the members of my immediate family who unhesitatingly volunteered to serve their country when it needed them most. Their motives were the same as those of many other families: patriotism, adventure, humanitarianism. They all came home physically unscathed.

To my grandfather, Major Michael O'Malley (World War I and II); to my grandmother, Nursing Sister Anne Wilson Wallace O'Malley (World War I); my step-grandmother, Captain (and matron) 'Nan' Childe O'Malley (World War II); to my dashing uncle, Lt John O'Malley, SAAF (World War II); to my adored father, Capt Arthur Pearce, SAAF (World War II) and to my brother, Detective Patrol Officer Miles Pearce, BSAP (Rhodesian War)

RECRUITS WANTED
FOR ALL RANKS OF THE
S.A. MEDICAL CORP
APPLY TO YOUR LOCA
RECRUITING OFFICE
MAGISTRATE, OR POLICE STATIO

Contents

1941

Foreword

A COUNTRY AT WAR 1939–1945 is an interesting and original book and I was very pleased to be asked to contribute a brief foreword to it. The number of South Africans who lived through those momentous years is getting rapidly less and certainly those of us who, like me, were more than thirty years old when war broke out are now few indeed. For us it is fascinating to have these events so vividly recalled, while for the great majority of younger South Africans they tell of a world and of a country which is quite outside their experience.

Naturally the books written about the Second World War are innumerable in number and in scope, but I know of no publication which reflects directly as this one does not only the impact on those South Africans involved in the armed forces but also on South Africans at home, of the social and political background against which this great drama was played out.

We entered the war as a deeply divided country. Indeed that South Africa entered the war at all was a close-run thing. Had it not been for the chance that for extraneous procedural reasons, Parliament happened to be in special session during those fateful days, South Africa might well have embarked on a different and, to my mind, quite disastrous course.

South Africa is still, unfortunately, a deeply divided country, but the grounds for division are quite different from what they were during the war years. While even then there were certainly some of us who realised that the most important issue facing the country was the relationship between black and white, the fact is that when in 1939 South Africans talked – as they often did – of 'racialism' they would normally have been referring to the quite different problem of relations between the Afrikaans and English-speaking white South Africans. In those simpler and happier times the term apartheid had not yet been invented and indeed it may well be thought that when, soon after the war, the apartheid policy was initiated, this happened not so much in order to solve the problem of black/white relations but as a step in the long struggle to build up the power of the white Afrikaans-speaking tribe.

This book therefore is not only interesting in giving a clear understanding of how South Africans of all races and colours looked on the part they played in what I believe will prove to be the last of the great wars initiated on account of the quarrels of the nations of Western Europe, then clearly still the centre of the world; it also helps to provide an essential background against which the national development of South Africa, and indeed of all South Africans, must now be judged. The book is therefore not only interesting and arresting, it is also a work of fundamental importance.

H F Oppenheimer
1992

Author's note

I interviewed over eighty people in the process of writing *A Country at War*. I put one question to them all: 'Why did you volunteer?' The answers differed, but in the end they boiled down to one, best summed up by a SAAF navigator: 'I went to war for adventure, brass bands and women.'

They seemed to go together, he said. 'What about patriotism?' I asked, again and again. The men who were in their late twenties and early thirties in 1939 all said patriotism came first. The younger men agreed that patriotism played a part, but only later when they realised exactly what it was they were fighting for.

Men and women alike, part-time SAWAS, fighter pilots, privates, generals, all said that the war years were the best years of their lives. 'There was a sense of purpose,' they said, 'belonging and a camaraderie impossible to find in civilian life.' For many of them, that sense of purpose and belonging dissipated once they were out of uniform and back in the slow slog of everyday life. The years of war were indeed their finest hours.

Why write a book fifty years after the war, when most people who took part in it are at least in their seventies? The answer is easy if you turn the pages of any school history book. The five and a half years of war are dismissed in a couple of pages. Talk to anyone under fifty now and ask them about Tobruk or Sidi Rezegh or the wartime 'fifth column'; ask them about Dan Pienaar or Sailor Malan and Ouma Smuts; ask them about the gallant Warsaw run by the SAAF, or glory bags or Japanese aircraft over Durban or ships torpedoed off the coast and they will look blank.

And yet the war was important in the brief history of South Africa. The foundations of modern industry were laid between 1939 and 1945. The schism between the white peoples of the country perceptibly widened during the years of war; Afrikaner nationalism, which came to a head in 1948, was firmly established by the beginning of 1939. The black squatter movement, the urbanisation of large numbers of blacks and the path towards militancy all took shape during those momentous five-and-a-half years. The South African history of this war has been greatly neglected, obfuscated for political reasons and generally underplayed.

It is not the purpose of this book to fill in all the gaps (the intelligence system within the country is one) but to describe across that broad canvas what it was like to be in South Africa in the war years, to present a general picture of a country at war: the men up north fighting, the Ossewabrandwag, a woman mourning the loss of her husband, a eulogy on Jan Smuts, a South African internee, a radio broadcast by a famous general. Such are the ingredients.

A Country at War makes no attempt to cover every battle, every aspect of the fighting troops, every women's organisation. It is rather the mood and the fabric of the country I hope to convey, the spirit, the energy and an atmosphere long since relegated to the past.

Acknowledgements

Behind every author there is a small army of people who, motivated by friendship, professional ability and generosity of spirit, offer unstinting help in spite of the demands on their own time. I have been astonished at the help I have received and am grateful beyond words.

With the help, the admonitions, the encouragement and the abundance of time which took her weekends and evenings for over a year, the contribution by my secretary, Carol Colley, has been enormous. Without her help it is doubtful whether this book could have met the publisher's deadline.

My thanks to the following are given in no particular order, but I warmly acknowledge their interest and their efforts: Trevor Kobrin, who rephotographed each precious photograph entrusted to my care; Betty de Lange and Barbara Worby of the South African National Museum of Military History; Arlene Fanarof of the South African Library; Carol Leigh of the Strange Library of Africana; Beverley Smith, Director of the Natal Region of the South African Red Cross Society; Cmdt Ossie Baker, formerly of the South African National Museum of Military History, whose help exceeded what was asked of him; Nicole Colley; Natasha Younghusband; Glynis Horning, who is always there when needed, as is Gorry Bowes-Taylor; Francois du Toit of the SABC Sound Archives; Vivian Rees-Bevan; Ethel Price.

Finally, my thanks to the many men and women who helped me with such zeal and patience through long interviews and tedious questioning.

Introduction

Ox-waggons, street battles and the Munich Crisis The beginning of it all, 1938

They came almost as pilgrims, to Cape Town. Thousands of men, women and children, thronging the length of Adderley Street on a winter day in August. Many of the women wore kappies; many of the men, even the young men, were bearded.

The crowd was thickest round two stinkwood ox-waggons; the sturdy oxen that would pull them already inspanned. Photographers milled round the austere figure of the bespectacled Hennig Klopper, founder of the Broederbond, a supposedly cultural organisation, and the man behind this, the culmination of the centenary celebrations of the Great Trek of 1838.

As the waggons slowly pulled away from the statue of Jan van Riebeeck on the Foreshore, hymns mingled with cheers. Following more or less the original route the trekkers had taken out of the Cape colony a hundred years before, through the magnificent desolation of the Karoo, through the sweet and seemingly endless veld of the Orange Free State, the grass tawny under a deep blue late winter's sky, the waggons rolled triumphantly through Johannesburg and towards Pretoria.

There, in the shadow of Monument Koppie, the flags of the old Boer republics flying proudly in the sky, the solemn singing of thousands of people and the muffled rhythmic tread of hundreds of hoofs as commandoes escorted the waggons to their destination, the foundation stone of the Voortrekker Monument was laid on the day sacred to the *volk,* 16 December 1938.

Outwardly it was a magnificent spectacle. But it was much more than a mere centenary pageant. The four-month trek which began in Cape Town on 8 August was a clear signal to anyone who cared to look beneath the rough pageantry that a new and powerful movement in the Union of South Africa had come into being: militant Afrikaner nationalism. It completely overshadowed another birth, that of the still puny though no less militant spirit of black nationalism.

The fusion government, under J B M Hertzog, had ruled the country since 1934. In the formidable hands of Hertzog and his Deputy Prime Minister, Jan Smuts, the country had prospered economically and come through the Great Depression of 1929–1932.

The Union was now off the gold standard, and the national income rose sharply. Gold-mining boomed and, as a consequence of the rise in the standard of living and the substantially increased output of new companies such as ISCOR and AECI, white and black workers flocked to the towns.

Under the fusion government poor whites had prospered, though poor blacks living in rural poverty had not. The 'native' acts of 1936 had effectively ended black representation in the House of Assembly and had furthered the cause of racial segregation.

But the year 1938 was dominated not so much by increasing prosperity or by the ox-waggon trek as it was by events in Europe, the prelude to a war that would sweep old Europe away and divide in great bitterness the white peoples of the Union.

Beneath the ancient symbol of the swastika the Third Reich had risen from the ashes of the Great War. Ruthlessly suppressing dissent and filled with the conviction that the Aryan race was superior to all others, by the time of the Munich Crisis Germany was the most powerfully armed and disciplined country in the world.

The National Socialist (Nazi) Party under its chancellor, Adolf Hitler, swept all before it. Already Austria had fallen under its yoke. Anti-Semitism had been turned into a systematic domestic policy. Few heeded the warning signs.

In September 1938, as the two stinkwood ox-waggons with a column of outriders and reporters increasingly disturbed by the message implicit in the slow progress of the trek north, moved slowly through the Karoo, the rumbling crisis in Europe came to a head.

On New Year's Eve 1937 Hitler blandly assured the world that the armed might of Germany, as a guarantee of peace, would continue to be the keynote of his international policy in 1938. But Goebbels, the Minister of Propaganda, uttered a more overt threat: 'There is no nation in the world that would dare attack us.' He was right.

Less than twenty years before, the shining youth of Europe died in their millions in the mud of France and Flanders. The memory of that horror had yet to fade in the minds of Britain and France. Pursuing a policy of peace at all costs, their appeasement of Hitler's every aggressive move disgusted clear minds and resolute spirits everywhere. 'The West is sick in body and soul, impoverished, desperate, disrupted,' Smuts told the peoples of the Union, 'her peoples milling round in confusion.' The impoverishment of spirit and confusion reached its nadir in September 1938.

Smuts delicately refrained from mentioning that the same confusion and impoverishment of spirit existed within the Union. The general election of 18 May was described as 'the dirtiest election campaign in the history of the country'. It was won by the United Party with 111 seats against the 26 of the National Party and it clearly indicated a distinctly pro-Nazi movement. The Nationalists under the leadership of the dour Dr D F Malan called for a republic (though not in the immediate future) and for an end to the immigration of Jews into the Union (those already there would be treated fairly, said the manifesto). 'The fact that they appear in their manifesto at all must serve as a warning to the electorate that the Nationalists are a disruptive and intolerant party, with strong leanings towards a Nazi-Facist outlook, the enemies of democracy and, as such, must be crushed . . .' wrote Arthur Barlow in the *Daily Express.*

And although *The Times* pronounced that 'South Africa decided for a united nation and sanity as against division and racialism', the future division and racialism of the country was clearly to be perceived in the emotions stirred up by the ox-waggon trek.

Hitler had given a pledge of 'no war' to Britain in May, but with a caveat: it would depend on the Czechs. The new King, George VI, and his Queen, Elizabeth, with a stunning all-white wardrobe, made a state visit to Paris in July. On 1 August a map of the 'impregnable' Maginot Line was published with the headline 'The Maginot Line – A Menace to Peace'.

On 6 August thousands of fans stormed the gates at Ellis Park in Johannesburg to watch the first rugby test between Britain and South Africa. (The South African XV was captained by the pugnacious Danie Craven). But on 17 August Nazi troops moved to the Czechoslovakian border. It was all right, soothed Hitler, the Nazis were merely playing war games. Smuts, recognising the threat to democracy presented by the belligerence of the Third Reich, assured the British that if a war should come, South Africans would fight with her. The Nationalists were outraged. 'Has he forgotten 1914?' asked Tom Visser, a member of the Transvaal committee of the Nationalist Party. 'Has not enough Afrikaner blood been shed for its freedom? Afrikanerdom sal en moet besluit'.*

By 7 September, as the Nazis continued their 'war games' along the Czechoslovakian frontier, two and a half million troops were under arms in Europe as frantic efforts were made to preserve the uneasy peace. The trouble centred on the Sudetenland, within the borders of Czechoslovakia but inhabited mainly by Germans. They were being

* Afrikanerdom must and will decide.

mistreated, claimed Hitler, and no Aryan could be mistreated by anyone, particularly by those whom he regarded as *Untermenschen*.

Oswald Pirow, the South African Minister of Railways and Defence, was openly pro-Hitler (who was, according to Pirow, 'perhaps the greatest man of the last thousand years') and contributed vastly to the national defence by believing the men could effectively be equipped with bows and arrows and he actually issued them with ox-drawn bush waggons (bush barrows), to the mirth of the Active Citizen Force Units. South Africa would go to war, he said, only if it were essential to protect the vital interests of the Union and then only if Parliament were given an unambiguous mandate by the people. 'Disagreement with fascist methods and ideals would not be sufficient excuse for taking up the cudgels on behalf of any democratic state.'

On 10 September European capitals prepared for war in the wake of a defiant speech by Hitler; on 14 September the Royal Navy was mobilised, and Czech troops were rushed to the border. In London the War Council met; on 16 September Dr D F Malan appealed to Afrikaners throughout the Union to stand together to prevent South African participation in a European war; on 17 September an observer commenting on the flying visit of Neville Chamberlain to Hitler's Berchtesgaden eyrie in the Bavarian Alps said: 'War – or shameful temporary peace?' On 22 September Winston Churchill told Africopa, a South African news agency: 'The partition of Czechoslovakia amounts to a complete surrender by the Western Democracies to the Nazi threat of force. The idea that safety could be purchased by throwing a small state to the wolves is a fatal delusion.'

On 24 September violent anti-Nazi riots broke out in central Johannesburg when five men wearing blackshirt uniforms and swastikas collided with a cyclist. 'Down with the Nazis,' shouted the crowd, and they stormed the car. 'Lynch them!' 'Nazi spies!' following the men down to Marshall Square police station. On 29 September Neville Chamberlain flew to Munich in a last attempt to avert war.

The meeting took place between the Führer, the Italian 'Duce' Mussolini, the French Prime Minister, Daladier, and Neville Chamberlain. Hitler played his cards well. By the end of the meeting France and Britain had agreed to the dismemberment of the Czech state on condition that Hitler did not invade the country. Solemnly he agreed. He even signed a piece of paper, the same piece of paper Chamberlain waved triumphantly at the crowd when he flew back to Britain*.

This act of political cynicism was greeted with great relief all over the world. Chamberlain – until the realisation of what he had done sunk in – was hailed as a hero.

---

* Now in an obscure file in the Imperial War Museum, London.

RAND DAILY MAIL, FRIDAY, SEPTEMBER 30, 1938.

SPECIAL EDITION

IT'S PEACE!

AGREEMENT REACHED AND SIGNED 2.30 a.m. TO-DAY

Photo by air mail last night.

BRITISH PRIME MINISTER'S SECOND VISIT TO GERMANY: Herr Hitler is here seen greeting the British Prime Minister, Mr. Neville Chamberlain (back of head shown) on his arrival at the Hotel Dressen, Godesberg, for his second talk with the Fuehrer on the Czechoslovakian question.

AGREEMENT HAS BEEN REACHED AND SIGNED ON THE SUDETEN QUESTION, STATES REUTER

SOUTH AFRICAN PRESS ASSOCIATION—REUTER

Munich, Friday.

GERMAN TROOPS will begin to occupy predominantly German districts of Sudetenland to-morrow October 1. By October 10 German troops will occupy all such areas.

The future of all the plebiscite areas will be decided before the end of November.

All areas where plebiscites are to be held will be controlled by an International Legion, commencing on October 10.

The region to be surrendered is to be handed over without destruction of any property, and the Czech State will be held responsible for any damage.

OTHER MINORITIES

Negotiations regarding the question of the cession of territories claimed by Hungary and Poland are still pending. The settlement of this question would lead also to a solution of the question of an international guarantee for the remainder of Czechoslovakia.

It is learned, says Transocean, that the Western Powers would declare their complete disinterestedness in the Czech question if the Prague Government should reject the plan agreed upon by the four statesmen.

It is furthermore learned that Mr. Chamberlain received the Czech Minister in London, M. Jan Masaryk and the Czech Minister in Berlin, M. Mastny, last evening during the pause before the resumption of negotiations and informed them of the results of the earlier discussions.

SAVED WORLD FROM WAR

MR. NEVILLE CHAMBERLAIN, WHOSE UNTIRING EFFORTS FOR PEACE CAME TO A TRIUMPHANT TERMINATION EARLY TO-DAY.

FULL TEXT OF THE AGREEMENT

SOUTH AFRICAN PRESS ASSOCIATION—REUTER

Munich, Friday.

The Four Power Conference ended this morning, having reached agreement of which the following is the text:—

Germany, the United Kingdom, France and Italy have agreed, taking into consideration the agreement already reached in principle for the cession to Germany of Sudeten Territory, agree on the following terms and conditions governing the said cession, and by this agreement each hold themselves responsible for the steps to secure its fulfilment.

1

Firstly, evacuation will begin on October 1.

2

Secondly, Britain, France and Italy will agree that the evacuation of the territory shall be completed by October 10 without any existing installations having been destroyed and that the Czechoslovak Government will be held responsible for carrying out the evacuation without damage to the said installations.

3

Thirdly, conditions of evacuation will be formulated by an International Commission composed of representatives of Germany, Britain, France and Italy and Czechoslovakia.

4

Fourthly, occupation by stages of predominantly German territory by German troops will begin on October 1. Four territories marked on the attached map to be occupied in sequence. The remaining territory of predominantly German character will be ascertained by the aforesaid International Commission forthwith and will be occupied by German troops by October 10.

5

Fifthly, the international commission will determine the territories in which the plebiscite is to be held, these territories to be occupied by international bodies until the plebiscite is completed. The commission will fix the conditions under which the plebiscite is to be held, taking as a basis the conditions in the Saar plebiscite. The commission will also fix a date, not later than the end of November, on which the plebiscite will be held.

6

Sixthly, the final determination of the frontiers will be carried out by an International Commission. This commission will also be entitled to recommend to Germany, Britain, France and Italy in certain exceptional cases minor modifications in strictly ethnographical zones to be transferred without a plebiscite.

7

Seventhly, there will be the right of option of going into and out of the transferred territories, the option to be exercised within six months from the date of this agreement. A German and Czechoslovak commission shall determine the details of the option, consider ways of facilitating the transfer of population, and settle questions arising from this transfer.

8

Eighthly, the Czechoslovak Government will within a period of four weeks from the date of this agreement release from their military and police forces any Sudeten Germans who may wish to be released and Sudeten prisoners serving terms of imprisonment for political offences.

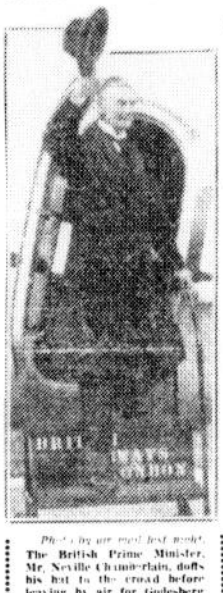

Photo by air mail last night.

The British Prime Minister, Mr. Neville Chamberlain, doffs his hat to the crowd before leaving by air for Godesberg for his second discussion with Herr Hitler on the Czechoslovakian question.

Guarantees

An annexture to the agreement states: The British and French Governments have entered into the above agreement on the basis that they stand by the offer contained in paragraph six of the Anglo-French proposals of September 19, relating to the international guarantee of the new boundaries of the Czechoslovakian State against unprovoked aggression.

When the question of the Polish and Hungarian minorities in Czechoslovakia is settled, Germany and Italy, on their part, will give a guarantee to Czechovakia.

The 2 Other Minorities

The heads of the Governments of the four Powers declare that the problem of the Polish and Hungarian minorities in Czechoslovakia, if not settled within three months by agreement between the respective Governments, shall form the subject of another meeting of the heads of the Governments of the four Powers present.

A supplementary declaration states: All the questions which may arise out of the transfer of the territory shall be considered as coming within the terms of reference of the International Commission.

ITALY HAILS "PEACE OF EUROPE"

Rome, Friday.

The "Giornale d'Italia" appeared as a special edition last night with an enormous headline "Peace of Europe Assured."

Commenting, Signor Gayda says: "The Munich agreement is the result of intimate harmony created between Italy and Germany by the axis, which is now more vital than ever before. It is also the result of the cordial nature of relations between Italy and Great Britain."

HOLD POSITIONS ON EBRO

S.A. Press Association—Reuter

Barcelona, Thursday.

All key positions on the Ebro River front have been retained by the Republican forces, despite two months of Nationalist counter-attacks, according to the Spanish Press Agency. It is declared that the Nationalist positions remain almost as they were when the Republican six-day offensive ended on July 30.

PREPARING FOR THE PEACE TALKS: German workmen hoisting a Union Jack at Godesberg in preparation for the second visit of the British Prime Minister, Mr. Neville Chamberlain, to discuss the Czech crisis with Herr Hitler.

GEN. HERTZOG'S MESSAGE

SOUTH AFRICAN PRESS ASSOCIATION—REUTER

London, Thursday.

MR. CHARLES TE WATER, Union High Commissioner in London, handed to Mr. Chamberlain before he left Heston, the following message from General Hertzog: "Allow me to congratulate you most heartily on your efforts to secure for humanity the blessings of peace.

"I wish you every success in your high mission and to express my greatest admiration for the great-hearted and statesmanlike manner in which you dealt with the situation."

Points From Official Communique

The Four Powers, taking into consideration that a settlement has already been reached in principle concerning the cession of the Sudeten districts, have agreed as to the conditions and procedure to be followed and declare themselves individually responsible for guaranteeing the steps necessary for its fulfilment.

Firstly, the evacuation of uncontested Sudeten districts is to begin on October 1.

Secondly, Britain, France, Italy and Greece will see that evacuation of the region is completed by October 10, without the destruction of any existing installations.

Thirdly, in districts where the German population is less dense an international commission will decide the localities where a plebiscite shall be held. The same commission will trace the new frontier.

Fourthly, the commission is to be composed of the German Under Secretary of State and Foreign Affairs, the British, French and Italian Ambassadors at Berlin and a Czechoslovakian representative.

Fifthly, Britain and France will immediately guarantee the new status of Czechoslovakia.

Sixthly, Italy and Germany will likewise guarantee the new status of Czechoslovakia when the claims of Poland and Hungary have been satisfied.

Seventhly, territories in which plebiscites will ultimately be held will be occupied by international bodies until the plebiscite is completed before the end of November.

Eighthly, for three months the right of option is to be exercised by the populations into and out of the transferred territories.

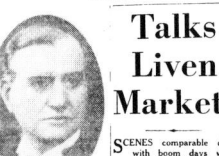

M. DALADIER looked grave. The possibility of severe criticism at home is believed to be worrying him.

HERR HITLER: An appeal made to him by Signor Mussolini on the strength of their "indissoluble friendship and union of hearts" is believed to have pacified the Fuehrer.

Talks Liven Market

SCENES comparable o... with boom days w... witnessed when the Johann... burg Stock Exchange ope... yesterday morning.

Encouraged by the news of Munich conference, buyers sha... bid up prices while sellers kept in the background. Most st... began at much higher levels ... Wednesday's closing prices, speculative counters heading ... general advance.

West Wits were up 20s. at the ... at Western Reefs 7s., Western ... ines 4s. 9d. and Marievales 4s. while other rises ranged from 2... 6s.

One of the most remarkable fea... of yesterday's High 'Change was ... although buyers almost ran riot a... beginning, many purchasing o... were held back in the hope ... abatement in the early rush. ... however, prices continued to adv... later in the morning, the rema... buyers also came into the ma... pushing quotations still higher.

FRESH LONDON SUPPORT

Although London appeared ... nervous at midday, Johanne... took little notice. Later in ... afternoon fresh support be... noticeable from the London ... and the day ended with a fresh ... of buying.

Symptomatic with the atmosphere of optimism at the opening of the Munich conference, states a Berlin message, was the reaction of the Bourse. The average increase was five points, some registering ten points, and Daimler as much as 13 better.

On balance, West Wits rose 26... Western Reefs 8s. 6d., Vlakfontein... Sub Nigels 7s. 6d., and Anglo... Other high class developing mine... dividend-payers also advanced ... stantially. A full list of yeste... advances will be found in the n... page.

How we reported the results of the Munich Crisis: with euphoria. Newspapers brought out special editions and sold many papers direct from newspaper offices to the crowds that thronged the streets of the main towns. (South African Library)

Johannesburg celebrated with a riot between pro and anti-Nazi factions, broken up only by the arrival of troops of the Transvaal Scottish who, with fixed bayonets and to 'ironical cheers', broke up the riot and guarded the entrance of the Union Ground to prevent the crowd from re-forming.

These running battles, displaying the same elements of thuggery and anti-Semitism that characterised Nazi Germany,* broke out all along the Reef, in Benoni and Boksburg, Potchefstroom and Johannesburg, and continued well after the declaration of war the following year.

The battles were fierce and ugly, and made more bitter by accusations that the police were in the main sympathetic, if not to Nazism (which some of them undoubtedly were) at least to Afrikaner nationalism. As the street battles in the Union intensified and as the country belatedly turned some of its thoughts towards rearming, the year of the Munich Crisis and the ox-waggon trek came to an uneasy end.

There were 246 days of peace left.

---

* In an orgy of violence and pillage, *Die Kristallnacht* (Night of Broken Glass) took place on 9 November at the urging of Goebbels, the greatest pogrom in the history of Germany. Over seven thousand Jewish shops alone were smashed and looted.

CHAPTER

1

1938

'We had everything to lose if South Africa went Nazi'

Civilian against civilian

South Africans played hard in 1938. They believed that they deserved it. The depression was over. State coffers were bulging. The price of gold had risen to nearly £8 the fine ounce. Jobs (for whites and in particular 'poor whites') had vastly increased, 'Africans' in the Cape had been deprived of the right to vote, and we lived under fusion, the coalition government of the South African and National Parties, commanded by their respective generals, Barry Hertzog with his white moustache and Jan Smuts with his familiar goatee.

On the surface all seemed well. We holidayed at Uvongo and St James, slept beneath sweet-smelling thatch in the Kruger Park and mostly travelled by train. Sir Ernest and Lady Oppenheimer entertained at Brenthurst and newspapers gushingly recorded the comings and goings of socially prominent South Africans and minor English nobility. Fostering the myth that all was well within the Empire, they reported in lavish spreads the doings of the new king, the stammering and pitifully shy George VI, his queen, Elizabeth and of course the little princesses, Elizabeth and Margaret Rose.

We listened to the ever-so-smooth Noel Coward, and some of us even believed in the stately homes of England and crumpets (with honey) for tea. Certainly for the most part we still believed in the Empire which daubed the map of the world with great splashes of red, and we took comfort in the might of the Royal Navy, the greatest in the world, there for our protection as well as for that of Britain.

But the increasing prosperity of the Union, the rise of institutions such as Santam and Iscor, the idyllic life of white-gloved house servants for the better-off, the sense of belonging to something larger than the country itself, was offset by the increasing turbulence in both Europe and South Africa.

The Munich Crisis, a clear preliminary to war, came and went. So also did the symbolic trek from Cape Town to Pretoria. But as the Voortrekker Monument began to take shape a new phenomenon also took shape in this restless country: growing Afrikaner nationalism, which walked in tandem with a strongly pro-German sentiment.

Afrikaner men wore beards like those of their forefathers and refused to speak English. The Broederbond was formed, an organisation that originally set out to restore and promote Afrikaans culture. So also was the Ossewabrandwag, although it soon acquired a paramilitary character. Young Afrikaners* wore brown or grey shirts with swastika armbands, and many of them displayed the same sinister anti-Jewish sentiments as the Nazis of the Third Reich, all over the country, but predominantly in the Transvaal. At their meetings they preached anti-Semitism; they were bitterly anti-British; they called for National Socialism in South Africa; they wanted the Vierkleur raised high again and an independent country modelled on the Boer republics of old.

The meetings turned into riots, some of them ugly. The police, it was suspected, were largely in sympathy with the brownshirts. But the running battles that were so characteristic of 1938 and 1939 did not always go the way of the South African Nazis. Angry fellow South Africans, appalled at what the brownshirts stood for, attempted, often successfully, to break up the meetings and to oppose the messages of hate that preceded the onset of war. The anti-Nazis were just as well organised and just as determined as the brownshirts to have their own way.

‘Things were changing rapidly in South Africa, but I didn't really notice it until the centenary of the Great Trek was held. It went on for months . . . It was about the time of Munich, and the Nazis were very much in the news. And I was Jewish. I wasn't very religious, but I was proud of my blood and full of fear for members of my family in Europe, in Lithuania. Some of them just disappeared . . .

'We lived in Benoni, which became a hotbed of pro-Nazi nastiness. I was a medical student in Johannesburg, and I noticed the Afrikaans students suddenly growing beards and refusing to speak English. They were all part of this movement which wanted South Africa for the South Africans, to re-establish the old Boer republics and to break away from Britain. I agreed with their thinking there, although there was still the bond of Empire and my father had fought for the British in the Boer War.

'But suddenly, wherever you went, in 1938 and 1939, there were these groups of greyshirts, young thugs, with swastikas on their arms,

* In the volunteer army 1939–1945, 60 per cent of the men were Afrikaans-speaking.

and they were preaching poison. They were slavishly pro-Hitler. I went to a few of their meetings, and I was shaken. They would march into the town hall or outside, buy quart bottles of beer, and when they were tanked up they would start talking hate against the Jews. "Where do you think your daughters are tonight?" they would ask the crowd. "We'll tell you where: they're sleeping with Jews in the back of their cars on Boksburg Lake."

'If South Africa was Germany, I thought, this sort of thing could spread. It was no use complaining to the police or to the government. They just ignored us. Hertzog was in power and the impression we got was that there was, at the very least, sympathy for these thugs. So we decided to take matters into our own hands.

'Most of us were Jews, a lot of us medical students, and we had everything to lose if South Africa went Nazi. We couldn't infiltrate their ranks, but we could break up their meetings, make it impossible for them to talk. We became well organised. Fortunately, General Smuts was Minister of Justice; he was all for us and he armed us. We got revolvers and ammunition. More men joined us, some of them very fine young Afrikaners who were appalled at what was happening.

'We always wore hats to recognise each other, lined with thick cardboard and stuffed with newspaper because the police used to hit us on the heads.

'There were about four hundred of us. We didn't bother with a name, but we certainly had a purpose. The first meeting that we broke up was in Benoni, where the police attacked us. They arrested some of us and charged them with creating a disturbance . . . But that didn't deter us. We created a medical section. We had doctors, we had cars and at the Cecil Hotel we had what amounted to a medical corps. We didn't want our men to go to any hospital if they were hurt, because the police would come and ask them where they got hurt. We treated each other.

'We had our spies everywhere and we were very fit. We went out to farms and trained ourselves, marching, drilling . . .

'As soon as a meeting began, and some of them were pretty big, with five to seven hundred people, we would wade in, push over the table and knock the speakers over, and there would be a free-for-all. One of their men was badly hurt, with broken ribs, and had to be taken to Boksburg Hospital.

'Eventually they got a bit fed-up with having their meetings broken up. The Greyshirts would put an advertisement in the local paper to say that they were holding a meeting on such and such a night in, say, Benoni. But our spies would tell us that all the police were going to Boksburg, so we got into a convoy of cars and went there. They never outwitted us. I think they were afraid of us. This was all before Robey Leibbrandt returned to South Africa, of course.

'Men would get knocked out. Some of our fellows were arrested after one particularly angry meeting. Three of us went down to the Boksburg police station and told the policemen to let them free – or else. They were so scared that they opened the cell doors and our fellows just walked out. I think we would have killed those policemen if they hadn't released our men. We had to break the greyshirts because if we didn't what they were saying would affect not only the Jews but the whole country. We weren't going to take anything lying down, as so many of our relatives did in Europe. This was my country too, and it was worth fighting for.

'Eventually the movement petered out, on the surface at any rate. Smuts passed some stringent laws forbidding such meetings, so I was able to get on with my medical studies.

'Then South Africa declared war on my 23rd birthday, 6 September 1939. I had been sitting my finals and a crowd of us went pub-crawling in Johannesburg. There was a pub at every corner of Rissik Street. You could get gloriously drunk for 2/6. A bottle of brandy cost 6/-. I was on my way back to Benoni after celebrating and one of the chaps with me, not very sober, said "Let's go and join the army."

'We didn't really know what we were doing, but we all thought it was a good idea, and we went to the Drill Hall and joined up on November 20th. I couldn't remember a damn thing about it until my call-up papers arrived. I rushed off to the Drill Hall and collared the recruiting sergeant and said "What's all this about?" waving my papers under his nose. "Is that your signature?" he asked; and to my astonishment it was. So I was in the army. A lot of Jewish fellows volunteered.* We weren't fighting only for our country – we were fighting for something very personal. ’

• Interview, 1990.

---

* Out of a Jewish population of about a hundred thousand no fewer than 9 400 men and 600 women volunteered during the period 1939-1945. Jews comprised 4,8 per cent of the South African volunteer army. Three hundred and fifty seven were killed, 143 were mentioned in despatches.

CHAPTER

2

'The renaissance of extreme Afrikaner political nationalism'

Harry Klein, the 1938 trek, scoops, and military intelligence

On 8 August 1938 two ox-waggons drew slowly away from an excited crowd in Cape Town. By the time the trek ended, after a triumphal journey of four months and something like a state entry into Johannesburg, at the foot of a hill outside Pretoria on which the Voortrekker Monument would be built, a new spirit of Afrikaner nationalism was running through the country, together with the belief that South Africa was a white man's land.*

A month after the trek began, the Czechoslovakian crisis became more acute. Germans living in the Sudetenland were encouraged to riot and make protest marches along Czech streets, anything that would give the Germans a pretext to invade and 'protect' their teutonic brethren. The world shifted uneasily as the Prime Minister of Great Britain, Neville Chamberlain, flew back and forth between England and Germany. On 27 September he addressed the British over the BBC: 'How horrible, fantastic, incredible it is that we should be digging trenches† and trying on gas masks here because of a quarrel in a faraway country between people of whom we know nothing.' In effect, what Chamberlain was saying was that Britain and France would do nothing to prevent the invasion of Czechoslovakia. The country, created in 1918, was being abandoned.

In South Africa the slowly evolving catastrophe was front page news, and stole the thunder off the centenary trek. If Britain went to war, it was assumed by many that South Africa, as a dominion and part

* Similar, in fact, to the Nazi belief in *Untermenschen:* blacks, Russians, Jews. On 10 September 1938 Hermann Goering, the head of the *Luftwaffe,* told a crowd in Nuremberg that the Czechs were 'a miserable pygmy race . . . oppressing a cultured people.'

† Hyde Park looked like a mole colony at the time.

of an Empire on which the sun never set, would do her bit as she had so valiantly done in World War I.

The Führer delivered an ultimatum to Czechoslovakia, to expire at 2 p.m. on 28 September. The lugubrious-visaged Chamberlain was addressing a subdued House of Commons when he was handed an invitation from Hitler asking Chamberlain to meet him in Munich. 'Herr Hitler has just agreed to postpone his mobilisation for 24 hours and to meet me in conference with Signor Mussolini and Daladier,' he told the House.

In Munich, while the world waited for news of peace or war, Chamberlain and Daladier ritually washed their hands of Czechoslovakia. Hitler signed the meaningless document; and Chamberlain believed that he had won 'peace for our time'.

In an extra late edition (5 p.m.), the *Rand Daily Mail* devoted an entire page to the news from the Munich conference. 'It's Peace!' announced the huge headline. Hertzog fired off a telegram to Chamberlain: 'Allow me to congratulate you most heartily on your efforts to secure for humanity the blessings of peace . . .'

As the British got ready their sandbags and fire-extinguishers, vacuum-flasks and adhesive tape for pasting across windows, first aid kits and government-issue gas masks, South Africans in the country were frantically trying to get a passage home. Some returned via the USA, so full were the ships plying between Southampton and Cape Town.

In the heart of the Karoo the neo-Great Trek, with all its symbolism, was slowly moving towards Graaff Reinet, the 'Athens of the Karoo'. Accompanying the waggons there was a crowd of reporters from both English and Afrikaans newspapers. If they had thought at the beginning of the trek that they would be observing a pageant, they were by now thoroughly disabused. Some, especially those of the English press, were becoming alarmed. Greeted as it was by commandos at every little dorp, by men carrying flaming torches in Bloemfontein and singing the new Afrikaner anthem *Die Stem* in Pretoria, the trek had assumed a disquieting, almost religious, fervour.

One of the journalists was Harry Klein. Some of his reports to the *Sunday Express* were quietly passed on to the still infantile intelligence unit of the Union Defence Force. Klein was approached by Intelligence officers and asked to report to them. It was not spying, he was told, but information-gathering – sensing and reporting the mood of people in different areas. He readily agreed.

At that time Intelligence was divided into three areas: the Shooting War (or The Battle), the Production War (or The Battle for Supplies and Materials) and the Intelligence War (or The Battle for Information).

'Do not confuse security with intelligence,' said a little book called *Field Security*. 'Security is defensive, intelligence is offensive.'

The head of South African Intelligence was Col B W 'Bartie' Thwaites, for twenty-five years News Editor of *The Star* and a former Sandhurst man. In 1940 he was appointed Director of Military Intelligence.* Working for Thwaites were men and women like Harry Klein, information gatherers. And then there were the spies, on the lookout for people who would pose a security problem if South Africa went to war. These spies were taught to look out for anyone living above his means, for people with extravagant tastes (gambling, horse racing, women), for people taking an unusual interest in troops or who entertained them excessively – and of labourers and hawkers working next to or within a military camp.

Harry Klein, reporter, gatherer of information and soldier, tells his story:

'I was profoundly disturbed by the implications behind the Voortrekker Centenary Trek. It was without question a magnificent pageant – no other nation I know of had honoured its pioneers so magnificently – Voortrekker waggons drawn fifteen hundred miles across the country by ox spans which were changed every twenty or thirty miles. All the journalists covering the trek were very impressed with the spectacle, but as the trek progressed we became very concerned with the underlying message, which was one of extreme Afrikaner political nationalism.

'At the beginning of the trek, Mr Klopper† told me that I would "see things on this trek I would never have believed I would have seen", and he was right . . . Before the trek began I decided to enter into the spirit of the thing and work up a bit of publicity for the news service. I bought a horse in Cape Town, a big white horse I called Africopa. He became quite famous. I said that I would ride this horse with the waggons from Cape Town to Pretoria, but he nearly drove me mad. We would start the day with a prayer at 5 a.m., trek to a village for breakfast, trek to another village or town about midday with a party in the afternoon and a party in the evening, and I had to find a stable for this horse, feed it and groom it AND write my story, then get the story to the post office before the lines closed . . . But I'd built the wretched beast up and everybody knew him.

---

* Little historical evidence of the work of Intelligence in South Africa during the war exists. There are reports that on the night before the Nationalist government took over power, huge piles of documents at military headquarters all over the country, particularly at Roberts Heights outside Pretoria, were burnt. It made little difference: English-speaking South Africans in the Defence Force were systematically got rid of.

† H J Klopper, Chairman of the Executive Committee of the Afrikaans Taal en Kultuur Vereniging, leader of the centenary trek and later Speaker in the House of Assembly.

'We got to five hundred miles from Cape Town, somewhere in the Eastern Province, when the government veterinary officer came up to me and said: "Mr Klein, I've read all about Africopa, I've heard about him on the radio and how you're going to ride him to Pretoria – but I've got a shock for you. You've ridden him into a horse-sickness area, and you will have to leave him here in quarantine." I've never known such relief. "My friend, he's yours," I said.

'At the beginning of the trek* a hundred thousand people in Cape Town came to see the two waggons off. All traffic was stopped, people hung over balconies to cheer, and a mounted commando with Oswald Pirow, Minister of Railways, Harbours and Defence at its head, clattered through the streets. Klopper made a speech, appealing to the nation to attend the centenary celebrations in the spirit of the promise made by Charl Cilliers on the eve of Blood River. "We . . . ask the whole Afrikaner nation to take part in the celebrations. Let us go to the monument as a nation, and let us take the monument to Afrikaner hearts," he said. And then we set off on our way, through dense crowds to Goodwood, where the first outspan was made. It was a jamboree, with camp fires, bands playing, fires cooking boerewors and more than ten thousand people singing Afrikaner songs. The journey was like that the whole way, crowds large and small, men riding out to greet the waggons, receptions and astonishing emotionalism. Gradually we reporters realised that we were seeing the beginning of a new Afrikaner fervour, of something totally new and very worrying.

'I believed that the trek was the spark-point for the renaissance of extreme Afrikaner political nationalism.

'The courageous pioneer exodus from the Cape to the wilds of the Transvaal and Natal was deified and dramatised out of all proportion to its intrinsic merit. A new God was created to be worshipped at the great new Voortrekker memorial shrine on the hills overlooking Pretoria.

'I was so concerned that I wrote to Arthur Barlow, the Editor of the Express group of papers: "You are seeing the birth of a new South Africa, a new political South Africa."

'The waggons reached a little place called Rooi Rivier, about a hundred miles south of Graaff Reinet, at the time of Munich. We were standing on the brink of an abyss. Schalk Pienaar† and I decided to tell our worries to Klopper. "Mr Klopper," I said, "when we interviewed you in Cape Town you told us we would see things on this trek that we would never have believed . . . I believed that those things were to

---

* 8 August 1938, at the Van Riebeeck statue in Cape Town.

† Later Editor of *Die Oosterlig* (1946), *Die Beeld* (1965–1974) and *Beeld* (1974–1975). At the time Pienaar was reporting for *Die Burger*, and became parliamentary reporter to the paper in 1941.

The reporter Harry Klein on Africopa, the horse he rode on the first part of the ox-waggon trek from Cape Town to Pretoria in 1938. (Harry Klein)

be great symbolic pageants, but what we have seen is nothing less than the birth of a new political fervour in South Africa."

'"Yes," he said, "out of this trek will arise a new South Africa." He beat his chest with a clenched fist. "God will show the way. There will be a new government. There will be a place for Smuts. There will be a place for Hertzog. There will be a place for Pirow." He went on and on. So I said to him: "Who's going to lead this new government?" And he said, beating his chest again: "God will show."

'As a result of this conversation I wrote a big story. Arthur Barlow sent me a telegram saying the press was going to expose the whole political background. I warned Klopper that the *Sunday Express* was going to publish the story. The trekkers rushed off to get the first editions of the paper, and they were horrified. They withdrew the hospitality of the trek from me. But because I was an accredited member of the press party they had to withdraw it from everyone, and there was an unpleasant rift . . . Then, in the midst of all this and the drama surrounding Munich, I went down with appendicitis.

'I was an idealist and my ideals were being shattered . . . I joined the trek again in the OFS and wrote what I suppose was my "seminal" piece on the trek.'

The article appeared in the *Sunday Express* on 16 October 1938; an extract from which appears (re-reproduced) below:

All S. Africa Has Trek Fever

RELIGIOUS PASSION IN "CRUSADE OF AFRIKANERDOM"

Women, in Emotion, Wipe Grease from Axles On Their Handkerchiefs

BY HARRY KLEIN

WAGON WHEELS ARE TURNING THE DESTINY OF A NATION. THAT IS THE DOMINATING THOUGHT ENGENDERED BY EVENTS OF THE VOORTREKKER CENTENARY OX WAGON TREK NOW ON THE ROAD TO PRETORIA AND BLOOD RIVER.

THE COMMEMORATIVE TREK IS SWEEPING THE SENTIMENTS OF AFRIKANERS IN AN UNPRECEDENTED WAVE OF RELIGIOUS AND NATIONAL EMOTIONALISM.

The character of the trek has openly changed from merely being a symbolic pageant into a crusade of united Afrikanerdom.

As the wagons roll north "Op die Pad van Suid Afrika" (on the Road of South Africa), everywhere Afrikaners are finding a new pride in their name and traditions and are proudly marching forward with deep religious ideals to new unknown heights of nationhood.

At trek celebrations and functions the great crowds that gather to do homage to the Voortrekkers dramatically exhibit religious passion in greeting the trekkers.

This deep emotional wave engendered by the trek has to be seen to be appreciated. Crowds greater than those which assembled to greet visiting royalty gather at every point along the trek route, and as the wagons roll by many of those cheering thousands can be seen wiping tears from their eyes.

Bearded old men and their bonnetted womenfolk hobble to roadside halts, and with hands trembling and feeble from age, touch the wagons, as if the dust-covered vehicles were sacred idols. Grease from the axles is surreptitiously smeared on handkerchiefs to be cherished evermore as a memento of an unforgettable pilgrimage.

On Sundays, churches are filled to overflowing by devout worshippers, and on many an occasion the passionate exhortations of the ministers create an aura of absolute fanaticism that can be sensed by the cool observer.

ABOVE: An armed commando escorts the waggons into a village. Wild celebrations greeted them wherever they went. (Harry Klein)

LEFT: Outspanned for a night in the bush. Often farmers from neighbouring farms would ride out and join the trekkers for the evening meal. (Harry Klein)

'I joined the waggons again at Newlands, as the waggons came in from Roodepoort on 3 December. To my mild surprise, Klopper welcomed me. "Come and sit on the leading waggon with me," he said, "and you will see how the people of the city of gold, the Jews, the infidels, everybody, will welcome this trek." They did, of course, with crowds of a hundred thousand, three hundred horsemen dressed in corduroy klapbroek, floral waistcoats and heavy jackets with Transvaal Vierkleurs and Free State republican flags held above their heads. Johannesburg welcomed it as a wonderful pageant, and no more.

'There was a large press contingent at Monument Koppie waiting for the laying of the cornerstone. T C Robertson (representing the *Rand Daily Mail*) introduced me to a man in a curious uniform of his own design: Gen Manie Maritz. He said to me in English: "You people will be amazed by what will come out of the Afrikaner sentiment raised by this pageant of history."

'When the trek had ended I was posted to Pretoria as bureau chief for the *Express* newspapers. One morning a man came into my office. I never knew who he was. He leaned over my desk and said: "If you want the scoop story of the year, Manie Maritz has written a book. He's staying with a man named Piet van Rooyen in an eastern suburb of Pretoria. If you can get hold of that manuscript before the book is published, you've got a national scoop."

'So I went to see Maritz.*

'I told Maritz that I'd heard about his book and if the book had any historical merit I would like to have a preview of it. He balked at first, but he lent it to me. The book was called *My Lewe en Strewe* (My Life and Struggle). It wasn't a good book, because he gave full reign to his hatreds, but I thought the first few chapters were magnificent, of great historical value. I wrote a story on those chapters, and called him the storm petrel of South African politics. While I didn't put a halo round his head, I didn't ridicule him. The morning the story appeared I was very nervous of what he would do to me.

'He marched into my office and took my hand in both of his and said: "Man, I never thought an English newspaper would write so well about me. Come and drink coffee."

'We went to Turkstra's tearoom, the political gossip headquarters of Pretoria. . . . He mentioned that he thought there was going to be a war and that Germany would be all-powerful again, and perhaps those who participated in the 1914 rebellion would be able to gain what they wanted

---

* Salomon Gerhardus (Manie) Maritz, 26.7.1876–19.12.1940, was descended from the Voortrekker leader Gerrit Maritz. He volunteered for service at the time of the Jameson Raid, fought in the second Boer War with Theron's Verkennerskorps and was made a general by Smuts in 1902. He refused to take the oath of loyalty to the British Crown, but was allowed to return to South Africa in 1907. In 1912 he was gazetted a major in the new Union Defence Force. As a Lt-Col in 1914 Maritz helped to plan a *coup d'état* which, with German help, was to overthrow the government. In the end his was the only defence force unit to rebel. He was tried for high treason and sentenced to three years' imprisonment, of which he served only three months. He was a man of great impetuosity, personal magnetism and courage, but his ruthlessness, arrogance and pathological racial prejudices made him an uncomfortable associate. He espoused the Nazi cause and joined the greyshirt movement in South Africa, but resigned in 1934 to form the SA National Democratic Movement. He made frequent speeches attacking Jews and Freemasons. In 1939 his book, *My Lewe en Strewe*, was published. He was living in Windhoek at the time, and he was charged in the Windhoek High Court with causing racial hostility. Friends paid his £75 fine. At the outbreak of the Second World War Maritz was in the Transvaal and became associated with various anti-government, extraparliamentary organisations, and he was proposed as a leader of the Ossewabrandwag. Maritz was a founder of the anti-parliamentary Volksparty and a joint founder of Die Boerenasie. He died in a car accident outside Pretoria in 1940. On his granite boulder headstone is engraved: 'Vat my hand dat ek kan opstaan vir my volk.'

as a result of the coming war. We met for coffee almost every day. It certainly aroused comment, me, a Jew, working for a Jewish newspaper, having coffee daily with this committed anti-Semite.

'About the middle of 1939 I was in my office when two men walked in. They said they were senior men from Intelligence. I got a terrible fright. They impressed upon me that I could be a valuable source of information. They weren't seeking my services as such, they said, only my co-operation. War was coming – it was only months away – and I still had the taste of the centenary trek in my mouth. It didn't occur to me not to co-operate with them. I was in daily contact with people on both sides of the political division and if my impressions could be helpful to the Intelligence then it would be a small contribution to the future of the country.

'Just before war broke out the *Express* newspaper empire folded and I was out of a job. Instructions were given that I was to be found a job on any newspaper that I wanted. But I decided to work my way through Africa via Kenya and get to London and work on Fleet Street if war didn't break out. As it was, on 3 September 1939 I was standing on the quay at Lourenço Marques and listening to the British declaration of war relayed from a Dutch boat.

'I returned to Johannesburg. Lt-Col B W Thwaites (of the Imperial Light Horse) was News Editor of *The Star* and Director of Intelligence at Defence Headquarters. He knew what I had been doing. "What I'm looking for is a chap like you," he told me. "I want you to act as a political correspondent investigating stories. I just want you to drift about and pick up anything that could be of interest politically that would help us to gauge the mood of the country."

'They gave me a car and I was a free agent. One day Thwaites called me: "We're getting garbled stories from Louis Trichardt. All sorts of things are supposed to be happening there. Just go there and see what you make of it."

'I said: "If I need help, or any communications, who should I communicate with?" He told me to communicate with *The Star* and to introduce myself as a reporter from it.

'At Louis Trichardt I made contact with a man whose name I had been given. I asked him to organise a car for me; I wanted to go to German mission country in the lowveld. There had been rumours that the missionaries might be stirring up trouble with the blacks. Then I went to the Hotel Louis. Who should I see there but Piet van Rooyen, Maritz's host in Pretoria. He greeted me warmly, and we sat and drank most of the afternoon. We got quite tight.

'Every time he picked up a glass he said: "To hell with the King." I sat and drank with him, but said nothing about the King. Then I noticed some youngish men drifting into the bar and taking up a position facing us. It was getting dark and Van Rooyen said to me: "Kêrel, kom sit, ons nou begin." I went to his car and he lifted some karosses on the back seat. There were rifles and ammunition boxes, and he said again: "Ons begin!" Then he drove off into the night. I was bloody shaken. I thought: "Are they going to start another rebellion?"

'Next day I drove to the lowveld and introduced myself as a reporter if I had to, otherwise I said I was collecting material for political articles. I wasn't spying – that is something altogether different. I was getting the feeling of the mood and making contacts – no more than that. It was a terrible time in South Africa: neighbours informing on neighbours, people being put into internment camps on hearsay evidence. I satisfied myself on what I had come to see or hear and drove back to Louis Trichardt.

'As I walked down the street, I saw a policeman on the other side. I realised he was shadowing me. I went to my local contact. He wasn't pleased to see me. "Get out of town, you're a bloody Maritz agent. Get out." I was flabbergasted.

'"What are you talking about?"

'"Don't give me that. Everyone knows you were drinking in the bar yesterday with Van Rooyen and everyone knows he is a Maritz agent. They're stirring up trouble. Get out!"

'It was about five in the afternoon. I went back to the hotel and walked into the bar. There was a large group of young men there, officers in the Zoutspansberg Commando. I sat down and had a drink and then they closed in on me. They accused me of being a Maritz agent. I told them I was merely drinking with a man I had met in Pretoria. They didn't believe me, and the mood was not of the friendliest, so I told them I was working for *The Star* and they could telephone to verify that.

'Well, they did, and came back grim-faced. *The Star* had confirmed that they knew me, but not that I was working for them. Thwaites had forgotten to tell them about me. I began to get worried. They wanted to put me under arrest. In desperation I told them to telephone Thwaites. They did, and he told them to leave me alone, but they didn't. I didn't know if they knew Van Rooyen had weapons in his car. I had been drinking with him while he was damning the King. At last I was hauled to my feet, and they put me on the train to Johannesburg. When the train stopped in Pietersburg another group of men got on board to see that I was still there, and they were threatening about the people I knew. I wasn't frightened, but I certainly felt very insecure.

'I reported to Barney Thwaites at Defence HQ. He told me to put it all down in a report. "I'll do a report," I told him, "but first I'm going into town and I'm going to have some tea and I'm going to have a haircut, because whenever I'm troubled a haircut does me good."

'So down I went to Turkstra's. Who should I see there but Maritz? I wanted to tell him to go away, but I didn't. He said: "Klein, I heard they arrested you last night in Louis Trichardt. If they had kept you, I would have brought a commando to get you out." I went back to Thwaites' office and wrote a detailed report. When I'd finished it I said: "I don't want to go on doing this work."

'I knew that it was important work, and I knew it was necessary and I knew I wasn't informing on people. But I was influencing thought, and my information, after it had been sifted, was sometimes acted upon; and I didn't like it. I didn't feel clean.

'It was early 1940; I was offered a job in the Tank Corps, and I took it. I felt a lot safer. ’

• Interview 1990

As Commanding Officer of No 1 SA Armoured Car Co, Major Klein saw service in East Africa, Abyssinia and the Western Desert. He was seconded to the British Political Warfare Executive and the American Psychological Warfare Branch of the US State Department for Specialist Services, and served in North Africa and Italy. As a Lt-Col, he served as Chief Psychological Warfare Officer on the Staff of Gen Sir Arnold Alexander's 15th Army Group Staff and later on Gen Mark Clark's staff when Clark succeeded Alexander as Allied Supreme Commander in the Mediterranean theatre. He was awarded the American Bronze Star.

CHAPTER

3

1939

'Put your hand into the hand of God'

To the sound of bells, cheers and the singing of *Auld Lang Syne* the New Year of 1939 began. Many people were certain that it was the last new year of peace.

Behind the festivities there was much uneasiness. Would Hitler's promise of peace hold good? After all, the Third Reich had considerably extended its boundaries in 1938 with the seizure of Austria and the Czechoslovakian Sudetenland. What (and who) would stop Hitler from looking yet further afield?

Opinion was now steadily hardening against Germany. There was a steadying of resolve and a resurgence of national pride. In Britain, respect for Neville Chamberlain evaporated. The voice of Winston Churchill, after years of frustration in the political wilderness, was heard more strongly.

All the crisis of 1938 had bought was a little time to rearm and to prepare. The Union, still firmly on the side of the forces of democracy looked to its manpower, its weapons and its coast defences. There were virtually none.

South Africa had at least a new General Officer Commanding the Union Defence Force, Maj-Gen Sir Pierre van Ryneveld. The Permanent Force itself consisted only of 4 500 indifferently trained men, of whom 313 were officers and only a handful were trained staff officers. The Active Citizen Force (ACF) had twenty-seven infantry battalions numbering fewer than fifteen thousand.

Seventy-one field guns and howitzers, six two-pounder anti-tank guns and eight three-inch anti-aircraft guns, most of them from the 1914-18 war and with only enough ammunition for one day's moderate fighting completed our defences. The total armoured strength was two obsolete medium tanks and two armoured cars. But we had 622 ox-drawn bushcarts.

The South African Air Force was in an equally poor condition with four modern Hurricane fighters, one Blenheim fighter, six obsolete Hawker Fury fighters, eighteen twin-engined Junkers 86s, 63 obsolete Hartbees biplane light bombers and one single-engined Fairy Battle bomber. There were 173 officers and 1 664 men in the SAAF. Coast defences scarcely existed.

Women were among the first to prepare themselves for a possible war. The South African Women's National Service Legion* was formed in September 1938; by the time war broke out there were seven thousand members. The African Explosives and Chemical Industries (AECI) at Modderfontein set up machinery for filling and pressing .303 percussion-caps and to supply the peacetime needs of ten million rounds of .303 rifle ammunition. Orders were placed by the War Supplies Board for 174 howitzers with local manufacturers, car dealers expressed their willingness to organise transport battalions, and amateurs enrolled on a special register for wireless operators.

In Europe the French sat in false security behind the Maginot Line, a line of fortresses stretching from Switzerland to Longuyon, where the Ardennes Forest begins. Like Britain, France had begun to rearm. Then, on 15 March, all vestiges of complacency were swept away when German troops crossed the border into the Sudentenland and the rest of Czechoslovakia. Prague was occupied. Next day Hitler declared: 'Czechoslovakia has ceased to exist.'

'The blow has been struck,' wrote Churchill a few days later. Hitler had 'broken every tie of good faith with the British and French who tried so hard to believe in him. The Munich agreement, which represented such great advantages for Germany, has been brutally violated . . . A veritable revolution in feeling and opinion has occurred in Britain and reverberates through all the self-governing Dominions . . . it was not an explosion, but the kindling of a fire which rose steadily, hour by hour, to an intense furnace heat of inward conviction.'

In South Africa the 'intense furnace heat of inward conviction' was confined mainly to the English-speaking people; the Afrikaners remained, in general, implacably opposed to engagement by the Union in a European war.

No matter. Hitler was now eyeing Poland. On 31 March Britain and France declared a joint guarantee to Poland and Romania against German aggression, reinforced on 25 August by the Anglo-Polish Mutual Assistance Pact. Neither Britain nor France knew it, but 25 August was the day marked by Hitler for the invasion of Poland. The invasion was cancelled when Mussolini, who had invaded Albania

---

* The forerunner of the South African Women's Auxiliary Service (SAWAS).

on 5 April (and Abyssinia in October 1935) declared that Italy was not prepared for war.

Seven days later the now inevitable happened: at 4.45 a.m., without any declaration of war, forces of the Third Reich burst across the Polish frontier and a new word entered all the languages of the world: *Blitzkrieg*, an invincible combination of speed and shock with co-ordinated air, tank and infantry attacks.

South Africans read about the invasion in special editions of the newspapers. On the morning of 2 September the news was yet grimmer: 'British Ultimatum to Reich: Withdrawal of German Troops Demanded.' Conscription in Britain was extended to include all men between the ages of eighteen and forty-one, and a War Cabinet was formed in which Winston Churchill was First Lord of the Admiralty.* That night London was under the blackout that was to last for the next six years.

The British ultimatum to Hitler was to expire on the morning of Sunday, 3 September. As that clear spring Sunday dawned in the Union, churches everywhere were filled. Key points all over the country were guarded, and the entire strength of the South African Police (SAP) had been placed on special duty throughout the Union, nearly five hundred in Johannesburg alone.

Most people stayed at home listening to the news; in hotels, little knots of people gathered round the radio; in cafés radiosets were turned on and Sunday newspapers that had earlier displayed 'It will be War' headlines now waited for the news to bring out special war editions.

At 12.15 p.m. local time the British Prime Minister came on the air. 'I am speaking to you from the Cabinet Room at No 10 Downing Street,' he said, with a quaver in his voice. 'This morning the British Ambassador in Berlin handed the German Government a note stating that, unless we heard from them by 11 o'clock that they were prepared to withdraw their troops from Poland, a state of war would exist between us. I have to tell you now that no such undertaking has been received, and that consequently this country is at war with Germany . . .'

But the British declaration of war did not mean that South Africa was at war, although Australia, Canada and New Zealand almost immediately declared their support for Britain, and France declared war five hours after Chamberlain's announcement.

By chance, the South African Parliament had been recalled for a special sitting to provide for the continued existence of the Senate. As news filtered into the House of the invasion of Poland, it was immediately apparent that more than the life of the Senate would have to be

---

* 'It's the Admiralty,' Churchill told his wife Clementine. 'That's a lot better than I thought.' He fired off a salvo to the Admiralty Board immediately: 'I shall take charge forthwith and arrive at six o'clock.' 'Winston is back,' the Admiralty signalled the Fleet.

HEADLINES:

British Decision 18
Vital S.A. Statement 11
Poles Hold Firm 13
Dominion Rally 13
New Conscription Bill 14
Naturalisation Rush 11
Love Shooting Drama 7
S.A. Takes No Chances 11
Stop Press 26

56 PAGES

African Postal Union 2d. Elsewhere 4d.

Sunday Times

A PAPER FOR THE PEOPLE

"PHYSICAL PERFECTION" SHOES 49/6 Bally CUTHBERTS ELOFF STREET MAIL ORDERS TO P.O. BOX 1177, JOHANNESBURG.

Founded in 1906. No. 1,746. JOHANNESBURG, TRANSVAAL, SEPTEMBER 3, 1939. REGISTERED AT THE GENERAL POST OFFICE AS A NEWSPAPER. Price Threepence.

THE PEOPLE'S COLUMN

Monkey Business

WILL THIS DOOR KEEP THE SKELETONS IN THE CUPBOARD?

It is an interesting fact that this cartoon is based on the "Sunday Times" cartoon of September 6, 1914—just a quarter of a century ago. It was then prophetic, for Famine, Bankruptcy and Revolution overwhelmed Germany at last. Now, however, they are close at hand.

The Passing Show

Sunday Sallies

ROAD TO PEACE IS END OF THE UNCLEAN

By R. F. S. DEWDNEY

IT is near at last — this final showdown which democracy has long expected but has not feared.

And there's a strange calmness about it all.

That's because it's not so much war as a holy crusade, something unpleasant that has to be done to pluck out something rotten that sought to infect our whole clean-living civilisation.

To-day is not as in 1914. Then, nation fought nation. To-day there is no war against Germany's people; only against Nazi Party that seeks to impose its law of rubber truncheon, murder and oppression on half the world.

When that era passes, there'll be peace.

So there is no shouting, no hysteria, no undue excitement among democracies; only calm resolution to end this unclean thing as swiftly as possible and allow us (and Germany's people with us) to return once more to peace, contentment and liberty for all men.

It had to come, one way or another.

It is not written that a handful of throwbacks should indefinitely flout God and man in a lust for power; this world is too good to allow sadism to run on unchecked.

Now it is checked.

Soon the light will come again.

Not War · Relief · Breaking Point · Fencing · Out of Alignment · Blunder · From Inside · Prophecy · Small Man · Our Part · Normality · No More Taxes? · Striking News

The early edition of the *Sunday Times* of 3 September 1939. It contained much speculation but little news, apart from that coming from Poland. Staff worked long hours to bring out a special edition once the British Prime Minister, Neville Chamberlain, had spoken to the world. (South African Library)

DAY TIMES, September 3, 1939.

SPECIAL EDITION

Sunday Times

SPECIA EDITIO

A PAPER FOR THE PEOPLE

unded in 1906. No. 1,746. JOHANNESBURG, TRANSVAAL, SEPTEMBER 3, 1939. REGISTERED AT THE GENERAL POST OFFICE AS A NEWSPAPER. Price Threepe

WAR DECLARED

GERMANY IGNORES ULTIMATUM

"I am Certain that Right Will Prevail"— *Chamberlain*

WAR WAS DECLARED AT NOON TO-DAY (SOUTH AFRICAN TIME) BETWEEN GREAT BRITAIN, FRANCE AND GERMANY.

The official announcement was made at 12.15 p.m. by the British Prime Minister, Mr. Neville Chamberlain, speaking from 10, Downing Street, London, in a world-wide radio broadcast.

The British Ambassador in Berlin, Sir Nevile Henderson, at 10 o'clock this morning (South African time) informed the German Government that unless Germany suspended all hostilities in Poland by noon and withdrew their troops, a state of war would exist between the Allies and Germany from that ho[u]r.

No such assurance was received.

In his address, Mr. Chamberlain said: "We have a clear conscience. We have done all that any country could have done to establish peace..... And now we have resolved to finish it. I know that you will all play your part in calmness and courage..... May God bless you all..... I am certain that Right will prevail."

In his broadcast, Mr. Chamberlain said:

I AM speaking to you from the Cabinet room at No. 10 Downing Street. This morning the British Ambassador in Berlin handed to the German Government our final Note stating that unless we heard from them by 11 o'clock this morning (British summer time) that they were prepared at once to withdraw their troops from Poland a state of war would exist between us.

I have to tell you now that no such undertaking has been received and that consequently this country is at war with Germany

You can imagine what a bitter blow it is to me that all my long struggle to win peace has failed. Yet I cannot believe that there is anything more or anything different that I could have done which would have been more successful.

Up to the very last it would have been quite possible to have arranged a peaceful and honourable settlement between Germany and Poland.

Made Up His Mind

But Herr Hitler would not have it.

He had evidently made up his mind to attack the Poles and although he said that reasonable proposals were rejected by the Poles, that is not a true statement.

The proposals were never shown to the Poles nor to us, and although they were announced in the German broadcast on Thursday night, Herr Hitler did not wait to hear comment on them, but ordered his troops to cross the Polish frontier the next morning.

This all goes to show that there is no chance of expecting that this man would ever give up his intention of using force to gain his will. He can only be stopped by force.

We and France are to-day, in fulfilment of our obligation, going to the aid of Poland to resist this wicked and unprovoked attack. We have a clear conscience.

We have done all that any country could do to establish peace.

The situation in which no word coming from Germany's ruler could be trusted and no people or country could feel itself safe, has become intolerable, and now we have resolved to finish it.

I know you will all play your part with courage.

At such a moment as this the assurances of support which we have received from the Empire are a source of profound encouragement.

When I have finished speaking, several important announcements will be made on behalf of the Government. Give these your close attention.

Will Carry On With Work

The Government has made plans under which it will be possible to carry on the work of the nation in the days of stress and strain that may be ahead, but these plans need your help.

You may be taking your part in the fighting services or as a volunteer in one of the branches of civil defence. If so, you will report for duty in accordance with the instructions you will receive.

You may be engaged in work essential to the prosecution of war, or in the maintenance of the life of the people, in factories, in transport, in public utility concerns, or in supplying other necessities of life.

If so, it is of vital importance that you should carry on your jobs.

Now, may God bless you all, may He defend the right. We are fighting against brute force, bad faith, injustice, oppression and persecution.

Against them I am certain that Right will prevail.

Sunday Times Opinion

The Mad Dog of Europe

THE Mad Dog of Europe has set his life upon a cast. It is certain that he will lose the hazard of the die. Hitler has been given very opportunity to behave wisely, but instead has elected to ontinue the evil that has marked his career from the day when e emerged from obscurity until now—when he is faced by estruction.

No dictator or other ruler in historical times has been urrounded by such personal and general hatred as Hitler. The ildest among right feeling men has a sense of bitterness in regard o this professed Antichrist, whose every action and promise is a e.

Germany, a nation that contains many decent people, is swept illy-nilly into the abyss created by her leader. A leader, moreover, who holds his position only by dint of false ballots and the rotection of his personal bodyguard of trained murderers. His nemies in his own land are counted in their millions.

The position of Germany at this hour of conflict is dire. She s besieged by the tremendous might of Britain and France, two of he greatest Powers in the history of the world. Germany has a arge man power, weapons and munitions. But these are ephemeral ossessions that will suffer great wastage in the early hours of the onflict. Then Germany will be without the replacements vitally ecessary after every battle. She has neither gold nor materials nd small reserves of food.

The Allies, on the other hand, have these in abundance and may range the wide world for replenishment, while Germany emains friendless and besieged. In addition, the Allies possess he immensely valuable quality of honesty and righteousness. The orld is their friend; it is the enemy of Nazi Germany.

In this hour there is wisdom in stating the case for South Africa. We have, unfortunately, a section who would even now ebate the point of remaining neutral—who urge that this Dominion hould remain passive while all other races of goodwill, in or outside the British Commonwealth, are ready to fight for their freedom nd for the removal of a blemish on humanity. Such a policy is ot only wrong but intensely dangerous.

It is a matter for calm reasoning. We should elect to play our part in this great conflict with steadfast faith, as is being displayed now by the other democracies. It is necessary that all shall join hands to overcome the powers of evil.

(Written by Guy Gardner, 155, Jeppe Street, Johannesburg.)

Heroic Stand by Polish Garrison

SAPA-REUTER REPORTS RECEIVED TO-DAY GIVE THE FOLLOWING FLASHES ON THE WAR POSITION ON THE POLISH FRONTS:—

Latest news confirms that the garrison of Wasterplatte successfully resisting German attacks by land, sea and air. The garrison's heroic stand has aroused tremendous enthusiasm throughout Poland.

BERLIN

German Claims

A communiqué states that the German air force raided Gdynia, Cracow, Lodz, Lublin and Posen. It adds that the railway stations and lines were also bombed as well as retreating Polish troops and that several Polish military aerodromes were bombed and destroyed.

The communiqué adds that the Polish Air Force "is so seriously damaged that the German air force is now ready for further measures to protect Germany."

WARSAW

37 Nazi Planes Down

According to a Warsaw radio spokesman, the Polish General Staff communiqué claims that 37 German planes were shot down and 100 German tanks were destroyed, while the Polish lost 12 planes.

Polish "Lourdes" in Flames

"We will win this war because Pilsudski taught us how to win liberty and how to defend it," declared the Prime Minister, M. Skladkovski in a statement at a meeting of both Houses of Parliament.

"The unconquerable Polish Army will defeat the historic enemy of our nation and crush Teutonic arrogance and haughtiness," he added.

At the close of the session members rose and sang the Polish National Anthem and the song of the Pilsudski legionaries.

PARIS

"We Will Win"

A communiqué issued by the Polish Embassy states that the town of Czestochowa, which is the "Polish Lourdes," is in flames.

The famous 16th century convent which contains the miraculous status of the Black Virgin and is a place of pilgrimage for all Poland and Central Europe, was bombed several times on Friday and Saturday by German planes.

"Czestochowa contains no military objectives whatsoever," the communiqué concludes.

LONDON

Undefended Towns Bombed

A later statement issued by the Polish Embassy here says that Polish troops held positions tenaciously in the face of the German advance. The most serious threat, it is added, lies in the concentration of the main mass of the German Air Force against Poland, not only lines of communication and military objectives being bombed, but certain towns and villages continuously and indiscriminately raided, although they are of no military importance whatever.

BERLIN

Nazi Denial

The semi-official German news agency "D.N.B." denies the reports that a German airman bombarded the children's hospital in Warsaw, and states that the air force is adhering strictly to orders to attack only military objectives.

TURKISH SHIPS CALLED HOME

Istanbul, Saturday.

Turkish Naval authorities have instructed all Turkish ships at present in the Mediterranean to return as soon as possible to Turkish ports and there await further orders.

Japanese Ambassador Leaves Rome

Rome, Sunday.

THE Japanese Ambassador to Rome is being recalled.

The official explanation is that he is going to report on the European situation, but Japanese circles in Rome do not hide the fact that the recall is due to the attitude of the Japanese Government towards the Axis Powers following the ratification of the German-Soviet pact.

Mr. Chamberlain Thanks Canada

S.A. Press Association—Reuter

London, Sunday.

IN reply to a telegram from Mr. Mackenzie King, Prime Minister of Canada, Mr. Chamberlain said: "My colleagues and I have received with deepest appreciation the statement of policy issued by His Majesty's Government in Canada and contained in your telegram to me on September 1.

"In these critical and anxious hours it has afforded us the greatest possible encouragement to know that His Majesty's Government in Canada are at one with us in their determination to resist aggression."

Hitler Receives Soviet Ambassador To-day

Berlin, Sunday.

IT is officially announced that Herr Hitler will receive the new Soviet Ambassador, M. Alexander Chkvarzeff, to-day. The ambassador will be accompanied by the Soviet Minister Plenipotentiary in Berlin, General Maxim Purkajoff.

PARIS THEATRES CLOSED

Paris, Sunday.

Transocean states that all Paris theatres have closed down and that in many cases cinemas have been unable to open owing to lack of staff.—Sapa.

Pirow Can Say Nothing

Interviewed by long-distance telephone immediately after the outbreak of war, Mr. O. Pirow, Minister of Defence, told the "Sunday Times" that at the present stage he was unable to say anything regarding South Africa's position.

England-S.A. Airmail Once a Week

S.A. Press Association—Reuter

London, Sunday.

THERE will be two services weekly in each direction between the United Kingdom and Sydney and one weekly in each direction between the United Kingdom and Durban and the United Kingdom and Kisumu.

What Japan Hopes to Get Out of the War

Tokio, Sunday.

IT IS believed here that if a general war breaks out in Europe it will not affect Japan as much as the last great war, says "Asahi Shimbun," according to the Domei Agency.

The paper says the general opinion is that there will be nothing like the boom which Japan enjoyed during the world war, but Japanese neutrality would bring political and economic advantages, while the weakening of Britain in the Far East could be counted on as favourable to the Japanese cause in China.

Japan would reap some advantage in exports, but there would be attendant difficulties in obtaining some imports, which are badly needed by the nation.

SWISS NEWSPAPERS SLATE GERMAN AGGRESSION

Geneva, Sunday.

STRICTEST neutrality has been declared by the Government, which has forbidden the export of arms and munitions and organisation of propaganda in favour of belligerents.

The Government has warned newspapers to exercise prudence, nevertheless editorial articles are almost unanimously favourable to Britain, France and Poland, and, in outspoken condemnation of what they describe as the latest German aggression.

Air Raid Sirens Over London

Chamberlain in House of Commons

LONDON, SUNDAY.

SHORTLY AFTER THE PRIME MINISTER HAD [...] HIS BROADCAST, THE AIR RAID SIRENS WE[...] ACROSS LONDON AND IMMEDIATELY THERE WA[...] QUICK BUT ORDERLY EVACUATION OF PEOPL[...] SHELTERS TO BASEMENTS.

When Parliament met at noon, the all clear sirens were heard. These drowned the opening sentences of the Prime Minister when he rose immediately to declare a state of war with Germany.

Greeted with loud cheers, Mr. Chamberlain said:

"When I spoke last night to the House I could not but be aware that in some parts there were doubts or bewilderment as to whether there had been hesitation or vacillation on the part of the Government.

"If I had been in the same position as Members and not in possession of all the information I might have felt the same. We were in consultation all day yesterday with the French Government, and we felt that the intensified actions which the Germans were taking against Poland allowed of no delay in making our own position clear.

"Accordingly we decided to send our Ambassador in Berlin instructions which he was to hand at nine o'clock this morning to the German Foreign Secretary, which read as follows:

"Sir,—In the communication which I had the honour to make to you on September 1, I informed you on instructions of His Majesty's Principal Secretary of State for Foreign Affairs that unless the German Government were prepared to give satisfactory assurances that the German Government would suspend all aggressive action against Poland and were prepared promptly to withdraw their forces from Polish territory, His Majesty's Government of the United Kingdom would without hesitation fulfil their obligations to Poland.

Mr. Chamberlain announced that France had joined Great Br[itain in] the war against Germany.

He then repeated his annou[ncement] that Britain was at war with Ge[rmany].

Further News in Stop Press Co[lumn] Page 4

Japanese Ships Wil[l] Shun German P[orts]

S.A. Press Association—Re[uter]

Tokio, Su[nday].

JAPANESE shippers, includi[ng] Nippon Yusen Kaisha, are [leaving] nothing undone to meet the E[uropean] situation, says the Domei Ag[ency].

The N.Y.K. liners Kashi[ma], Hakone and Noto Maru hav[e been] ordered to stand by at B[...], Athens and Columbo respectiv[ely].

It is understood that shipp[ers] risking transportation of car[go to] Europe under a special clause [...] insurance policies.

All cargoes for German ports [...] unloaded at neutral ports a[ccording] to "Hochi Shimbun," which s[...] man and Polish ports will he[nce] be avoided by Japanese ship[s ...] further orders.

4-PAGE NEWSPAP[ERS]

Paris, Su[nday].

According to Transocean [...] newspapers have now been li[mited to] four pages by order of the ce[nsor].—Sapa-Reuter.

ALLIES WILL NOT BOMB OPEN TOWN[S]

SOUTH AFRICAN PRESS ASSOCIATION—REUTER

London, Sunday.

A COMMUNIQUE issued this mor[ning] states that the Governments of the Un[ited] Kingdom and France solemnly and pub[licly] affirm their intention to conduct hostilities [with] the firm desire to spare civilian populaton [and] to preserve in every way possible monumen[ts of] human achievements, which are treasured i[n all] civilised countries.

In this spirit they welcomed with deep satisfaction President Roosevelt's appeal on the subject of bombing from the air.

Some time ago they sent explicit instructions to the commanders of armed forces prohibiting bombardment from air, sea or land of any except strictly military objectives in the narrowest sense of the word.

SUBMARINE WARFARE

As regards the use of naval forces, including submarines, the two Governments will abide by the Submarine Protocol of 1936. They will only employ aircraft against merchant shipping in conformity with recognised rules applicable to the exercise of maritime belligerent rights by warships.

Finally, the two Governments reaffirm their intention to abide by the terms of the Geneva Protocol of 1925 prohibiting the use of poison gases and bacteriological methods of warfare.

Enquiry will be addressed to the German Government asking whether they are prepared to give an assurance to the same effect. In the event of the enemy not observing restrictions imposed on British and French forces, the two Governments reserve the right to take such action as may be deemed appropriate.

GERMAN GO[LD] STOCKS DOW[N]

Berlin, Su[nday].

THE Reichsbank returns for t[he week] ended August 31 show an [...] of 2,197,800,000 reichsmarks co[mpared] with the previous week.

The proportion of gold and [foreign] exchanges to the note circula[tion has] fallen by .17 per cent. to [...] cent.

At a meeting of the [...] Directors of the Reichsbank h[eld yes]terday the Reich Minist[er of] Economics, Herr Funk, declar[ed that] the German financial syste[m and] money market had shown n[o] [...]ions which might give rise to [...]

The German people, he stat[ed, had] complete confidence in the [...] financial system, which was pr[oved by] the fact that there had been [no] any panic withdrawals from [...]

He told the directors th[at the] situation would entail a rise [in the] fiduciary issue and that the [Govern]ment would exercise control o[f ...] and prices.

The special edition of the *Sunday Times* announcing that Britain had gone to war. Many copies were sold direct from the Johannesburg offices to a large crowd outside. (Rand Afrikaans University) debated. The Cabinet had met at 4 p.m. on 1 September; when the two-hour meeting broke up it was apparent that the cabinet itself was split over the question, with five members, led by Gen Hertzog, in favour of non-belligerence and seven, led by Gen Smuts, in favour of co-operation with Britain.

That night there were ugly scenes in Johannesburg as police with drawn batons charged a crowd of seven hundred that had surrounded the German Club at the corner of Loveday and Plein Streets. Tear-gas bombs were thrown, and a running fight broke out before the riot was broken up.

On Monday, 4 September, after air-raid sirens had already been sounded in London (it was a false alarm), the House was filled for this historic session. As the debate bounced back and forth, shops closed their doors, factory machines stood idle, ports were strictly guarded and anxious crowds gathered outside newspaper offices and, in Cape Town, outside Parliament itself. In Johannesburg large crowds gathered outside the Drill Hall, inside which men of the Active Citizen Force waited tensely for the decision of Parliament.

As time dragged on and as traffic came almost to a standstill (people were listening on car radios for the news, stopping and obligingly letting pedestrians listen), British nurses at the Johannesburg General Hospital were recalled to Britain to serve for the duration. German nationals in the Union were ordered to stand by in readiness to leave for Germany, and offices of the Department of the Interior were besieged by anxious Italian and German citizens applying for South African nationality.

In Worcester, while the Union waited for the news, Kaas Willemse, a spry 106-year-old, was charged with being drunk. He had been celebrating the war, he explained. 'At your age,' scolded the magistrate, 'you should have learned a little wisdom and should be an example to young men of seventy or eighty.' Plain-clothes men were out in force, sniffing out 'spies', and in Mossel Bay Nazi propaganda took the form of envelopes delivered to selected bigwigs with a drawn swastika inside and the words 'Money spent with Jews never returns to gentile pockets.'

According to the German propaganda station, Radio Zeesen, broadcasting in English and Afrikaans, 'A special session of the South African Parliament was called to discuss a motion introduced by Dr D F Malan, the National Socialist leader, that South Africa should remain neutral, and the House unanimously adopted this resolution.' The report was premature.

At last, after nine p.m., the tension broke. Gen Smuts's amendment was carried by eighty votes to sixty-seven. 'It is in the interest of the Union that its relations with the German Reich should be severed,' stated part of the war policy of the new coalition government, 'and that the Union should refuse to adopt an attitude of neutrality in this conflict.'

In the Drill Hall in Johannesburg there were three cheers for Smuts, a few bottles were broken out and plans by rebellious members of the ACF to revolt if the vote had gone the other way were burnt. Johannesburg celebrated with a riot of two thousand in the city centre, and in Cape Town good-humoured policemen urged drivers to continue on their journey home.

RIGHT: The new Prime Minister, Gen Jan Smuts. The photograph was taken on the day when the Union formally declared war on Germany, 6 September. The General, his face worn with the pressures of the last few days, also became Minister of Defence. *(The Star)*

BELOW: On Sunday, 10 September, this cartoon, illustrating the struggle between Smuts and Hertzog, appeared in the *Sunday Times*. The division lasted for the rest of the war. *(Sunday Times)*

On 6 September under the coalition government led by Gen Jan Smuts, the Union formally declared war on Germany.

Three months later, halfway through the 'Phoney' war, King George VI broadcast his Christmas message to Britain and the Commonwealth. The King, keeping his stammer under control, ended with a quotation from a poem written by an American poet, M Louise Haskins. It was a moving declaration of his faith and his belief that good would prevail: 'And I said to the man / Who stood at the gate of the year; / "Give me a light / That I may tread safely into the unknown". / And he replied: "Go out into the darkness / And put your hand into the hand of God. / That shall be to you better than light / And safer than a known way."'

CHAPTER

4

'Where the bloody hell are the mobilisation orders?'

Brigadier Eric 'Scrubbs' Ponsonby Hartshorn, September 1939

No one knew better how ill-prepared the Union Defence Force was for a war than the men of the Active Citizen Force (ACF). The purely voluntary part-time soldiers of the ACF numbered about fifteen thousand altogether. Their training, hampered by lack of equipment, nonetheless assumed a new urgency after the Munich Crisis.

Relations with the Permanent Force became strained in 1939, when the ACF begged for modern weapons to fight a war and were consistently refused. Senior officers of the ACF also believed, with some justification, that by no means all the Union Defence Force would fight if war broke out.

On the day after Britain declared war on Germany, the Drill Hall in Johannesburg seethed with activity. Volunteers queued at the doors; but no mobilisation orders had been given and no orders had been received to permit the ACF to take on more men. Senior officers of the ACF, some of whom had fought in World War I and who had tasted the bitter trench warfare at first hand,* had every intention of fighting. As the doors of the House of Assembly closed for the historic debate that would either lead South Africans into war or leave them on the sidelines, a handful of officers planned to take extreme steps in the event of Parliament voting for non-belligerence.

One of these officers was the colourful one-armed Eric 'Scrubbs' Ponsonby Hartshorn, an officer of the Transvaal Scottish. No matter what the cost might be, he was determined that the ACF should fight.

---

* It had been calculated that if the Imperial dead of the First World War were to march four abreast past the Cenotaph in London, it would take them three and a half days to pass it.

And they were determined to take whatever steps they could to ensure that a South African policy of 'neutrality' would not be as shameful as the British policy of appeasement. Eric Ponsonby Hartshorn was one of those men.

As a private in the Manchester Territorials in 1914 Hartshorn saw action in 1914–18 war in the Dardanelles (Gallipoli), Egypt, Palestine and India. He was wounded seven times (which led to the hypotheses that he was immortal) and, as a result of picking up an enemy hand grenade thrown into a group of his fellow-soldiers, he lost his right arm, which earned him the Distinguished Conduct Medal.

The flamboyant 'Scrubbs' Hartshorn was determined to go to war even if it meant taking the Active Citizen Force to the top of Majuba. Fortunately it wasn't necessary. (South African National Museum of Military History)

While he was living in South Africa between the wars he joined the Transvaal Scottish in 1928 as a volunteer and became a junior officer. He moved steadily upwards in seniority. In civilian life he was a commercial artist (he learnt to draw with his left hand), and was deeply angered at the *laissez-faire* attitude of the government towards the coming conflict. As the following extract from Hartshorn's controversial book (*Avenge Tobruk*, published by Purnell & Sons) clearly reveals, he and his fellow officers determined that no matter what the cost might be, the Active Citizen Force would fight:

'Some minutes past 9 p.m. on 4 September 1939, South Africa reached the historic decision which made her declaration of war on Germany inevitable.

'To three men in Johannesburg, of whom, today, I am the only survivor, that parliamentary decision ended nightmarish weeks of cloak-and-dagger activity, of meetings behind sentry-guarded doors, of couriers going to and fro with messages and orders that could not be exposed to the danger of their almost certain extraction by government authorities from normal mail channels. It meant, above all else, that the order we dreaded issuing – one that we had drafted in cold-blooded realisation of its possible implications of civil war – could now safely be consigned to limbo as an unwritten fragment of South Africa's turbulent history. Of its own volition, albeit by a majority of only 13 votes, South Africa had saved its national honour by aligning itself with the forces of civilisation and decency, rejecting the Nationalist demand for neutrality that could have had but one outcome at the time – enslavement to the Nazi doctrine, clothed though it undoubtedly would have been in hypocritical protestations of liberty and economic prosperity.

'This bizarre episode which, unquestionably, would have diverted the course of South African history had it materialised, has never before been written. Even today, 20 years later, much of its detail must remain undisclosed; the names of the other two principal architects of the plan are secret, for, though they are dead, their descendants are carrying on the family tradition of serving South Africa to the very best of their ability, and nothing must be allowed to prejudice them.

'Six years before the war started, when I was Adjutant to Lt-Col M G McCalgan, DCM, commanding the 1st Battalion Transvaal Scottish, we had produced a paper for Defence Headquarters showing the urgent necessity of training a Volunteer Staff Corps and to organise forthwith volunteer brigade staffs, and later divisional staffs. We pointed out that the Permanent Force was far too small to fill all the Staff appointments needed for such a force as South Africa could raise. Verbally, McCalgan, in my presence, informed the Chief of the General Staff, General Sir Pierre van Ryneveld and his senior staff, that the brains of the majority of Senior Regular Officers were atrophied and they were quite incapable of administering or leading an army.

'As a result the ACF were allowed to form Brigade Staffs, the first of which was the 5th Brigade (Witwatersrand), with McCalgan commanding and myself as Brigade Major, with a staff of war-experienced businessmen. But the definite training of a Volunteer Staff Corps was denied us until after the war had started.

'The spanner in the works was always the Permanent Force's desire to sanction nothing that might remotely challenge their holding all the senior military staff postings while relying on the commercial and industrial world to provide all ranks for the fighting forces, including the officer leadership which they so grievously lacked. ACF Brigade Staffs were formed, but definite Staff Course training was denied until after the war had started. By then, of course, there was insufficient time for anything resembling effective training. South Africa was to pay a heavy price for this wilful act by the authorities entrusted with the defence of a nation.

'We formed the Senior Officers' Club, and held fortnightly discussions to debate the strategical and tactical necessities in the event of war, fully aware though we were of the sterile fate that awaited our recommendations from the moment they were referred to the defence authorities in Pretoria. Undeterred by continuous frustrations, we carried on our duty as we conceived it.

'25 August 1939, was a decisive day in the drama that was unfolding in the Johannesburg Drill Hall. On that day the British Government proclaimed a formal treaty with Poland, confirming the guarantee that she would come to her armed aid should she be the victim of German aggression. By this time, details of our plan, hundreds of them, were in the process of being worked out. When the BBC announcement of the British treaty came over our radio sets, we knew that war was now certain and imminent. We pressed on with our plan, alarmed now that time might run out on us.

'We had already had further proof, if any were needed, of the Government's obvious predilection for neutrality. Fulfilling my function as Brigade Major and Mobilisation Officer for the Witwatersrand Area, I decided to check on the amount of ammunition available for issuing on mobilisation. There was none, or rather virtually none. Something like 23 000 rounds of .303 was available – roughly two rounds per man. There were no mortar shells, no mills grenades and no artillery shells. Enquiries elicited the fact that, while I was away on private business, an order, said to have emanated from the Minister of Defence himself, had resulted in practically all reserve stocks of ammunition being collected and removed to the Grand Magazine in Pretoria.

'I was dumbfounded. I immediately gave orders for the urgent indenting of new supplies of reserve training ammunition for all arms. Every request was ignored. Furthermore, we learned that the only regular infantry force in South Africa – the Special Service Battalion stationed at Voortrekkerhoogte – was being permitted to guard the Grand Magazine and that all other members of the regular force of gunners and the Air Force had been instructed to remain on a "stand by" basis. There could be no doubt whatever now. The Government, or rather a section of it, determined on neutrality, had taken timeous steps to forestall the possibility of anti-Government action by the volunteer soldiers of the Active Citizen Force, who, the authorities had so rightly divined, would wish immediately to throw in their lot on the side of Great Britain.

'The implications of our plan were now frighteningly apparent. Our volunteer soldiers, we determined, must be placed in a position whereby they could, if they wished, fulfil their dictates of conscience and duty to the cause for which the free world was now mobilised. That the Government would oppose any such move with ruthlessness was more than a calculated risk. It was a virtual certainty and it could bring in its train, we knew only too well, civil war. Brother would be fighting against brother. South Africa would be split into two warring factions. I had seen too much of the horrors of civil war in Palestine, India and Egypt to accept lightly the responsibility of being an organiser of civil strife in South Africa – a country which I now loved as my own and for which I was prepared to lay down my life, if necessary. But what were the alternatives? National dishonour, the prospect of South Africa becoming a slave with the certainty of death for all who dared to oppose Nazism. The alternative was unthinkable. There could be no turning back.

'There now began the final stages of the secret planning and scheming, which, though unaware of it at the time, automatically fell into the pattern which later in the war was productive of so many amazing systems and operations by which secret agents and underground workers were able to operate behind enemy lines. We committed to paper, for example, as little of the detail as we possibly could. No papers were entrusted to a messenger or orderly. They were carried by me or one of the other officers personally, and the escort was, as often as not, my son in a St John's College cadet uniform. Such typing and duplicating as were necessary were done in my business office by my private secretary.

'The plan in its entirety was known to the three of us and to no one else. A few other senior officers knew details in varying degrees, but none was in possession of sufficient knowledge of the overall scheme to jeopardise it by irresponsible talk.

'This was the plan, or rather as much of it as can prudently be disclosed. For obvious reasons neither the names of the principal individuals nor of the organisations which had assured us of their support can be given. The first phase entailed the "calling up" of all members of the Active Citizen Force units based at the Johannesburg Drill Hall, and their assembling at a given hour at the Union Grounds. The methods ordinarily adopted in the case of mobilisation – the posting, or personal delivery, of cards – were, of course, impracticable in our case. Instead it was so arranged that officers of every unit, upon receiving a certain message, would immediately assume the responsibility of rounding up and transporting to the Drill Hall all the men of his unit living in his particular district. The officers would be issued with lists of the men they would be required to contact, and had full knowledge of where to go to get the necessary transport.

'Phase two involved the participation of a large number of well-trusted men, most of them ex World War I soldiers, to whom had been confided certain code words. It was arranged that if they received a telephone message from a particular individual intimately known to them, and that in the course of their conversation the word "Growl" was mentioned, the following steps would immediately be taken. They would contact certain organisations on the Witwatersrand and, in accordance with previously made plans, would ensure that petrol-driven vehicles, able to transport large numbers of men, would be in readiness for an immediate move. This stage was to be accomplished with as little disruption as possible of the ordinary services being carried out by the vehicles so as to avoid arousing undue suspicion.

'Personal contact had earlier been made with the heads of certain organisations on the Witwatersrand which controlled large fleets of petrol-driven vehicles, and they had promised to make these available should the emergency we were providing for ever arise.

'On receipt of the code word "Bark" all the vehicles would immediately be called in, drums of petrol and cans of water and oil stowed aboard and the vehicles held in readiness for a move the moment the third and final code word was received. This was "Bite". It would have sent all the vehicles moving at once to the Union Grounds, where waiting men, already formed up into parties, would be assigned to their particular vehicles. All the men would, of course, be virtually unarmed, except for their empty rifles and bayonets. We would not have been completely without ammunition however. Several officers, in the weeks preceding, had been preserving as much as they could of the ammunition of World War I vintage, which was made available, without formal indenting, to the Active Citizen Force for training purposes, but which was of such poor quality that it was for use in machine guns only. It would have had little practical value if we were called upon to fight, but just knowing it was there was a boost to our morale.

'Where to go? That was the cardinal point to which all else was subordinate. Rhodesia was the obvious choice. But it was a day's journey by car to Rhodesia along a route straddled by aerodromes of the South African Air Force. The special Service Battalions and other regular units stationed at Pretoria could easily and rapidly be deployed to thwart our northward movement, and we had little doubt that, to a government, self-righteously convinced that it would be acting under the mandate granted it by the majority vote of a democratic parliament, would resort to force, utterly and ruthlessly. To expose our force, without ammunition, to such a fate was unthinkable. So it was that Natal became our final choice. In sentiment it was more pro-British than any other province of the Union, and had the strategic advantages, from our point of view, of the sea, which might well, in an extremity, provide the only possible escape route.

'Our master plan, disarmingly simple by the very virtue of the fact that it was impossible to divine what reaction it would provoke in a completely unpredictable group of Nationalist fanatics, with the might of the regular armed forces at their disposal, was this. If General Smuts failed to obtain a majority vote in the crucial debate in the House, orders would be issued, and it was hoped that within a few hours the column of volunteer soldiers would be flowing down the road to Durban.

'It was intended that the vehicles should drive straight down the main road towards the Natal border. With their tanks already filled, and additional supplies in drums aboard each vehicle, we were confident that they had sufficient fuel to reach their destination without stopping. Their destination? It was to be Majuba, the historic Boer War battlefield that lies just over the Transvaal-Natal border. It had many advantages, not the least being the sentimental associations of fighting for freedom which its very name would evoke in South Africans. It was, too, a heavily wooded, mountainous area, with only one really good road giving access to it, and we would have been able effectively to conceal very large numbers of men. On arrival at Majuba it was our intention to inform every man of the action we had taken, and the reasons for it, and to give everyone the opportunity of returning to Johannesburg immediately in the transport should they wish to do so. No compulsion of any kind was to be imposed. Knowing the men of the units as we did we felt confident that, in our enclave on Majuba, we would have at least 8 000 or 9 000 men willing and ready to share with us the gamble we were taking.

'Our plans did not envisage fighting except as a last desperate resort. Not only were we almost unarmed, for all practical purposes, but we would have been no match at all against the Air Force and other weapons that the Government would undoubtedly employ if it decided that our action constituted civil war and justified it in taking armed action against us. What we were relying upon to win the day was the moral force that would be exerted by so spectacular a demonstration on the part of the country's fighting men.

'It was clear that politically the country at this time was almost equally divided and that a vote in Parliament for neutrality, or against it, would be a very close thing. We believed, therefore, that the effect of our demonstration would be to sway emotionally to our way of thinking so decisive a section of the nation that it would rise up and demand that the Government resign and go to the polls on the issue of war or neutrality. That was the political weapon on which we were relying not only for achieving success but in protecting the lives of the men. No Government, we reasoned, would possibly be so politically inept as to try and enforce its will by attacking with arms the men of Majuba. But we could not be sure.

'In the last, climactic, few days during which Germany invaded Poland, and Great Britain issued its ultimatum to Hitler, the Johannesburg Drill Hall became the focal point of seething masses of ACF soldiers, in uniform, going about the tasks they had been trained for – cleaning weapons, dismantling and re-assembling machine guns and generally engaged in activities, in an atmosphere of mounting tension, that instantly transported my mind back to another day, 4 August 1914.

But I had no time for memories as I stepped into the Drill Hall, having driven overnight from Port Elizabeth.

'"Where the bloody hell are the mobilisation orders?"

'The question was slung at me from all sides, from senior officers, from adjutants and staff officers as I shouldered my way upstairs to the office of the Permanent Force Officer who held the post of Officer Commanding, Witwatersrand Command. Lt-Col "Karlie" Ross, DFC, a World War I veteran, who had played a distinguished part in the famous Van Ryneveld Royal Flying Corps Squadron, was sitting at his desk – in mufti!

'He had an enormous black Guardsman's moustache, which threw into relief an unnatural whiteness of his drawn face as he grimly answered my "What orders, Karlie?" with "No orders, Scrubbs. No orders at all. We are not mobilising. I cannot face the regimental COs or the men . . . I'm just sitting here praying that the Government will change its mind and join Britain or else make some sort of announcement. Please do what you can to quieten the men. Persuade them to go home. Tell them we'll make some plans to keep things moving . . ."

'Soldiers continued to pour into the Drill Hall, some from as far afield as Rhodesia. Women drivers voluntarily filled up their cars with eager young men anxious to get to the Drill Hall with the least possible delay. Some even arrived by bicycle. All were actuated by one motive: To get cracking. Knock the hell out of Hitler and preserve South Africa and the Commonwealth. No other course seemed even remotely possible to them.

'It was heartbreaking to disillusion them, to tell them that no orders for mobilisation had yet been received. Two Brigade Commanders, Colonel F L A Buchanan and Colonel Alex Hayton, had arrived by now and they, too, heard the news in silent disbelief.

'In this atmosphere of anti-climax the men dispersed to their homes.

'On the afternoon of Sunday, 3 September, the South African Cabinet met at Groote Schuur, the residence of the Prime Minister. As night fell, with the Ministers sharply divided, we learned that the great debate would take place the following day in Parliament. South Africa's destiny would be decided any time from 4 p.m. onwards. The word went out to the ACF officers to foregather the following afternoon.

'The Union Ground filled rapidly on that historic day. From far and wide cars, motor-cycles and other conveyances converged on the Drill Hall. Parked vehicles jammed the vicinity for blocks, while in the Drill Hall itself and its immediate environs a vast mass of men – Officers, NCO's and other ranks – milled and shuffled waiting the answers to the questions that were on everyone's lips: "What gives? What are we here for? Any orders?" For all that vast crowd there was a strange stillness that was broken by the metallic chattering of radio sets that had been plugged in to get the news of the drama that was reaching its climax in the House of Assembly in Cape Town.

'I sat alone in my office. On my desk was a box containing the detailed orders that would – or would not be issued, depending on the fateful words that any moment now would come from the little radio by my side. My old .45 revolver, loaded, lay in my shoulder holster, its rough caress imparting a comforting stability to my racing thoughts and to nerves tensed to breaking point. What if something should be wrong with the plans? What if they were already known to the authorities and counter-measures were at this moment in operation? What if those men, totally unaware of the extraordinary web that was being woven around their immediate destiny, should be butchered? What of their wives, their children?

'At exactly 9.10 p.m. came the fateful announcement that, by 13 votes, General Smuts had won the critical debate.

'From below came one roaring, shrieking burst of yelling, cheering and shouting. The old building vibrated with a rising paean of joy. My door burst open and my co-planners rushed in. One of them, one of South Africa's great soldiers who was to die on the battlefield of Sidi Rezegh* had, with his genius for meticulous planning, not overlooked the essential need that such a contingency would demand. He produced a bottle of Scotch and thrust it into my hand.

'"Here – take a couple of slugs of this. It'll do you a lot of good . . . and for God's sake stop shaking." I was speechless. Tears were streaming down my face. The whisky was choked by the lump in my throat. The other, whom I buried high up in the mountains of Abyssinia, was already tearing up the now useless orders, muttering "Thank God, thank God!"

'On the verandah adjoining my office stood an empty 44-gallon drum. It was there for a purpose. Quickly we took and scattered the papers loosely into the drum. A match was applied and, as a final valediction, a slug of whisky was poured on the papers already beginning to curl and blacken with the heat. We stared at those papers as they burned, stirring them every now and then to ensure that no half-charred page, no tell-tale line would ever remain of an episode that from now was to be locked in the souls and minds of the three of us.

'As we turned to join the roaring, shouting, hilarious tension-free crowd in the huge hall below, I looked back for the last time on those ashes from which, I jubilantly told myself, there would soon rise,

---

* The South African Delville Wood of World War II. See 'What can you do to a tank with a Bren Gun?'

Phoenix-like, the pride of a free people ready and anxious to take their rightful part in the great struggle for justice and liberty.

'Then we got drunk.

'There is a sequel to this chapter. Months later, in East Africa, talking in the secure knowledge that our words were being shared only by the bird and animal denizens of those vast, unyielding tracts of desert, I cautiously sounded out a South African Air Force Squadron Leader on what he thought the probable reaction would have been by the Air Force but the event – "utterly improbable, of course, old man" – occurred of a break for Rhodesia by units of the Witwatersrand ACF.

'He looked at me and then said quietly: "You poor bastards . . . if you had only known. We had every Nationalist supporter in the Air Force carefully marked . . . We had all our aircraft ready with every scrap of ammunition that we could carry and we were going to fly every aircraft in South Africa to Rhodesia . . . The few British fighters in Rhodesia were actually standing by to escort us in . . ."

'"When was this to have taken place?" I asked as matter-of-factly as I could manage with a throat suddenly constricted with emotion.

'"On 4 September," he replied. "We would have flown out the moment we knew that the vote in Parliament had gone against Smuts."'

Avenge Tobruk (Purnell & Sons)

Neither General Smuts, any Member of Parliament or of the Permanent Force nor any government official had been admitted to any part of this plan.

'Scrubbs' Hartshorn began the war as Brigade Major of the 1st Brigade under Dan Pienaar. At Gilgil (Kenya) he was appointed to command the 1st Transvaal Scottish. Awarded the DSO during the Kenyan/Abyssinian campaign, he was amongst the first troops into Addis Ababa. At El Alamein, Dan Pienaar appointed him Reserve Brigade Commander, ready to deputise for any senior officer in an emergency. Prominent in the advertising world after the war, Hartshorn died in Swaziland in August 1974.

CHAPTER

5

'Miss Ouida Snoek our first war bride'

Dewdney in the first week of war, South African style

There wasn't much humour to spare in that first week of war. Men, many of them under age (the youngest was a boy of fourteen; his age was only discovered when he reached Kenya nearly a year later. He was sent home with a mild rebuke) had already joined up and had promptly been sent home, there being no machinery to process them, no uniforms and no guns to train them.

The week was marked by panicky housewives rushing to buy everything in sight. 'Hoarders!' screamed the newspapers, but even under pressure from shopkeepers the women simply spread their shopping circle wider and went to four or five shops instead of one. Bully beef, tea, coffee and even caviar temporarily disappeared off the shelves until sanity restored itself.

R F S Dewdney, the *Sunday Times* columnist, helped to put matters into true perspective. On Sunday, 10 October his weekly column, *The Passing Show** satirised the scene, Radio Zeesen, food hoarding, Miss Ouida Snoek and all:

* Dewdney volunteered early in 1940. His place was taken by A B Hughes, who wrote *The Passing Show* until 1945, when Joel Mervis, later editor of the paper, took it over and, in the 1990s, is still writing it.

The Passing Show

War Horror

There appears to be every possibility that Miss Ouida Snoek (nee Haddock) will be our first war bride – provided Hitler doesn't stop the war when he hears about it.

The official announcement of her engagement was made from the German radio station on Thursday in 234 languages, but it sounded just as bad in all of them.

"This wedding," declared the announcer, "is another typical example of British perfidy, for we had always understood Miss Ouida would remain neutral. Why should her neutrality be violated in this way?"

In order to counteract the effect of this news, the German station then declared another 56 victories and announced that General Goering was out at the front and quite a bit at the sides as well.

Love Comes

It seems, however, that Miss Ouida has at last met her dream man. Indeed, she told us yesterday he seems too good to be true – or too true to be good, she couldn't remember which.

Anyway, the fact remains that last week he called around and confessed his feelings for her and declared she was, his long-felt want. He then offered Mr Snoek six cups of beef-tea and a mutton cutlet as lobola, and the deal was concluded.

During the last war he was a private in a Highland regiment in Egypt, where he found his kilt enabled him to enter harems with impunity.

He joined up again last Tuesday, but he isn't as young as he used to be and this time he chose the Marines because he prefers being told things.

The marriage will probably be performed by the National register and, to add to the military atmosphere, Mr Snoek will stand by with a shotgun.

The best man will be Mr. Blug, the well-known retired rioter, and the honeymoon will be spent on army rations.

How to Grab

For the benefit of those who have had no previous experience of buying up all the food in town so nobody else can get any, we have secured the services of an eminent food hoarder to answer readers' queries.

Send in your query, together with £5 for our War Relief Fund – our staff need the money.

FOOD HOARDER'S CORNER

Snaffle (Von Brandis). – 500 tins of lobster should be ample for the next fortnight; but don't forget 15 cwt. of bicarbonate as well.

Jitters (Parktown). – It was indeed very rude of the lady standing next to you to grab 54 tins of jam out of your bag; some people have no sense of public duty.

Windy (Melrose). – A good way to ensure your five barrels of caviare doesn't go bad is to cat it. It would be an awful waste to give it away.

Brought Down

The news that a German airman forced down in Warsaw, had been arrested by a traffic cop, presumably on an illegal parking charge, reminds us of several odd incidents during the Great War.

Lieut.-Colonel Wallaby Wallop (Indian Army, cashiered), who was serving at the time with 49th (Demechanised) Lancers, is considered to be one of the few men who have brought down a low-flying enemy aircraft with a pike or halbert, a feat that won the Kadir Cup in 1917.

When Major "Fruity" Rhumbetow was transferred from the same regiment to the R.F.C. he used to fly around slashing at hostile aircraft with a polo stick, until he was worsted in an exciting chukka by a Fokka.

CHAPTER

6

'Weren't we clever boys?'

Major G R Bozzoli and the development of radar, 1939

The last stand of the Active Citizen Force, wild and improbable though it may have been, was averted by the entry of the Union into the war, formally announced by the Governor General, Sir Patrick Duncan, on 6 September.

'Our primary duty,' said Smuts, his face lined with the strain of the last few days, 'is to place our own defence in the highest state of efficiency and we can best serve the cause for which we stand by so strengthening our own defences, and by so surveying our national resources as to render the Union safe against any inroads from the enemy.'

The problem was there were no defences. The registration of reserves began immediately, with an estimate of the shortage of trained infantrymen in the region of thirty-nine thousand – and no instructors to teach them, there being only 104 other ranks in the SA Instructional Corps. There were no coast defences of any practical use against marauders such as the German battleship *Graf Spee*, which sank the *Africa Shell* and gave Walvis Bay the jitters by sinking the *Doric Star* 884 kilometres to the north-west. Indeed, it took another three years before 3.7-inch anti-aircraft guns were mounted.

Plans were immediately begun to place the Defence Force on a modern war footing. General Headquarters would be based in Pretoria, with one divisional headquarters, including its three infantry brigades, and all medical and service corps units would be based at Premier Mine outside Pretoria.

But as volunteers, many of them under age, queued to join up all over the country (in the main it was adventure that called; patriotism came later when they realised how high the stakes were), a project developed in the greatest secrecy was already well under way.

Radar had been developed in Britain in 1935. Range and Direction Finding (RDF), as it was then called, was developed in the greatest secrecy. Its first important success was in June 1935, when an aircraft was tracked to fifteen miles and, a month later, to thirty-five miles. It was also possible to estimate the number of aircraft in a group and to measure the height of a target. By the time war broke out Britain had a chain of RDFs operating from the Isle of Wight to Edinburgh, the length of the vulnerable east coast.

By the beginning of 1939, radar was already fairly well advanced. The British Government informed Commonwealth countries that a top secret system of aircraft detection had been developed and invited top scientists to visit Britain to learn about it.

Brigadier (later Sir) Basil Schonland, the man who began the secret development of radar in the Union in the early months of the war.

On the *Winchester Castle* when war broke out was a New Zealand scientist, Dr Ernest Marsden. He had with him notes that he had made on the course in Britain and about fifty pages of diagrams. Marsden was met at Cape Town by Dr Basil Schonland, Professor of Geophysics and Director of the Bernard Price Institute for Geophysical Research at the University of the Witwatersrand.

Closeted with Marsden on the Cape Town to Durban leg of the voyage, Schonland learnt what he could. He had already been ordered by the new Prime Minister, General Smuts, to train suitable staff to operate the secret equipment. But, Schonland protested, how could he train people when South Africa had no radar apparatus? Clearly it would have to be developed in the Union.

Marsden agreed to let Schonland make photocopies of his notes and diagrams. The moment the *Winchester Castle* docked in Durban, Schonland rushed to Natal University College* and, using cumbersome glass plates, copied Marsden's notes. The reproduction was so poor that the notes were hardly decipherable; but they were all that Schonland had.

Impressed by both the secrecy and the urgency of his task, Schonland returned to Johannesburg and reported to the Defence authorities. It was decided to set up a secret service, the Special Sig-

* Now the University of Natal, Durban.

Maj G R Bozzoli; working with Schonland and three others, he helped to pioneer radar. By December 1939 the first set, JB1, was operational.

nals Service, a branch of the SA Corps of Signals, whose first job would be to develop radar in South Africa.

The facilities of the Bernard Price Institute at the University of the Witwatersrand were turned over to Basil Schonland.* There, he approached a newly appointed lecturer in Light Current Electrical Engineering, G R Bozzoli.

'I had never heard of radar before. The first time I heard the word was when Basil Schonland called on me at Wits and asked me if I would come in with him on developing this new thing, range and direction finding.

'I said I would be delighted, particularly because my father was an Italian citizen. I was at Wits when war broke out and some of my companions came to see me and said: "Ah, you're the enemy," and this fairly knocked me. I realised I could be in a peculiar position, because my father was a subject of an enemy country. So when I was invited to work with Schonland and do something for South Africa I was very happy indeed, and I climbed in, boots and all.

'It was very exciting. We had to work very fast, using these impossibly bad photostat copies of Marsden's, because Schonland believed that the sooner we got people trained the better, and we had to get the thing built. There was an urgency about, it, and that in itself was exciting.

'The first thing we had to do was get equipment – and that was the most difficult thing of all. Radar worked at very short wavelength at very high frequency. In 1939 we were used to broadcasting wavelengths of 500 and 600 metres, and shortwaves might have gone down to 15 metres, but this was one-metre stuff. At one metre, the frequency is about 30 megahertz, very high, and the ordinary valves available didn't work at that frequency. The special electronic equipment that we needed wasn't available except in amateur radio shops.

'There were about five or six such shops in Johannesburg, and

* During the war he carried the rank of Brigadier; later he was knighted.

we raided them – casually, of course. We managed to buy amateur transmitting valves which worked. We bought stocks as soon as they arrived, mostly from America.

'We began work in October, and by December the first mock-up on 90 mHz gave us something to test with. We worked in great secrecy, reporting regularly to Col F Collins, Director of Signals, who in turn reported to Smuts.

'I had just got married, and my wife and I were expecting our first child. I said to my wife: "What am I going to say to my children when they grow up and say: 'What did you do during the war, Daddy?'" I said I would say to them: "I was a secret."

'We worked right through Sundays and public holidays.* With our mock-up, we now had something to test with and special arrangements were made for an aircraft to follow a carefully planned route. Because the project was so secret, the pilot had no idea of what was going on. We began the test, five pairs of eyes staring at the cathode-ray tube for two solid hours – and it was blank. Where had we gone wrong? We discovered later that the pilot had flown to one of the Reef towns where his girlfriend lived. He just couldn't see why he had been asked to fly along this particular route.

'On Dingaan's Day† we were in the Bernard Price Institute again. Within minutes we saw a picture, a reflection, for the first time. It was a clear echo from the water-tower at Northcliff. There were only two of us in the room then, Schonland and myself. There was a lot of excitement. Many years later I sent him a reminder of the day.

'"Remember Dingaan's Day 1939?" I wired him. He wired back: "Yes, weren't we clever boys?"

'We adjusted the set again and received strong echoes from the Magaliesberg range about sixty miles away and then a less strong signal from something 25 miles away, to the east of the range. It didn't move, and looking at a map we could find no hills in the area. In a moment of exuberance Schonland called it "Bozzoliberg"‡ – it turned out to be the hill alongside Lanseria Airport!

'By March 1940 we had built a complete mobile radar unit. It was mounted inside two military vehicles together with a diesel-driven power unit, and we tested it to our satisfaction on aircraft at a site south-east of Johannesburg. We called it JB1.

---

* Basil Schonland's team consisted of his senior geophysicist, Dr R G Gane, Mr W E Phillips of Natal University, Mr Noel Roberts of Cape Town University and Prof Bozzoli. Six months later they were joined by F J Hewitt, a physics graduate from Rhodes University.

† 16 December.

‡ Oddly enough, years later Bozzoli bought a piece of land in almost exactly the same position.

'A medium-sized plane could be seen at sixty miles when flying at three thousand feet with a limit of eighty miles at an altitude of six thousand feet above ground, so a fighter doing 300 mph could be detected twenty minutes before arrival, which was acceptable. We got five kilowatts out of our transmitters, and that was remarkable.

'The research team had now become militarised. We suddenly became captains in the army. We had to learn how to drill and march, and we weren't any good at either. It was quite traumatic. We were still working in the greatest of secrecy when arrangements were made to operate this outfit on Signal Hill in Cape Town for trials over sea water and to introduce operational radar to the coastal defence authorities.

ABOVE: The first radar set in the Union, JB1, on Signal Hill, Cape Town, early in 1940. JB1 was later moved to East Africa, where it was used operationally.
LEFT: Working JB1, Signal Hill, Cape Town: the operator, display and antenna-turning gear.
Charcoal sketches by Geoffrey Long, *c* 1941.
(South African National Museum of Military History).

A photograph taken in secrecy of the JB1 radar installation at Cape Point, 1940, designed and built at the Bernard Price Institute and based on a design first tested on 16 December 1939.

'On a wet winter day with visibility down to a few yards and the Mouille Point foghorn blasting away, we were able to detect two ships making for Table Bay. The JB1 could see quite small craft – minesweepers, tugs and fishing boats up to and slightly beyond the optical horizon. That really determined the role of the JB1 round our entire coastline.*

'We also did successful trials on The Bluff, Durban in mid 1940. We had already had our first intake of trainees in January. Then Smuts realised that there was no radar in East Africa at all† and so a unit was formed and went up there.

---

* Radar units were installed from Lamberts Bay to north of St Lucia in Natal.
† The 1st SA Infantry Brigade left Durban for Mombasa on 16 July 1940. The SSS Unit, under Capt F J Hewitt, was based at Mambrui in Kenya.

'By April 1941 our entire operation had to move to the Middle East. Three JB radars were installed on the Sinai coast and they were operationally fully integrated with the RAF filter room at Ismailia. These stations were in use there for over a year until the new large radars coming into production in the UK replaced them.

'It was certainly exciting and it was certainly a considerable achievement. But for me the most exciting part of the war was the Sunday night summary of the week's war by A N Wilson*. Everybody sat by their radios at 9 o'clock. His programme would begin with the V for Victory sign. He was a remarkable narrator and summariser.The radio was left on all day, programmes interrupted by the V sign and then a brief bulletin would follow. It was tremendously exciting. '

• Interview 1990

Professor Bozzoli continued with his academic career at the University of the Witwatersrand after the war. He became Vice-Chancellor of the university in 1969.

---

* A N Wilson of *The Star* had a devoted following. His *News Topics of the Week* came on the air at 9 p.m. on Sunday. When he was appointed head of the Information Bureau the country mourned his loss to radio.

CHAPTER

7

'A movement to link South Africa up'

Lucy Bean and the SAWAS

The declaration of war ended the trips abroad overnight. Gone were the paragraphs in the social pages of the day noting who had departed and who had arrived. It was, although no one could conceive it then, the end of an era.

The Johannesburg Stock Exchange, which had suspended trading on Monday, 4 September, reopened on the 11th to confused and lethargic trading. It was a situation that continued for the duration of the war. Durban Deep was 56/3, Anglo Americans 34/4, Consolidated Murchisons 10½d and Randfonteins 39/4.

Plans were already in being to convert factories and to build new ones to supply the wartime needs of an army: everything from food to bullet-proof tyres. Men, and many schoolboys, tried to volunteer, but were told to come back later when a coherent system for intake had been formed. But in the confusion and the excitement of the early days of war* one body was already organised and ready to work: the South African Women's National Service Legion, later renamed the South African Women's Auxiliary Services, known to everyone as the SAWAS.

The foundations of the SAWAS had been laid in 1938 by two women, Lucy Bean, a woman's page journalist on the *Cape Argus* and Mrs E Kane Berman, Chief Commandant of the South African Red Cross.

Both had been to Europe before war broke out; both returned home determined to form a woman's organisation similar to those that they had seen in Britain, organisations providing a backup for an army and with a wide range of duties such as running canteens and typing services.

* Marked by the despatch of the British Expeditionary Force of 158 000 men to France on 30 September and by the sinking of HMS *Royal Oak* in Scapa Flow.

In the summer of 1937 Lucy Bean was walking through St James's in London with a friend, a senior officer in the Ministry of Health. Pausing in their walk, he turned to her. War, he said, was coming. 'When you go home, do what you can to get your people to prepare. For we shall be in it. This will not be a little war. Hitler is out to break the Commonwealth. You at the Cape are on the highway between East and West. You will be in the thick of it whether you want to be or not.'

A year later Mrs Kane Berman was approached by the Matron-in-Chief of the British Army Nursing Service with a view to organising a similar service in South Africa and to keep in contact with the British organisation in the times ahead. 'I would like to see about ten thousand trained women and girls in South Africa ready to play their part in the next war,' she said on her return to the Union.

On 20 April 1938, at two huge meetings organised by Lucy Bean in the Alhambra in Cape Town, four thousand women enrolled. In Johannesburg Mrs Kane Berman was busy setting up an organisation of women workers. By September 1939 the Women's Legion had seven thousand members.

The Department of Defence, attracted by the thought of unpaid women working voluntarily part-time, suggested that all existing women's war work should be co-ordinated by one body, working under the broad aegis of the Department. The SAWAS came into being.

Those working full-time were put into uniforms: an unattractive brown skirt and jacket with sky-blue stripes on the shoulders denoting rank and a dark-brown felt slouch hat. Ordinary auxiliaries wore tunics on duty. The same drab brown, to their sorrow.

Organised into twelve commands, the main sections of the SAWAS were auxiliary nursing, motor transport, canteen services, secretarial services, crèche and welfare services, civic services, hospital requisite services, general and specialised services. But, most of all, the SAWAS are remembered for the hospitality that they gave to the men and women who landed on our shores from the early days of war from convoys of grey ships.

By the end of the war the SAWAS numbered 65 000 women and had tended, comforted, fed, watered, entertained and sometimes married over a million men. 'I look upon SAWAS as a spiritual bequest to us,' said the new Prime Minister, Jan Smuts, '... it will become a movement to link South Africa up.'

Lucy Bean, who became Provincial Commandant of Command 13 (the Cape Peninsula) tells her story:

'The New Zealanders were the first to come, about ten thousand of them, mostly medical people en route to Britain for further training. We thought we were organised, but really we simply had no idea of what the numbers would do to Cape Town. Sometimes we had between sixty and seventy thousand men in the city, and that is an awful lot of young men to feed and entertain and keep out of mischief.

'We coped with the New Zealanders all right, because their numbers were relatively low, but when the convoy which included both the *Queen Elizabeth* and the *Queen Mary* came in it was another matter altogether. My flat was in Gardens, and it overlooked the city. I opened my bedroom window one day and I saw this hull come round the corner of Signal Hill. It went on coming and coming – a fantastic sight. I gulped when I thought of the boys on board just itching to get off the ships and into Cape Town. The convoy that had come in just before the *Queen Mary* and *Queen Elizabeth* convoy had taught us a lot.

'In the first place, we didn't know they were coming: the authorities were very concerned about security ("Don't talk about ships and shipping") and they hadn't let us know in advance. The result was that the men weren't dispersed; they were all in the centre of Cape Town and it was quite a sight, drunks lying all over the place. They headed straight for the bars and stayed there until they were pushed out and then just lay down on the pavements. One man tried to take a little black baby with him back on board. He was stopped at the gates to the docks and asked for an explanation. He said he had bought it, for a shilling, as a mascot for his unit. We spent the whole of the next day trying to find the mother and return the baby to her.

'When the next large convoy came in we were organised. We had a canteen built near the dock gates as the first port of call. Then we engaged special trains to take the men to different areas. We also organised a fleet of buses for them, but never *en masse* to one place. And by then there were also five hundred women on our lists with cars; they had a special petrol allowance, and they would be waiting in a line for the men to come off the ships and would whisk them away.

'Local councils gave us halls, free of charge, for the duration of the war, and we ran them as canteens. No alcohol, but tea and coffee and buns and sandwiches, music, a place where they could relax and feel at home. I said no alcohol, but of course we did have some. Every mess was issued with a drop of brandy. We called it "Ouma's Blood" or "Iss" (issue brandy) and we used it when one of the boys was a bit weepy. We'd talk to him and give him a bit of comfort and a glass of Iss. Some of the boys were homesick, but most of them buoyed each other up – they were very supportive. In one canteen someone was playing a sentimental tune on the piano and there was this young boy sitting there on his own with the tears rolling down his cheeks. He was just seventeen. He got a glass of Iss and it perked him up no end.

'The canteens were very well organised. The women would come down in the morning and open them up. We asked the Navy to see

The indomitable Lucy Bean, a photograph taken towards the end of the war.

that none of the men was let off the ships until 10 a.m., to give us time to get ourselves organised – not that that made any difference when the Australians hit us – and by the time they arrived there would be piping hot tea and coffee. At lunch time other women would arrive and they would take four or five of the boys home with them for a proper meal, because we couldn't do full meals. The men either spent all day with the women and their families, sometimes they went on a drive, or they would come down to the canteens again because we had a dance in the halls every night.

'When the first convoy came in, with the New Zealand nurses, we hadn't enough men for a dance, so I rang up the camp at Wynberg. I asked them to send their young men down to the City Hall where we held the dance. Everyone had a good time: the girls were pretty and the boys were pleased. But when the next hospital ships came in they were filled with British nurses. I telephoned Wynberg again and asked them to send their men down for another dance. But when I saw the nurses coming off the ship, I realised that the men wouldn't be too excited: they were all grey-haired, and some of them were somewhat stout. The men were very good about it, though. One of them danced up to me and just said: "Not up to standard, Miss Bean," and let it go at that.

'Those British nurses ... cheeky. They pinched all our glasses because they apparently were terribly short of glasses on the ship.

They tucked them under their breasts and tried to walk out like that. Well! We realised what was happening, so we stood at the door as they went out and just got all the glasses back. We hadn't got enough ourselves. We had to organise all the knives, forks, cups, saucers and all that for the camps all over the place, and we were terribly short. We had to get cups and saucers from South America, it was so bad; so we weren't going to let the British girls walk off with anything.

'But it wasn't often we had to look for men. It was the other way round most of the time. The girls in Cape Town had a wonderful time. Just imagine, sixty thousand men in town at any one time. They were very much in demand, I can tell you. There were lots of high jinks, lots of fun and quite a lot of engagements. The sea transport people were very good about these engagements. They would ring me up – by then we knew exactly how many were coming in and when, all in code, of course – and they would say "so and so is coming in" and I would alert the girl and we would leave them to their own devices.

'I suppose there was hanky-panky. The nearest I ever got to it was one night at the Mayor's Garden* when I was standing at the door and a young Tommie came up to me and asked me to dance. I was only in my early thirties, but I said "I'm old enough to be your mother, go and ask someone else," and he looked me slowly up and down and said, "Madam, if you let me, I'll make a mother out of you tonight ..."

'I had two telephone numbers and I was available there day or night: 2-0041, my office number, and 2-2608, my home number. I was very fortunate in that the SAWAS head office in Cape Town – we were Command 13 – was on the upper floor of the old Supreme Court, only about a block away from the *Cape Argus*† offices. The newspaper was very good to me during the war years. I was allowed to do all the SAWAS work provided I did the women's page. So I would go into the *Cape Argus* first thing and do some writing and put everything together and lay out the pages (I was in a slightly curious position because I was both making the news and writing it) and then I would walk to the SAWAS offices and come back late in the afternoon to check the layout and prepare for the next day.

'It used to be a very emotional sight for all us women seeing the convoys coming in, and even more emotional when they went out, because you knew that on board would be some of the boys that you had met and they were almost certainly going to be killed or torpe-

* A canteen built by the City Council in a former parking space behind the City Hall. In 1943 seventy thousand eggs were cooked in this canteen in one month alone for visiting troops.

† Now *The Argus*.

doed. And they were so very young, for all their nonsense. After the Battle of Crete in May 1941, three thousand survivors were brought into Cape Town. They were dressed in white shorts, vests and solar topees, and that was all. They had nothing. We used up all our stocks of clothing on them and we still hadn't enough, so some of the SAWAS whose own sons were serving up north gave the men their sons' flannel trousers and sports jackets.

'HMS *Ajax*, with the wounded on board after the Battle of the River Plate* came into Cape Town – that was very stirring – and so did the cruisers *Cumberland, Cornwall* and *Dorsetshire*.

'We had terrible memories of the Australians. They had come to Cape Town in the First World War and they had been very tough. We had a lot of fun with them this time. They would march up to the traffic policemen in Adderley Street and cut their braces. A beer lorry was stopped and they handed the beer out to everyone and then commandeered the lorry to look for more. Cape Town responded very well.

'All this time, of course, we were knitting like mad, supplying things to Ouma's Gifts and Comforts Fund. Because of the shortage of wool, we got out old spinning wheels from retirement and set to spinning. We used to knit in the City Hall, and one room was set aside as a storeroom for all the spinning-wheels and bits and pieces.

'Altogether over nine thousand women in Cape Town became SAWAS. Even the socialites, who were a bit toffee-nosed in the beginning, mucked in. I don't think any city offered as much as Cape Town did over these years.

'All anyone had to do was call us. A typical call would be like the one that I got from Major "Tank" Ransome of the Royal Marines. He telephoned me once and said: "Two cruisers will dock within half an hour. Please will you do something to entertain the sailors besides car

---

* *The Graf Spee*, a 'pocket' battleship with a crew of 44 officers and 1 050 men under the command of the gentlemanly Captain *(Kapitän zur See)* Langsdorff made her way into the southern Atlantic and from 26 September 1939 until she was brought to battle off Montevideo on 13 December 1939 off the River Plate, had caused havoc among Allied shipping. Langsdorff considered that the Atlantic was becoming too hot for him and he headed for the Indian Ocean, passing Cape Town at 4 a.m. on 3 November 1939. He considered an attack on the South African coastline and a bomb attack, by means of a seaplane, on the oil tanks in Durban, but he made for the area north-east of Lourenço Marques. Only one ship was sunk, but for the senior British naval officer in Durban this seemed to confirm the presence of the *Graf Spee*. After sinking two more ships, the battleship made for the River Plate. At 6.07 a.m. on 13 December she opened fire on HMS *Exeter*, which was accompanied by *Ajax* and *Achilles*. Less than 45 minutes later the valiant *Exeter*, severely damaged and smoking copiously, was firing from only one turret. *Ajax* was also badly damaged, though *Achilles* got off more lightly. The *Graf Spee* broke off the action and made for Montevideo. At 6.15 p.m. on Sunday, 18th, *Graf Spee* left the harbour and as the sun set scuttled herself. In Buenos Aires the next day Langsdorff shot himself.

drives?" I said: "Like what? And when?" All he said was: "Tonight. Pretty girls and beer." And we did, for nearly seven years, because we were only stood down in 1947 after the Royal visit. ’

•Interview, 1990

In spite of the rapid mobilisation of the SAWAS, both the Government and the Defence Force were struggling to make plans and to honour promises made in terms of men to Britain, which would take the country effectively into the war. Hampered by a bitterly divided country, no one was more aware of the difficulties ahead than General Smuts. One of his main tasks in the years ahead would be his attempt to unite the country.

CHAPTER

8

'The tragic division among us'

General Jan Smuts's New Year's Eve broadcast, 1939

No one knew better than the Prime Minister, Jan Smuts, that South Africa was unprepared for war. Apart from the political division, which grew wider and more acrimonious as the early years of war progressed, neither the Permanent nor the Active Citizen Force was in any state to go to war.* But the country rapidly prepared itself.

One month after the outbreak of war a technical committee with Brigadier O J Hansen, Chief Engineer of Iscor as chairman, was appointed to inquire into and report on the acquisition and production of war material. The committee recommended that a centralised control should be established to oversee the methods of creating and procuring war supplies. As a result of the recommendations of the committee Dr H J van der Bijl was appointed Director-General of War Supplies on 24 November 1939.

Van der Bijl gently but firmly commandeered the services of businessmen to fill the senior positions on his staff. None of them in the early days of the war could have foreseen how difficult their jobs would become. When the war broke out South Africa expected war supplies, in the main, to be provided by Britain. After the fall of France in May 1940 and with most of Europe subjugated, the supplies simply never came. South Africa had to buckle down and, with an exhilarating mixture of improvisation and work round the clock, was able to come up with the goods. The record, even seen from the distance of 1992, was an astonishing one.

---

* The figures were horrifying: the Permanent Force had 352 officers and 5 033 other ranks, the ACF had 13 490; the SAAF had 131 officers and 1 605 other ranks; the Royal Navy Volunteer Reserve (SA) had 57 officers and 743 other ranks and the eight ACF field ambulance units of the Medical Corps had only 89 officers and 1 141 ORs for the training year 1938-39. Coast defences scarcely existed, and industry, so vital in war, was totally unprepared.

By the time the 1st South African Division left for the Abyssinian campaign at the end of November 1940, local industry was not only manufacturing weapons and clothing but providing thousands of vehicles of different types, and general service waggons, soon to be the envy of the British forces in the north.*

The key to the expansion of industry and the equipment of the South African fighting men was the steel and munitions industries; for example, South African Railways and Harbours, which managed to produce an ambulance train within six weeks from the date of order in January 1940, and the Royal Mint in Pretoria, installed a complete plant for the manufacture of small arms and ammunition and remained throughout the war the main supplier of accurate gauges.

Within ten days of the outbreak of war, and certainly not receiving as much attention as the volunteers steadily offering their services all over the country, National Emergency Regulations were published on 14 September 1939, permitting the Minister of Commerce and Industries, on the advice of the National Supplies Board, to regulate and control the economic resources of South Africa. Among other measures, the Board acted to prevent hoarding and (not very successfully) profiteering, exercise control of imports and exports, food supplies and rationing and the obtaining of supplies both inside and outside the country.

Amid this activity, much of it confused in the early days of the war, the Prime Minister moved with apparent serenity, although his work load was formidable by any standards. He was deeply disturbed by the divisions within the country and, even early in the year, by the threat of sabotage by South African citizens. Smuts, with the slight figure of 'Ouma' by his side, retreated to his farmhouse at Irene outside Pretoria whenever he could.

With its verandah running round the house, his simple, even austere bedroom and the casual and warm entertainment that the couple offered to great and small alike, the house was a haven of peace, even though it gave Smuts's security advisers nightmares.

From a book-lined room at Irene, then, the Prime Minister sat down on New Year's Eve 1939 to deliver a message to the country, broadcast by the South African Broadcasting Corporation. For eight minutes Smuts, with his fine command of the English language, cajoled, chided and gave hope to the people of South Africa in this, their first wartime New Year of the Second World War:

---

* The waggons carried the full equipment of a certain number of men, including their food. They were based on an idea of Smuts's, an updated version of the old commando idea, and they allowed great mobility in the field.

ABOVE: General Jan and 'Ouma' Smuts's farmhouse at Irene, Pretoria. (*The Star*)

LEFT: The Prime Minister at his desk. (*The Star*)

'Good evening, my friends. May I wish you all a Happy New Year, although that wish is not unmixed with deep concern. We are glad to part with the old year, which has brought us and the world so much bad luck, brought us a long series of fears and alarms ending at last in a great war.

'The calamity which so many of us had considered unthinkable, that of another great war within a few decades of the end of the last World War, that calamity is upon us in all its horrid possibilities. We looked upon August 1914 as the black date in history and prayed never to see the like again. It may yet be that September 1939 may stand out as no less black and sinister.

'But this war has, after four months, proved full of surprises, and has in many ways been entirely unlike what we had expected it to be. And so it may be to the end. The devastating attack with which it was to open has not yet come. While in the last World War the first four months of the war saw some of the greatest battles of all history, so far no great battle has been fought in this war, on land or sea or in the air. On both sides there is a curious hanging back from the fatal clinch.

'And although we see little prospect of peace, still we should never cease to hope. Who knows whether 1940 does not hold some surprises and may not witness some unexpected turning of the corner, some fruitful peace effort backed by heaven's high blessing and the frail bark of our western civilisation may unexpectedly sail out of the storm into smooth waters.

'One dare not hope for so much, but at this moment one may at least hope and pray that 1940 may continue the surprises of the last four months and may bring the world luck. In that case, how we shall hold our breath and bless it as the happiest surprise of history. The age of miracles is never past, but it would not be wise to build our hopes on miracles. Let us at any rate be thankful that the worst has not yet happened and that some unseen hand has stayed the blow of blows which would finally extinguish all hope of peace before the bitter end.

'Even politics, which some wag has called our premier national industry, shows no signs of flagging. The outbreak of the war, far from sobering our people into a sense of responsibility and calling a halt to our excessive party politics, seems to have coincided with a fresh impetus to our party's strength.

'This is the sadder side of our national life. In the moment of danger, instead of uniting round our leadership, we do our best to break it down. People do not seem to have realised yet that this country is really at war. That war is no longer an open or debatable question for us, but a decision has been taken by Parliament which is an irrevocable fact, a fact which may influence the future of this country more deeply than any other political decision it has ever taken.

'The point I would specially emphasise is that this country is at war, that we should realise that fact with all its consequences, and that our whole situation should be viewed from that angle even though our actual share in the war still remains comparatively small. In times of war our slogan is 'my country, right or wrong'.

'The question is no longer whether we are rightly at war, as if the rights and wrongs of our being at war can still be debated as an open question. That issue is decided and closed, and every patriotic South African, whatever his views as to the rights and wrongs of the question, and whatever his politics, can now only put the interests and well-being of his country first and foremost in his thoughts and actions.

'"Let the consuls declare that no harm befalls the state", such was the ancient war formula of the Roman Senate and such must be the first thought of all our political leaders of whatever party. Our first duty therefore is to prepare for war and to put this country in a thorough state of defence. For four months now that has been our main task, and right nobly has the young manhood of South Africa listened to their duty.

'Tonight it is my privilege gratefully to bear testimony to the wonderful volunteering efforts of the last four months. I should never have thought that so much could be done to put our house in order in so short a time.

'I close with a few words aimed more specifically at my Afrikaans-speaking friends and all parties involved.

'I have spoken about our choice in the war. That choice with all its overwhelming responsibility was relatively easy for the English-speaking Afrikaners to make, their hearts agreed with their heads.

'On the contrary, for Dutch Afrikaners the choice was a crisis which hit deep, causing the tragic division among us.

'But don't allow the crisis to become a tragedy. Don't allow the division to turn into judgment. In the words of Oliver Cromwell: Let even the bitterest opponents concede that it may be possible for them to be wrong.

'Don't allow the division to become a chasm which will undo a lot of good work done during the last couple of years. Until 4 September it was our deep understanding that our national direction was the right one.

'Let us hold on to the light which saw, tested and followed us through those years of working together with the races and old parties.

'Years of peace and blessing and progress for the whole of South Africa. ’

• SABC Archives.

CHAPTER

9

1940

Mobilisation, embarkation, blood, toil, tears and sweat

We were halfway through the Phoney War. Nothing much, other than the sinking of the German battleship *Graf Spee*, had happened. For the Union, as well as for Britain, the five months of martial inactivity which followed the declaration of war was a godsend. It gave us time to prepare ourselves for the fighting that would surely come.

The South African Air Force (SAAF), it was envisaged, with its 131 officers and 1 605 other ranks (including 800 apprentices) would be expanded to thirty squadrons.* Coast defences were to be modernised, 382 motor ambulances, six ambulance trains and two hospital ships were needed for the medical services. The shortage of automatic weapons was put at 833 Bren guns, 780 anti-tank guns (twenty were available); 548 three-inch mortars would be needed.

Minimum requirements for armoured fighting vehicles were put at 22 light tanks (two obsolete ones were all the Union possessed) and 67 armoured cars (again, there were two, dating back to 1925). In the end 5 770 armoured cars were built in the Union during the war years.

As African Explosives and Chemical Industries (AECI) expanded to cope with war production; South African scientists, working in the utmost secrecy at the Bernard Price Institute at the University of the Witwatersrand were independently developing radar. New training camps were being built all over the country for the expected flood of men, and all key points in the Union were guarded.

Instructions were issued that no volunteer was to be turned down, even if men were called up a month later. Between seven and eight hundred men a day were volunteering at Witwatersrand Command; not nearly enough for the planned divisions.

---

* Thirty-five SAAF squadrons were formed during the war.

The Union Defence Force wasn't the only force to be slowly mobilising. The Ossewabrandwag, formed as a cultural organisation, was assuming distinctly militarist lines, organised like the commandos of old. Later the Ossewabrandwag would create the *Stormjaers,* shock troops, trained and ready for action against fellow South Africans. The first Commandant-General of the OB, Col J C Laas, was succeeded by the formidable J F J van Rensburg, a man who had met Hitler and was openly pro-German.

The Phoney War ended abruptly on 9 April when German troops invaded Denmark and Norway, followed on 10 May by the invasion of the Low Countries.

As the mining industry shelved plans to open a new goldfield in the Orange Free State and turned its attention instead to making munitions (43 mine workshops, non-profit-making, contributed to the war effort), the British Prime Minister, Neville Chamberlain, resigned.* He was succeeded by Winston Churchill, the right man at the right hour: pugnacious, ruthless, arrogant, self-indulgent, difficult, talented and with rare oratorical powers, Churchill stood fast and steadied his beloved sceptred isle when it needed it most. He promised nothing but 'blood, toil, tears and sweat' and finally 'Victory at all costs, victory in spite of terror, however long and hard the road may be.' The Commonwealth, like Britain, thrilled to his words. On 14 May, the day after Churchill's speech, the unimaginable happened.

Bypassing the Maginot Line, the Germans broke into France through Ardennes Forest† and pushed south towards Paris and west towards the Channel. As the British Expeditionary Force fell back towards the Channel towards the French seaside town of Dunkirk, the South African government realised that they could expect no help from Britain, either in men or military equipment. Henceforth, as Britain stood alone against the might of the Third Reich, South Africa would have to fend for herself.

As the British were retreating towards Dunkirk the 1st SA Infantry Brigade was mobilised, together with the newly formed Tank Corps, the SA Artillery Corps and the Engineering Corps. On 29 May, as the evacuation from the beaches of Dunkirk began,‡ thousands of South Africans joined up.

General Smuts spent his seventieth birthday (24 May) cutting cakes and attending a banquet in Johannesburg held in his honour. It was the first time that he had been seen in uniform in this war – the

---

* He died of cancer in the autumn of 1940.

† Where, four years later, the Battle of the Bulge took place, the last real resistance offered by a nearly defeated German army and its once proud Panzers.

‡ The evacuation was completed on 5 June. Over 200 000 Britons and 140 000 French and Belgians were saved.

same carefully preserved uniform that he had taken off in 1918. And in that dark month of May 1940 the first South African servicemen to take the Red Oath (which enabled them to serve anywhere in Africa) proudly bore the orange flashes on their shoulders – like a red rag to the Ossewabrandwag bull, for they set upon servicemen wearing them whenever they could.

Key men (such as those employed on the railways, the post office, the electricity and water supplies, mines, hospitals, banks, building) chaffed at their enforced civilian status. Those who attested – took the Red Oath – were given a round metal lapel-badge with the words 'On Service' and 'Op Diens' on it and a small orange flash suspended below.

As South Africans struggled to come to terms with the execrated National Loaf, an unappetising grey in colour and often with gelatinous lumps inside (it was made partly with fishmeal and went sour overnight), and coped with the irritating shortages of pins, lavatory paper and soap, the skies over the south of England were filled with the whines and vapour trails of Spitfires and Messerschmitts: the battle for Britain had begun.

While most of the Union troops were undergoing their training and the public again learnt with pride the names of historic regiments (the Transvaal Scottish, the Natal Carbineers, the Botha Regiment, the Dukes, the SA Irish), other South Africans were already fighting, principally those who had joined the RAF ('Sailor' Malan, who flew from Biggin Hill during the Battle of Britain, was one of them), and an advanced guard already in Kenya.

We listened to the wireless like junkies. There was the 6 p.m. news: first the chimes of Big Ben and then: 'This is the BBC, London. Here is the news and this is Bruce Belfrage reading it …' A N Wilson of *The Star* had a devoted following with his weekly *News Topics of the Week* at 9 p.m. every Sunday. And then were was *Snoektown Calling* by Cecil Wightman, and the forces' programmes, which have changed little in the fifty years between the war and now. Later in the war news broadcasts from London were prefaced by the opening chords of Beethoven's Fifth Symphony, the morse code for V for Victory.

Ouma (Isie) Smuts's Gifts and Comforts Fund was launched, likewise the Governor-General's War Fund which, by the end of the war, had raised millions of pounds. The country echoed not only with the beat of marching feet but with the click of knitting needles: *everyone* knitted and carded (some women even spun the wool). Housewives were persuaded to hand in aluminium and copper saucepans (to make aeroplanes) and in Cape Town a two-minute pause at noon was instituted; to remember, to pray and to think. The pause began when the noonday gun on Signal Hill was fired and it ended with a bugler play-

Mrs I W Schlesinger (wearing the hat) presents a cheque for £58 000 to 'Ouma' at Libertas. With the two women are Mr I W Schlesinger and Jan Smuts. The money was given to the SA Gifts and Comforts Fund from money received from Ouma's Birthday Party organised by African Consolidated Theatres. Fund-raising was a full-time occupation for many; so was the Gifts and Comforts Fund. Later in the war, Gifts and Comforts' 'glory-bags' were even handed out to German wounded in South African military hospitals in Italy. (*The Star*)

NUWEJAAR · NEW YEAR · 1945

These metal boxes were distributed to troops 'Up North', supplied by the SA Gifts and Comforts Fund. They were used as New Year fillips to morale.

GREETINGS FROM SOUTH AFRICA
We rely on you and are grateful.
Ons vetrou op jou en ons is dankbaar.
GROETE VAN SUID AFRIK

ing the Last Post. Opponents of the war chose this two-minute silence to wander across the streets, yawn and scratch their heads.

In July ninety German aircraft were shot down in six days over Kent. By August the Battle of Britain was coming to an end. Hitler decided to bomb British towns in reprisal for the bombing of Berlin. That decision saved the fighter stations that were vital to Britain. 'The gratitude of every home in our island, indeed throughout the world,' Churchill told his peoples on 20 August, '– except in the abodes of the guilty – goes out to the British airmen who, undaunted by odds, unwearied in their constant challenge and mortal danger, are turning the tide of battle by their prowess and devotion. Never in the field of conflict was so much owed by so many to so few.'

In the Union came the day that everyone had been waiting for: in what was the worst-kept secret of the war, the 1st SA Infantry Brigade* entrained for Durban. Singing 'So Long Sarie, So Long' and much else that was unrepeatable, they embarked on a dull grey convoy at night in full blackout for Mombasa and thence to Gilgil in Kenya for further training. It was 16 July 1940; and from then on a steady stream of men in khaki went north. 'Up North' was an expression that lasted throughout the war.

They were going to meet the Italians who, in theory, had the ability to bomb Johannesburg and who had invaded British Somaliland on 4 August. Few of the men had heard of Abyssinia or Somaliland; no one had heard of El Wak, or Mega or Marsabit of Sololo. But they would.

By the end of September the Battle of Britain was over and the Blitz intensified in fury. The 2nd SA Division was formed in October and, on 1 November, just as the folks back home were watching Judy Garland tripping the light fantastic down the yellow brick road in *The Wizard of Oz,* the East Africa Force under Lt-Gen Sir Alan Cunningham, and including a substantial South African force, was formed; and the 1st SA Division was on its way Up North to Kenya.

Affluent Johannesburgers, dressed in swanky evening clothes, held (legal) roulette and poker evenings for war funds. Next year, they told each other, the *real* fighting would begin. And we wished the men luck as we waved them goodbye.

---

* 1st Royal Natal Carbineers, 1st Duke of Edinburgh's Own Rifles, 1st Transvaal Scottish.

CHAPTER

10

'Fraudulent enlistment'

George O'Neill, volunteer, deserter, volunteer

Everyone who supported the war was doing his bit, though in some confusion. Defence Headquarters in Pretoria announced that the Active Citizen Force would be expanded to thirty battalions; a Special Service Reserve Battalion for men over forty-five (the equivalent of the British Home Guard, or Dad's Army) was formed for guard and protection duties, freeing younger men for the volunteer army, and war production was getting into its stride – three-inch mortars were already being supplied by March 1940 to East Africa and Rhodesia and later to the Middle East.

With a projected figure for the ACF of thirty thousand, double its 1939 figure, plans were also in operation to house recruits during their training. One of the first was at Potchefstroom, where the Artillery School was established as early as October 1939 with the arrival of the Transvaal Horse Artillery.

Although men were steadily volunteering, there were not nearly enough to make up the numbers for the projected four divisions, and mobilisation was delayed because of the shortage. Recruiting took place all over the country; Permanent Force officers such as Col Dan Pienaar* toured the country for recruits, often in the face of great hostility.

Recruits eager to do their bit also faced hostility, not only from the now open militant Ossewabrandwag but sometimes from their Permanent Force officers. One of the problems of a volunteer army† as opposed to an army of conscripts was the men's determination to be placed in a regiment of their own choice. One of the men who volun-

* Who took over command of 1st SA Infantry Brigade on 19 June 1940, the beginning of an illustrious but short-lived war career. See 'He was so deeply loved'.

† In spite of the high hopes of the Union Defence Force for white volunteers, it was obvious even from early 1940 that Indians, Malays, blacks and Coloureds would have to be drawn upon if it were to operate at all. In May 1940 the Cape Corps was reformed, and in June the Native Military Corps with eight battalions was formed. None of them was permitted to carry arms.

teered at the very beginning of the war was George O'Neill, and he, like many another recruit, had a pretty rough time. After all, in the early days of 1940 it was an army trying to shake off the image of Pirow's bushcarts and the outdated methods of the 1914-18 war. O'Neill's first few months of war were a foretaste of things to come:

'It was while visiting a friend, on that historic Sunday the 3rd September, that I was to hear the announcement over the radio, that England had declared war on Germany. With a rising sense of excitement and anticipation, I started to plan how I could join up as soon as possible. I wanted to work my way over to England on a ship so that I could join one of the glamour regiments like the Guards or the Black Watch!

'That plan was knocked on the head because I was on the "A" class Permanent Force Reserve. It was therefore only on 5 December 1939, that I attested at Potchefstroom with the South African Artillery. Conditions were grim, eight men to a bell tent and sleeping on ground sheets only. We had 18-pounder split-trail guns, which at the time were the most up-to-date field guns in the Union, and beautiful Permanent Force horses at first, but eventually we were given remounts which we had to break in ourselves. We also had mules to pull "Pirow's Bush Carts". After a number of courses at Roberts Heights I was made a troop sergeant. A special harness was made to pack 3-inch mortars on the horses and special ammunition pouches.

'Potchefstroom, and especially the University students, were very anti-soldier and many of our chaps were badly beaten up while passing through the grounds at night. Once we went to a dance and I asked an attractive young student for "the pleasure of the next dance". She looked up at me and without a word spat in my face. The laughter of her companions was short-lived when I pulled her boy-friend off his seat and knocked him to the floor. There was a free-for-all in which the soldiers gave a very good account of themselves …

'Our training took us to Klerksdorp and Parys. We were not very welcome there and had many a set-to with members of the Ossewabrandwag. Their favourite weapons were sjamboks. We would retaliate with our leather bandoliers, the pouches filled with blocks of wood, a very effective weapon but only at close range, so you had to take a few whiplashes to get in close enough for action.

'A new Commanding Officer – Major Van – arrived on the scene. He was one of the many Permanent Force officers who would not take the oath to serve anywhere in Africa. He had two sergeants, who also had not taken the oath, who we discovered were carrying tales from the Sergeants' mess to Major Van. One night Sgt Minter and I confronted these two and in the ensuing mêlée they got a frightful beating up, while Minter and I lost our stripes a few weeks later! Major Van disliked me intensely for a number of reasons. As troop sergeant I had been allowed a choice of horses, but as Commanding Officer he of course could take whichever horse he desired, and when he took the one I had chosen and I objected, he was furious with me.

'Once when I was bringing a squad from foot drill I passed him and gave the command "eyes right", he just ignored it and walked on. I stopped the squad, went up to him and demanded to know why he had not returned my salute. I thought he would have a stroke, but I stuck to my guns until he admitted he was wrong.

'A couple of friends and I went to investigate a dance that was being held in "The Afrikander Club". We were thrown out, after being bashed about a bit and told what they thought of Smuts's "Khaki Riders". We then went to the Soldiers' Club and rounded up about forty men and marched back to Afrikander Club, forced our way in and stopped the dance. There were a few fights, but it was broken up by the MPs and the SAP. I was taken to HQ next day and had to do a bit of explaining.

'In the Potch Show Grounds, next to our perimeter, stood a girls' school hostel. The night guards always tried to make a date with the girls. One of our amorous hopefuls was told by a girl he was trying to get off with, to climb up the pipes to a certain room at 11 o'clock that night and knock on her window. The window was on the second storey, and when he knocked the house matron opened the window and emptied a chamber pot over his head! He got such a fright that he fell and broke his leg!

'In Harrismith we were warned that the OB were about to rebel, so guards were doubled and live ammunition was brought into the camp. We were there for nearly a week. A dance was given for the

The military camp at Potchefstroom. Pirow's bushcarts can be clearly seen. (George O'Neill)

Battery in the City Hall, and during the evening I was dared to ask the Major's wife for a dance. I walked up to her and requested the pleasure of the next dance. She was charming, and we had three dances one after the other, but when I took her back to her seat the Major was livid! Next day at Van Reenen he got the Battery together and spoke at length about other ranks dancing with officers' wives. I found myself cutting chaff at all stops until we arrived at Ladysmith.

'On the first night there, lightning struck a piquet line and killed a number of our horses. Next day a man was drowned while watering the horses at the river. Later we were told by General Smuts that it was nice to see there were still horses and horsemen in the country, but that in warfare the day of the horse was over and the mounted units would be kept for Home Defence.

'Next day I asked Major Van for a transfer to a mechanised unit. He turned me down flat and added that my Christmas leave was not granted. It was then that I decided to desert and join another unit, which at my subsequent court martial was termed "fraudulent enlistment". Charlie Povey and I decided to go together; I handed all my kit to the quartermaster but Charlie said he could not be bothered to do so. A step he was later to regret. We got a lift to Durban, had a lovely holiday over Christmas, and on 6 January 1941 we joined the Natal Jocks, Armoured Fighting Vehicles Unit (AFV).

'About three months later Charlie had to go to Pietermaritzburg for something or other and was spotted by someone from the Battery, and next day the MP's came for us. The OC of the Natal Jocks was very sympathetic and told me he had wanted to promote me to corporal. He also said he would give me a good report and request that I should be transferred to the Natal Jocks.

'Major Van now overplayed his hand on two counts. He got the Battery together and told them that when he was finished with me no

one else would ever want to desert. He also said I was too dangerous to keep under guard in a tent and had me locked up in the Ladysmith SAP cells for over a week. During the court martial both of these counted against him, besides the fact that he was not completely truthful in giving evidence. We were sentenced to only three weeks' detention at Roberts Heights.

'The first night there I showed Charlie how to make enormous blisters on his feet with a dry towel so that next day we were given "light duties only". After a week I was called into the office and told that after a review of my case all charges were to be expunged from my record and I was free to go.

George O'Neill shortly before he deserted and volunteered again. The photograph was taken in Durban. (George O'Neill)

'In the meantime the Battery had to be disbanded because of desertions or whatever and had returned to Potchefstroom, without the horses and equipment, but with the Major still at the head of the remnants, which were to become replacements. I had excused duty because of my blisteɪs and waited for Charlie to return. The day he arrived we bumped into Major Van between two bungalows, with no one to see or hear us; we saluted smartly and came to a halt right in front of him. He turned pale and bit at his moustache and told us to get those "silly things" off our heads and get Artillery caps. I asked him if he thought Scottish Tams were silly; he blustered and said he could have us arrested for insubordination. I said: "Look, Major, you have blotted your copy-book enough already, so don't bite off more than you can chew." He hissed something through his teeth about getting his chance. Charlie said: "Not unless you get yourself a pair of Red Tabs."

'After our embarkation leave we began preparing to go up north as replacements in the Mechanised Transvaal Horse Artillery (THA). A few days before we were due to leave, Recruit Depot challenged us to a game of rugby. Charlie accepted against my advice and consequently the day we left he was in the sick bay with a broken leg! Tears streamed down his face when I went to say goodbye to him, he was really very upset. I saw him in a POW camp many months later, and he swore that Major Van had been overheard saying as we left, "Good riddance, I hope the buggers rot up there". Major Van, of course, never went "Up North". ’

George O'Neill's war was eventful. He sailed for Egypt with the Transvaal Horse Artillery in June 1941, just in time for Operation Crusader. He was captured at Sidi Rezegh and survived the sinking of the *San Sebastian* (see 'What the hell had happened'), Dysentery Acre and arrived at Bari in Italy as a prisoner of war, and he immediately began to make plans to escape. After one failure, he found himself in the Italian countryside, moving from village to village with the help of the Italians.

He was recaptured by the Germans at the end of 1943. With the possibility of a death sentence from the SS, he was billeted with the Jäger Panzer Regiment while awaiting a military tribunal. To his astonishment he was invited to the regimental Christmas party. 'At midnight,' he later wrote, 'They sang "Stille Nacht, Heilige Nacht". To me it was the most beautiful rendering of the song I have ever heard. Looking down the rows of suntanned combat soldiers' faces, I saw that many were wet with tears – I also felt mine beginning to flow.' On 21 January 1944 he escaped again, and after many adventures he reached British headquarters. He returned home on 3 September 1944.

•George O'Neill, *Enough for Survival*, 1985.

CHAPTER

11

'Outside the limits of South Africa'

The Africa or 'Red' Oath, March 1940

Within months of the outbreak of war, it was already envisaged that South African troops would be serving beyond the borders of their country. Although, for the time being, South Africa was not at war with Italy, a close watch was being kept on the Italians in Abyssinia and Somaliland.

If they moved further south, into Kenya, for example, or operated from the Belgian Congo, Tanganyika, Madagascar or even Portuguese West Africa, their aircraft, with a range of nearly two thousand miles, could bomb Johannesburg.

On 7 February 1940, General Smuts got to his feet and told Parliament that it was 'South Africa's policy to extend operations as far as Kenya and Tanganyika, using volunteers if necessary'.

On 29 March 1940 officers and men were invited to take a new oath, which became known as the Africa or 'Red' Oath, undertaking to serve anywhere in Africa for the duration of the war. The oath would be optional for those already serving (a significant number of men refused to take it) but in future no man would be permitted to join any branch of the South African Defence Force without taking the oath.

The famous red tabs, proudly worn by South African volunteers during the Second World War, whether they went abroad or not.

The African Oath was administered for the first time in May; the men who took it were then distinguished by strips of orange flannel on their shoulder-straps – the famous red tabs. The oath, which varied slightly between officers and other ranks, was to the effect:

'That in accordance with the resolution of Parliament, I will serve in the South African Permanent Forces and/or the Coast Garrison Forces and/or the Active Citizen Forces in Africa, whether within or outside the limits of South Africa, for the duration of the present war.'

CHAPTER

12

'In short it was a horrible experience'

Joshua 'Sticky' Furman and the Jocks, June 1940

May and June 1940 were momentous months in both Europe and South Africa. On 10 May Luxembourg, Holland and Belgium were invaded by the Germans. On that same day, as the news of the invasion came to South Africa via Reuters and radio, Neville Chamberlain resigned and Winston Churchill was asked by George VI to form a government.

On 13 May, as France sheltered behind what it fondly hoped was the impregnable Maginot Line, Britons and South Africans listened to the first of Churchill's great wartime speeches. He rose to a packed and silent House of Commons. 'I have nothing to offer but blood, toil, tears and sweat,' he told the House.

'We have before us an ordeal of the most grievous kind. We have before us many, many long months of struggle and suffering. You ask what is our policy? I will say: It is to wage war, by sea, land and air, with all our might and with all the strength that God can give us: to wage war against a monstrous tyranny, never surpassed in the dark, lamentable catalogue of human crime. That is our policy. You ask, What is our aim? I can answer in one word: Victory – victory at all costs, victory in spite of all terror, victory, however long and hard the road may be; for without victory, there is no survival. Let that be realised; no survival for the British Empire; no survival for the urge and impulse of the ages, that mankind will move forwards towards its goal. But I take up my task with buoyancy and hope. I feel sure that our cause will not be suffered to fail among men. At this time I feel entitled to claim the aid of all, and I say, "Come, then, let us go forward together with our united strength."

And united strength was needed as the Dutch capitulated and the German Panzers burst into France through the Ardennes. On 20 May

South Africa called up the 1st SA Infantry Brigade (1st Transvaal Scottish, the Dukes and the Carbineers) for continuous training. On 29 May, the evacuation of the British Expeditionary Force from the beaches of Dunkirk began. Less than two months later, on 16 July, the 1st SA Infantry Brigade left Durban for Mombasa – and war.

Joshua 'Sticky' Furman, a post office worker in the Free State, had joined the 2nd Transvaal Scottish early in 1940. Like many men, and against orders, he kept a diary from the day he joined up until he was invalided home with diabetes shortly before the calamity at Sidi Rezegh.

His hitherto unpublished diary, written in a sloping hand that closely covered the pages of his pocket notebook, reflects both the frustrations and the excitement of the disorganised days after mobilisation.

He did not write every day; this extract was written soon after his arrival at Zonderwater on 18 June 1940, before his training and embarkation for Mombasa, where he arrived on 27 November 1940:

‘ **18 June 1940**

General Mobilisation was evident. Battalion followed Battalion to Zonderwater for full-time service. The 2nd TS was the last to be mobilised of the Tvl units. Every inch of ground in Premier Mine and Zonderwater was occupied. Military equipment could not be manufactured fast enough to enable the Defence Dept to equip all the men. This sad state of affairs that now existed was due to the work of a former Defence Minister* who spent or rather "forgot to spend" the money voted by Parliament in previous years for the Defence Vote. The only thing this particular Minister is known for is the equipping of the SA Army with "bushcarts". Some of these stand outside the military college at Roberts Heights as a remembrance to the futile work of an absolutely incompetent Minister. Pietermaritzburg was the training centre for the 3rd Tvl Scottish, known as the "East Rand's Baby". This young and newly formed battalion under the able leadership of Lt-Col W Kirby, was undergoing intensive training during May and June. The authorities mobilised this unit at about the same time as its sister Battalion, the 2nd.

'Lt-Col Dalrymple, OC of the 2nd TS in a man-to-man talk with us in the Drill Hall in Johannesburg told us one fateful Tuesday evening on 10 June 1940 that at last we were mobilised. Possibilities of our meeting the enemy were discussed, and the high traditions of our Regiment would be upheld in the field when facing the enemy. All this sounded dramatic, and many a heart beat faster. Every man had to make final arrangements, and by Thursday the 12th had to notify the

---

* The unlamented Oswald Pirow. Hitler was his idol.

Officer Commanding of his willingness to serve on full-time service. Artisans and key men were withdrawn. Lads under 18½ had to get their parents' consent before they would be accepted. Huge strides ahead had to be taken in those two days.

'Thursday night soon arrived, and every member of the 2nd TS was present. Again we were marched into the Drill Hall. Something had gone wrong with the organisation. The Officer Commanding was depressed; his tone was unnatural. The matter was soon brought to a head and the 2nd TS found itself demobilised.

'This spelt disaster to many. Some had given up jobs, others had given notice to landlords; there was chaos among the men, and there was an air of great disappointment. Some compensation had to be arranged. It was impossible for the men to go back to their employers and ask for their jobs back again.

'However, all trained men and those who desired to go could transfer to the 3rd TS. This unit was now on full-time service and needed men to bring it up to war strength. It lost a few hundred of its men who had been recalled as artisans and key men.

'About two hundred men, including officers such as Maj Southey, Capt Jones and Lollip and others all went across to the 3rd. The cream of the old Battalion left. Those who stayed behind thought of promotion and their own ends. Many privates were offered stripes if they transferred. Most of us were disgusted with the internal organisation of the 2nd TS and gladly transferred.

'In fairness the 2nd TS deserved some gratitude in that it acted as a feeder battalion to both the Jock regiments on fulltime service.

'We all gathered outside the Drill Hall in the rain, ready to move. We were ordered to change into battle dress and leave all "revue order" uniform behind.

'There was great confusion: two hundred men all searching for their kit-bags, changing into battledress and cursing loudly. The Drill Hall was like an Indian bazaar.

'Col Kirby took over the command from Col Dalrymple and welcomed us. He looked a proper soldier. His manly way of talking impressed us, and we were confident in his leadership.

'One section was bundled into army vehicles and were off to "do a job of work". No one knew their destination, but the general feeling was "action". It seemed incredible that we should be going into action without proper equipment, etc. Many were surprised when they arrived at the Portuguese East African border, and did patrol duties at Komatipoort.* Meanwhile the rest of us were marched through the streets to Park Station. When we got into our train a multitude of

* It was believed that there might be an invasion from Portuguese East Africa.

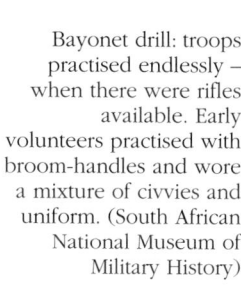

Bayonet drill: troops practised endlessly – when there were rifles available. Early volunteers practised with broom-handles and wore a mixture of civvies and uniform. (South African National Museum of Military History)

In training, 1940. Many of the men went to Barberton for training. Route marches up and down the steep hills were killers. (South African National Museum of Military History)

people gathered to wave us goodbye. Mothers and sweethearts were a pitiful sight with tears flowing down their cheeks. We were surrounded by civilians wishing us luck, waving Union Jacks patriotically and shouting "Leave some for me", at the same time pushing a packet of 10 cigs into one's hand.

'Again the army failed to cater for the men. No arrangements were made for grub; and here I must say a word of appreciation for the Women's Auxiliary Service* for the excellent work that they did. The sandwiches and cigs that that ladies dished out to us were a god-send. Hats off to the ladies!

'Amid cheering and singing we left Jo'burg for Zonderwater. The train pulled out about 11 a.m. It was cold and rainy.

'The boys were all in high spirits. After having a bite to eat they all settled down and made themselves comfortable. Old friendships were renewed and new ones were started on this trip. Here a few played bridge, while over on the other side some would swop yarns and tell tall stories.

'It was bitterly cold when we arrived at Zonderwater that afternoon, with a biting wind.

'We stood on the platform, clad only in a shirt and battle togs, waiting for orders, our hands and feet numb. At intervals it rained, which made matters worse. In short it was a horrible experience.

'The advance-guard of the 3rd Jocks then arrived. Everyone had a greatcoat on and was warmly clad. We saw that these fellows had men in charge who looked after them.

'I expected to see some of the older men drop out from exposure. Some of them weren't used to the hard life of the army, and it was surprising to see them all standing up to it. Most of us had had our intensive training a few weeks before and we were toughened up a bit.

'We were marched through mud across wet fields to the Premier Mine camp two or three miles away. Walking at a brisk trot soon warmed us up and the blood in one's body started circulating briefly.

'When we arrived at the camp we were cheered by our comrades. It did a lot to raise the morale of the rookies. To me it seemed silly; as if they took us for soldiers returning from a battlefield

'We were now the guests of the 1st who put us up for a night in their mess-hall, three hundred of us. The camp site had been condemned by the MO. We were given three blankets each.

'One night turned out to be four. Every single man had a cold by now. Some got pneumonia and were taken to hospital. No wonder, as we were sleeping on cement floors.

---

* The newly formed SAWAS

'Fatigue parties went over daily to Zonderwater, erecting huts and carrying out various duties, etc. It was a relief to sleep on Mother Earth again. The old 3rds had a few days' leave to settle their affairs. On their return those of us who stayed behind had the camp in tip-top order: all the tents pitched, the parade ground cleared and the QM stores unpacked and so on.

'The health of the men was at a low ebb and the authorities thought it best to give them five days' leave to recover. We made the most of it, with reunions and dinners in Jo'burg. We had a very fast life during that period.

'The rest did us the world of good, and on our return we were ready and fit for anything. '

CHAPTER

13

'Would the camp be ready for us?'

Private Dick West in training, Premier Mine, Zonderwater and Barberton, 1940

In 1899, at the beginning of the Second Boer War, the Boer forces had 97 guns. In 1939 South Africa had 65 mostly obsolete guns. The shortage of weapons was put at 833 Bren guns, 780 anti-tank rifles, (twenty were available) and 548 three-inch mortars. Reserves amounted to only twelve thousand men, and the South African Instructional Corps had only 104 officers and men dispersed all over the country.

Instructions were given for the building of new training camps to accommodate Active Citizen Force volunteers. Col B F Armstrong was ordered to form a camp at Barberton to accommodate the 5th SA Infantry Brigade. On 13 August, a month after the 1st SA Brigade sailed for East Africa, the 1st Division, comprising the 1st, 2nd and 5th SA Infantry Brigades, was formed under the command of Brig-Gen George Brink (promoted Maj-Gen in 1940).

It was into this state of unpreparedness and confusion that thousands of volunteers marched. One of them was Dick West, who joined the newly re-formed South African Irish Regiment. With other volunteers, members of either the Irish, the 3rd Transvaal Scottish or the 2nd Regiment Botha, he arrived at Premier Mine in bitterly cold highveld weather to begin training. Nothing was ready for the men. In civilian clothes Dick West and his fellow-soldiers ate, drank, drilled and froze.

'It was bitterly cold, a steely mid-winter's day, when we marched into the barracks at Premier Mine. The accommodation was as hard as the weather – asbestos-walled buildings with bare cement floors and not a bed in sight and all of us with nothing but our civilian clothing. With not even a blanket between us we were expected to sleep on the freezing cement floors.

'Luckily I had brought with me not only a leather overcoat but an eiderdown; and even then I nearly froze. How the men with only the clothes they stood up in coped I don't know. A lot of them fell ill, some seriously, with colds, 'flu and pneumonia. Nothing had been prepared for us.

'We were there for a few terrible days. No one knew what to do with us, so they gave us lectures. One sergeant-major told us with relish all the things we could be put on the peg for, including "dumb insolence". We thought this was rather daft, because we were all volunteers and were itching to get down to soldiering. After the lecture he ordered us to pick up every cigarette-end and match lying on the ground. That was enough to make me want to go for him and desert immediately. You leave your comfortable office and volunteer because you want to do your bit for your country; and then you are set to picking up cigarette-ends – it just wasn't the game.

'Fortunately our stay at Premier Mine was brief if bleak. We were ordered to march to Zonderwater which, to our dismay, was in the same state of unreadiness. There weren't even asbestos huts, just a maze of bell-tents, forty men to a tent. We were like sardines in them, body squashed to body with just enough room for your feet to meet the pole in the centre when everyone was lying down. God help any man who had to get up to go outside ... it evoked the most terrific abuse, because he literally had to walk over the fellows.

'To call it spartan would be an understatement. There were showers all right, but because it was midwinter everything froze at night, so when you went shivering into the showers before parade there was no water. We went on parade – in our civilian clothes – dirty, and when we came off parade, even dirtier, we were too tired to wash. The stink of unwashed feet in the tent at night was nauseating.

'We had expected to be thrown into drilling, but we did very little, simply because there wasn't enough space for it. They set us to marching up and down the road, dry and dusty, and we did some arms drill, miming the actions because we hadn't been issued with any weapons.

'We Irish were among the fortunate ones not to have to drill with a broom-handle.* After a few days we were given rifles and bayonets. My rifle was a 1916 .303, with a date stamp. Someone before me had shortened the butt and it suited me perfectly, a lovely little rifle. It stayed with me until I was ordered to break it up in Tobruk when I was captured.

'Our instructor was in the permanent force. His fetish was to get us all into a circle to demonstrate arms drill; and if he thought you weren't paying attention he would suddenly throw the rifle, with a

---

* Unlike the 2nd Regiment Botha, which found drilling with broom-handles first funny, then ignominious and ultimately infuriating.

bayonet on the end, straight at you, bayonet first. If you didn't catch it, it would go straight into your chest. My first response was to throw the thing right back at him; but then I remembered the sergeant-major's lecture at Premier Mine and thought better of it.

'The food was skilly.* All the meat was dumped into a 44-gallon drum, then it was boiled until the fat came up to the surface, with a nice green tinge. We were each given a ladle of skilly and mixed vegetables. After the first few samples of this military repast we gave it a miss and went to the canteen to buy tins of fruit and cream or, when we had a pass, go into town for a decent meal. Breakfast wasn't too bad.

'I can't say I felt like a soldier, not in my civvies. One day we were issued with a jacket, a pair of army boots and a greatcoat. I wore the greatcoat all the time because it concealed my civvie trousers and I wanted people to know I was a soldier. Then came the day we were issued with our caubeens. There's this caubeen placed at just the right tilt on your head, it has a green shamrock on it and an Irish badge and a green hackle sticking up and I felt like the bees knees when I put it on. Suddenly I felt I was part of the Irish.

'Now the Irish were mighty fond of medical examinations. We never stopped having them. My first taste of this was when we were ordered to go for injections.

'We marched to the medical tent, a huge marquee with three tables in it. Behind each stood men with bowls of needles and serum. I stopped at the first table, and as I filed past the orderly behind it stuck a needle into my arm. Then I walked to the second table, where a syringe was screwed into the needle, I was given the injection, and the syringe was unscrewed. With the needle sticking out of my arm I went to the last table where the orderly pulled out the needle. There was blood flowing all over the place and a lot of the chaps fainted. Curiously enough, we never saw the chaps who fainted again.

'Not before time, we received orders to go to Barberton, which was to be our permanent training camp. We left in high spirits, singing at the tops of our voices, crammed into a convoy of trucks. We slept in the open at Middelburg and reached Barberton the following day. The big question was: would the camp be ready for us?

'It wasn't; but it was pretty, and warmer, at the foot of the Makonjwa mountains. We'd been hoping to be housed in finished bungalows, but there were only wooden shacks, still being built. I looked at the one I was assigned to incredulously. It had four wooden walls, a door, an earth floor and no roof. When they built the roof later I pinched some of the wood and made a bed for myself.

---

* A thin broth flavoured with meat.

'The three regiments* at Barberton made up the 5th Brigade. There was tremendous camaraderie and tremendous rivalry, even antagonism at times between us. Of the three regiments, it was the Scottish which had the aura of glamour and the tradition behind it. We were still building ours.†

'Slowly, through the months of training, we grew to love our regiment, to feel a part of it and proud to be serving with it.

'Our days began with reveille, with all the dogs accompanying the bugler in an early morning sing-song. There would be a rush for the showers and a quick shave, then we'd be on parade. After that the day would be varied. We might go for bayonet practice, a sinister activity, it might be arms drill, it might be target-shooting, or it might be a route march with compass-bearings. I most enjoyed being taken out into the veld and given the chance to use my own initiative, like being told to take a hill no matter what.

'There was a fair bit of weapons training, hand-grenades, target-shooting. Unfortunately for me I had a good eye, and when we first got to the shooting range I hit the bullseye and much to my disappointment I wasn't allowed to practise again but set to helping the others. We did a lot of route-marching, some of them quite arduous, but by now most of us were pretty fit. A lot of men dropped out of a thirty-mile march from Barberton to Nelspruit; but that was mostly from blisters.

'At last we were issued with our full uniform. All the trousers were in one pile, and when you found one that fitted you you went off and registered it. There was no case of correct sizing – you got it either too big or too small, and whichever was the most comfortable was the one you chose. When we were fully kitted out, complete with caubeens, we were very smart. The officers, of course, had more glamorous uniforms.

'We went into Barberton quite a lot. There were lots of parties, some of them pretty wild. One of the jobs that I enjoyed was being on stick parade, when you patrolled the town with a bayonet (but no rifle) and you could go into the cinema and make eyes at the girls or into the pub.

'I was on duty once with the Provost Marshal, 'Tiger' Burns, a big chap who had been a boxer and wasn't averse to using his fists. We went into the pub at the Transvaal Hotel‡ , and someone swore at him.

---

* The South African Irish Regiment, 2nd Regiment Botha and 3rd Transvaal Scottish.
† The South African Irish Regiment was raised as an infantry battalion in 1914, but was disbanded after the German South West Africa campaign. Raised again in 1939 under Lt-Col S F K Dobbs, the regiment was badly mauled at Sidi Rezegh and ceased to exist. Survivors were taken into Regiment Botha and 4th Field Regiment SAA.
‡ Now the Impala Hotel.

'His response was to punch the chap, who crashed to the floor. We picked him up and threw him into the back of the truck. When we had a full truck we went back to the camp and he said protectively: "These boys are not to be charged. Take them to their bungalows and let them sleep it off." And that was that. We were the best of pals, the Irish.

'At night in the bungalows there was a lot of chatting and a lot of gambling, mostly poker. We'd spread a blanket on the floor and play. By then we had electric light, so things were more comfortable.

'I joined the South African Irish because I had an Irish grandmother and also because everyone in my office was volunteering for the Scottish. All the time we spent in Barberton getting fit, learning to use weapons, learning how to become soldiers was valuable, but for me the most valuable thing of all was learning about camaraderie. By the time we left for East Africa one really did believe that under fire one would give one's life for another bloke.

'When the lights went out and everyone was asleep I lay wondering what it would be like when I came under fire, how I would react. I didn't know. My biggest terror was getting into a bayonet charge or being attacked with a bayonet. I didn't like the thought of cold steel: a bullet would be greatly preferable. I was offered promotion while we were at Barberton, but I turned it down simply because I was so unsure how I would behave under fire, especially if I were leading men and responsible for them when, for all I knew, I might turn round and run. I remained a private.

'When I joined up on 17 June 1940 it was with the firm conviction that we would be going to France. The papers at that time were full of Dunkirk and the fall of France, and it seemed logical that at some time we should be going there. But while we were at Barberton I realised that it would not be France but north, in Africa. The 1st Brigade was already at Gilgil, and there was a growing sense of frustration at Barberton that we weren't already on our way. We believed we were ready for anything.

Private Dick West of the South African Irish, caubeen and all, shortly before he embarked for East Africa on 30 November 1940 with the 1st SA Division under the command of Maj-Gen George Brink. (Dick West)

'It was General Smuts who told us that we would go up north. The whole of the 5th Brigade was on parade, and as I listened to him I had a sinking feeling. Suddenly we were faced with the real thing. It was a very emotional moment, listening to this great man who had been a great soldier. He told us we were embarking on an adventure, the greatest adventure of our lives, and that we would remember it for ever. None of us, he said, would ever regret it; and very few of us did.

'After our embarkation leave, the highlight of which was a big parade through Johannesburg and a concert at the 20th Century cinema, where Ivy Tresmond sang to us and was made an honorary Colonel of the regiment, we reported back to Barberton, and then promptly had to go back to the Reef, where we entrained. Most of the men had said goodbye to their families before we left, so there weren't too many scenes at the station, but some of the wives came, and of course there were tears.

'The last reception we were given before we reached Durban was at Knight's station where there was a tremendous welcome by the SAWAS, with tea and cakes and good wishes on the platform.

'When we got to Durban we marched straight on board the *Llanstephan Castle*. We stood at the rails as the ship pulled out. All the tugs in the harbour sounded off in farewell, and we sang as we slowly

South African volunteers before entraining. There were wild scenes at the docks as the camouflaged ships left harbour. (Africana Library)

moved out of the harbour, three passenger ships and a destroyer. As I watched the palms of Durban gradually shrinking it crossed my mind that I night not see South Africa again. ’

• Interview 1990.

Private Dick West fought with the South African Irish through the East African campaign and his regiment stood fast at Sidi Rezegh on 23 November 1941. He was one of the few to escape. He was ordered to take a wounded gunner to the Regimental Aid Post, and arrived there to find it occupied by Germans, who waved him in. 'Who are they to give me orders?' he thought indignantly; and he swung his truck round, headed for the open desert and came under direct fire from a German tank. After a night in the desert, with severely wounded men, he found the 4th Armoured Brigade and safety. He was later taken prisoner at Tobruk.

CHAPTER

14

'We now go forth as crusaders'

General Smuts's speech to the 1st SA Infantry Brigade, Zonderwater, 14 July 1940

From the moment when the Governor General, Sir Patrick Duncan, delivered the South African declaration of war on Germany on 6 September 1939 General Jan Christian Smuts, the Prime Minister and Minister of Defence, had worked ceaselessly to get a South African force into the field. It wasn't simply a matter of recruiting and training men: the whole of South African industry had to be galvanised to equip the men: guns, armoured cars, boots, food, medical supplies and so on ad infinitum.

But now, in July 1940, the 1st South African Infantry Brigade was ready. Fit, trained and equipped, impatient to enter the fray, the Brigade was warned on 27 June to prepare to entrain. Frustratingly, final orders for them to move were received only on 13 July. Many of the men would not see home again for five years. The 1st Brigade comprised the 1st Transvaal Scottish, the Royal Natal Carbineers and the Duke of Edinburgh's Own Rifles, each with its own proud history.

The Transvaal Scottish were raised in Johannesburg in 1902 and served in Zululand (1906), German South West Africa and, heroically, at Delville Wood in the 1914–18 war.

The Carbineers were raised in 1855, fought against the amaHlubi clan in the Drakensberg, in Zululand (1879), the Second Boer War, in Zululand (1906), in German South West Africa and overseas theatres in the 1914–18 war. Although none of the Carbineers assembled at Zonderwater in July 1940 could know, theirs was to be the only unit of the Union Defence Force to serve throughout the East and North African and Italian campaigns without the need to amalgamate with other units to keep up to strength.

The Dukes were raised in 1855 as the Cape Rifle Corps, and they served in the frontier wars, in the Transkei (1879), Basutoland (1880–1), Bechuanaland (1897), the Second Boer War, German South West Africa and overseas theatres in World War I.

And so they stood on the parade-ground at Zonderwater on 14 July 1940, before General Smuts, Sir Pierre van Ryneveld, Chief of the General Staff, and Brigadier-General George Brink, Director of Army Organisation and Training. Was it mere coincidence that the farewell parade was held on Delville Wood Day, 24 years after three thousand-odd South Africans had gone into battle in Delville Wood on that fateful July of 1916, to emerge after six days of bloody battle with 2 815 casualties?

Perhaps the memory of Delville Wood and the men who lived and the men who fell was with Smuts as he addressed his men off to fight in another war. His moving and stirring speech was brief, from one soldier to another on the brink of battle:

‘I have looked forward to an opportunity to say goodbye to you before you leave for the front. I therefore welcome this occasion to bid you a very heartfelt farewell.

‘I do so personally, because as an old soldier I know what your service as soldiers in the far north may mean to most of you. I do it also in my official capacity as head of the Army and of the Government.

‘In all these capacities I express to you the gratitude of the people of South Africa for the choice you have made and the service you are prepared to offer your people and your country. More no man can do than offer his life for his friends. That offer, the highest and most solemn offer a man can make, you are making. We are proud of you.

‘You have done so freely and willingly. You are volunteers of your own choice. No compulsion of law has been laid on you. You go forth as free men and serve your country in that highest duty of the citizen – to defend his country, even unto death, if necessary.

‘Speaking to you today on this solemn occasion of parting, a parting which for some of you will be final, I can but wish you Godspeed from the bottom of my heart and say: God bless you, God bless your great enterprise.

‘From personal experience I know what awaits you. I know what war means – seven years of my life have been spent in wars. They were among the hardest years of my life, but they were also full of the richest experience that life can give. I would not exchange my war experiences of the Anglo-Boer War and the last Great War for all the gold of the Rand.

‘You are going to face danger, hardship and sacrifice – perhaps death itself – in all its fierce forms. But through it all you will gather that experience of life and enrichment of character which is more valuable than gold or precious stones.

‘You will become better and stronger men. You will not return the same as you went. You will bring back memories which you and yours will treasure for life. Above all, you will have that proud consciousness that you have done your duty by your country and rendered your contribution to its future security and happiness.

'You will not be mere items in the population; you will come back as builders of your own nation, of its best traditions, of its lofty national spirit and of its national pride.

'Your children will be proud of you. A nation is never proud of its "hands-uppers", its fence-sitters, its players for safety. We South Africans reserve our respect and pride for the bitter-enders, for those who go all out; who take their life in their own hands for country and people. And in the free choice you have made you will take your place in that select company of whom South Africans are instinctively proud.

'You are going north to meet the enemy where he can be found, not where he comes to find you – in your own homes. That, too, has been the tradition of South Africa. We did it in the last war.

'Many of you will revisit familiar haunts in the north. But to most of you that will be a new world, full of great interest of all kinds. You will see the vastness of this continent, its immense variety, its richness and grandeur of scenery, its magnificence in every respect. You go to it now as the strategic rampart and defence lines of South Africa.

'But in the years to come your service there will forge links between north and south which will inevitably open up wider horizons

An old soldier saluting the new: General Jan Smuts after addressing the 1st SA Infantry Brigade, immediately before their departure for Kenya on 16 July 1940.

and establish larger interests for South Africans. From every previous war South Africa has emerged a greater country, and this war will prove no exception. Your work will carry further the tradition of Briton and Boer alike.

'But we are endeavouring to do more. In taking our part in this war we are not merely defending ourselves, our country, our future. We are also standing by our friends in the Commonwealth of Nations in all loyalty and good faith, as we know they will stand by us.

'But we are doing more: we are also safeguarding that larger tradition of human freedom, of freedom of conscience, freedom of thought and freedom of religion which is today threatened as never before in history by the Nazi menace. That tradition is the spiritual rock whence we were hewn.

'We have fought for our freedom in the past. We now go forth as crusaders, as children of the Cross to fight for freedom itself, the freedom of the human spirit, the free choice of the human individual to shape his own life according to the light that God has given him. The world cause of freedom is also our cause and we shall wage this war for human freedom until God's victory crowns the end.

'In conclusion, just one word more. Wherever you may be or whatever you may do, remember that you are South Africans and that our name and honour are in your care. Keep it safe and high. Farewell, my friends; and may God bless and prosper the Right. '

CHAPTER

15

'Train after train steamed out of the stations'

Uys Krige and Conrad Norton with the boys *en route* to war in July 1940

Throughout 15 July steam engines hauling carriages filled with the men of the 1st SA Infantry Brigade clacked towards 'a point of embarkation'. It was supposed to be secret, as were the movements of troops, but everyone knew the men were off to Durban.

Not for a holiday along the Golden Mile, but to embark on steel-grey troopships and, with a strong escort of Royal Navy ships, to sail north to Mombasa and war.

Most of the men said goodbye to their families at home, but some were nonetheless treated to the poignancy of a wartime farewell on station platforms. The trains stopped several times *en route* for Durban. At each stop, SAWAS had commandeered station platforms and lined them with tables covered with mugs of tea and coffee, with sandwiches and buns. They were cheered as the trains steamed in and cheered when the trains steamed out.

One or two hapless civilians who had come to the stations to wave the boys farewell were lured on to the trains, held down as they left the station and released (with apparently no hard feelings) when the soldiers disembarked in Durban. All along the tracks through the Drakensberg and the lush countryside of Natal little groups of people stood and waved.

Durban was already on a war footing. Four six-inch Mark XII naval guns had been installed at Lighthouse Battery on the Bluff (unfortunately the lighthouse had been built in the middle of the arc of fire) and the eighteen-pounder of an armoured train was placed on the South Breakwater to guard the harbour entrance. A Railways and Harbour Brigade had already been established with a large Operating Group and two infantry battalions. The SAWAS were in action, and the women of Durban had begun entertaining troops passing through the town for destinations unknown.

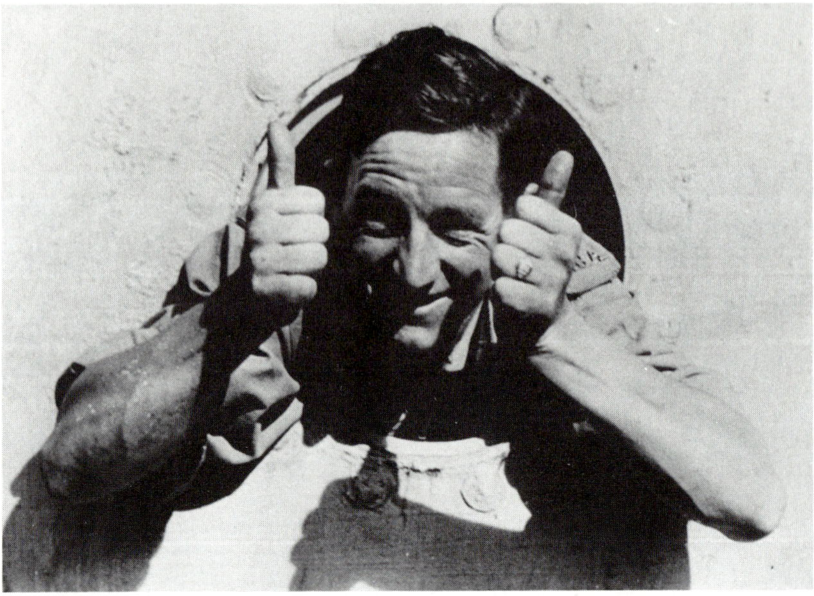

'Goodbyee!' (Africana Library)

As the men of the 1st SA Infantry Brigade walked towards the grey hulls of the ships which towered above them, a live broadcast by the SABC went out over the air. The sounds on the spot told their own story: marching feet, whistles, singing: 'Die Alibama', 'Sarie Marais', 'Tipperary', 'Land of Hope and Glory'. Then came the sounds of ships under way, cheering … and then silence.

Uys Krige and Conrad Norton, reporting for the Bureau of Information, together with other reporters and cameramen, travelled with the troops. They were careful to omit the name of Durban. This is their description of the journey to Durban and the north, which ended at Gilgil in Kenya.

'For a second time in a generation troops' trains began rumbling across the South African countryside bringing to the port of embarkation thousands of cheering, laughing young men to whom this day – July 15 – was the unforgettable culmination of six months' hard training. There had been many false starts, many galling disappointments, necessary in the interest of the safety of the long convoys that would soon be steaming northwards, but all was now forgotten in the tremendous adventure that lay before them. Train after train steamed out of the stations headed for the coast. The news of the passage of the troops had gone before and at small sidings, at unknown halts, and at big railway junctions crowds of people were gathered to wish Godspeed to this happy, singing army. Far into the

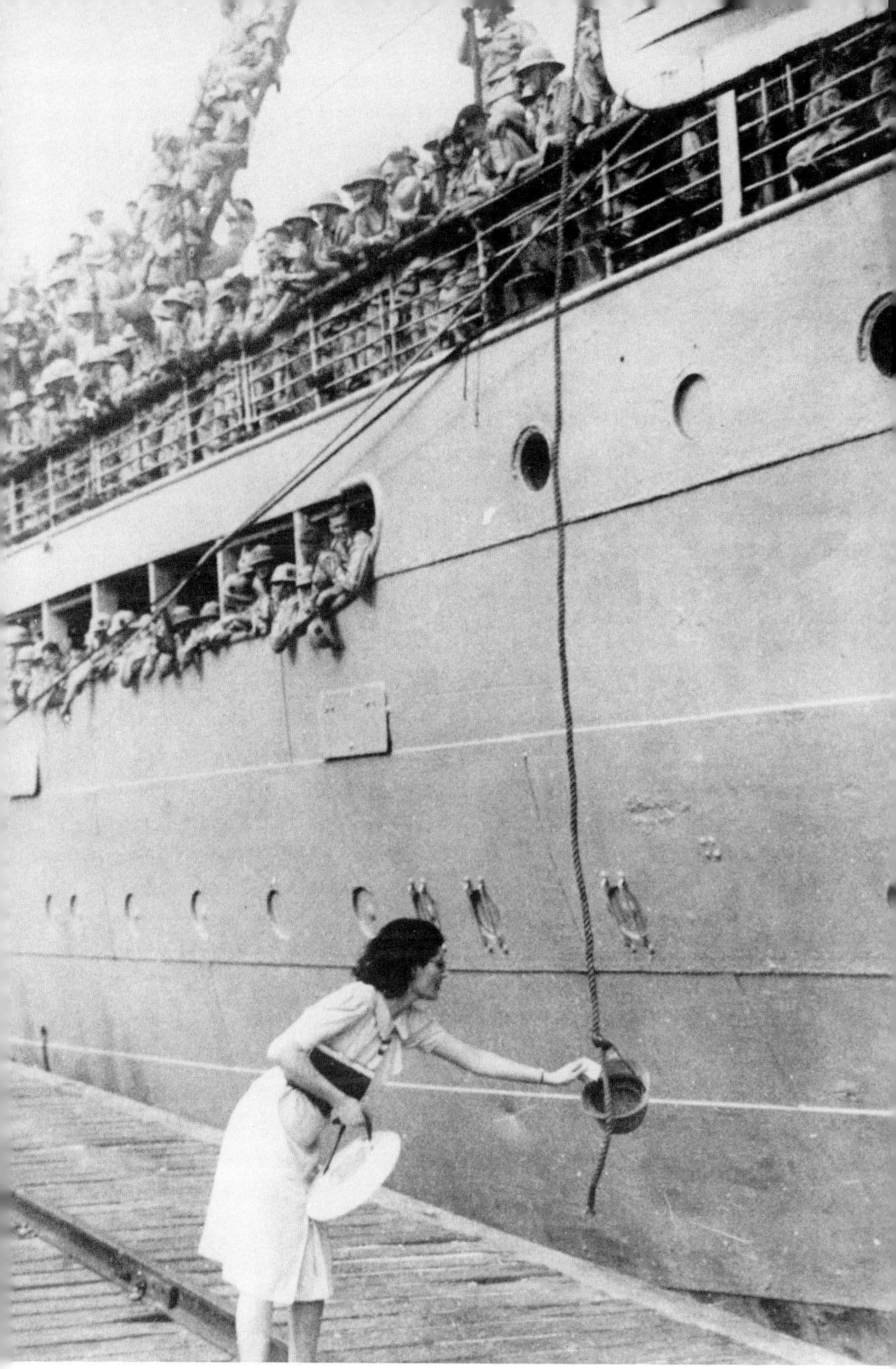

The troops set sail from Durban, supposedly in secrecy, but everyone knew they were going. (Africana Library)

night the troops were roused by the cheering crowds who had stood for hours in the cold of country stations to watch this historic scene.

'The trains, that followed each other in an endless stream, came to a stop on the quayside alongside giant, black, pointed liners into which enormous quantities of war material were being ceaselessly loaded. Soon thousands of khaki-clad men began streaming up the gangways, and the scene resembled a gigantic hive in which activity never ceased for a moment. Behind barbed wire enclosures crowds of civilians stood and watched this amazing scene, cheering each group of soldiers as they marched by. Within a few hours the black ships had sunk lower in the water and from every porthole, from every inch of deck space and from every part of the rigging, no matter how precarious his position, cheerful, singing soldiers jostled each other and waved and shouted to the crowds below.

Uys Krige, reporter, prisoner of war, soldier and, later, playwright. (*The Star*)

'At four o'clock the last gangway of the leading ship had been raised and then slowly, reluctantly almost, as if yielding to the hundreds of coloured streamers that linked those on board with the crowds on shore, the ship pulled away into the bay. Soon it was steaming towards the open sea to the accompaniment of the deafening singing and shouting of the troops, who were crowded ten deep on the shoreward side decks taking their last glimpse of home, for no-one could say how long.

'Within ten minutes of reaching the open sea the realities of war were brought home to those on board. There was a shrill whistle, and soon all were at their lifeboat stations, their life-belts resting clumsily on the shoulders of the soldiers. The lifeboats were swung out level with the decks and the captain and officers of the ship inspected the ranks, explaining to the men what they would be expected to do in the event of an emergency. Anti-submarine guards were mounted, watchers for enemy aircraft patrolled the upper decks and at the stern an Imperial gunnery officer was training a group of enthusiastic South

Africans in the handling of a long muzzled gun that could, he assured them, blow any submarine right out of the ocean.

'As the sun dropped below the shore line, throwing into silhouette the high buildings on the sea front, the five ships with their escorting armed merchantmen headed northwards. All on board soon settled down to the routine which began at six o'clock every morning with the reveille. Inspection followed and before a day had passed there was not a soul on board who did not realise the vital importance of absolute cleanliness in this tiny world in which thousands of men would live together for more than a week. Over the blue vastness of the ocean the other vessels were weaving strange patterns as they zigzagged, while in front the escorting cruiser darted to and fro like a great sheep dog watching its flock.

'During most of the daylight hours the ship was a playground, every known – and unknown – deckgame that ingenious soldiers could devise taking place. When night fell, however, the grimness of war again obtruded and the ship was rigidly blacked-out. Not a pinpoint of light was allowed. The decks became as black as pitch and woe to him who dared smoke a cigarette anywhere outside the heavily shuttered lounges and cabins.

'Day after day the voyage continued, as pleasantly and uneventfully as any peacetime cruise. On the morning of the seventh day, however, the sight for which the troops had been straining their eyes for days, suddenly came into view. It was the deep green rolling countryside that lay directly ahead. As we drew nearer to it palm trees – an excitingly exotic sight to most of the troops – came into view and soon white stone buildings that shimmered in the haze could be detected. Overhead droned aircraft of the South African Air Force – a friendly, protecting squadron of heavy bombers and fighters which ensured complete safety from enemy air attack.

'An hour or two later the scenes which had taken place at the port of embarkation were being re-enacted at the Mombasa docks, only here the scene was made more picturesque by the addition of colourfully dressed Arabs, vividly uniformed Askaris and the white drill suits of the civil officials. Soon troop trains were crammed with excited men and one after the other they set off for the hinterland which lay behind rolling hills of the deepest green speckled with vivid red of Hibiscus.

'It was a remarkable journey through beautiful countryside where every wayside station provided new interest and new impressions for those eager young soldiers. All through the night the trains rumbled and the next morning Nairobi came into view. A brief stop only was made and a few hours later the deeply impressive Great Rift Valley was entered. On the left lay the volcanic crater Longonot – soon to become familiar to every South African – and below it the beautiful Naivasha

Lake. Small buck, ostrich and hundreds of head of Zebra and Wildebeest scampered away from the side of the line as the trains raced by. That afternoon, hot, dusty and tired troops streamed out of the trains at Gilgil station and made for the camp that was to be home to them for more than two months.

'The next morning the rolling hills around Gilgil echoed to the skirl of bagpipes and to the tramp of thousands of marching feet as the troops took up their position at King's Parade to hear a message from the King.

'On a dais Sir Henry Monck-Mason Moore, Governor of Kenya, attended by many senior officers, read this message: "Once again forces from the Union of South Africa have come to East Africa to take part with the other members of the British Commonwealth in the fight for the future of their own country and for the safety of all freedom-loving peoples. As you enter the field of war I send you my best wishes, confident that with your help our cause will triumph."

'The King's message was read in Afrikaans by Brigadier Dan Pienaar and then the troops returned to their camp to settle down to the most intensive period of training they had so far experienced. From dawn to nightfall in the days which followed, khaki-clad men could be seen streaming over the hills, fighting mock battles, learning the tactics for war in the desert and toughening themselves for the physical hardships that lay ahead.

'Within a few days of their arrival the Gilgil camp soon breathed the spirit of South Africa and street names familiar in dorps and towns of the Union were given to the roads, various sections of the camp became known by the names of South African cities and all the hills in the vicinity lost there native names to more nostalgic titles.'

• Bureau of Information

CHAPTER

16

'It was very moving, singing to them'

Peggy Timmons, singing to the troops

If the First World War is remembered in song, it is 'Pack Up Your Troubles in Your Old Kit Bag' and 'Roses are Blooming in Picardy' which captured the imagination of the troops. In the 1939–45 war we also sang the haunting 'Lili Marlene', sung by German and Allied troops alike, Vera Lynn's 'There'll be Blue Birds Over the White Cliffs of Dover' and the incomparable Glenn Miller.

In South Africa we had singers who sang to the troops, raised money for war funds and comforted the wounded. Who could forget Perla Siedle Gibson, in her white dress and red ducoed straw hat singing her heart out from the Durban dockside as the troops left and returned? Peggy Timmons, a nineteen-year-old girl when the war broke out, was billed as the South African 'Forces' Sweetheart'. She sometimes gave three concerts a night to men in uniform and to the wounded to help to raise money for war funds throughout the war.

'Whenever I stood on a stage and looked out on a sea of young men's faces I would get the briefest of lumps in my throat. When I heard Chamberlain telling the world that Britain was at war I thought it was a dreadful thing. I felt so sad that my generation would bear the brunt of the fighting. We were all only eighteen or so, and so were many of the boys I was singing to.

'As soon as I heard that war had been declared I went to my father. I told him I wanted to join the Entertainment Unit, but he wouldn't hear of it. "You stay in Durban, my girl, and do your bit here." So I did.

'I had first sung to soldiers in 1937, when I was seventeen. On Armistice Day, 11 November, there was always a march-past through Durban. It ended up at the cenotaph in the City Gardens, where a service was held. After the service there was a concert in the City Hall, the audience being men who had seen service in the Great War. They were all middle-aged by then, but it was very moving, singing to them.

'After war was declared in 1939 it was no longer middle-aged men who marched through the streets, but boys of my own age. They went in their thousands, smiling and laughing, to the station where trains would take them to the camps to begin their training. And I would see them later, fitter and leaner, boarding the converted liners that took them up north. Many of them never returned … it was a time of heartache, of tears and joy.

'I had been singing since I was a toddler. When I was 2½ I would sit at the piano and bang on the keys and sing at the top of my voice – I turned out to be a coloratura soprano – and say: "All clap, please." When I was sixteen I trained with Keppoch MacDonald, who got me into the chorus of "The Desert Song", so I was quite ready to sing when war began.

Peggy Timmons, who sang to the troops from 1939 to 1945. She was billed as the Forces' Sweetheart.

'Working in the offices of the Receiver of Revenue in Durban, I knew right from the very beginning of the war that my best contribution was to use my voice. Singing can do so much, remind one of home, give hope for the future or just give fun and perhaps take away, even if it was for a short while, fears for the future and memories of the past.

'Durban very quickly became a town awash with khaki. When the convoys arrived, the town would be flooded with 35 000 young men. What a time, and what goings-on! And the marriages: a quick decision, three weeks to prepare and have the banns called, then the wedding, with everyone helping with the catering, a few days' embarkation leave or a weekend for the honeymoon, and then the boys were off.

'Much of the entertainment was organised by the Municipal Entertainments Department led by Jock Duff, who also started the series of Happy Night Shows. Edward Dunn was in charge of the orchestra, which he divided up to play at different places. For the variety concerts in the City Hall the Theatre Orchestra would play in the pit, with the dance band on the stage. The military band played in the parks or

Peggy Timmons beneath the bandstand, 'chasing the blues away' with the Durban Municipal Dance Band in a 'bright and breezy programme' at South Beach every Tuesday evening from 5.30 to 8.30 p.m. Chairs cost 6d, but the singing was free.

on the beach bandstand on Sunday mornings, and all sections would come together for the Thursday evening symphony concert in the City Hall. What a feast of music it was!

'What did I sing? Nearly everything, but most often the light classics or the haunting Vera Lynn songs. They always brought the house down, especially with the boys from Britain.

'There were hundreds of concerts for war funds – it was a constant round of charity work, but I loved it all. One exciting evening a concert was given to the navy down at the Seamen's Mission. The guest of honour was Noël Coward. To my eternal sorrow I sang his songs in the first half of the programme and he wasn't there to hear me, but later on he signed my music of "Some Day I'll Find You".

'There were also regular broadcasts from the broadcasting studio in Aliwal Street, and I sang with the Studio Orchestra, conducted by Leonard Pearce. The broadcasts went out live, and so did many of those from the City Hall, and it was quite nerve-racking. Once I was singing "The London I Love", a new song that I had just learnt, and when I came to the verse I couldn't remember a single word. I knew I had to continue, so I just improvised the words as I went along, and I don't think anyone noticed except the conductor who looked a little puzzled.

'I also sang to the boys just before they went up north. The Royal Durban Light Infantry* was based at Oribi Camp in Pietermaritzburg. Major Leslie Leon, who worked with the YMCA arranged these concerts. After finishing a day's work at the Receiver of Revenue in Durban, I would pile into a car with the members of the orchestra and we'd leave in convoy for Pietermaritzburg. If we left Durban early enough after 5 p.m. and if the weather was good, we'd escape the dreaded mist, but often, especially in winter, we were enveloped in a thick white cloud as we made our way gingerly along the road.

'When I first started going to Oribi Camp I sang from a makeshift stage out in the open, with the boys standing around in their greatcoats whilst I shivered in my cotton or silk dress. Later a YMCA hut – a hall, really – was built and that was a wonderful improvement. They also built a YMCA hut in Ladysmith and I sang there, too.

'Sometimes I sang with Perla Siedle Gibson, "The Lady in White" at the City Hall. She had a ladies' choir and I would be introduced as the young star in the show. She was a very charming person, the only one to be given permission to sing at the docks.

'But it wasn't just singing to the convoys or the men in the camps. I also sang, often, at the military hospitals. Whenever I saw the big white hospital ship with its huge red cross nosing its way into Durban harbour, I knew the hospitals would be crowded with the wounded. We didn't go straight away, the men had to settle in and recover from their journey. It was always terribly difficult, trying to be cheerful and seeing so many badly wounded men. I suppose I had sung to some of them before they went up north.

'After one of those concerts I was asked if I would return as soon as possible, because a young Irish boy had heard that I could sing Irish songs (my father was Irish) and would I go to his ward and sing there? I did, without any accompaniment at all, and I had such a lump in my throat that I thought I wouldn't get through. But I did, and perhaps I brought him some little comfort. Once, at George V Hospital, the whole of the front row of my audience were all in wheelchairs. They'd lost their legs. I couldn't sing for a few moments. I had to compose myself.

'The cinemas were packed with men. There were not enough "shorts" to accompany the main film in many of the cinemas, and I

---

* Raised in 1873 as the Royal Durban Rifles and renamed the Durban Light Infantry in 1889. It received the Royal title in 1935. The 2nd Battalion was mobilised in May 1940 and fought with the 4th SA Infantry Brigade until it was captured at Tobruk. The 1st Battalion was mobilised in June 1940 and fought at Bardia, Gazala, El Alamein and in Italy until the war ended.

sometimes provided the interlude. When *Shipyard Sally*, with Gracie Fields, was on at the 20th Century cinema, I sang the popular song from the film "Wish Me Luck As You Wave Me Goodbye". Keppoch MacDonald worked with me late into the night to teach me the song, for we received the music only the day before the cinema wanted me to start.

'We were supposed to be on for only three nights, but the interlude was so popular that the run was extended by several weeks. I was singing the top notes an octave higher than the score, as Gracie Fields did, so Keppoch suggested that I should swallow a raw egg before I sang. When we finished there I couldn't look another egg in the face.

'My name was up in lights for the first time when I appeared at the Metro Theatre with the Wurlitzer organ. The film was *The Ziegfield Follies*, and I had to sit on top of the huge organ as it came out of the pit. I was dressed in white tulle covered in silver stars and with a headdress of a silver crescent moon and stars, like the outfits in the film. With the spotlight playing on us in the darkened cinema, filled with troops, it must have looked very dramatic.

'By the middle of 1940 I was being billed, rather flatteringly, as "The Soldiers' Sweetheart", and I was asked to be the singer for a series of SABC concerts called "From a Soldier's Camp". They chose a

The *Natal Daily News* of 14 July 1941 described Peggy Timmons in her 'song scene' at the Metro as 'seated on the organ in a costume which was a replica of one of those used in the feature film "Ziegfield Girl", delighting her audience with the range and purity of her singing'. The organist is Tommy McLennan. The show brought the house down and was extended from a few days' run to weeks. (Peggy Timmons)

camp at the end of the Bluff where there was a large encampment of men from the SA Coast Artillery, and in September we all went there for a concert.

'The hall was crowded, and I had just finished singing when there was a terrific explosion and the alarm bells began ringing. Within seconds the hall was cleared and every man was at his post. We artists were forgotten, so we rushed out, too, and saw this huge ship caught in the searchlights from the battery. The ship was going astern, with white foam surging up from a pitch-dark sea. It was an awesome sight. It was a Spanish ship that hadn't replied to any signals, and a warning shot from one of the huge coast-defence guns had been fired across her bows. They were afraid that she might be scuttled in the harbour mouth and block the shipping. When the excitement was over we went on with the concert. At the interval I was introduced to a handsome officer, Captain George Ellis, whom I married a year later.

'I travelled all over the place, singing, often for war funds, to Pietermaritzburg, Ladysmith, Underberg. It was a continual round of concerts, and I never seemed to stop rushing. But it was very satisfying, feeling I was doing something for the war. I spent hours learning the latest Vera Lynn numbers, which the troops loved.

'Just before I turned twenty-one my singing teacher, Keppoch MacDonald, said to me: "Peggy, if you never sing another note, you will have done more than many people could have done in their lifetime." I just couldn't say no to a deserving cause. It was wartime, and you had to do your bit.'

• Interview 1990

CHAPTER

17

'A lot of bullets and things from planes'

Irene, June and Brian Nicholls, West Wickham, August–September 1940

When war broke out in 1939, there were many South Africans in Britain. Commonwealth men of military age mostly chose to stay and fight with British forces rather than return home to join up. Others, particularly those with families, rushed for ships to take them home, to Canada, Australia, New Zealand or South Africa.

But some as a result of circumstances had little choice but to stay. One of those families was that of the Nicholls. Hedley Nicholls, a fitter at Sub Nigel mine, was amicably divorced from his wife Irene. With their two young children, June and Brian, Irene went to Britain on a long visit in 1937. The visit proved to be longer than they had intended.

Unable to obtain a passage back to South Africa, Irene and the two children settled into a council house in West Wickham, fifteen miles from London. Biggin Hill, the sector station of Fighter Command, was only a few miles away.

The excitement and the fears after the British declaration of war had abated in the Phoney War that followed. There was a *frisson* of excitement during the battle of the River Plate and the sinking of the *Graf Spee* in December 1939, but it was not until the German invasion of the Low Countries and the fall of France and the heroic rescue of part of the British army from the beaches of Dunkirk that civilians felt that the war had really begun.

And begun it had, with a vengeance. The European continent was now firmly under the boot of the Third Reich. Germans walked the streets of Paris, Amsterdam, Oslo and Prague. Italy was in thrall to Mussolini. With France occupied and Vichy France allowed a limited and precarious freedom, Hitler turned his attention to Britain. He was determined to conquer her before turning the armed might of Germany towards the hated Russians, and he ordered the preparation of Operation Seelowe.

But before German troops could march in triumph down the Mall, the Royal Air Force had to be destroyed. Operation Adler (Eagle) was therefore put into effect. The German Air Staff considered that it would take four weeks to smash the RAF, leaving the middle of September 1940 free for the proposed invasion.

Air attacks began as early as the first week in June, but it was only from the middle of August that the might of the *Luftwaffe* was unleashed upon the British people, whose main defence was a thin blue line: a thousand young Spitfire and Hurricane pilots (of whom South Africa's gallant Sailor Malan* was one).

On 13 August there were 1 485 German sorties; the following day there were 520 bomber and 1 270 fighter sorties over Britain. The battle, in autumn sunshine, raged mostly above the fields of Kent. On 7 September the Germans, frustrated at their inability to cripple the RAF, switched tactics: their target became London: the Blitz had begun. The first bombs to fall on London were dropped on the night of 24 August. 30 September saw the last major raid on the capital, although bombing continued until May 1941. Other targets – most notably Coventry – took the brunt. But the Battle of Britain had been won. Forty thousand British civilians were killed in the Blitz, 46 000 injured, and more than a million homes damaged.

In the midst of this mêlée – but fortunately not in the very centre of the attack on London – lived the Nicholls. In letters to Hedley Nicholls back home in a South Africa untouched by bombs, they described as best they could, how they were living:

‘97 Addington Road
West Wickham, Kent
17 6 40

My Dear Hedley,

Many thanks for your letter received to-day, expressing your sympathy with us in this terrible time. – You have no doubt heard most of

---

* Adolph Gysbert ‘Sailor’ Malan ended the war as a Group Captain, the fifth-highest scorer among the Allies with 35 confirmed victories (Sqn-Ldr Pat Pattle, another South African, died in his Hurricane over Greece, with over 41 kills to his credit. He had the highest score of all the Allied air aces). By June 1941 Sailor Malan was the highest scorer of Fighter Command, with 29 victories. He was the first air fighter of the Hitler war to win the DSO and bar and the DFC and bar. In the RAF, 11 August 1940 is still known as ‘Sailor's August 11th’ – the third day of the Battle of Britain, when he and his squadron of twelve Spitfires attacked and shot down or damaged 38 enemy aircraft over England. He issued a booklet: *Ten of my Rules for Air Fighting*, the first of which was ‘Wait until you see the whites of his eyes.’ Sailor Malan died of Parkinson's Disease in Kimberley Hospital shortly before his 58th birthday.

the news from Enid, but things are certainly looking very black just now. We have started a poultry farm, and have 400 birds at present. The children are at home with us, as you know except Derrick, who is in Somerset at school. As we have had no air-raids to speak of the children don't realise that there is a war on and treat all this gas-mask business as rather a 'silly performance'. Brian goes to school in the morning and June in the afternoon, as this school has to take school children from other areas as well as here now, and so the children cannot go for a full day.

All the sign-posts have been taken down here and barricades of barbed wire complete with trenches are halfway up Corkscrew Hill, (Aunt Minnie knows where that is) – 2 minutes' walk from our house – as we are on the main Folkstone road. We have troop camps on Hayes common 5 minutes away, and everything is looking pretty grim.

We have heard today that Mr Renaud has resigned, and are wondering how much longer the French can go on fighting – knowing full well that it is to be our turn as soon as Hitler has finished with them. We all feel confident that good will prevail over evil and that we cannot lose, and we are prepared to stay here and fight until we are killed or bombed out. My main worry is the children. I wish I could get them to safety, but in England if Hitler comes there will be no safety anywhere. If it was possible to have sent them back to you I would have done so – but in any case the war seems to be extending to Africa now, and they probably won't be any safer there – Canada sounds the only fairly safe place at the moment, but I can't send them away to strangers anyway, so we must all take our chances together.

If anything should happen to me – my will is with the Westminster Bank, Hayes – Kent. The children have my annuity as you know – and I have an insurance policy with Prudential. Their identity numbers are as follows:

June W.B.D.A. 75–10
Brian W.B.D.A. 75–17

Our food supplies are quite good, although sugar is very scarce, (which is particularly painful to me). Prices are very high of course, petrol is now trying to climb to the Durban prices – 1/11½ per gal when it was 1/4 – 1/5. However, it can't be helped; we are lucky to get any.

The children are quite fit and Brian has gained 7 lbs since these photos were taken, and he looks 100% better. He had an accident a few weeks ago when a boy at school was throwing stones and one hit him in the eye. It bled profusely and he complained he could not see. I took him to an eye specialist, who said that although no severe injury had been done, he had concussion of the eye and he must go to bed for 10 days and have Atropin instilled twice daily. All is well now and he says it has completely recovered.

Well I think that is all for now, I am sorry the war news is not better. I hope you are well.

Yours very sincerely,

Irene

Dear Daddy,

I hope you are well. Here is a piece of shrapnel for you. We have not got any windows broken. We have had a lot of bombs around here but not as many as they have had in London.

We go to school from 9 a.m. to 2 p.m. and we do our work in the shelters. The shelters are very wet at school, and the water comes in. I would like to see you and I expect you would like to see me, but perhaps the government will be sending the children next year.

I used to think you were black but know you are white. It's a pity I cannot see you. Well goodbye.

With love from

June

9.00 pm Thurs. September 12th 1940

My Dear Hedley,

Just a line to let you know that we are all still alive so far. After six days' continuous day and night bombing we are still managing to keep our end up. The raids are brutes! But last night was far and away the noisiest as, for the first time they had all the mobile guns in action. The sirens went at 8.30 pm and the all-clear at 5.35 am. The guns *never stopped* all night. They are all around us, and today our gardens are full of shrapnel, and pieces of bombs. The Jerries come right over here on their way to London and again on their way back. So far tonight the sirens have not gone, so perhaps we may get an hour or two's sleep before they go.

We have had a number of bombs dropped at Wicklaw and Hayes (our other little shopping place). On Saturday night we had one 150 yards from our house. It did give us a shaking up I can tell you – (there go the sirens now). It completely demolished six houses and has wrecked about 60 or 70 others all in the vicinity. Luckily we have been spared that. Next door to us were the first to escape the blast – now tonight the police have been round to say we have an unexploded bomb in the playground which backs onto our garden, and we must not use the backs of our houses if possible. But as the kitchen is at the back what can one do? We are waiting for it to go off.

The Nicholls family taking a breather at the coast, 1940. (Brian Nicholls)

Brian Nicholls, 1941, after the worst of the blitz had ended. Both he and his sister June, trapped in Britain for the duration of the war, wrote frequently to their father in South Africa. (Brian Nicholls)

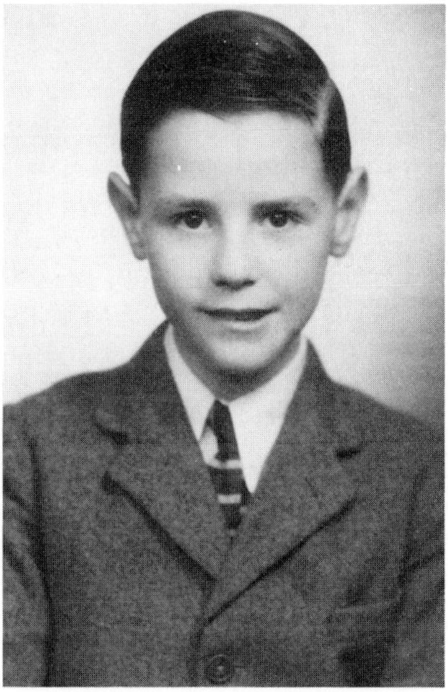

June Nicholls. It was years before she saw her father again. (Brian Nicholls)

London has had a dreadful time, the fires round the docks have been burning for days and lighted the roads even in this district 15 miles away. Buckingham Palace has been bombed.

The children take the raids marvellously well. We all sleep downstairs in one room. I put the children in a little cupboard under the stairs, as our air-raid shelter is too small for us all to sleep in, and besides it is getting rather cold.

Mr Churchill told us that we must expect to be invaded this coming week, so I felt I must try to get these letters off as one never knows what may happen. We live with our lives in our hands from one day to the next – praying each night that we may live to see the morning. We eat snacks, as, and when we can get them, as when the sirens go all the shops close, and as they go about seven or eight times a day you can imagine how difficult it is to stop and prepare meals. There go the guns again, they are kicking up hell's delight. We went to town on Monday. There was no gas anywhere in the city as the mains had been struck. How I wish the children had not got to go through it all, although they sleep through it all at night.

Fred has been called up, and left yesterday. He is 1st Lieut. Dorsetshire Regiment. I have to run the chicken farm in between the raids, but it seems as if as soon as I get up to the farm the sirens go and I have to dash back Our air-force are simply wonderful – bless them – and we only pray to have the guts to stick this hell (for that's a mild description of it) out to finish.

Friday

All clear from last night went at 5.45 am. Sirens again 9.30 – all clear 2.15 pm. Sirens again 4.0 pm – all clear 4.30 pm. Sirens just gone again and it is 9.0 pm. The night is as clear as a bell, and a beautiful moon is shining to light up his targets for him. They got Buckingham Palace again today and damaged it rather severely it was announced on the wireless tonight, but time bomb still not gone off yet.

Saturday

All clear 5.30 pm. They got the shops in W.Wickham High Street last night, about twenty with their windows out and some partly down.

Monday

Sorry this letter has still not gone. We had an awful night – it sounded as if hundreds and hundreds were passing over. The guns went non-stop and the house shook and shook. They have *entirely demolished* Hayes station and the beautiful new inn that was opposite is to the *ground* and you can imagine the damage all round. Two killed, eight seriously injured. We heard the bombs coming, they make an awful rushing sound and gives one the feeling that the bomb must have your name and address *alone* on it. Actually there were five dropped there. It shook us all out of bed anyway.

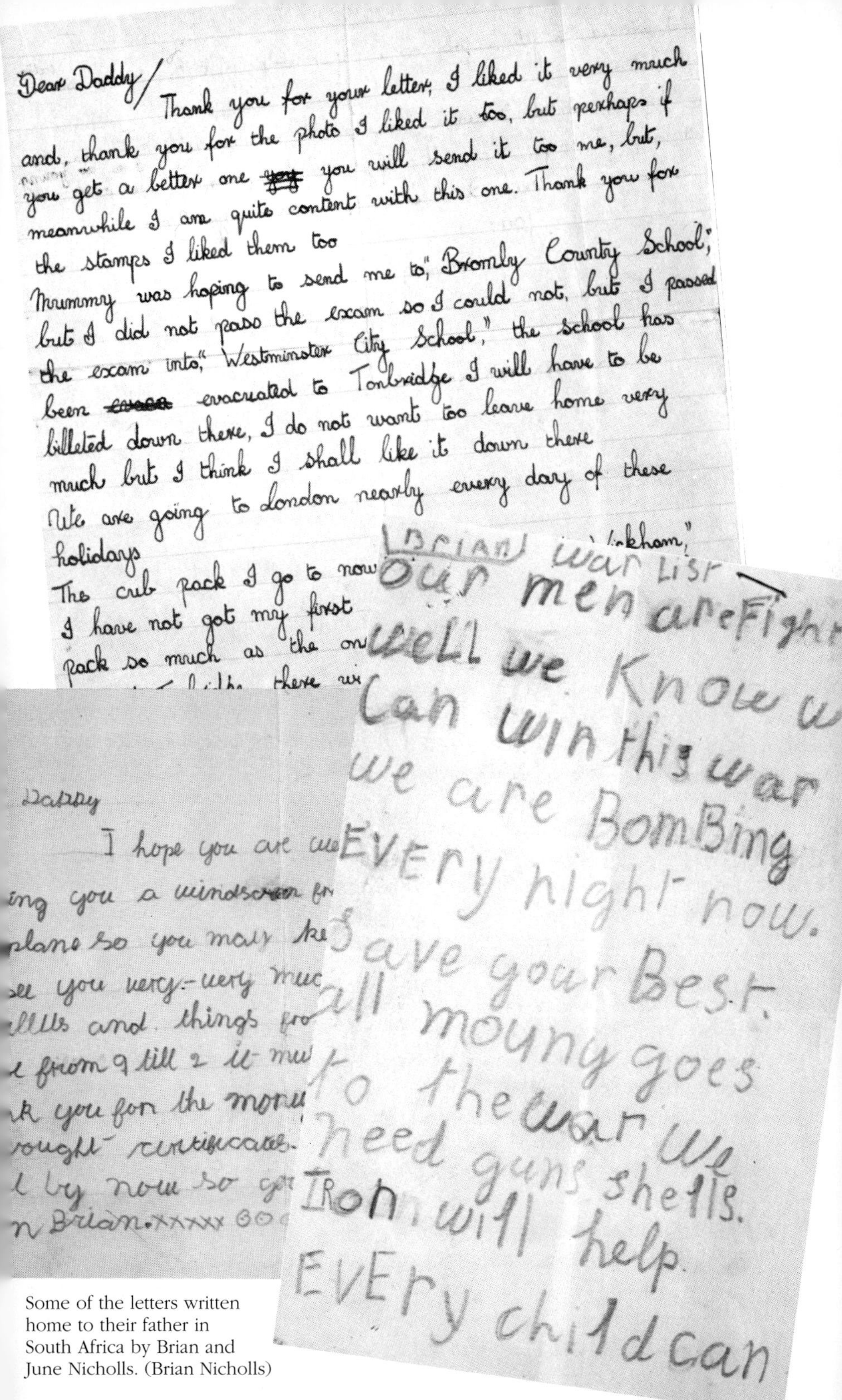

Dear Daddy/
Thank you for your letter, I liked it very much and, thank you for the photo I liked it too, but perhaps if you get a better one ~~you~~ you will send it too me, but, meanwhile I am quite content with this one. Thank you for the stamps I liked them too
Mummy was hoping to send me to "Bromly County School" but I did not pass the exam so I could not, but I passed the exam into "Westminster City School," the school has been ~~evacu~~ evacuated to Tonbridge I will have to be billeted down there, I do not want too leave home very much but I think I shall like it down there
We are going to London nearly every day of these holidays
The cub pack I go to now ... Wickham,"
I have not got my first ...
pack so much as the on...
... there w...

Daddy
I hope you are we...
...ing you a windscreen fr...
...plane so you may ke...
...ss you very-very muc...
...llls and things fro...
...e from 9 till 2 it mu...
...k you for the mone...
...rought certificates...
...l by now so go...
...n Brian.xxxxx ooo...

BRIAN war LIST
Our men areFight...
Well we Know w...
Can win this war
we are BomBing
EVEry night now.
Save your Best.
all moung goes
to the war we
need guns shells.
IRon will help.
EVEry child can

Some of the letters written home to their father in South Africa by Brian and June Nicholls. (Brian Nicholls)

Well we all send our best love to Aunt Minnie, Ronnie and Jean. Please pass this letter to them all.

Kindest regards to yourself.

Yours very sincerely,

Irene

Dear Daddy,

I hope you are well. I am well. I am sending you a windscreen from a german airoplane so you may keep it. I would like to see you very-very much. I have a lot of bullitts and things from planes. We go to school from 9 till 2. It must be very hot in South Africa. Thank you for the money you sent me. We bought certificates. I must say goodby now so goodby with love from Brian.

Dear Hedley,

London is in a pretty fine mess, it bears the scars of a real battlefield, and the guns all round makes you think you are in the front lines on the Western Front. I am sure Aunt Minnie would not recognise today as half the important places are all down to the ground. At Elnes End and Annerly (near here but not us) the water mains have suffered badly and the people are having to fetch every drop of water in pails from one main tap in the one road. What a queue! You think twice before you wash. Anyway the jerries haven't beaten us yet and are not likely to either. The team spirit of the people is wonderful, and I'm proud to be British and I'm sure you are too, if you could see how these poor bombed people can 'take it'. A patient of mine last week with her baby less than 24 hours old was bombed out in the night. The A.R.P. people found her and three of her other six children with her (all of which are under the age of eight) and she carrying the new baby in the street in her nightgown, with no shoes and stockings on trying to walk to her mother at Norwood (about three miles away). She was badly cut with glass but otherwise alright – her husband was in the army and she was alone in the house – I nearly wept when I heard about her, as this was on Sunday night at 7.30 pm and the baby was delivered on Saturday at 10.0 pm. She was such a cheery soul too. However – that's war, I suppose. The A.R.P. people put her in the ambulance and took her, and she is doing well now, thank goodness, and still cheery.

Well I hope you are all fit and well.

Well, all the best for Xmas and the New Year – so cherrio.

Irene

P.S. I thought you might be interested in Brian’s idea of helping to win the war. It was entirely his own effort, and apart from being asked how to spell one or two words, I did not know the contents until I have just read it.

BRIAN – WAR LIST
Our men are fighting
well we know we can win this war
we are bombing every night now
Save your best
all money goes to the war
We need guns shells
Iron will help
Every child can help
We must have it airplanes. We buy of America
But we must have the money.
Turn out your pockets
Every sixpence will help
We must pay the men. Buy savings stamps.
It is money and iron.
If you save we will win. Give pennys for the red cross
that helps to win the war.
Every penny goes to a gun.
We must do our best as well as our men.
We can do it so dont think we can not we can
save your best. ’

Irene, June and Brian Nicholls survived the war, though not without mishap. Early in 1941 their council house was hit by a five-hundred-lb bomb. It was 1 p.m. and they were sheltering in the tiny broom cupboard under the stairs. As Irene heard the bomb whistling down towards them, she flung herself across the children. Although the house collapsed about them, they were unhurt apart from superficial cuts and bruises. Within minutes police and ARP men were digging them out. A primus stove boiled water for a cup of tea, which they drank amid the smoking rubble. Other accommodation was found for the family in Sidcup – only to be damaged when another bomb levelled three houses on the opposite side of the road. The two children eventually returned to South Africa.

CHAPTER

18

'A cockpit of minor but intense action'

Percy Baneshik and the SABC, 1939–45

The Second World War was fought in the South African Broadcasting Corporation with an intensity, not quite comparable to the action in the field of battle, but with nearly the same degree of animosity.

The SABC had been set up as an independent body only a few years earlier, in 1936, after conversion from a private undertaking, the African Broadcasting Company Ltd (ABC) owned by the country's then reigning entrepreneur, I W Schlesinger.

The character of the new corporation was determined by a report made to the government of the day (the Hertzog-Smuts coalition) by Sir John Reith, Director-General of the British Broadcasting Corporation, who had been invited to South Africa to recommend a policy for a national broadcasting service.

His report resulted in the establishment of a "public utility" corporation modelled on Reith's own BBC. Its responsibility to government was merely to allow the Minister of Posts and Telegraphs to appoint members of its board of governors and for them to present an annual report in the House of Assembly.

Thus, when three years later South Africa declared war on Germany and joined the Allies in September 1939, the SABC also was expected to declare its allegiance to the prosecution of the war.

Which it did. But, as in the rest of the body politic in South Africa, there were great schisms of opinion among the staff. Percy Baneshik was News Editor of the SABC during the war. Here he recalls a divided corporation:

'The first Director-General of the SABC was Rene S Caprara, a man whose experience was rooted in orchestral music. He was a crack flautist with the Cape Town Municipal Orchestra, and his work often took him into the Cape Town studios of the old ABC. Mingling there with the staff, he became interested in the technicalities of wireless and later, by a sort of osmosis, in the administration of the station.

'Despite his Italian name, Caprara was English-born and trained at the Royal College of Music in London before he joined the Cape Town Orchestra. On the Cape Town airways he took part in children's programmes as "Uncle Bonzo", with a young woman, Gladys Dixon, who was known as Auntie Lex and reputed to be Caprara's mistress.

'Soon he became manager of the Cape Town station.

'With the establishment of the quasi-governmental body, the SABC, the Cape station was incorporated in it along with the Johannesburg and Durban equivalents, and Caprara, by then well versed in the administration of a radio station, was appointed Director-General of the new national body.

'Auntie Lex came to headquarters in Johannesburg and was appointed Director of Programmes.

'Until then Afrikaans had been represented on the air only in a minor way, with programmes limited to one night a week. But with the new dispensation an entire new second channel was instituted – a revolution in broadcasting, giving Afrikaans parity with English.

'Staffing this new service was a problem, since a body of Afrikaans-speaking broadcasters scarcely existed. Hasty recruitment of Afrikaans talent for the new job netted mostly male teachers emerging from the *onderwyserskolleges*.

'The head of the new Afrikaans service, however, was an Afrikaans barrister, though not yet practising at the Bar: J F ("Kowie") Marais.

'Mr Marais, like many of the young men of that era, hot-heads not long after from the Great Depression and still smarting from defeat in the Boer War only forty years behind them, was a zealous Afrikaner nationalist. His superior intellect soon began to exert a perceptible influence on the SABC.

'On the outbreak of war and the need for the SABC staff to support the war effort, he was obliged, however, to suppress his feelings; though as Hitler's conquest of Europe progressed that became increasingly difficult.

'War news began to take precedence in the bulletins, and some of the stories reporting unfavourably on the enemy (though not yet full-blown propaganda material – that was yet to be developed) was anathema to Marais and his supporters among the staff.

'That put me in a tricky position, since at that time, and throughout the war years, I was News Editor of the SABC network, in charge of all news bulletins. The news was supplied in English by Reuter and the South African Press Association and translated for the Afrikaans

Percy Baneshik, a news editor with the SABC during the war. (Percy Baneshik)

newsreaders by translators in the same department.

'Marais was therefore often present in the newsroom, supervising the translations. This led to frequent clashes between him and me, when for example, early in the hostilities, he objected to a report of German sailors being captured by the Royal Navy which described the new prisoners of war as "shambling, hulking fellows". He ordered the phrase to be deleted from the Afrikaans version.

'This was but a symptom of the subterranean feeling among the Afrikaans staff. With the advance of the German forces and Marais' encouragement, they began to let their anti-Allied feelings surface boldly and, since many of them were well-versed in Nazi doctrine, they were a real problem to one such as myself in the lower echelons of the organisation.

'They had long been keen students of Hitler's philosopher of Aryanism and the *Uebermenschen,* Alfred Rosenberg, Streicher's *Der Stuermer* and Hitler's *Mein Kampf*, and they could top any argument by direct quotation of chapter and verse.

'Whether Caprara was aware of that is uncertain. He himself had leapt eagerly into the spirit of the war and got himself gazetted as a major; home-based and non-belligerent, but he appeared daily at his office in uniform.

'That once led to a delightful misunderstanding, when the actress Marie Ney, a refugee from the war in Malaysia, called at Broadcast House to take part in a radio production of Shaw's *Major Barbara.* A horny-handed son of the platteland appointed in those times of shortage of manpower as a security guard, intercepted her.

'"Where are you going?" he asked.

'Imperiously the actress replied, "I'm here for *Major Barbara*".

'And since there was only one major he knew of in the building, she was escorted to Major Caprara's office.

'But expediency (as he once told me in an unguarded moment) was his watchword; and when a call came for recruits to join the South African volunteer army he blocked the applications of a dozen or so members of technical staff to join the Signal Corps (for which they were especially well qualified) and got them declared "key workers" necessary to the war effort at home.

'There was considerable resentment at this, and some left their jobs to enlist, forfeiting their rights as provided by wartime law to continue to receive civilian pay while serving.

'But that was incidental to the growth of the anti-war faction in the SABC. It increased in step with Nazi successes, and the attitudes of the pro-Nazis grew more truculent.

'One English-speaking figure in the administration, L M ("Buster") Brown, was the studio manager at Broadcast House. He had been an officer in the Royal Flying Corps in the 1914–18 war, and he was proud of his wounds and now a keen supporter of the new war against Germany. Resentment at the paradings and posturings of the pro-Nazi staff smouldered within his breast, and he discussed their activities with the loyal staff.

'Word of this conflict of sentiment spread to the Press. For years the animosity within the SABC simmered, but there came the point at which a Johannesburg journalist, George Heard*, of the *Sunday Times*, exposed the story in a sensational article.

'The government were eventually forced to act. They appointed a commission of enquiry presided over by a retired magistrate, and evidence was given before him in a big studio in Broadcast House.

'The accused staff were cross-examined, and Caprara and Brown, with counsel to support them, were called on to testify. (So was I; it was a very tense situation, for at that point Germany appeared to be winning the war.)

'The outcome of the enquiry was a triumph for the faction supporting the war effort; the allegations of "parading Nazi sympathies" within the SABC while the organisation was legally committed to supporting the war effort were found to be proved.

'Kobie Marais, as the leading pro-Nazi, was dismissed from his post and interned with two of his staff in the camp for dissidents at Koffiefontein and life at the SABC went on much as before.

'But as a reward for bringing to light the parading of Nazi sympathies by the sacked employees, Buster Brown was summarily dismissed from his job.

'Soon after the war, in 1948 when the triumphant National Party came to power, Marais was released with honour, proceeded to the Pretoria Bar and within a year or two was elevated to the bench. He proved an excellent judge.

---

* Heard disappeared in Cape Town at the end of the war in a mystery that has not yet been solved.

'The other Nazi supporters rooted out of the SABC and interned at Koffiefontein were also released at the end of the war. One, Louis Wiesner, became a film-maker and produced a film, *In die Lente van Die Lewe*, depicting student life at the Afrikaans universities. He spent years making it, and when it flopped he was bitterly disillusioned.

'The other political internee, who spent the latter years of the war in Koffiefontein in company with John Vorster, later Prime Minister of South Africa, dropped out of sight.

'Caprara remained head of the SABC for several years after all this, but with the growing strength and ultimate triumph of Malan in the immediate post-war history of South Africa, he soon found himself under extreme pressure from the Nats and retired.

'Apart from all these shenanigans, the war years at the SABC were pretty routine. Programmes were devoted to maintaining morale, and they included many imported from Britain, such as Tommy Handley's *Itma* (*It's That Man Again*). The British view was reflected in South Africa by the regular relay from London of the BBC news every evening. As always, the BBC style was calm, reflective and comforting.

'The relay was effected by the establishment of a "diversity receiving station" on a large tract of land north-west of Johannesburg called Panorama. The principle of "diversity" reception was that a widespread array of masts bore aerials receiving the shortwave signal from Britain.

'The signal, which arrived in uneven billows of volume bouncing off the Heaviside layer (otherwise the ionisphere) was picked up at its optimum on at least one of several aerials, so that undulations were smoothed out and the level of reception was kept constant.

'So remote was Panorama from Broadcast House that the maintenance engineer, a man called Morris, living alone on the property, relieved his boredom by cultivating vegetables. Pretty soon he was carrying on a thriving trade on the side as a market gardener.

'Direct coverage of the South African forces in the war zone "up North" was carried out by two senior men of the earlier peacetime programmes: an Englishman, Bruce Anderson, and an Afrikaner, Con Lamprecht.

'Anderson had been hired by Caprara as a producer of musicals, since he had first come to the country as the leading tenor in a stage show, *White Horse Inn*. He and Lamprecht were assigned to the forces as official war correspondents.

'Both left for the war zone with a large van equipped with the only system available at that time for recording the sounds of battle and the correspondents' commentaries – cumbersome turntables on which huge acetate discs revolved while a heated stylus cut a spiral groove in the surface.

'Despite the difficulties, Anderson recorded sounds of battle direct and brought something of the realities of war back to South African listeners.

'Otherwise the material consisted mainly of personal messages recorded by the *Boys up North*, bringing some sort of comfort to their families back home. And, of course, the morale-sustaining programmes broadcast locally were directed and lots of encouraging messages from their families to the boys not yet sent abroad.

'These programmes were run by a "Sister Sunshine" character, voiced by a woman called Gladys Kenyon and another called Noreen Purdon. Both became great favourites of the boys.

'Perhaps the sharpest reminder of the realities of the Nazi waves of aggression were the nightly broadcasts from Radio Zeesen.* There a barrage of blatant propaganda was directed at South Africa by a personality whose voice, similar to that of the notorious Lord Haw-Haw, sowed dismay. Listening to Radio Zeesen became a nightly exercise in masochism among South Africans.

'Every broadcast from Zeesen was eagerly, if morbidly, discussed next day. To counter it, the Smuts government appointed an official Information Officer, one Mr A N Wilson, who regularly broadcast an analysis of progress in the war. It was not, I fear, much of a counter-blast to the high-powered Goebbels propaganda from Zeesen.

'He did some effective homework, however, and was able to discover the identity of the renegade South African who voiced the anti-British propaganda. The disclosure was publicised in a broadcast trailer (nowadays in TV parlance it is a "promo"), and all South Africa was glued to its loudspeakers to hear his identity.

'My own responsibility throughout the war was heavy but never dangerous. My worst problem was the primitive distribution system, by which each news bulletin was supplied to the Cape and Natal studios to be read by a local newsreader.

'The news was telexed to the coastal stations over telephone lines subject to violent interference. Electric storms were not the only cause; one constant problem was identified as "the crow fault" caused by birds perching on the wires and shorting them out.

'Once the animosities of the different allegiances I have described broke into violence, when one of the Afrikaans-speaking staff punched me in the jaw over an imagined affront – nothing to do with the war, but simply a boiling-over of suppressed hate.

---

* Received clearly in South Africa and understandably discouraged by the authorities. The chief announcer of the Afrikaans broadcasts from Zeesen was a former teacher from Natal of German extraction: Erich Holm. Like Robey Leibbrandt, he was tried and sentenced and after the Nationalists came to power, released.

'Caprara investigated the incident and brought us together in his office, bade us shake hands and then, as I departed, called after me as the door closed, "I'm sure Van Wyk was provoked". [Van Wyk was not the aggressor's name.]

'That was Caprara's notion of equity.

'Wartime service in the SABC was stimulating, often frightening and a cockpit of minor, but intense, action within the broader context of a world at war. '

CHAPTER

19

'There'll Always be an England'

Jean Lawrence and the British child evacuees, September 1940

On 17 February 1940, in the midst of what Winston Churchill, still a backbencher in the House of Commons, called the 'twilight war', Britain made arrangements to remove four hundred thousand children from London to rural areas.

In the main these children came from poor urban areas, predominantly the East End of London. Families with money found homes for their children in the Dominions, especially in Canada. When she was asked whether Princess Elizabeth and Princess Margaret Rose* would stay in the United Kingdom and face not only the expected heavy bombing but a possible invasion, Queen Elizabeth† replied simply: 'The children won't leave without me; I won't leave without the King; and the King will never leave.'

As one of the Dominions, South Africa declared herself willing to take in British children. The Child Guest Scheme, as it was called, was administered by the Department of Social Welfare in co-operation with the National Advisory Council of the Overseas Children Reception Administration.

Altogether 357 children, 308 from England, 45 from Scotland and two from the Far East, arrived in South Africa in September 1940. Local committees in the areas where the children were sent watched over their progress and welfare and submitted reports to the Council, which in turn passed them on to the Children's Overseas Reception Board in London and thence to the parents. The children stayed with selected hosts.

When it was announced that children would be arriving in South Africa and would need homes, the South African Overseas Children's Reception Administration was flooded with applications. Many of them, however well meant, were unsuitable. Jean Lawrence, wife of Harry

* Now Queen Elizabeth II and Princess Margaret.
† The Queen Mother.

Lawrence, Minister of the Interior and of Public Health, was Vice-Chairman of the Reception Administration:

'We were told originally to expect at least twenty thousand child-ren. But in the end, mainly because the ship taking one of the groups of evacuees to Canada was torpedoed and sunk, very few children actually arrived. The sea voyage was just too dangerous.

'I made many broadcasts asking people for help, for money and provisions, and I made speeches all over the country. The response was amazing – we got thousands of offers of homes. It was an unbelievable response. The main difficulty, of course, was finding suitable homes, the sort that the children were used to.

'They mostly came from towns, such as London and Glasgow and Edinburgh, and we felt we couldn't put the children into a wealthy home and then send them back to a poor home after the war. And we couldn't put the children with very aged foster-parents, either – we tried to fit like with like. Of course, there were some obviously unsuitable applications, such as the one we received from a farmer for seven healthy lads. He was obviously short of labour, and needless to say he didn't get his seven boys.

'We had no idea of when the children would be arriving, so we got everything organised within as short a time as possible. I thought they shouldn't be separated the minute they arrived, and here we were very lucky, because Lady Duncan, the Governor General's wife, offered Westbrooke in Rondebosch and then Lady Michaelis offered Monte Bello in Newlands, and a large sum of money, to house them. The Cape Town Jewish Orphanage also offered accommodation.

'The children came out in a convoy under appalling conditions: blackout, lifeboat drill and great danger. We received 24 hours' notice in the end and it was a hard job to get everything ready. When they arrived they looked surprisingly fit, although most of them had very few clothes with them.

'We took all the children to our two 'hostels' in a fleet of cars that I had arranged with people prepared to drive them at a moment's notice. The hostels were filled with beds and stretchers, and there were a few cases of measles, and we had to get the children into hospitals, all sorts of problems like that.

'They were so cheerful when they arrived. They had obviously been taught on board ship to sing "We Are Marching to Pretoria", because they sang that for us and "There'll Always be an England", which left us all with lumps in our throats.

'On the first afternoon of their arrival we gave a party for them. There was singing and lots to eat and drink. One little girl was sobbing because she had lost her sister. Eventually we reunited them. After the

Jean Lawrence, Vice-Chairman of the Reception Administration, at Westbrooke, Rondebosch, on the day when the child evacuees arrived. More were due to arrive but the threat of sinkings due to submarines, the Battle of Britain and the blitz meant that no further evacuees from Britain arrived. (Jean Lawrence)

party had begun, about five in the afternoon, Albion Springs across the road set off their siren, a signal for the workers to stop work. All the children disappeared under the bushes – they thought it was an air-raid siren. We couldn't persuade them to come out, so I hurriedly telephoned the manager and asked him to sound the all clear, which he did and the party continued.

'The children were taken to the places that they had been allocated to. Wherever possible we kept members of a family together. I never saw any of them again, but I kept track of them through the committees all over the country. We looked after them very well.'

• Interview 1990.

The South African hosts were generous. They paid school, university and college fees. In January 1942 the Department of Social Welfare accepted money sent by the children's parents. All the children, with the exception of thirty-two who stayed permanently in the country and twenty-four who were finishing training courses, were repatriated by January 1946.

CHAPTER

20

'I was taught to be proud of being a Boer'

Manie Maritz and the Ossewabrandwag

The Ossewabrandwag was formed in Bloemfontein in 1938 in response to the urge for Afrikaner nationalism manifested by the centenary ox-waggon trek that year.

There was an Old Testament ring to the objectives of the Ossewabrandwag: the 'perpetuation of the ox-waggon spirit in our land'; the 'maintenance, extension and realisation of the traditions and principles of the Afrikaner'; the 'protection and advancement of the religious, cultural and material interests of the Afrikaner'; the 'cultivation of patriotism and national pride'; and the 'linking up and stringing together of all Afrikaners, families as well as males, who subscribed to these ideals and were willing to work energetically for them'.

Afrikaners flocked to the banner of the Vierkleur in pursuit not only of nostalgia but of an identity that they believed had been submerged after the Second Boer War. By 1941 the membership of the Ossewabrandwag under its leader Dr J F J (Hansie) van Rensburg was between three and four hundred thousand.

South African participation in the war was bitterly opposed by the Ossewabrandwag. Within months of the declaration of hostilities the Ossewabrandwag was being organised along military lines: the Boer War commandos. It was led by a Commandant General, the first of whom was Colonel J C Laas, an officer serving in the South African Defence Force. Under him each province had a general. Units, each led by a commandant, helped by three field cornets and between three and nine assistant field cornets, fell under the generals.

Laas was succeeded in 1941 by Dr Van Rensburg, a brilliant scholar, aged thirty when he was appointed Secretary for Justice and thirty-seven when he became Administrator of the Orange Free State (1936). Like Oswald Pirow, Van Rensburg attended the Olympic Games in Berlin, where he met Hitler.

Under Van Rensburg's leadership the Ossewabrandwag formed a military wing, the Stormjaers (shock troops), independent of the Ossewabrandwag but consisting of handpicked men recruited from the parent organisation. The similarities to the Nazi Party's *Schutzstaffel* (SS) were obvious.

The Ossewabrandwag was certainly a force to be reckoned with until 1943, when its power base began to crumble. But in spite of the Stormjaers the organisation achieved little of military value other than petty acts of sabotage, the beating of men in uniform – particularly those wearing the distinctive red tabs – occasional riots, the most serious of which were in Johannesburg, and adding to the tensions within the country during the war.

Where was it all leading to? Speeches by Dr Van Rensburg, at loggerheads not only with Smuts but with Dr D F Malan, leader of the Purified National Party, left the country in little doubt about the future if the Ossewabrandwag were to triumph, and again, the speeches were uncomfortably similar to the aims of the National Socialists under Hitler.

'The aim of the Ossewabrandwag,' he said in May 1942, 'is to found a one-party, authoritarian and disciplined state in which the people will not be allowed to say, write or do as they please to the detriment of the people and the government'. And concerning the Ossewabrandwag's predilection for things German: 'The Ossewabrandwag is of the opinion that a German victory is an obvious condition for an Afrikaner republic to come into existence. Liberation can happen only as a result of a German victory.'

There is little doubt that much of the story of the Ossewabrandwag during the war is still to be told. Whether they could have made a national rebellion is debatable; certainly it had the numbers, the trained men and the desire.

One of these men, a member of both the Ossewabrandwag and the Stormjaers, was young Manie Maritz. He was the son of General Manie Maritz and an associate of Robey Leibbrandt, passionately determined to ensure the line of the Boers and passionate about Afrikaner nationalism:

'A wrong thing happened in the history of South Africa on the day she went to war with Germany. That should never have happened. It's true that my family was politicised … we knew what was going on, especially my father General Manie Maritz, a real patriot.

'He never stopped hoping that we would get the Boer republics back again. He didn't sign the Treaty of Vereeniging, but he was in agreement with those who would do anything to get the republics back again. They tried in 1914 and it didn't work, but that didn't put men like my father off.

'When the centenary trek was going on in 1938 and the Ossewabrandwag was being founded, they felt it was a good time to start working again to get their freedom. We felt we were sowing the seed for a free nation and the Republic of South Africa.

'Smuts was a traitor, I can't call him anything else. He was fighting with the Boers a few years before and he betrayed them. Now he was betraying us again. We were enemies of the British and we certainly didn't want a war with Germany. But in spite of the feeling in my home about Smuts, I was never allowed to speak disrespectfully of him or tell jokes about him. I was never allowed to call him Ou Jannie. If I talked about him I had to call him *Generaal* Smuts. My father wouldn't stand for anything else, in spite of his beliefs.

'His beliefs were very strong. He wanted me to go on the student exchange we had before the war, by which youngsters like me could go to Germany and join the German army to be trained. It never happened because of the war. Instead, I stayed on at school, at Grey College in Bloemfontein, the same school that Robey Leibbrandt went to. I was a member of the Ossewabrandwag Youth Movement, and there were many camps in the Bloemfontein area where we went for training.

'It was flat country round there, not really bush. We would go to one of the farms and sometimes we would pitch tents and sometimes we would just roll ourselves in blankets and sleep on the ground. There were a lot of lectures, mostly about being Afrikaners and being proud of that. We would sit in the open for the lectures. We talked about many things. About President Kruger and Piet Fourie and who we were and what we were. We wanted to maintain our identity as Boers. That was very important to us.

'My whole family believed in that: that they were Boers, that we were members of a white nation in South Africa. I was a rebellious kid.

'We also did military training – we had no weapons, the big blokes had those. We had drill parades and we learnt how to *spoorsny* [track], how to start a fire and at night how to find our way by the stars.

'We were being taught not only to be proud of our birth but to stick together. That was very important. We were a select group, a closed group, and we all had to support one another. And our training was to prepare us for what might come, maybe a rebellion, maybe a war. But not the British war.

'My father was planning rebellion. That was no secret among us. He was planning it as early as 1938. He was a member of the Ossewabrandwag, of course, and he was considered for the leadership, but Van Rensburg was chosen instead.

'The Grootraad must have had its reasons. Certainly the Ossewabrandwag conducted itself very differently during the war under Dr

Van Rensburg than it would have under my father. My father believed in confrontation. He started a semi-military organisation called Die Boerenasie and I was in that too.

'So, from 1938 my father was organising a rebellion. If the Government carried on with the war against the Germans, he wanted to do something inside South Africa to stop it. He thought we should do *anything* to stop it. It wasn't a small thing. We had camps all over the place and there were a lot of very important people in the movement.

'We young people were told to pack bullets. We didn't do that at the camps, we did it privately, in secret. We got hold of a lot of rifles and we gave those to the leaders and we began to plan blowing up power stations.

'When the road convoys were going up north, to Northern Rhodesia and Kenya, there were certain steep hills in the Warmbaths area, and we would hide at the side of the road and wait for them. We would jump on to the back of the trucks – they were well apart and moving very slowly – and we could steal the supplies on the trucks, especially the drums of petrol. We needed petrol because it was short in the country and the leaders needed to drive about a lot, and they couldn't without coupons.

'I wasn't at all frightened. It was an adventure. It was just something we did, like going to war. We did more important things later. And we did everything with our parents' knowledge. I was frightened only once. I was at school and the police took me from there to the police station and held me for about six hours, questioning me. My father had a radio transmitter and the police knew he had it, but they wanted to know more. Eventually they had to let me go. They didn't get anything from me and I never told my father about it.

'All this time men were joining the army and going up north to fight. But most of them didn't volunteer. They had a sword over their heads. A lot of teachers, a lot of railway workers, a lot of the government people had this sword over their heads. If they didn't take the red oath they would lose their jobs, so what else could they do? A lot of the people in the Ossewabrandwag with me also had fathers in the Ossewabrandwag, and their fathers were forced to go.

'Most of the time, of course, I was at school. We felt very strongly about Britain. We had cadets at school, but I refused to drill. That caused a scene, but eventually I was told I could sit at the side. My headmaster was very understanding. I drew up a petition at the College to say that if they didn't expel a lot of the Jews then the boertjies who signed the petition would all leave.

'The headmaster heard about the petition and called me to his office. "Manie, if you hand me that petition I shall have no option but to expel you immediately. Give it to me and we will say no more about it," he said. I went to my room and got the petition. It had nearly 240 signatures on it. He just tore it up in front of me.

'We never stood for God Save King. I would go to the bioscope and just walk out. I had a lot of fights on the road, but I could look after myself. When I played rugby against St Andrews, the English school in Bloemfontein, they booed me and shouted: "You're bloody Ossewabrandwag;" but when we played against Centraal, the Afrikaans school, they booed me too, shouting, "You're a Jewish boertjie," because there were so many Jews at Grey College. I enjoyed it.

'There was a cadet shooting match at school and all the weapons were locked in rooms before the match. That night three of us broke in and stole all the .22s and ammunition. There were more than forty rifles, and we couldn't get them off the grounds that night, so we hid them. There was a terrible bother about the rifles, and I think one or two of the teachers suspected us, but they never said anything. I was in contact with various groups, and that night I handed the weapons over to them. Robey Leibbrandt was with them. He knew the school grounds well, having been a pupil there.

'I didn't hate the English as such, but I hated the idea of being under their yoke. If you think something is right and you are in the minority, that doesn't necessarily make it wrong. We were taught that we wanted to be our own rulers. I was taught to be proud of being a Boer, to be proud of being a rebel, to try to get what was rightfully mine. That was the big thing.

'My father never wore a German uniform and in that he was different from Robey Leibbrandt. We didn't want the Germans here to start a German colony. We were happy to use the Germans, but we wanted to be a free country, not a colony of another country. My father would say "An English jingo is just as bad as a German jingo", and I thought Leibbrandt was too much of a German jingo. His heart wasn't really in the Afrikaans movement. He admired Hitler, and we had a few differences about that, but he was a great man.

'Leibbrandt wasn't in South Africa when my father was organising the rebellion. As I said, he had a lot of important people working for him, and some of those important people were at Roberts Heights. My father told me that was where the rebellion would begin. He had a lot of inside information about Roberts Heights, for a lot of men there, including instructors, were working with him and came to his meetings. That was to be the centre of the rebellion.

'But it never happened, because my father was killed. It was a road accident, but none of us believed that it was an accident. About two months before he died my father was crossing the Jukskei Bridge near Pretoria and six men tried to stop him as he drove across it. He drove straight through them; and he said when he got home that they were out to get him.

'And there was evidence that about ten days before my father was killed, murdered I should say, a person driving the identical car to his, a little Volkswagen, was killed in a crash in Pretoria.

'We were staying at the Erasmus's boarding house* in Warmbaths on the night of 17 December 1940. They were close friends of ours. Later we went to our farm in Naboomspruit. My father left early that morning. Maybe he had a premonition. He said to me: "Ou Beck, you must remember one thing. If something should happen to me, you must look after your mother." He said it so clearly. The police arrived that evening to tell my mother that my father had been killed in a road accident. After they had gone, she said it wasn't an accident, he had been killed by Smuts's men.

'My father always drove his own car. That day was one of the very few times someone else was at the steering wheel, a man called Piet Joubert. After the accident, they just left him lying at the side of the road, and two army officers picked up my father and took him away. What happened to him? When we next saw him, he was dead.

'If anything, I became more involved after my father's death. I stayed with the Ossewabrandwag, but I also became associated with Robey Leibbrandt. I was staying with the Erasmus family at Warmbaths one night – Johannes Erasmus was one of my father's men – and I was dozing in bed when Hendrik Erasmus walked into my room with this big man. He introduced us. "This is Jan Smit," he said. I looked at this bloke but I didn't say anything.

'Next morning I went to Hendrik† and I said, "Hendrik, the man you introduced to me as Jan Smit – I want to correct you. He wasn't Jan Smit, he was Robey Leibbrandt." Hendrik's mouth fell open. I was a sports-mad kid and Robey Leibbrandt had been an Olympic boxer, and I had recognised him the moment I saw him. That's how I became a member of the Leibbrandt group. If I hadn't, I would have been a risk to them.

'We were hard on people we thought were traitors to us. We gave one bloke a thrashing with a sjambok because he had got out of line. And we cut telephone wires. One night we blew up a post office.

---

* The Eldorian, owned by Johannes Gerhardus Erasmus. Johannes Erasmus and his two sons, Hendrik and Theodorus ('Doors'), were to become staunch supporters of Robey Leibbrandt, who stayed there in August 1941. Both Hendrik and 'Doors' were killed, Hendrik by the police on a farm in the Waterberg where he was hiding in November 1941 and 'Doors' on Sunday, 14 December on the Denneboemspruit railway line, when an explosive that he was laying went off prematurely.

† Hendrik Erasmus was one of the first men Leibbrandt met on his return to South Africa on 10 June 1941 and his most trusted lieutenant.

There were five of us. We took a stick of dynamite and put it in front of the door of the post office. It had a long fuse. When we were three hundred yards away we lit the fuse and it blew up. We were part of an underground army, you see.

'I had my mother's full support. She was a great, great patriot. If she had had the time and the energy she would have blown things up too. She went to Lourenço Marques* after I saw Leibbrandt at the Erasmus's boarding house because Dr Van Rensburg approached her and asked her to go to the German consulate and talk to them. She came back with a lot of messages.

'One of the main reasons why the Ossewabrandwag never managed to do anything really big in the country was Dr Van Rensburg. He was too much of a gentleman, he wouldn't do anything to hurt. But he wasn't a traitor. Some people thought he was a Smuts man working under cover, but I think he was just very honest and kind-hearted. Van Rensburg and my father weren't so much pro-German as pro-Boere. But Leibbrandt was pro-German.

'I was in court when he was sentenced on 11 March 1943. Leibbrandt was sure that *Generaal* Smuts wouldn't let him hang, because his father was close to Smuts during the Boer War. Even so, when they sentenced him to death it was something to see. It wasn't so much the sentence of death as Leibbrandt's attitude that was so astounding. He didn't turn a hair.

'I left South Africa before the war ended. I was in the police in Windhoek. I used to warn Germans there that there would be a police raid at such and such a time. I worked through a young baker. I'd go to the bakery and pass on the message for them to get out and he would warn them. At the end of the war I still thought that we could have had a rebellion.

'The Ossewabrandwag had the power. It had the people. But was Jerling† to be trusted? What were other men's parts in the Ossewabrandwag? Weren't they persons planted by Smuts to do things to prevent us from rebelling? Weren't they the people who were holding us back?'

• Interview, 1990

---

* Dr Luitpold Werz, former German consul in Pretoria, was stationed there.
† Advocate Pat Jerling, a general in the Ossewabrandwag, and the man who betrayed Leibbrandt to the government.

CHAPTER

21

1941

'The Roll of Honour lengthened'

'Thank God the tide is at last turning,' General Smuts optimistically told his troops in a New Year's Eve broadcast from Nairobi. He was wrong. 1941 turned out to be one of the grimmest years of the war, a year of almost unrelieved gloom as the Germans and Japanese appeared to be seizing the world.

It began cheerfully enough, though, with a romp by South African forces through northern East Africa, Abyssinia and Somaliland. By the end of January, with the South African Air Force playing a vital part, Union troops had cleared the not remarkably heroic Italians from Kenya. To the north lay Abyssinia and Somaliland, with their vast and rugged terrain.

In the late afternoon of 31 January 1941 the 2nd and 5th Brigades moved into Abyssinia. Their first actions, helped by army co-operation aircraft, were on enemy positions at El Gumu and the Gorai crater. The Beau Geste fort of Mega was the next objective: it also fell, and sixteen hundred colonials and Italians were taken prisoner. The South Africans swept forward in atrocious weather; in the armoured cars temperatures reached 130°C. As they advanced through Abyssinia a German general was despatched from Italy to North Africa. His name was to become legendary: Erwin Rommel.

The 1st SA Brigade, separated from the 2nd and 5th Brigades, occupied with the Italians in southern Abyssinia, was under the command of the 12th African Division. On 18 February the Brigade crossed the important Juba River in Somaliland, and from there swept aside all Italian resistance. It was a rout. After taking Mogadishu on the coast of Somaliland the Division turned inland toward Addis Ababa in Ethiopia, which surrendered on 6 April 1941. South African infantry battalions marched through the streets together with the 22nd East African Brigade after an astonishing advance of eighteen hundred miles in fifty-three days. There was jubilation at home.

On the day when Addis Ababa fell Britain despatched sixty thousand troops to Greece, now threatened by the Germans. The *Luftwaffe* devastated Coventry a few days later.

Remnants of the Italians fought on under the command of the Duke of Aosta. The stronghold of Amba Alagi at an altitude of ten thousand feet held out. The South Africans approached it from the south over mountainous terrain, the Indians from the north. On 18 May 1941 the Duke of Aosta surrendered. The Italian General Staff, followed by more than eight thousand soldiers, were marched into captivity between a South African guard of honour and to the sound of the pipes of the 1st Transvaal Scottish. Seventy-three South Africans were killed in the campaign. The war in Abyssinia formally ended on 21 November 1941, but by that time the South Africans were fighting a very different war in the Western Desert. The bad news was about to begin.

While British and Commonwealth forces were sweeping through Abyssinia and Somaliland, the little-known garrison town of Tobruk with the Mediterranean on one side and the desert on the other, withstood a ferocious assault by Axis forces.

By 2 May British troops had withdrawn from Greece. Worse was to come. Crete, the jewel of the Mediterranean, fell to the Germans by airborne assault. By the end of May Crete was in German hands; but at least the German navy was short of one battleship, the *Bismarck* having being sunk by the Royal Navy on 27 May.

On 22 June, a mild European midsummer's day, German troops invaded Russia along a front of two thousand miles. It looked as though nothing on earth could resist the great German war machine.

The 2nd SA Division under Maj-Gen I P de Villiers had been seen off on its way north, not to Kenya or Somaliland but to North Africa, by the Lady in White, singing the Division out of Durban harbour. The men responded by singing 'Sarie Marais' and 'Tipperary'. As a birthday gift to General Smuts, King George VI promoted him Field Marshal on his birthday, 24 May. But to the soldiers he was still Oom Jan, or the Oubaas.

June was also to be remembered in South Africa for another reason. On 10 June the former South African Olympic light-heavyweight boxer Robey Leibbrandt secretly landed on the coast of South West Africa. Operation Weissdorn, the German-inspired plot to assassinate Smuts and other South African leaders, had begun. A world apart from Leibbrandt, Wing Commander A G 'Sailor' Malan, DSO, DFC and bar, serving with the Royal Air Force, became its highest-scoring air ace with a bag of thirty-five German aircraft.

Isie Smuts, who had been married to Jan Smuts for forty years, was affectionately known as Ouma. She was a small, slight figure with a mop of curly grey hair, devoid of make-up or frivolity and with her skirt never higher than mid-calf. She turned the public rooms of Libertas and Groote Schuur into workrooms for the Gifts and Comforts Fund, of which she was president.

The shy and retiring Ouma took the troops to her heart. They were her boys, and she conscripted women ruthlessly to her cause. Three thousand women in Johannesburg alone worked for Gifts and Comforts, making glory bags for the troops, stuffing the bags with cigarettes, handkerchiefs, hand-knitted socks, tinned food, razor-blades – anything to bring a touch of comfort to the fighting soldiers. By the end of the war Ouma's Gifts and Comforts Fund had distributed over three million cigarettes alone (C to C, Springbok and Max), and one-and-a-half million pairs of laboriously knitted socks.*

For five years the Union, divided by a chasm into pro and anti-war factions, struggled to find enough men to fight up north and to man the units needed at home to guard the coast, provide security inland and guard the increasing numbers of prisoners of war (mostly Italians) and suspect South Africans interned for the duration. The Native Military Corps was accordingly expanded, but not armed; they served mostly as cooks, batmen and, with bravery, as stretcher-bearers. Plans were also announced to ease the manpower shortage by expanding the Women's Auxiliary Defence Corps from eight thousand to thirty thousand.

There were plenty of scares off the long South African coast. A suspected German battleship four hundred miles off Cape Point sent a 32 Flight Maryland on a seven-hour wild goose chase. Houses were opened to the shocked survivors of torpedoed ships and to the men spilling off convoys. 'Don't Talk About Ships and Shipping!' warned posters. As many as thirty ships berthed and unberthed in a day.

Great warships such as HMS *Prince of Wales* and HMS *Nelson* were seen in Table Bay for the first time. The liners *Queen Mary* and *Queen Elizabeth* also anchored there. Aircraft-carriers, battleships and merchantmen in need of repairs went into the graving docks at Durban, the largest between Gibraltar and Singapore. Convoys streamed in: twenty-one ships in one convoy alone entered Durban harbour, and in September 1941 HMS *Repulse,* escorting a convoy of troopships bound for the Middle East, left from Durban on her last voyage. As many as forty thousand men at one time came off the convoys, and turned Cape Town and Durban into organised bedlam while they were there. The hospitality that these troops received in the coast towns was

---

* In addition to the glory-bags, families sent a constant stream of parcels up north. For 3/6 a man could get a packet of ginger snaps, a quarter-pound of assorted sweets, a quarter of crystallised pineapple, a quarter of chocolate wafers, a quarter of nutty toffee, 2 oz nuts and raisins. Postage was a shilling.

affectionately remembered by soldiers from as far away as Australia, Canada, Britain and the USA, even though great indignation was expressed by the people of Cape Town at the stuffy decision of the Cape Divisional Council not to allow dancing at roadhouses on a Sunday.

As the Roll of Honour lengthened in the daily papers (reduced in size because of paper shortage and only recently having replaced the traditional front page filled with advertisements by news), the historic declaration of the principles of democracy known as the Atlantic Charter was made in August by Winston Churchill and F D Roosevelt. Black nationalists in the Union seized on the Charter as a declaration of rights, much to the annoyance of the government.

Letters home, strictly censored, came from the hundred thousand South African personnel now in North Africa. The men, they assured their wives and girlfriends at home, were bearing up in the desert world of sandstorms, scarcity of water, against the hawkers of Cairo and in the night clubs of Alexandria. But it wasn't until November that the realities of war came home to both the fighting men and their families.

On 18 November Operation Crusader began, an attempt to push the Afrika Korps to the west and to relieve the beleaguered town of Tobruk. As the 8th Army cut through the wire that divided Egypt from Libya on 18 November, South African troops, many of whom had fought through Abyssinia and Somaliland, were to the fore.

Out in the desert, at Sidi Rezegh, men of the 5th Brigade (2nd Regiment Botha, 3rd Transvaal Scottish and 1st SA Irish) were overwhelmed by a surprise attack by two Panzer divisions. On Sunday, 23 November the 5th Brigade ceased to exist; its men in some cases fought German tanks with nothing more than a machine gun. By the end of a day filled with horror, the men of the proud 5th Brigade who survived the battle were mostly prisoners of war. When the news of the disaster reached home, belief in the invincibility of the South African troops was shattered. We were mortal, after all.

By the end of 1941 the South African Air Force, part of the Desert Air Force, had flown 5 727 sorties. With sea lanes threatened by U-Boats, Britain alone lost over three million tons of shipping during the year. On 7 December, as families waited anxiously to hear what had happened to men posted missing at Sidi Rezegh, the war assumed another dimension: Japanese carrier-borne aircraft attacked the American Pacific Fleet at Pearl Harbour.

Next day Britain and the United States declared war on Japan, and on 11 December, the day after the great British warships *Prince of Wales* and *Repulse* were sunk by the Japanese, the USA at last, to the great relief of Britain, declared war on Germany and Italy. The knowledge that the Yanks were in it with them put heart into everyone, even

A German propaganda postcard circulated in the Middle East in 1941. It shows a dim and bloated Britain, easy prey for the lithe Teutons of the Third Reich.

though the British withdrew from Penang and Hong Kong fell to the Japanese on Christmas Day. But the far-eastern disasters were offset by Hitler's maniacal declaration of war on the USA.

While South African women complained about the quality of lipstick – the local product being a poor substitute for the vanished imported brands – and yearned for the new nylon stockings and snivelled over Alice Duer Miller's *The White Cliffs*, work began in Chicago and Los Angeles on the Manhattan Project: the development of the atomic bomb.

Good news? Well, there was Able Seaman Just Nuisance; occupation: Bone-Crusher. Just Nuisance was on the regular strength of the Royal Navy at Simonstown, holder of a season-ticket on the Simonstown train and on the Navy's register and pay-list. He became a father.

To raise morale, two of his progeny were sent on a tour of the Transvaal to do their bit for Naval War Funds. It helped a little to take the collective South African mind off the crisis Up North.

CHAPTER

22

'It was poignant saying goodbye and it was poignant saying hello'

Valerie Back, looking after the troops

By January 1941 the troops who had left with such a fanfare the year before had been in Kenya for over six months; training and training, they moaned in their letters home. In the Union it was left to the women to step into jobs previously held by men, to support those on active service and to give … and give they did, even their aluminium saucepans, piled in huge drifts outside the municipal halls in the big towns to raise money for the war funds.

The Governor General's National War Fund, started on 15 July 1940, gathered momentum in 1941.* Its purpose was to help financially the families of men away fighting, to help with children's education, to help returning soldiers get back on their feet when they came back home, and as the casualties mounted towards the end of 1941, to help bereaved families.

Money was raised in the usual ways: bingo, cake sales, street collections, fairs, morning markets, dances and gambling. The prohibition of gambling in the Union was unofficially lifted during the war years, and Johannesburg in particular rushed to the tables with zest. The gambling parties were held in private houses at first, and then in clubs. The roulette tables were run professionally – Eric Gallo was a big gambler, and he guaranteed an audience when he approached a table. Altogether over a hundred gambling evenings were held in Johannesburg; they raised £23,614 for war funds.

Money was also raised by sweepstakes; and again the authorities turned a blind eye. Winners were drawn in front of an audience from a revolving drum, and each number was checked by two independent

---

* £7,782,783 was raised direct from the public. From 1943 the government matched pound for pound for every contribution. A final appeal to the public was made after VE Day (8 May 1945). It resulted in over £1 million in thirty days.

recorders and also against the stubs of the books. By the end of the war £1 229,757 had been raised from sweepstakes alone.

Women also knitted, cooked, packed glory-bags for the SA Gifts and Comforts Fund and played host to hundreds of thousands of young servicemen of all nationalities who passed through the country *en route* for somewhere else, usually to North Africa. It wasn't just the men off the convoys who were looked after (the Australians, who had passed through the Union during the 1914–18 war were remembered with certain qualms by the older women. When they arrived in the 1939–45 war they did not disappoint their daughters either), but also over thirty thousand pilots, navigators, observers and gunners who were trained in the Union under the Joint Air Training Scheme.

Valerie Back was one of the nine thousand SAWAS in Command 13, the Cape Peninsula, who cooked, washed up, typed, wrote letters, made tea, comforted the wounded and entertained soldiers, sailors and airmen in her family home, on call from Sunday to Sunday:

'I remember those words broadcast by Neville Chamberlain on Sunday, 3 September 1939 as if they were yesterday: "We are at war with Germany." We were having lunch, my husband and I and a nursing sister. I had just had my first child, Jennifer. Sister Charlton was English; when Chamberlain finished speaking she burst into tears and left the table.

'My husband, Rubin, was a manufacturer, on war supplies. He joined the home guard at once. A lot of my friends also had small babies, and even though their husbands volunteered and many of them went away to war, they pitched in to help the war effort. I decided to join the SAWAS and filled in all the forms; and because we lived in Kenilworth I joined the Wynberg branch under the command of Nicolette Bairnsfather and became an assistant section-leader, clerical.

'"Clerical" was a misnomer, because we were called upon to do anything and everything from washing dishes and serving meals to the soldiers to toasting buns and making tea at Wynberg Military Hospital; meeting and entertaining soldiers and sailors off the ships in convoy, or driving Daisy, a very unwieldly mobile canteen.

'I had a nanny for Jennifer, so I had a lot of time to spare. I'd be down at the SAWAS office in Wynberg by 9 a.m. and do whatever secretarial work there was – helping wives of South African soldiers with problems, typing. I'd work until about one and then go home, or sit knitting, knitting everything, even though my fingers always got tangled up with the wool. I wasn't the world's greatest knitter, but I managed scarves without difficulty.

'That was on the days when there were no convoys or men to entertain. The arrival of a convoy was a hush-hush affair. Only the heads of the SAWAS were told when one was coming in. Our only instruction was a telephone call to say "Be at the usual place [which was the docks] this afternoon". We never talked about the convoys, we were very security-conscious. There were large posters everywhere saying "DON'T TALK SHIPS OR SHIPPING" and "CARELESS TALK COSTS LIVES".

'When the convoy was due in I would drive down to the docks and we'd all wait there until the men came out of the dock gates, hundreds and hundreds of them. We'd take as many as the car would hold and go off for a drive and tea. If the weather was bad we would take the men home and give them a good meal and a bit of family atmosphere. There were so many men coming and going in our house that Jennifer, when she was older, used to call them Daddy. I very seldom took officers, for they were well looked after and had the *entrée* to all the clubs.

'In the end I entertained about four hundred men, and I wrote to every single one of their mothers, their wives or their girlfriends; just a short letter to let them know that their boy was well and being looked after. If I had any film in my camera, and if it was available, for we were very short of film, I would also take a photograph and send that back home. Home might be Britain, New Zealand, Australia or even Java.

'The Australians ... they arrived on the *Queen Elizabeth* and the *Queen Mary* and other ships in a convoy of about sixty thousand. They'd been cooped up for some time and they had a lot of spare energy. They painted Cape Town red. There was one poor traffic officer directing traffic at the top of Adderley Street. Two Australians with a bag of oranges stood in front of him. Every time the officer put up his hand the soldiers would put an orange into it. The Aussies would go into the bars, swallow their drinks and not pay. "Charge it to the Australian Government," they'd say and walk out.

'They turned over a beer lorry and opened the stopcocks, so that beer flowed down the streets. Discipline was much more lax than in the British army. When it came to sailing time it was very difficult to round them up. Some were found on trains as far away as De Aar.

'One miserable winter evening my husband and I were driving up Plein Street when we saw two very disconsolate-looking soldiers hunched up in the rain. We stopped the car and picked them up and took them home to dinner. As we sat in front of the fire, one of the boys, a thin, weedy-looking fellow, told us he had been a jockey and had been warned off every course in Australia for doing what he shouldn't do. Neither of them wanted to go back to the ship that night.

'I always kept the spare bedroom ready for that kind of thing, with pyjamas and toothbrushes, so it was no problem to put them up.

The troops entertained left mementoes behind with their hostesses. Here an autograph album is filled with couplets, doggerel and leaves from a silverbush picked in Cape Town.

Margaret Fricker also entertained the troops. She was presented with an 'award' by some of the men she entertained. Most of the men wrote 'thank you' letters, and many of the women wrote to parents and wives telling them that their boys were well.

Whereas on a day in the month of May in the Year of Our Lord One Thousand Nine Hundred and Forty Two certain Soul Weary Sea Sick and Dispirited Footsloggers were deposited on the Quayside in the Ancient City of CAPETOWN

AND WHEREAS Miss M. Lamont did faithfully provide for the aforementioned Footsloggers swift moving Transport that they might traverse the Land in Indolence Dignity and Sybaritic Luxury

AND WHEREAS the said Miss M. Lamont did further provide for these Footsloggers such Entertainment and Refreshment as were Needful and which in their Variety and Profusion did Amaze and Overwhelm the Footsloggers

BE IT THEREFORE KNOWN to all men that for her Virtue and Charity and after due Observance of the fitting Ceremonies the said Miss M. Lamont has been admitted to Membership of the Ancient and Most Illustrious and Noble Order of the Little Ray of Sunshine

AND BE IT FURTHER KNOWN that on such occasions as may be permitted by the Manners and Customs of Good Society the said Miss M. Lamont is enjoined to indicate her Membership of the aforesaid Ancient and Most Illustrious and Noble Order by appending to her name the letters "L.R.S."

IN WITNESS WHEREOF we the undersigned have hereto subscribed our Names and Seal

Signed:

Master of the Ancient
and Most Illustrious and Noble
Order of the Little Ray of Sunshine

Countersigned:

Chairman.

Secretary.

Awards Committee.

Witnessed: Manchester, England

Master of Ceremony

Office Boy.

Rubin went into their room to see if they were comfortable and saw the little jockey putting a knife under his pillow. "What are you doing with that?" he asked. He replied that he always had a knife on him because, after all, they didn't know what sort of a joint they were coming to.

'We locked our bedroom door that night, which I'm sure wasn't necessary; but one couldn't be too sure, and friends of mine had had rather unpleasant experiences with some of the soldiers.

'We entertained Indian officers, American negroes and students from a naval college in Java who were being evacuated from that part of the world. Because of the colour bar in South Africa special arrangements had to be made for these men, for there was really nowhere to take them out for tea. We were on duty every day of the week and on call at all hours.

'I didn't only entertain, though. One of our jobs was to fetch officers in charge of supplies on the ships and drive them to the various suppliers. They had to victual the ships to the Middle East and back to Cape Town. We were given petrol coupons for that sort of work, and we drove all over the place. There were always shortages of food after a convoy left, but nothing very serious.

'Once I entertained officers, and that evening there was a dance for them at Kelvin Grove. I was asked to bring the men I had had at home that day. During that evening, unexpectedly and unannounced, General Smuts arrived. After welcoming everybody, he said he wanted to congratulate the Japanese. There was a sudden hush – we couldn't quite believe what we were hearing. Then he continued: "Because they have brought our friends the Americans into the war." It was just after Pearl Harbour.

'I worked with Ouma Smuts when she was starting the Gifts and Comforts for the troops – the SAWAS were very involved with that. The General's secretary, Sally Richardson, had been seconded to Ouma and she needed an assistant secretary, and that was me. I was greatly honoured. It was interesting work, a lot of organisation. Ouma was very appealing, very unaffected and natural. She had an appointment to visit Pollsmoor military camp and have tea with "her" boys. Then she realised it was on a Monday, and she asked Sally to telephone to say she couldn't come as she always did her washing on a Monday; she would come another day!

'We saw the other side of the war too. Some of the men who had been blinded in battle were being cared for and trained to do certain jobs – before returning home – in a lovely old house near us. I used to go and read to them and dance with them and take them for walks. They often used to come home for meals. Most of them were wonderfully brave and uncomplaining, although a few were very angry. Some of them had lost an arm or a leg as well. Sometimes one just didn't think when one said something. Frank was blind and often used to come to the house. I was taking him back to St Dunstan's one night, in the blackout, and I stopped the car outside the house and said "I can't see a thing." Frank just said: "Give me your hand. I'll take you."

'There was a lot of fun and games and entertainment, but there was also a lot of heartache and sadness. We never knew whether the youngsters we entertained would survive the war. I used to say good-bye to them, laughing and joking and making arrangements for after the war, and I would wonder if they would be alive in a month's time.

'I entertained a delightful naval man, very young; he was on the *Prince of Wales* which was lost with all hands. And I would hear of a battle up north and wonder which of those laughing boys who had shared a meal with me had been killed. It was very poignant saying goodbye, and I suppose it was very poignant saying hello. One never knew, and I felt very protective towards them.'

• Interview 1990.

CHAPTER

23

'The cool blue hills of Abyssinia'

Carel Birkby and the first news from Abyssinia, January 1941

The newspapers in the Union had been drastically reduced in size because of the shortage of newsprint and the Paper Controller, who doled out stocks. In 1940 the advertisements that had filled the front pages of newspapers were placed inside the paper, and for the first time news occupied the front page. Since space was so short there were no screaming headlines; even the biggest stories looked modest compared to those of the 1990s.

Nonetheless it was on newspapers and the radio that the population depended for news of the war and other events. The wedding in Durban in 1940 of Sir Delves Broughton, Bart, and Miss Diana Caldwell was given wide coverage before the couple left for Kenya.

So when the news of the murder of the wildly attractive Earl of Errol and the arrest of Sir Delves came over the wires, it was promptly put on the front page of most English papers. The murder had everything: sex (a flagrant affair between Lord Errol and the former Diana Caldwell, a beauty thirty years younger than her husband), high society and money (Sir Delves was rich, and Lord Errol, the Deputy Director of Manpower and the Military Secretary in Kenya, had given Lady Broughton a £30 000 pearl necklace).

Surely, South Africans speculated, Sir Delves wouldn't have crept out of the house, run down the road, flagged Lord Errol down and then shot him in the neck? It provided dinner-table gossip for weeks.*

Meanwhile, far removed from the world of high society and polo and all-night parties, South African troops were slogging it out in northern Kenya, wondering when they would be going into real action.

---

* The trial became the longest and most famous in Kenyan legal history, lasting six weeks. In the end the verdict was not guilty, and Sir Delves was acquitted. Forty years later the film *White Mischief* recalled the murder.

News of their doings was faithfully reported in the South African newspapers, thanks to the war correspondents who accompanied the units. At the beginning of the war the Bureau of Information appointed two official war correspondents, Conrad Norton (English) and Uys Krige (Afrikaans). The South African Press Association (SAPA) appointed Carel Birkby as its first (but by no means last) war correspondent in the field. Birkby, a reporter on the *Cape Argus* during the 1930s, was appointed general war correspondent to the Argus group, and after an officers' training course at Roberts Heights he was seconded to SAPA for the duration.

Birkby went north with Krige and Norton on the first troopship to leave Durban with South African men aboard (16 July 1940). Invidious though it is to single out one journalist from the many who covered the war for South African papers, Birkby stands out for the quality of his journalism, a certain reckless zeal and for his exposé of the Sidi Rezegh débâcle,* which earned him the intense dislike of Smuts, who attempted to suppress the full extent of the battle; and it was at Sidi Rezegh that Uys Krige and Conrad Norton, with other South African reporters and cameramen, were captured.

He also achieved a little *coup d'éclat* in January 1941 for his anonymous despatch, written on 29 January and published in the Stop Press edition of *The Star* on 4 February 1941. What made this short report so special was that it was the first written in Abyssinia.

Birkby and the other correspondents with the 2nd SA Infantry Brigade† (including Uys Krige, who wrote verses in his spare moments) were based in the middle of nowhere on the inhospitable border of Abyssinia. In a shallow depression at Dukana the correspondents, like everyone else, were waiting for the orders that would send South African troops across the border into enemy territory proper.

In almost unbearable heat, and fighting off the torpor that it produced, Birkby sat down at his portable typewriter to write a sort of all-is-well-with-the-boys despatch. Finding it almost impossible, he wrote for his own amusement (but also knowing that nothing is ever wasted and that the copy could be used later, as it was in *Springbok Victory*, published in 1941) an account of what life was really like in the Northern Frontier District:

‘Here we sit, sizzling in the heat on the Abyssinian border. When I lift up my eyes I see the cool blue hills of Ethiopia which loom before the South African troops like Canaan before the Israelites when their fortieth year in the wilderness was drawing to

---

* 23 November 1941 in the Western Desert.

† 1st Field Force Battalion, 2nd Field Force Battalion, 1st Natal Mounted Rifles.

a close. When I look back at my typewriter I find that the sweat from my brow has dropped on the paper: it is not like perspiration but yellow liquid dust. I change the paper on the typewriter with moist, impatient fingers, while a dust devil sweeps through the tent we have improvised below a tarpaulin. I pause, watching anxiously whether the tent, which is being sucked up as though by a giant vacuum cleaner, really will go flying away this time like a magic carpet leaving me (unfortunately) behind. I write a passage saying that Smuts's "happy warriors" stand ready in this wilderness, gladly enduring all trials outrageous nature can devise because they are crusaders in the sacred cause of democracy and they are advancing for the destruction of the Fascists, whose hearts are as black as their shirts or the lava blocks which surround this sun-scorched camp.

Carel Birkby, war correspondent. He covered the war for Sapa from the beginning to the end of the war. (Estate of Carel Birkby)

'Now I find I have written all the above on the wrong side of the paper because this infernal wind has come up again and twisted my foolscap. I wonder what the temperature is. Down there in the shallow *lugga* the armoured-car fellows have a thermometer which registered 150° this morning. The thermometer under the tent of a three-tonner registered 130°. You can't touch the metal-work of a car or our fingers burn. Dixon, the newsreel cameraman, who is gasping beside me on a stretcher that seems to feel like a Turkish bath slab, complains that the emulsion will melt off his film. It will soon be lunch-time, but it will be hard to face the bully beef which, though in the shade, has already gone as soft and hot and greasy as though it were cooked. The tinned Kenya butter has melted into a liquid like ghee. Our cigarettes are so dry that the gummed paper seams come unstuck. Gandar-Dower, the Ministry of Information man, is killing a scorpion over there. Goodhouse or Komatipoort or the Californian Desert would seem arctic compared with this. I must have another mouthful of lime-juice. I wish I were swimming at the Cape. Why is it that every time I have to change the paper in the typewriter this wind comes up again? The Springbok troops here are listening on Bruce Anderson's receiver to the midday wireless news of the advance by the army of the Nile from Tobruk to Bardia but beg leave to doubt whether the heat in the Western Desert is ever anything like this. Perhaps I should make it plain it is really hot. If you sit in the shadow of an acacia tree the sun will turn you the colour of a nicely baked tomato. Here I am trying to write a sensible dispatch about conditions, but the sun beats so intensely through the canvas that I have to wear a sun helmet even in the shade of the tent. I think I'll go and visit the armoured cars mess – they've got the only refrigerator in 20 000 square miles. The sky outside our tent isn't the beautiful African blue you may imagine, it is almost white and blindingly bright. Sunglasses are your best friend, but you now and then lose them. With heat-frayed tempers you periodically feel like losing other friends too. We are limited to one gallon of water a day and we use it like systematic Scrooges. As a sergeant explained to me, "In a mugful you first clean your teeth, then shave, then bath, then strain the water through a sand-and-stone filter in an empty petrol can and finally you wash your bush shirt in it. You use what's left to water the garden." There, my carbon paper has just blown away. I would finish this dispatch to-night but there is a complete blackout throughout the camp. You sup at sundown, mourning the drought of beer. It is too hot to go to bed because the blankets feel like towels that have been warmed on an electric towel rail. It does not cool off until four o'clock in the morning, when it turns most chilly as is usual in deserts. After two hours of this coolness you get up and shave. The heat has turned the shaving cream curiously glutinous. The latter dries on your face before the blade gets a chance. Then you drink several cups of tea and face another day of this infernal heat. ... I have just thought of several personal experiences illustrating the fact that it's hot in these parts but it demands too much energy to go on writing. Besides, I think the first folio I typed has blown away already. I wish I were swimming at Durban. I wish the General would tell me when we are going to advance into those cool blue hills of Abyssinia. ’

Birkby tucked what he described as his 'incoherent composition' into his kitbag and strolled down the hill to see the Brigade Major, Eugene Maggs. Maggs told him he was sending out a sapper with an escort of Field Force Battalion men in two troop-carriers to reconnoitre a route across the lava and through the bush from Dukana to the border. Would Birkby like to go along? It would, said Maggs encouragingly, be the South Africans' first crossing of the frontier.

'Now men with red tabs on their shoulders had got to the country that had been their goal for six months,' Birkby wrote later in *Springbok Victory*, 'and as they went crashing through the bush into enemy territory they sang "We are Marching to Pretoria" as nonchalantly as though they were on a jaunt from Johannesburg to Pretoria.'

And then, he wrote, the men sang 'Sarie Marais' as the troop-carriers lurched across the rough country. After the reconnaissance the men returned without mishap. Carel Birkby wrote and sent this historic despatch:

SOUTH AFRICANS IN ABYSSINIA
Frontier Crossed in Force

'*Today South African advanced forces are nearer to Addis Ababa than to Nairobi.*

Behind the brief communiqués of increasing pressure along the whole Kenya front and constant patrol activity is the dramatic fact that the South Africans have expelled the Italian invaders from all parts of northern Kenya and have forced their way into Abyssinia. The men from Cape hamlets, from the Transvaal highveld, the Natal coast, and the Free State plains have crossed the threshold of the country that has been their goal for the last six months.

'Lean South Africans, now hardened to the sweltering heat of armoured cars in the desert east of Lake Rudolf, have trundled across the trackless wastes of lava rock into Abyssinia, with machine guns ready to spray the elusive Banda. Infantrymen who have already tasted the excitement of battle at El Yibo, have gone bucketing across rough country into what was recently enemy territory, their cheerful songs almost drowning the steady roar of the engines of their three-ton troop-carriers.

'As soon as the men realised they were north of the border they struck up "Sarie Marais", which is probably the first time this song has been heard in Abyssinia. The region was probably visited by not more than 100 or so white men before the war.

'The South Africans had to force their way through some of the most fearful country on earth – across deserts over a dead world on which volcanoes now extinct have spewed millions upon millions of tons of lava.

ETHIOPIAN REGIMENT

It is now possible also to reveal the part played so far by the first Ethiopian refugee regiment in Kenya. The regiment was formed from refugees who fled to Kenya after the collapse of Abyssinia.

'They received several months of intensive training, and under a sergeant-major who is an American, and Scottish sergeants, all belonging to a well-known Cape regiment, received musketry and infantry drill.

'They went into action towards the end of October in north-west Kenya on the eastern side of Lake Rudolph, against groups of Italian native irregulars holding a large area of country on the Kenya side of the border.

Birkby and other correspondents leaving for Up North. His coverage of the war, particularly his Sidi Rezegh despatch, was notable (Estate of Carel Birkby)

'The Ethiopians co-operated with the King's African Rifles and played a large part in the clearing out of Banda posts and driving the enemy back to the frontier in a few weeks.

'This action, which the Ethiopians carried out with dash and daring, permitted the native tribesmen of Kenya to return to their tribal grazing grounds and proved to be an important military development.

'Their attacks helped to pave the way for the successful South African attack at El Yibo.'

At 1 p.m. on 31 January 1941, the 2nd and 5th Brigades went into Abyssinia in three parallel columns, singing, according to Birkby, 'So Long Sarie' as they went.

CHAPTER

24

'Sirens, the Aussies – and Oom Boetie Jan'

An eleven-year-old's view of the war

South African children could hardly miss the fact that there was a war on. Men in uniform walked down every street. Schools followed the war through geography lessons and raised money for war funds. Fathers, uncles and brothers were either in uniform or away from home Up North. Compared to the children of Europe, though, the children in South Africa had an easy life. There was a shortage of sugar, but there were still sweets. There was a shortage of cream, but there were still banana splits.

If they lived on the coast, in Cape Town or Durban, they could hardly have failed to notice the men coming off the convoys. And every boy wanted to be a pilot in the SAAF.

Peter Younghusband, eleven years old when the war broke out, had an average sort of a war, as far as wars go. He spent his in Cape Town:

'We knew World War II had come to Cape Town when the authorities erected an air raid siren in the vacant plot beside our house in Clifton. The first time it went off the cat ran straight up the wall and my small brother wet his pants.

'My mother became formidable in her objection to the siren and made some remarkable attempts to telephone General Smuts about it. Finally, more to preserve their peace than ours, the authorities moved it to a more remote piece of wasteland.

'But the damage had already been done. Our next-door neighbour's parrot had learned to imitate the siren, and did so whenever the mood took it.

'No one quite knew what to do when the siren went off. We hadn't been told to dig trenches or bunkers, or anything like that. Nor was it ever made clear how we were to tell if the alarm was a practice or the real thing. Never mind, we were at war, and we had an air-raid siren, and Camps Bay did not.

Peter Younghusband in Cape Town 1939–1945: sirens, blackouts, expensive chocolate logs and banana splits, breadless days, the Aussies and Italian POWs. What more could any boy ask for? (Peter Younghusband)

'We also had blackouts each night. Cars had to have little hoods over their headlights and blackout screens had to be fixed over windows.

'My father, who had failed his first medical to get into the army, was given a steel helmet, a baton and an armband, and used to stomp around the neighbourhood at night shouting 'put out that bloody light.'

'To the relief of the neighbours my father passed his second medical, was given a rifle and ordered off to North Africa to fight the Italians.

'I was eleven when war broke out, and my brother was five. We suffered severe hardships. Chocolate logs and peppermint crisps went up from threepence to fourpence. Vanilla milkshakes and banana splits also became more expensive. It was hell.

'My Uncle Bill, who was my hero because he wore striped blazers and straw boaters and played the banjo and drove a splendid old Buick mysteriously beyond his means as assistant-head porter at the Mount Nelson hotel, gave all this up to join the air force.

'He came home after his first day in uniform with a black eye and a cut on his nose. He said he had met some newly recruited artillerymen who had derided the cloth badge on his shoulder depicting a propellor, and called it a powder-puff. This had required remonstration, which had ended in a fight. I remarked that actually the badge did look like a powder puff – and got my head smacked.

'My brother and I collected military badges and buttons from soldiers when convoys stopped at Cape Town.

'Among the first to arrive was a convoy of ships bearing Australians. These were magnificent men who appeared to a small boy to be gods. However they showed their mortality by rushing off their ships shouting "We want women".

'Not quite grasping the drift of this, my brother and I took them home to our mother, and I got my head smacked again. Once the misunderstandings were cleared up the Aussies were charming and courteous, and my mother gave them tea and lots of good food, and some lasting friendships were made.

'What we enjoyed most, my brother and I, was waiting for Australian soldiers outside the Clifton Hotel. We learned very quickly that when they became drunk they became very generous, and would cut off all their regimental buttons and badges and give them to us and then stagger back to their ships, where they would be arrested for being improperly dressed.

'The Australians took Cape Town by storm. They were always exceedingly generous, walking down Adderley Street drinking beer, which they tried to share with everyone in the street, and they would insist on helping old ladies to cross the street who didn't want to cross the street.

'One trooper, in an astonishingly athletic feat, climbed on to the roof of a double-decker tram car. The entire electricity supply of the city had to be cut off to prevent him from being electrocuted.

'Cape Town accepted all this with patience and tolerance. Everyone knew that these boys were having their last fling before beginning some very serious business, and that a lot of them would not be coming back. The hardships of war continued to afflict us. There was one breadless day and one meatless day a week, and sugar became scarce. My mother bemoaned the scarcity of silk stockings. From the point of view of my brother and myself, we were enduring these hardships without the excitement of being bombed and being able to watch aerial combat between Spitfires and Messerschmitts, like those lucky people in Britain.

'By and large the war was a dramatic event which we watched from afar like spectators on a hillside watching a rugby match on a distant plain. The only close-ups we had were at the Adelphi and Marine bioscopes, where a seat still cost eightpence on a Saturday morning and where cowboy movies were replaced by movies about the cruel Gestapo interrogating brave captured Britons.

'Those war years touched the lives of all of us some way or other, whether we lost a loved one or merely lost out on some luxuries; or ended up in a camp for being pro-Nazi.

'My aunt Miemie down on the farm near Moorreesburg was touched in quite an unexpected way by an Italian prisoner of war, one of two allocated by the Defence Department. He was a doe-eyed Neapolitan, lithe and slender and quite different from her husband, my Uncle Boetie Jan, who was a very large Boer.

'For my aunt it was a case of *Vive la différence* and things really got out of hand when Oom Boetie Jan awoke to what was happening.

To us the courage of the Neapolitan was remarkable, for we had been given to understand that Italians were not very brave, having not fought very well against us in North Africa. Also, Oom Boetie Jan was a giant of a man, much respected in the neighbourhood because he was able to pick up an anvil with one hand.

'Oom Boetie had the Italian tied across the tractor by his farm workers and personally flogged him with a sjambok. Whereupon the Defence Department sued Oom Boetie Jan for ill-treating their prisoner of war.

'There were exchanges in the Moorreesburg magistrate's court when Oom Boetie Jan told the magistrate that the court's jurisdiction did not extend to his farm, where only he could be judge, especially in matters relating to his wife and doe-eyed Italians. For this he was fined for contempt of court as well as for assault.

'Oom Boetie Jan was very angry and swore that, although he was not in agreement with the government in this matter of getting involved in a British war, he would now join the army so that he could kill as many Italians as possible. But Italy had already surrendered and the South African Sixth Division had moved on to fight the Germans.

'We got sadder news: my cousin Terry, who used to play football with me and help me with my homework, and whose passion for flying had led him to become the youngest bomber pilot in the South African Air Force, had been shot down and killed over Warsaw, dropping supplies to Polish partisans.

'Everything passes, as the Ethiopians say, and the war ended. It was for me at that tender age and time of no serious involvement, a fairly enjoyable war. I have certainly seen worse since. ’

CHAPTER

25

'Stay with me, God'
El Agheila, 1941

The First World War produced some of the finest war poetry ever written, and some of the most evocative songs. From Siegfried Sassoon to Rupert Brooks, from Robert Graves, to Wilfred Owen, they wrote about a carnage unsurpassed.

The Second World War did not produce as rich a crop of poetry; perhaps the poppies splashing red as blood against the Flanders fields grasses lent themselves more to imagery. But poetry there was, some of it very fine.

One of the best-known poems is anonymous. All we know about it was that it was blown by the wind across the desert into a slit trench at El Agheila during a heavy bombardment. It was almost certainly written by a British soldier, but thousands of soldiers in the Western Desert and even further afield took this poem to their hearts.

A SOLDIER – HIS PRAYER

ANONYMOUS

Stay with me, God. The night is dark,
The night is cold: my little spark
Of courage dies. The night is long;
Be with me, God, and make me strong.

I love a game. I love a fight,
I hate the dark; I love the light.
I love my child; I love my wife.
I am no coward. I love Life,

Life with its change of mood and shade.
I want to live. I'm not afraid,
But me and mine are hard to part;
Oh, unknown God, lift up my heart.

You stilled the waters at Dunkirk
And saved Your Servants. All your work
Is wonderful, dear God. You strode
Before us down that dreadful road.

We were alone, and hope had fled;
We loved our country and our dead,
And could not shame them; so we stayed
The course, and were not much afraid.

Dear God, that nightmare road! And then
That sea! We got there – we were men.
My eyes were blind, my feet were torn,
My soul sang like a bird at dawn!

I knew that death is but a door.
I knew what we were fighting for:
Peace for the kids, our brothers freed.
A kinder world, a cleaner breed.

I'm but the son my mother bore,
A simple man, and nothing more.
But – God of strength and gentleness,
Be pleased to make me nothing less.

Help me, O God, when Death is near
To mock the haggard face of fear,
That when I fall – if fall I must –
My soul may triumph in the Dust.

CHAPTER

26

'Jan he still remains'

Punch and the Field Marshal

He had a mind of steel, ice-blue eyes, a patrician face and the ability to make coldly logical decisions. Jan Smuts, the South African Prime Minister in wartime, was one of only a handful of South African political figures to gain world stature.

As he aged and as honours were heaped upon him, Smuts's ruthlessness was tempered by the passion and the compassion with which he regarded the country he loved so well. Revered by the troops, adored by many but by no means all South Africans, respected particularly in Britain (his bust still stands at RAF Cranwell and his statue in Parliament Square, London) he was by far the most colourful of the wartime leaders, with the exception of the big three: Churchill, Roosevelt and Stalin.

Even *Punch*, Britain's satirical magazine, occasionally permitted a note of sentiment to creep into its pages when it wrote about Oom Jan. This poem, published in *Punch* on 4 June 1941 after he received his Field Marshal's baton form George VI* written by Capt G D Martineau, affectionately salutes the man and the event. It was republished for a wider South African audience in the October 1942 issue of *Sparks* – the magazine of 64 Air School in Bloemfontein:

Oom Jan Smuts

Oom Jan Smuts, who was numbered with the foe.
Riding through South Africa some forty years ago.
Mounted on his pony, with his little Boer beard,
Slim as his *voorloopers,* and a fighter to be feared:
Quick and cool in action, ever working to an end,
Paladin of Africa. In whom we found a friend.

* Smuts's baton, and other wartime objects belonging to him can be seen at the South African National Museum of Military History, Johannesburg.

Oom Jan Smuts, who has always watched the Hun.
Rode von Lettow Vorbeck out of places in the sun.
Leading troops to triumph whom he once led by the nose,
Thinking for South Africa, as each new dawn arose.
Planning for posterity, that all men might be freed –
Thus we learnt to know him for another hour of need;

Oom Jan Smuts bears a baton for his pains,
Holds high place in history – but Jan he still remains,
Brown and hard as leather, though his beard is turning white,
Bringing new commandos into Freedom's grimmest fight:
Out again in harness for his own unconquered land,
Spirit of South Africa, and Christendom's right hand.

Published by permission of *Punch*.

Oom Jan Smuts, wartime Prime Minister of South Africa and Minister of Defence, seen through the eyes of one of South Africa's cartoonists. (EVO)

The person behind the pseudonym was Charles Evenden, cartoonist to *The Natal Mercury* from 1924 to 1953. Apart from being one of the most perceptive cartoonists, Evenden occupies a significant place in South African history as the founder of the Memorable Order of Tin Hats (Moths). In 1927 he drew a cartoon on the subject of Remembrance; it depicted a steel helmet surmounted by a burning candle. Round the flame of the candle were the words True Comradeship, Mutual Help, Sound Memory; words that inspired the formation of the organisation of former soldiers of all ranks. Evenden was given the title of 'Moth O'. The order, thanks to a cartoon and Evenden's lifelong support, spread to the United Kingdom, Zimbabwe, Australia and New Zealand. (Mrs J Keir/*The Natal Mercury*)

CHAPTER

27

'Hopes for a better future for the world'

The Atlantic Charter, 14 August 1941

By August 1941 the Abyssinian–Somali war had been all but won. Seventy-three South African soldiers had been killed in battle and 270 wounded. In general, the campaign had been an easy one, with soldiers and airmen flexing their muscles for the real battle to come. That lay ahead in the North African desert. Few South Africans could have predicted the course that the war there would take in the next two years, with bitter defeat before the hard-won victory.

Three battles became part of our history: The rout at Sidi Rezegh, comparable in bravery to Delville Wood; the capture of Tobruk, which dismayed Churchill and shook Smuts; the battle that turned the tide of war: El Alamein

But in that August of 1941 all that still lay ahead. The 1st South African Division had taken over the defence of Mersa Matruh, the first of a string of new names that the people back home would become familiar with. The 2nd South African Division, fresh from the Union, was at El Alamein, preparing a defensive position. Field Marshal Erwin Rommel, Commander of the Afrika Korps, had been in North Africa for six months. He had been flexing his muscles too.

Most of Europe lay within the iron grip of the Germans. Only Britain was still free, though badly shaken by Dunkirk, the Battle of Britain and the devastation of the Blitz. The British looked to their Prime Minister, Winston Churchill, to provide the leadership and inspiration they needed. And Churchill looked across the Atlantic to President Franklin D Roosevelt and the vast riches of America in both money and men.

In the August of that dark year of 1941 an event occurred the results of which are still visible in the governance of the West, and which was to have an immediate and unforeseen impact on South Africa.

On a ship in the cold Atlantic waters off Newfoundland Winston Churchill and Franklin Roosevelt met for the first time since they had assumed office. They were there to discuss among other things an agreement on a statement of principles. What emerged was the Atlantic Charter.

To avoid having to get approval by the Senate for the Atlantic Charter, Roosevelt called the Charter a 'release', not a treaty. Two weeks after this pregnant meeting, Roosevelt announced the joint declaration to Congress and the world:

'Joint declaration of the President of the United States of Ame-rica and the Prime Minister, Mr Churchill, representing His Majesty's Government in the United Kingdom, being met together, deem it right to make known certain common principles in the national policies of their respective countries on which they base their hopes for a better future of the world.

'First, their countries seek no aggrandizement, territorial or other;

'Second, they desire to see no territorial changes that do not accord with the freely expressed wishes of the peoples concerned;

'Third, they respect the right of all peoples to choose the form of government under which they will live; and they wish to see sovereign rights and self-government restored to those who have been forcibly deprived of them;

'Fourth, they will endeavour, with due respect for their existing obligations, to further the enjoyment by all states, great or small, victor or vanquished, of access, on equal terms, to the trade and to the raw materials of the world which are needed for their economic prosperity;

'Fifth, they desire to bring about the fullest collaboration between all nations in the economic field with the object of securing, for all, improved labour standards, economic advancement, and social security;

'Sixth, after the final destruction of the Nazi tyranny, they hope to see established a peace which will afford to all nations the means of dwelling in safety within their own boundaries, and which will afford assurance that all the men in all the lands may live out their lives in freedom from fear and want;

'Seventh, such a peace should enable all men to traverse the high seas and oceans without hindrance;

'Eighth, they believe that all of the nations of the world, for realistic as well as spiritual reasons, must come to the abandonment of the use of force. Since no future peace can be maintained if land, sea, or air armaments continue to be employed by nations which threaten, or may threaten, aggression outside of their frontiers, they believe, pending the establishment of a wider and permanent system of general

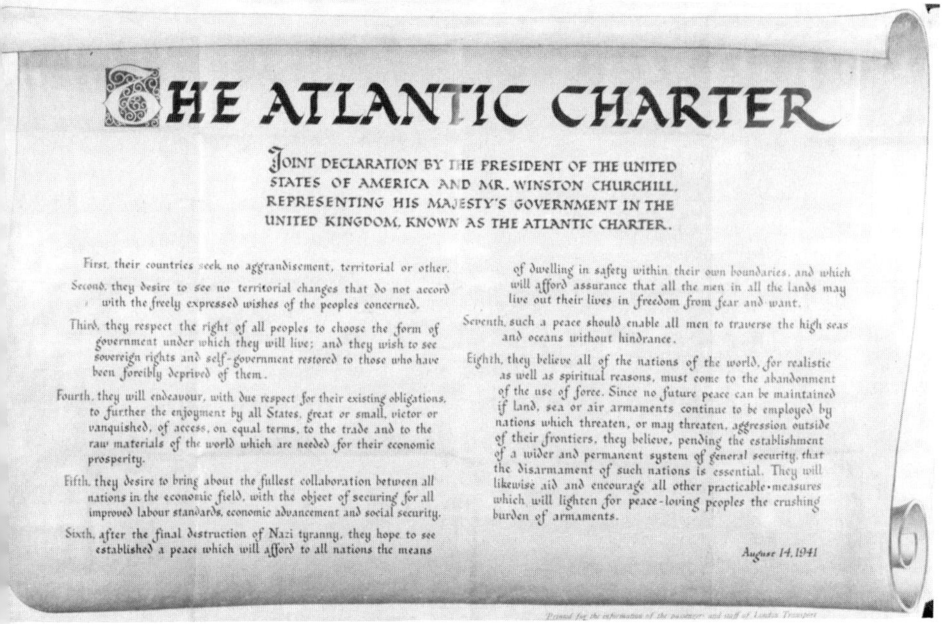
THE ATLANTIC CHARTER

JOINT DECLARATION BY THE PRESIDENT OF THE UNITED STATES OF AMERICA AND MR. WINSTON CHURCHILL, REPRESENTING HIS MAJESTY'S GOVERNMENT IN THE UNITED KINGDOM, KNOWN AS THE ATLANTIC CHARTER.

First, their countries seek no aggrandisement, territorial or other.

Second, they desire to see no territorial changes that do not accord with the freely expressed wishes of the peoples concerned.

Third, they respect the right of all peoples to choose the form of government under which they will live; and they wish to see sovereign rights and self-government restored to those who have been forcibly deprived of them.

Fourth, they will endeavour, with due respect for their existing obligations, to further the enjoyment by all States, great or small, victor or vanquished, of access, on equal terms, to the trade and to the raw materials of the world which are needed for their economic prosperity.

Fifth, they desire to bring about the fullest collaboration between all nations in the economic field, with the object of securing for all improved labour standards, economic advancement and social security.

Sixth, after the final destruction of Nazi tyranny, they hope to see established a peace which will afford to all nations the means of dwelling in safety within their own boundaries, and which will afford assurance that all the men in all the lands may live out their lives in freedom from fear and want.

Seventh, such a peace should enable all men to traverse the high seas and oceans without hindrance.

Eighth, they believe all of the nations of the world, for realistic as well as spiritual reasons, must come to the abandonment of the use of force. Since no future peace can be maintained if land, sea or air armaments continue to be employed by nations which threaten, or may threaten, aggression outside of their frontiers, they believe, pending the establishment of a wider and permanent system of general security, that the disarmament of such nations is essential. They will likewise aid and encourage all other practicable measures which will lighten for peace-loving peoples the crushing burden of armaments.

August 14, 1941

Printed for the information of the passengers and staff of London Transport

The main points of the Atlantic Charter were published all over the world. This stoutly made poster was stuck up in the London underground as soon as the Charter was made public. (Digby Hoets)

security, that the disarmament of such nations is essential. They will likewise aid and encourage all other practicable measures which will lighten for peace-loving peoples the crushing burden of armaments.'

FRANKLIN D ROOSEVELT WINSTON S CHURHILL ’

The black nationalists in South Africa, hitherto an inconspicuous force, read the Atlantic Charter very carefully. South Africa, as a member of the Commonwealth and an ally of Great Britain and the USA, they concluded, was morally obliged to adopt the letter and the spirit of the document. The government replied that the Charter was directed at Nazi oppression. The black nationalists then said that they saw little difference between the South African policy of racial segregation and that of Nazi Germany.

The government lay low on the subject and hoped that it would go away. But it didn't. In 1943 a document, *African Claims in South Africa,* was issued to members of the African National Congress and the Communist Party of South Africa. It was an interpretation of the Atlantic Charter from a black point of view. White South Africans, whether they supported the war or not, began to read about four young blacks, members of the African National Congress Youth League: Anton Lembede, Nelson Mandela, Walter Sisulu and Oliver Tambo.

CHAPTER

28

'I wore the Red Cross uniform '

Doreen Grantporteous, nursing aide

The Red Cross Society towers above all other humanitarian agencies, both in time of peace and war. But it is in war that its work is most needed, and it was out of war that it was born, in Geneva in 1863 by Jean Henri Dunant. In 1901 he was awarded the Nobel Peace Prize, and his organisation, distinguished by a red cross on a white background (the reverse of the Swiss flag) was described as 'the supreme humanitarian achievement of the 19th century'. The Red Cross won three other Nobel Peace Prizes: in 1917, in 1944 and on its centenary in 1963.

In South Africa the Red Cross was founded in July 1896 with the blessings of Paul Kruger. The Society saw two wars: the Second Boer War and the First World War; then it was caught up in the second great disaster of this disastrous century.

The Red Cross had agreed to supply the state with two hundred trained VAD nurses and two hundred ambulance-men in a case of emergency. That emergency turned out to be World War II and by the end of it the Society had far exceeded its modest promise to the state. It provided ten Red Cross Auxiliary Military Hospitals and the staff and the funds to run them, and three convalescent homes; and they gave help to civilian hospitals all over the country.

Its work literally saved South African and other prisoners of war from starvation, educated them and kept them in touch, however tenuously, with home.

The Red Cross nurse became a familiar figure in the Union after war broke out. Her distinctive red-lined cape and blue uniform were seen everywhere. Doreen Grantporteous was one of the Red Cross nursing aides who eased some of the pain of the wounded:

'My mother decided she had to do her bit for the war, so she became a nursing aide, training through the Red Cross in Johannesburg. I was working as a librarian and feeling rather restless because I

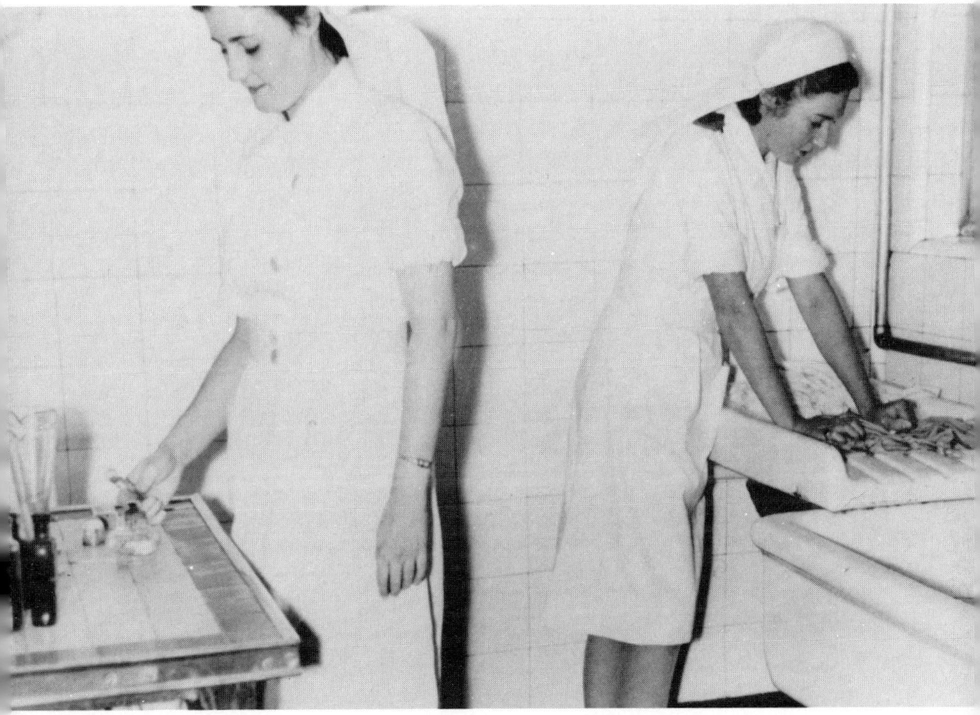

VAD nurses worked long hours, sometimes in trying circumstances. Without them the nursing sisters could not have coped. (South African National Museum of Military History)

wasn't contributing much to the war, and she persuaded me to become a nursing aide too. We were known as VAD nurses.*

'Most of our training was done in the local Scout Hall: basic first aid, then more complicated. I wore the Red Cross Uniform, blue with a white apron and a white veil. My first posting was to Brenthurst,† Sir Ernest and Lady Oppenheimer's house which they had turned over to the country as a hospital. My uniform changed, when I worked there, into a white uniform with a navy-blue red-lined cape and a short veil. We wore low brown shoes, and we searched all over Johannesburg to find a stout, comfortable pair.

'I was very excited about working at Brenthurst. I had read a lot about it and the work that Major Jack Penn was doing there, and I was very keen to be a part of it.

'My duties were very much those of a junior nurse. I came on duty with the other nurses at 7 a.m. We did the usual bedmaking, tidy-

* Voluntary Aid Corps, Nursing Division of the Red Cross. Over thirteen hundred VAD nurses from the Union served abroad in military hospitals.

† The Brenthurst Military Hospital for Plastic Surgery. See 'I'll leave it to you, Dr Jack'.

ing up wards, emptying bedpans, working in the duty room, where we might be asked to scrub up, bathing the men, giving them their meals – a host of things, under the supervision of nursing sisters.

'Each of us nursing aides was allowed to go into the theatre. When it was my time to go I got all scrubbed up and into a gown. I was in awe of being in the theatre itself. Dr Jack said to me; "Just stand behind me, nurse, but don't touch me." The operating theatre was very controlled, very busy. The man they were operating on was a young British soldier who had lost his jaw, his lip and his chin. It was a terrible sight. I'd never seen anything like that before. I stuck it out for most of the operation, then I passed out. I was thoroughly disgusted with myself.

'But Dr Jack was kind to me. At lunchtime he said to me: "The trouble was there weren't any windows open, were there, nurse?" He was a very down-to-earth man, not at all superior, in spite of his reputation.

'A lot of the men were very badly hurt, but the atmosphere there was quite jolly most of the time. Most of the men were very positive and they supported one another, but sometimes one would be really difficult. It really came from him fighting what had happened to him. There was one South African boy of nineteen who had lost both his arms above the elbow Up North. He was very angry. He used to jump on the beds after we had tidied them, just before matron came on her rounds. But we were taught that we had to give as much emotional care as nursing care to the boys, so we made allowances.

'They were allowed to walk about in the gardens, which were very beautiful, and they were encouraged to go out and meet people when they could. A lot of them never went out. They felt they were too disfigured. They had a blue uniform, blue trousers and jacket, which they had to wear when they went out. Very few of them had visitors, you see, because most of them were British.

'When they went to a dance, in the Drill Hall or somewhere else, we nursing aides would go with them. It was a psychological boost for them. We'd gang up if people made remarks or stared too much. We were taught to accept them as they were, although when you saw boys with no faces and no arms and other terrible wounds, it was difficult at first.

'When I was on night duty I would come on at 7 p.m. The boys had already had supper and they were in bed, just chatting to each other until lights out at 9.30. The wards had to be tidied up by then, of course. I found that if I could get half an hour's sleep before midnight I had no difficulty in staying awake for the rest of the night. We were allowed to sit in deck chairs in the dressing-room.

'The men had no buzzers, and we had to go out and check them every hour. If a man had had an operation we would "special" him, sit

Some of the men undergoing reconstructive surgery in the grounds of Brenthurst, the home lent by Sir Ernest and Lady Oppenheimer to Jack Penn for the duration of the war. Thousands of men were healed and helped there. (South African National Museum of Military History)

with him until he was conscious, but that was mainly during the day. The floors were all wooden, and we moved as quietly as we could, shining a flashlight quickly into each man's face to see if he was all right. It wasn't lonely, it was peaceful, and there was a sense that one was doing something useful.

'I was only twenty at the time, yet I felt like mothering the men. They were so badly shot up and they were the same age as me and I wanted to do everything I could for them. I wonder how many men were helped because of little Red Cross nurses like me? Nursing those men became an experience that I learnt from and was able to draw on after the war. So much suffering so bravely borne. '

- Interview 1990.

CHAPTER

29

'What can you do to a tank with a Bren gun?'

Corporal Howard 'Rusty' Balme and the battle of Sidi Rezegh, November 1941

In spite of the successes in Abyssinia and Somalia, the sinking of the *Bismarck* and the still unexplained flight of Hitler's deputy, the beetle-browed Rudolph Hess, to Scotland, the war was not going well for Britain and the Commonwealth.

The British withdrew from Greece and after a humiliating military fiasco were driven out of Crete; on 22 June the apparently invincible Hitler launched his invasion of Russia along a two-thousand mile front, By 3 September Leningrad was almost encircled. Then the mystique of British supremacy at sea, the aircraft-carrier *Ark Royal* was sunk off Gibraltar.

South Africans digested this news equably. All would be well, they reasoned, because their boys were now on their way to North Africa (the 2nd SA Division under Maj-Gen I P de Villiers left at the end of May). South Africans, as it seemed from their successes in Abyssinia and Somalia, were almost invincible. There was good cause to expect their successes to continue in the desert. There, in the vastnesses of the harsh landscape, Rommel had invested Tobruk, and in July Gen Wavell had been dismissed in favour of The Auk – Gen Claude Auchinleck.

Things weren't exactly calm at home either. Because of attacks by members of the Ossewabrandwag and assorted other louts, troops had been forbidden to go out alone. Robey Leibbrandt was pursuing this will-'o-the-wisp career all over the country, and there were persistent rumours of an impending armed rising. The Nazis seemed triumphant everywhere.

None of this mattered to the men of the 5th Brigade, moderately comfortable at Mersa Matruh and training in the desert. They were cock-a-hoop at their easy passage through Abyssinia and Somalia, and they could be forgiven for thinking that the desert campaign would be a similar breeze.

So it was with little trepidation that the Brigade* moved west from Mersa Matruh, through the wire that separated Egypt from Libya, and out into the desert. They were part of Operation Crusader, the main purpose of which was to relieve Tobruk. The Brigade made for the area south of an isolated tomb deep in the desert: Sidi Rezegh.

Near the tomb there was an airfield, in German hands, which had to be taken too. And somewhere out there in the desert, unaware of the advance of the British and Commonwealth forces, lurked the tough and well trained infantry and tank-crews of the Afrika Corps.

South of the escarpment, which fell abruptly to the Mediterranean, south of the beleaguered coast town of Tobruk and south of Point 178 on the southern edge of the escarpment, stood the 5th South African Infantry Brigade. They were in a 'box'† on the northern perimeter of which were the 3rd Transvaal Scottish; facing east was the 2nd Regiment Botha and to the west stood the 1st South African Irish. In the centre was Brigade headquarters commanded by Brig B F Armstrong; to the south was B Echelon and the Brigade's supplies. And, much further to the south was Dan Pienaar's 1st SA Infantry Brigade. Blooded in the East African campaign but unversed in the skills and rapidity of desert warfare, the South Africans, elated at getting through the wire virtually unscathed, waited for their orders.

'The battle has now reached its oasis,' Rommel wrote to his wife on the night of the 20th. 'I hope we get through in good order.'

Next day the planned outbreak from Tobruk was stopped by strong opposition from Rommel's 21st Corps and the approach of the Deutsches Afrika Korps (DAK), consisting of the 15th and 21st Panzer Divisions from the south-east under the command of the enterprising Gen Cruewell. The South Africans, who played little part in the battles of the day, spent a bitterly cold night under the desert sky on Friday, 21 November.

During the cold morning of 22 November the 3rd Transvaal Scottish received orders to advance and attack the German positions in a wadi east of Point 178. Among those who debussed at 12.20 p.m. and got into formation was a young corporal, Howard 'Rusty' Balme, a section-leader of 7 Platoon B Coy. In high spirits the Scottish moved forward, supported by 8th SA Field Battery and anti-tank guns, and the 1st SA Irish in readiness to advance against the escarpment west of Bir du

---

* 2nd Regiment Botha, 3rd Transvaal Scottish, 1st South African Irish.

† The 'box' was an elaboration of the infantry square used so successfully by British forces up until the end of the 1879 Zulu War. The men of the square faced outwards, the centre contained medical supplies, ammunition and water and the officers. The last time it was used was at the Battle of Ulundi on 4 July 1879.

Creimisa and the 2nd Regiment Botha moving round the right wing of the Scottish towards El Duda.

Howard Balme tells the story of 22 November and the next day *Totensonntag,* when the Germans remembered their dead, which was to become part of South African war history, and to shake the newly created Field Marshal Smuts and all South Africans waiting at home:

‘Who of us who fought at Sidi Rezegh will ever forget the days of 22 and 23 November 1941? And who of those who fought through those days and lived will ever forget our comrades in arms who died beside us?

‘After six months at Mersa Matruh we were decidedly pleased to get a chance to come to grips with the Afrika Korps. The Commanding Officer of the 3rd Battalion, Transvaal Scottish, was a very warlike fellow, Lt-Col Walter Kirby. He had no liking for Germans, having fought in the First World War and received the MC. The morning of the 22nd was quiet enough; but a little before midday Kirby was ordered to clear out a bunch of machine guns up a wadi: Point 178, just a point on a map, nothing more, south-west of the landing ground that the 60th Rifles had been battling for two days.

‘They'd had a very rough time there. On the other side there was this little tomb of Rezegh. I never saw the thing, there was so much dust and smoke, and anyway we never got as far as that. The desert there is completely featureless, like a billiard table, with little rises we called ridges, and not a blade of cover.

‘It was a cold, overcast day and we were wearing British battle-dress for the first time, and, also for the first time, steel helmets, issued to us in Mersa Matruh. For some extraordinary reason we were wearing gas-masks on our chests. Our strength was thirty-odd officers and about seven hundred other ranks.

‘The rifle companies had 27 Bren guns. Support Coy had two platoons of twelve three-inch mortars and one platoon of six Vickers guns. As a section-leader I was armed with a tommy gun, which may have been fine for Chicago gangsters but wasn't much use in the desert, with a very short range.

‘Alan Chilvers,* like me, was an old Hiltonian. There was a strong bond between us.

‘We went into action about midday,† when we debussed and shook ourselves into battle order, with the rifle companies in front and the Vickers and mortars of Support Coy manhandled behind them. Once we were organised we advanced in open order. The battalion

---

* Corporal H A Chilvers.

† According to the Transvaal Scottish records, it was 12h20.

advanced with my company, B Company, on the right, C on the left and A in reserve. We were enormously confident, full of fight and businesslike about the whole thing rather than excited. I was certainly too busy to concentrate on anything but the job in hand. When you are in command, even a humble one, you are so occupied with what you have to do, controlling the men, following the platoon commander and covering a certain distance in a certain time, that you have no time to worry about anything.

'The first thing that bothered us was the appearance of six Stukas just as we got out of our trucks. They came at us with their sirens screeching, dropping bombs all over the place, but they didn't do much damage, and they didn't hold up our advance, although two men were wounded,* our first casualties in a day that became a nightmare. As we advanced only the clatter of our boots and the machine-gun fire could be heard.

'Then we saw the German machine-gun fire in the beaten zone kicking up dust in front of us and that worried us quite a lot, for we knew that we had to go through it to take Point 178. We hadn't advanced very far, about six hundred yards, when all three companies were pinned down.

'The enemy were in entrenched positions on the ridge, and they soon made themselves felt with steady machine-gun and rifle fire that kept us pinned down. The supporting fire from the Transvaal Horse Artillery [THA] guns seemed to have little effect on the volume of their fire, because the enemy were well dispersed. As soon as we were pinned down they began mortaring us. We had been shelled before, by the Italians in Abyssinia, but this was our first sample of mortar fire. A shell comes at you slowly, and usually over you, but a mortar bomb goes up very high and comes down with a whoosh! on top of you. They are very unpleasant things, and most of our casualties were caused by the mortars.

'We had no time to dig in, and we couldn't lie flat because of the gas masks on our chests. We eventually threw them away. Even when we could find a little stone or a bit of a camel shrub we weren't completely prone. We were on the right flank. Over on the left, C Company slowly advanced until they moved over the lip of the ridge into a shallow donga, where they ran into a withering fire that killed the Company Commander† and some of the boys.

'Meanwhile some of our chaps took cover behind two burnt-out vehicles, a British Bren-carrier and a South African armoured car. It was the worst thing they could have done, because the enemy was

*Lance Corporal Don Morgan and Private Doug High.
† Captain Dudley Furniss.

able to get a fix on their fire and let loose their firepower on us. In spite of all that we were hammering away and managing to keep the Germans' heads down. We still had plenty of ammunition.

'Col Kirby, being the man he was, refused to take cover. He was walking about among us saying, "Try and get forward, try and get forward!" but we couldn't. No sooner had he spoken than he was hit, first in the hand, then in the body, then in the chest. He fell among us, mortally wounded. We had stretcher-bearers, of course, but they couldn't get to us because of the fire. There was no way I could help; I had no stretcher, no blankets, nothing. Some of our walking wounded, like our platoon sergeant, managed to crawl to the rear, but none of the badly wounded men could get out.

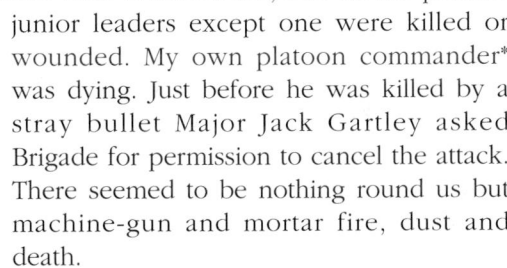

'All three Bren-gun teams were knocked out, and all the platoon junior leaders except one were killed or wounded. My own platoon commander* was dying. Just before he was killed by a stray bullet Major Jack Gartley asked Brigade for permission to cancel the attack. There seemed to be nothing round us but machine-gun and mortar fire, dust and death.

'We had nowhere to go. To advance over the four hundred yards of open ground would have been suicide, and to withdraw would have been no less so. As dusk fell we began to run out of ammunition; and of course our fire was diminished because so many of our chaps had been knocked out. But at the same time, in failing light, the enemy's fire abated, thank God.

'It seemed to me almost miraculous that I was still unscathed. Dusk was falling rapidly and it was becoming difficult to see, and we were thinking of getting out.

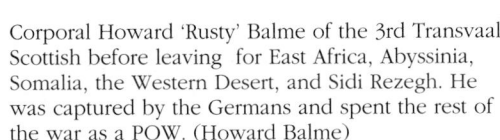

Corporal Howard 'Rusty' Balme of the 3rd Transvaal Scottish before leaving for East Africa, Abyssinia, Somalia, the Western Desert, and Sidi Rezegh. He was captured by the Germans and spent the rest of the war as a POW. (Howard Balme)

* Lt B Heatlie, whose place was taken by Lt Henderson.

Then suddenly when everything was fairly quiet, there was one crack of German machine-gun fire, and Alan Chilvers was hit in the back, in the kidney. He was in terrible pain; I knew he was dying, and I could do nothing for him. It is terrible to leave dying men on a battlefield, but we had to withdraw, leaving Alan, Lt Heatlie and the Colonel behind.

'I gathered the few men left in C Platoon and we went back to our lines, finding our way back in the dark, a thousand long yards, by holding on to the telephone wires that trailed back.

'I had to report to my acting Company Commander. He said to me: "Rusty, take twelve men from each platoon and go out and bring in the Colonel and anyone else who is still alive."

'So we went out again, together with the padre, Capt Wyles. The night was very still. We brought the Colonel out, in a blanket, the padre at one corner and a man at the other three, but he died later. Alan was dead. I hadn't realised when we pulled back that all the Bren-gun crews were dead, so we had to bring in all the guns as well, then go back again and bring in the wounded and take the identity discs off the dead. In my platoon alone twelve men out of forty were killed. I was numb.

'The Germans had come forward under cover of the dark and were digging in. We found a chap from C Company who was *in extremis*, and I left one of the men to sit with him until he died.

'When I got back to Coy HQ the acting Company Commander, Tiny Henderson, asked me to go out again and bring in the dead. I said: "No, I'm not going out again. My chaps have to dig in before the morning," and he sent somebody else out.

'We dug shallow scrapes, mostly in silence. It had been the worst day in the history of the regiment. The men were depressed and shaken, and we got very little sleep, two hours at most. All you could see were the white German flares hanging in the dark sky, and we knew we were surrounded. That night, although we didn't know it then, Rommel had begun to bring up most of his two divisions to the south of us. It never even occurred to us that the entire Panzer Korps would be thrown at us.

'It was pitch dark, and we could hear Jerry digging in on the ridge. You could hear the clink, clink, clink of the shovels. And they could hear us. There was the odd truck roaring behind us as our rations were brought up. We tried to sleep, but only fitfully.

'We woke to a bitterly cold overcast morning, *Totensonntag,* the second last Sunday in November, the day when the German army mourned its dead. This year it fell on 23 November.

'The new CO of the 3rd Battalion Transvaal Scottish was now Major "Rusty" Rosser, the new commander of B Coy was Captain Vernon Prankerd, and I was the new commander of 7 Platoon. As the sun came up I looked round and saw the men sitting in their scrapes, spread out over a wide area, a little disorderly because of all the stuff that we had to leave on the surface, gas masks (the few that hadn't been thrown away the day before), extra ammunition, and sticky bombs.

'They looked like big toffee apples, crazy things. You were supposed to take the cover off, rush up to a tank, stick it on the hull and run like mad, and then it would destroy the tank while it sat and waited for you to run back and forth to blow it up. I was wearing a thick shirt and battledress, with a gas-mask on my chest and on my back a small pack with my shaving stuff and a spare shirt and what not, and stuck on to that was a sticky bomb. I hastily put it in my slit, for if that were hit I would be scattered all over the place.

'We received our orders before breakfast: hold our positions. In spite of what had happened the day before, we were still quite confident. We had the THA with twenty-four guns in support, the 2nd Battalion Scots Guards, who had come in to help us, and bits and pieces of British artillery, which all added to the force. It didn't occur to any of us that we might be taken prisoner. In an infantry unit you think you might get killed or badly wounded, but not be taken prisoner.

'A hot breakfast came up from B Echelon, porridge and bacon in hot-boxes. But then the first shells began to fall about us, coming from the north, so we abandoned thoughts of breakfast and returned to our slits and ate the tinned foods that we had in our packs. There wasn't much that infantry could do, so we just sat under the rain of shells. By ten o'clock the shelling became general and heavy, but there weren't many casualties so far.

'By midday the shelling became frightful. We couldn't understand it. There weren't very many Germans on the ridge, so why were we being subjected to this terrible pounding with shells, mortars, tank fire, machine-gun fire, everything? We ate lunch (dry rations eaten in our slits) and then the German attack began, first from the north, though that turned out to be only secondary, and then with the main thrust of armour coming from the south-west. Two German armoured divisions were coming towards us.*

'We, the Transvaal Scottish, were manning the northern side of the 5th Brigade Box, with the SA Irish and 2nd Scots Guards on the west and the Regiment Botha on the east. We were supported by the 8th Field Battery of the 3rd Field THA, and their 25-pounders did wonderful work, selecting targets among the advancing armour and armoured infantry.

* The 15th and 21st Panzer Divisions.

After the battle: the ground was covered with burnt-out tanks, armoured cars, mortars, machine guns and bodies. The stand of the 5th Division against Gen Cruewell's 15th and 21st Panzers was heroic. In the end it was a Pyrrhic victory for Rommel. (The Rev Stanley Pitts)

'By now we were in the midst of an inferno, sheets of tracer, mortar bombs and shells raining down, dust, smoke and the terrible stink of cordite, and noise, the most inconceivable, utterly overwhelming noise. To communicate with each other we shouted from slit to slit all the time to see if anybody had been hit or to pass on a message. There wasn't much that the rifle companies could do, for it was almost impossible to see and the bren guns were our only weapons. I would look up every now and then, see a shadowy thing in the distance, a tank, and take a shot at it. What can you do to a tank with a Bren gun?

'The mortar platoons were helpless, because they were not properly dug in and trying to work the mortars in the open was suicidal; but the Vickers platoon under Sergeant Johnny Roos did great work, especially on the infantry supporting the tanks sweeping towards us.

'By now, late afternoon, the air was full of shot, shell and tracer bullets, and we were under a lot of strain. One B Coy man broke and stood up on his slit. He was immediately riddled with bullets. We had twins in our regiment. They were lying near me in adjacent slits. An artillery shell landed in one slit and killed one and left the other unharmed.

'Our main defence was still the guns of the THA. As long as they kept firing, as long as they still had ammunition, the enemy's tanks were kept off; but by about 4 p.m. they had knocked out most of the guns, killing the crews mainly with machine-gun fire. That was when we first saw the tanks through the dust and smoke, grinding towards our slits, almost on top of us and right behind them the German infantry, coming in very cautiously. Then our few remaining guns ran out of sharp ammunition and began firing smoke.

'The situation was desperate. Our acting Battalion Commander, Rusty Rosser, ran forward from Battalion HQ to C Company in front of him, now commanded by Lt Neil Webster, Capt Dudley Furniss having been killed the day before. Rosser spoke to Webster and decided very wisely to give the order for A and B Coys to withdraw to the east, while C Coy held their positions.

'That was more or less the order that came down to me, shouted from slit to slit: "Withdraw to the south-east, try to join up with the New Zealanders"; and then those fateful words that no soldier believes he will hear: "Every man for himself." We were to act on the firing of two Very lights, red over red.

'I was very nervous about this, for although I didn't want to get run over by the tanks, which were clanking closer every second, the stuff that was going over us was nightmarish, appalling, everything that the enemy had. Then the lights went up and we jumped out of our slits and ran like hell through the smoke. The chap next to me, Willy Weyl, was killed immediately by a shell. He just disappeared. I was thrown forward a few yards but was otherwise unhurt.

'Ahead of us other men were being cut down at the knee by a gracefully curving tracer. To my right, amid this indescribable chaos and death, a gun tender towing a 25-pounder was hit by a shell and disintegrated in a cloud of black smoke; the gunners clinging to it fell off like rag dolls.

'Beyond us some three-tonners of our B Echelon crossed our vision, going fast south-east. We ran towards them. I got the second. It was full of badly wounded gunners, short of arms and legs and all sorts of things. I leapt into the cab with the driver and said: "Go like hell," and we bounced across the desert, over shell slits and probably right through the Botha* lines, and through a cordon of German tanks. We thought we had made it, that we had broken through.

'Then we ran into the casualty clearing station of the 11th Field Ambulance, Red Cross flags and all. We drove straight into it, and got off the truck because we wanted to get the wounded into hospital. As soon as I got out of the cab I looked up.

'Two very short German infantrymen came out from behind a tent. All they said was "Hände hoch". My tommy gun was useless – we

---

* 2nd Regiment Botha on the east of the box.

were in the middle of a hospital. We were so numb we hardly felt a thing. We just went to sleep in the sand. ’

• Interview 1990.

The 5th South African Infantry Brigade no longer existed. Only a few men, including the future General Neil Webster of the Transvaal Scottish, managed to escape. The rest of the Brigade (those who survived) were taken prisoner. They were shocked, many of them were wounded and wearing only the light clothes they stood in, and they slept uneasily in the open that night, huddled together for warmth.

Next day they were grouped together. Rommel drove past the South Africans, a gesture that warmed many of them. But he told them they would be handed over to the Italians from then on. There followed the harrowing ‘Thirst March’ in which the men, unfed and without water, were marched for twenty hours under the blazing sun. Although by now South Africans at home knew that a devastating battle had taken place, mainly because of Carel Birkby's news report,* – that enraged Smuts who attempted to conceal the extent of the disaster – they had no means of knowing who had been killed, who had escaped and who was a prisoner of war. Families waited for months for news before their fate was made known to them by the Red Cross in Geneva.

Because the reporters Uys Krige and Conrad Norton were also among those taken, it wasn't until the end of the war that South Africans learnt of the Thirst March. Nor did they know of the horrors that stretched in front of their men: the sinking of the ship that took them from North Africa to Greece, with much loss of life (see ‘What the hell had happened?’) and a miserable stay in Greece before they arrived in Italy.

Sidi Rezegh destroyed the notion that the South Africans were invincible. From then on the word ‘war’ took on another meaning. But the disaster at Sidi Rezegh had another effect back home: a shortage of men. From then on the Defence Force, in spite of its volunteers, would be seriously short of men.

Within two days, South Africans knew, more or less, what had happened up north. They needed reassurance. They got that from a mild whimsical priest, Father Paddy Nolan of the 1st SA Irish.

His *Totensonntag* was seen from a different perspective from that of the men fighting through their longest day.

---

* His first was never published; the carrier was killed.

CHAPTER

30

'There was no waving of white flags'

Father Patrick Paddy Nolan and Sidi Rezegh, 23 November 1941

On 12 May 1940, the eve of the departure of the 1st Brigade for East Africa, General Smuts approved the appointment of twelve full-time chaplains. During the war 517 chaplains of all denominations served with the South African troops.

Father Nolan, who had arrived in South Africa in 1935, was one of them. He found himself with the South African Irish, and went with them to Barberton, then to East Africa and Abyssinia, thence to Egypt and Sidi Rezegh.

'Throughout my army career, which lasted from September 1941 to the end of the war, stark tragedy and exhilarating comedy have followed hard upon one another's heels.

'Take Sidi Rezegh. If ever there was stark tragedy and comedy, it was there. I had come to this place in the desert with the grand boys of the South African Irish, via Abyssinia and Mersa Matruh, because I wanted to be with men who were fighting and meeting death, not only my own South African boys but any Catholic boy, whether South African, Italian or German.

'I went through the wire in my own one-ton truck. I had with me a portable altar, a compact box containing the vestments, candles, candlesticks and books; and I lost everything at Sidi Rezegh. I had the breviary with me as well, the one I had from the time when I was a student, but because of the uncertainty of the times we were dispensed from the full recital of the breviary and replaced it with something much shorter that we learnt by heart. You said mass wherever you could, in the back of a truck, in a forest glade in Abyssinia or out in the desert.

'I entertained high hopes for my truck and left Matruh feeling well provided for, but from the day when we passed through the wire until we reached Sidi Rezegh I was pushed into battle. There was something wrong with the electrics of the vehicle, and notwithstanding all the good works of the mechanics I always had trouble with it. One moonless night, as we were on the march to Sidi Rezegh, stopping became a problem because I couldn't start her again. Some of the Irish drove behind me all the way, ready to give me a push. A cup of tea, then a push, a cup of tea, then a push, all the way into battle.

'I must say that I do not like being under fire, and there was plenty of that at Sidi Rezegh. I was very much with God when I was under fire, and there was also the thought of what my boys would say if I ran away. I was afraid, but I didn't want to be a coward and I certainly didn't want to die a sinner.

'We came under fire on the 19th, the day after we crossed into Libya, from Stukas. It was unfortunate for them that they did not realise the proximity of some of our planes, which dived upon them, and a wonderful dogfight ensued. I saw one German plane come down, and I drove across to see if I could be of any help. When I got there it was in smithereens all over the desert, and there was nothing left of the boy except a hand and his stomach, which was burning; a horrible, horrible sight.

'We came under more fire as the days continued. On the 22nd I thought we must be going into battle soon, so I went round the whole Brigade to hear confession. I walked up to the men wherever I found them and said: "Look lads, we're into battle any moment now, let's be prepared."

'When we got to our place in the 5th Brigade box, I found myself with the Regimental Aid Post [RAP] inside the left flank of the Irish. There was fighting ahead of us, but I could get no news of the casualties from there, so I went back a mile or so to the 11th Field Ambulance to see to the casualties, and there were many, mostly from the British lines ahead of us. My practice in a battle was to stay as near to the hospital as I could for the simple reason that all the men came there.

'Captain Du Toit of the 11th Field Ambulance was operating in a tent beside a truck. Singing at the top of my voice – one needs comfort – I crept under the camouflage net attached to his tent, but the song faded away when I beheld first the number of casualties and then Du Toit, operating on some poor fellow, his arms smeared with blood and the original colour of his apron judged only by a rare spot of white set within the red.

'There were a lot of wounded and dying to attend to on the 22nd, both at the Field Ambulance or the RAP or out in the field. There were so many young men smashed. I always carried with me a small blue stole and the holy oils. As soon as a boy saw me wearing the stole he knew who I was. A Catholic boy would know immediately what was happening and there would be no rebellion in his heart.

'My faith never faltered. War is war and a war is not fought with love. God gives life and God takes us to Himself when He is ready.

'It was a cold day, that Sunday, 23 November at Sidi Rezegh. I began it by burying an Italian who had died after being captured. His companions stood at the graveside. While I read the burial service an enemy plane hovered overhead, but saved his bombs until we had finished the service.

'As the day went on and the battle intensified many prisoners were brought in, Italian and German. As I always did, I went among them, saw they had food and drink and cigarettes and sat and chatted to them. All around were our own wounded bravely enduring their sufferings. I hardly heard a moan all the time I was with them, and it was pitiful to know that we could not get them out.

'Among the wounded was the OC of the 1st South African Irish, Lt-Col J Dobbs, a grand fellow. I went to him when he was brought in. What he had to say of the Germans was unrepeatable. He was badly wounded. "See here, Patsy," he said to me, "I went you to go to the ambulance and see to my boys. Go and tell them all I'm damn sorry for them." So I delivered his message and came back with their thanks.

'"What are you waiting for, man?" he said to me. Three times he called me and sent me away. Major Melzer, OC of the 11th Field Ambulance, asked me to take Col Dobbs and a badly wounded British officer away and lay them in shell-slits for safety.

'In the afternoon the battle became very intense. My friend Padre Wiles had brought in some dead. Our native troops dug graves for them. While the two of us stood side by side discussing whether the graves were deep enough to allow us to begin the burial service the battle reached its peak.

'As we were standing there, there was a terrific concentration of machine-gun fire and another artillery barrage. The only cover was the graves, in one of which we had to put Col Kirby of the Transvaal Scottish. In the grave nearest to me there was already a body, but still we leapt in. A little while later I heard a rumble that made me think that tanks were near. Raising my head from the grave I saw a heavy tank drawn up within ten yards of where I was lying. It came straight towards me. I jumped to my feet and waved it to stop, but it came on and on, and I threw myself on my side out of the grave and missed being crushed to death by a split second. I can assure you I said my prayers then.

'Looking behind me I saw a German tank drawn up near our wounded. I ran to the commander standing in the turret to explain that this was a field ambulance and the men lying about, some still in slit trenches, were casualties. He smiled and waved me forward with his pistol in his hand.

'We were marched back some distance under escort, taking with us our walking wounded. The officers and men were separated, but since most of the wounded were other ranks I told the guard that as chaplain I intended to stay with the men. He was Italian, and he nearly fell on my neck with joy. Another Italian came forward and then a German, all pleased to see me. They had been among the prisoners whom I had consoled earlier. They allowed me to do more or less what I liked. I wasn't afraid. There was no question of maltreatment.'

Father Nolan was put into a truck with forty other men and after much hardship he reached a prisoner-of-war camp in Benghazi, where he stayed until 24 December when it was relieved by the British. Bruce Anderson of the SABC talked to him after the relief of Benghazi. Father Nolan gave a talk to the people back home, still shaken by the disaster at Sidi Rezegh and many of them still unaware of whether their men had been killed, wounded or taken prisoner.

The dead of Sidi Rezegh. Father Paddy Nolan helped to bury some of them. (South African National Museum of Military History).

‘First of all let me assure you that many more of our gallant boys are alive and well than you may have at first supposed. Our death toll is not high. Quite a number of our boys escaped and others, not very many, are here with me now.

‘Please do not think that I am saying these things merely to console you. It will console you still more if you realise that I am more anxious to tell you the truth.

‘Yesterday morning, Christmas Eve, Major Boardman and I contacted the British troops. Can you imagine what our feelings were to know that we were relieved after a month of life as prisoners of war? It was overpowering; and when I returned to the hospital to tell the ninety men, British, New Zealanders and South Africans, their emotion was too great to permit themselves even to cheer. And here we are all together today, spending our Christmas in Benghazi, and even though we bemoan the fact that our Christmas parcels did not reach us, we are infinitely more happy with this Christmas present of liberty.

‘Before concluding my short talk, may I tell you along which lines I have been trying to get all my boys to think. I have insisted, first of all, on a deep sense of gratitude to the good God for having saved so many of us and we are grateful, I assure you.

‘Secondly, I have been getting the boys to think frequently of our dead comrades, who made the supreme sacrifice for the cause. Need I say how deeply we feel their loss, having rubbed shoulders with them for so long?

‘And thirdly, I have been getting the boys to pray for the broken hearts at home. God help those poor broken hearts and console them with the realisation that their sacrifice has not been in vain. The boys who fell, fell indeed as heroes. There was no waving of white flags.

‘Goodbye, totsiens.’

• Interview 1990

CHAPTER

31

'After all, we were part of the British Empire'

Miriam Markman and patriotism, Port Elizabeth style

Whether they agreed with it, no one in South Africa could be unaware of the war, and that included the schoolchildren. The news from North Africa made them more aware. Teachers told them about the rise of German patriotism, of the First World War and sometimes of Jewish pogroms in Europe and Russia.

Copies of magazines with pictures of the war – *The Illustrated London News* was a great favourite – were displayed. And of course there was the BBC news. In Domestic Science classes girls were taught to bake with the coarse flour then available and to make sauces without eggs; later they would be taught to cope with the meatless day a week decreed by the government. While their brothers drilled, the girls and their mothers knitted for the troops. Ouma Smuts's Gifts and Comforts Fund had an insatiable appetite, and the old lady with her round glasses and unruly grey hair was not used to hearing the word 'No'.

Although the spirit of republicanism was alive and growing, most of the English-speaking youth still regarded Britain as the mother country. They were loyal to the Empire and proud of belonging to the Commonwealth, and they responded with emotion to Britain in the dark days before El Alamein. Miriam Markman recalls the period at the Collegiate School for Girls in Port Elizabeth:

'We were unbelievably patriotic during the war, no matter what our age. Even though I was a schoolgirl of fifteen when war broke out I wanted to be involved. We followed the war on the newsreels, in the papers and on the radio. It was a ritual in my family to listen to the news. We were elated when Churchill became prime minister,* and we thought that was the most wonderful thing in the world.

'We had a map on the wall and we used to bring that up to date every day with little markers – what was happening and where. And then there were our teachers at school, who were very alert as to what was going on. One of them, my history teacher, would try and put it in perspective. She would draw comparisons about the German invasion of France with the Franco-Prussian war, where the Germans broke through at a similar point. Everyone knew what was going on.

'As a family we had links with Germany. We were Jewish, although that was kept in the background when war broke out. My brother-in-law was a German refugee. He was a political journalist there, and fled in 1935. We listened to the horrors of the invasion of France, then of the collapse of France and then, of course, Dunkirk and the Battle of Britain, and we had a real fear that Britain might go under. We were greatly influenced by Britain in the eastern Cape, and after all we were part of the British Empire. The Collegiate was an Anglican school and there was a very British attitude there; we celebrated Empire Day, for example.

'That's how we came to write the song. A friend of mine, Felicia Glago, was very good at music and she often used to compose little songs. I composed the words. We had an end-of-term concert coming up and Felicia decided to compose a patriotic song. I was with her one afternoon and she said: "Listen to this." I listened, and then I went home and wrote the words for it. It just came to me.

'We performed it at the school concert. The audience loved it. They cheered and clapped, and the teachers thought it was marvellous. Our singing teacher, Madame Fryer, was so impressed that she got in touch with the SABC, and they arranged for it to be broadcast from Grahamstown.

'Then the Red Cross invited us to perform at a fund-raising concert, and we went in our white dresses and black stockings and sang. It was fun; and, of course we really believed in the words of the song.

---

* At Buckingham Palace, after tea on 10 May 1940, 'His Majesty received me most graciously and bade me sit down,' wrote Churchill in his memoirs. 'He looked at me searchingly and quizzically for some moments, and then said: "I suppose you don't know why I have sent for you?" Adopting his mood, I replied: "Sir, I simply couldn't imagine why." He laughed and said: "I want you to form a Government." I said I would certainly do so. And at one in the morning of 10 May, Gen Maurice Gamelin, CIC of the French army, had been woken by a signal from a French agent behind the German lines. 'Colonnes en marche vers l'ouest.' The Blitzkrieg had begun.

Miriam Markman (bottom row, second from right), and Felicia Glago (bottom row, second from left). (Miriam Zanni)

The original words and score of 'Cheer Up', written by Felicia Glago and Miriam Markman, pupils at the Collegiate School for Girls in Port Elizabeth, and sung live on radio in 1941. (Miriam Zanni)

CHEER UP

If this war seems long and weary
And your hearts begin to doubt,
Though the days are dark and dreary,
Throw your chests right out and shout:

Chorus
Britain's going to win this war,
As she's always done before,
So cheer up and leave your cares behind you
Though your heart's feeling sore.

Three cheers for our lads in blue
And the Air Force brave and true,
Who with the Empire proudly stand,
Fighting on sea and land.

Fight until the end will we,
Fighting for democracy,
So thumbs up although the times are pressing
While we march to victory.

Don't despair, just stick together,
Hope and trust and do not fear,
Never mind disheartening weather,
Fight, for victory is near.

Chorus
Britain's going to win this war …

'I left school in 1941 and joined the Civilian Protective Services* with a friend. We went through an intensive first-aid course and had lectures on what to do in the event of an attack. That wasn't at all unlikely, either, because there were German submarines off the coast. At night you could see the searchlights sweeping out to sea, moving back and forth.

'Besides the first aid and the lectures we had to patrol the neighbourhood and see that no light was showing from any of the houses. There were no street lights, and cars had little hoods over the lights

* Part of the Home Defence Force, which comprised the National Volunteer Reserves a part-time military National Volunteer Brigade, the Civilian Protective Services, and the National Commando Volunteer Reserves.

and people made blackout screens with thick black material. We were also taught how to deal with civilians if an attack took place, where we had to go to, how to keep people calm and so on. Of course we had no air-raid shelters, although we had air-raid sirens. It was quite frightening.

'We were also very concerned about the Ossewabrandwag. The Seaview Hotel in Port Elizabeth was turned into a school for naval officers. There was also an air school for navigators and a lot of RAF mechanics came to be trained. The men from the Ossewabrandwag used to harry them.

'They used to gather in a tearoom called Die Koffiehuis, big burly fellows. When these young RAF and navy men walked past in the street, the OB boys would rush out of the tearoom and beat them up. A friend of mine, a big South African boy, was so angry that he decided to escort the RAF boys and take on the OB. He spent a good deal of time in detention barracks as a result of that, but he felt quite happy about it. Eventually instructions were issued that volunteers and the RAF and navy men had to walk in pairs.

'Not that that stopped the OB. They used to barge into the service clubs and cause chaos. But when the Americans came to town we didn't see much of the OB. The Americans were like locusts in the town. There were thousands of them. They bought everything in sight and the shops were shut because they were out of goods. But it was lovely for us girls. The Americans had the cheek to tell us we couldn't speak English! ’

• Interview 1990.

CHAPTER

32

'Not above the knee, sir?'

Reuby Cohen and the long journey home, November 1941

The casualties of war began to come home in late 1940. The casualties from the Kenyan and Abyssinian campaigns were so few that they went almost unnoticed. From November 1941 wounded men began to come home in greater numbers, through a complicated but efficient network of medical services that stretched from the battlefield back to South Africa.

The South African Medical Corps (SAMC) had come into being on 14 June 1912. In spite of twenty-seven years of existence, September 1939 found the Corps no better equipped for war than the rest of the Defence Force.

Only eight field ambulance units of the Active Citizen Force, which served the soldiers in the midst of battle, existed at the outbreak of war. They had a total strength of ninety officers and a thousand trained other ranks. Ambulances, equipment and the standard of medical training among the other ranks were entirely inadequate. In 1939 it was estimated that a minimum of 382 ambulances, six ambulance trains and two hospital ships would be needed, and that the medical equipment, much of which was still of 1914–18 standard, would have to be brought up to date.

The first step towards making the SAMC an efficient body was the appointment by Smuts in November 1939 of three doctors, A J Orenstein,* J H Orford and F Bester to give advice on the formation of a medical service for the East African campaign.

Under Colonel (later Major-General) Orenstein, a system for the evacuation of wounded and sick men was worked out. There were three zones: collecting, evacuating and distributing. In the collecting zone, in the battle area, travelling with the troops and operating often

---

* Later Director of Medical Services and the man to whom many men later owed their lives.

under difficult and dangerous conditions, was the regimental aid post (RAP) with its field ambulances and motor ambulance convoys. The advanced dressing station (ADS) was the second in line for the wounded, a few miles behind the fighting. From there the wounded were taken to the main dressing station (MDS), capable of dealing with over a hundred casualties.

After the MDS the evacuating zone took over. Casualties were taken by ambulance convoys to the casualty clearing station (CCS), the first place where the men came under the care of female nurses, and from there to ambulance trains, barges and aircraft to the distributing zone, which comprised general hospitals, convalescent depots, hospital ships and hospitals at home.

The first South African field ambulance unit to reach East Africa was the 10th Field Ambulance Unit,* which went into the field under Lt-Col D B Strachan as part of the 1st SA Brigade.

All this was academic for the men in the field. They knew that if they were wounded they would be taken care of somehow. One of the ambulance drivers in the 10th Field Ambulance Unit was a buoyant nineteen-year-old, Reuby Cohen. After serving in East Africa and Abyssinia he went through the wire in the Western Desert and found himself in the middle of the Sidi Rezegh battle.

Later he was severely wounded, and found the collecting, evacuating and distributing zones were no longer merely academic but a matter of life and death for him and the other wounded. This is his story:

‘The last thing I thought I would be doing after I joined up was driving an ambulance. And the last thing I thought would happen to me was that I would be severely wounded myself. Put that down to Reuby Cohen's luck. It all began on 25 July 1940, the day when I enlisted. Well, you couldn't not enlist, could you?

‘Every time you opened a newspaper the war jumped out at you: the Battle of Britain, the Germans overrunning France, Dunkirk, and South Africans getting ready to do their bit.† Reuby Cohen wasn't going to be left out. I was nineteen and I was fit, and there was a troop train leaving Cape Town that very night for Pretoria; and I was on it.

‘We were at Zonderwater for nine days. Training? Forget it. This sergeant comes up to a crowd of us and says: “Hands up all those who

---

* Destroyed at Sidi Rezegh. On 22 November 1941 the Unit had breakfast about a mile from the 5th SA Brigade. Next morning Gen Cruewell, the Panzer commander, issued an order: ‘21 Panzer Division will advance SW to destroy the enemy who has already been badly hit south of Rezegh.’ The Unit was taken prisoner, although a fair number of men were later recovered.

† The 1st SA Infantry Brigade left for East Africa on 16 July 1940.

can drive a vehicle." I held up my hand. Then he says, "Right, go to Broken Hill." So we get on a train to Broken Hill in Northern Rhodesia. When we get there, what do I see but the biggest vehicle park I have ever seen in my life. Thousands of vehicles. The minute we're off the train we're told, "Get into a vehicle, anything you like, just get into one and go, go, go." I said: "Pardon me, but where to?"

'"Nairobi," they said. "Just follow the one in front of you and go." I got into one, started the engine and set off, just like that. We drove through Northern Rhodesia, through Tanganyika and into Kenya. When we got to Gilgil we stopped.

'At Gilgil it was the same routine: "Hands up everyone who can drive." So I put my hand up again. "Right. You will be an ambulance driver." Well, I didn't know anything about medicine and I wasn't sure that I wanted to, but I hadn't got much choice.

'Each ambulance driver was supposed to have a medical orderly sitting with him when he went into action, but that didn't happen very often. Because we were a front-line unit we'd be right in the thick of the fighting, picking up the wounded, putting them in the ambulance and taking them back to the RAP and then further back when they could be moved. You learnt to do everything, drive under fire, leap out, haul out a stretcher, yell for someone to give you a hand, put the wounded in the back and then rush like hell to the doctor.

'There was no equipment in the ambulance, just four stretchers, a container of water if the men needed a drink, and I always kept cigarettes with me, great for calming a man down. Of course, they'd already been given morphine on the battlefield, so they were often dazed. We were always on the move, no time for anything fancy. We were the first into battle and the last out.

'We had this doctor Willem Steenkamp* attached to the 10th Field Ambulance, a legendary character, and I was very grateful for his care later. He couldn't care less that I had had no medical training. If he wanted me to look after a man I would look after him, and that was that.

'I first came under heavy fire in Abyssinia. We had set up the surgery at the bottom of a hill, where heavy fighting was going on. I spent the whole day going up and down, up and down, carrying

---

* Major Willem Steenkamp served in the Medical Corps of the Citizen Force before the war and was mobilised with the 3rd Field Ambulance. He was a Fellow of the American College of Surgeons, but he passionately wanted to be a gunner and applied to be transferred to the artillery. When he was turned down he applied to join the Tank Corps and was similarly refused. He was transferred to the 10th Field Ambulance and served in Abyssinia and in the desert. He abhorred authority and red tape. He returned to South Africa at the end of the desert campaign with chronic amoebic dysentery. His motto was 'We against the world'.

wounded men, loading the ambulance, then driving down the winding road to the surgery. All the men were lying outside, on the ground, on stretchers. Steenkamp was going round looking for the most seriously wounded men. "Bring this one to me immediately," he would say, or "Keep this one here until I call." He was under pressure and the wounded were building up.

'"Reuby," he said to me, "keep that man going."

'"What man?" I said.

'"That man," he said and he pointed. "Over there, that one. Keep him going until I can get to him."

'"Blimey," I thought, "I don't even know how to put a plaster on." The man was on a stretcher with blankets up to his neck and he was rocking backward and forward. He was doped with morphia; when I got next to him I saw that his whole jaw had been blown away. As I put out my arms to hold him the blankets fell away and I saw that both his arms had gone too. I went cold. What could little Reuby Cohen do for this man? I was afraid to touch him; I thought I would only hurt him more. I don't think he even saw me; he just went on rocking.

'I ran into the tent where Willem Steenkamp was sawing off a leg. I hadn't seen that before, either. "Tell me what to do for him," I said, but Steenkamp finished with the man he was working on and got this other man on to the table, and there was nothing more I could do.

'When the Abyssinian campaign ended we went on to Egypt, to Mersa Matruh. It was all a great adventure. How was I to know that it was nearly at an end?

'We went through the wire [between Egypt and Libya] on 19 November 1941. I got separated from the 1st Brigade because the rear axle of my ambulance broke, and by the time it was mended they had disappeared, which is how I found myself in the middle of the 5th Brigade and Sidi Rezegh. It was all bombs and shells and mortars and men screaming, the sound of tanks and me driving like a madman from the front to the RAP and then back to the CCS, about six miles back.

'Most of the casualties I took that day died in the ambulance. As soon as I unloaded them at CCS the padres wanted to know what religion the man was, so that they could bury him. But sometimes their discs weren't on them and they didn't know, so anyone buried them. It doesn't matter what last rites you have, does it? It was chaos, men all over the ground, moaning, the doctors working as fast as they could, vehicles burning all round. I never saw a German tank, but at the end of that day, the 23rd, I decided to get back to my unit and I drove off into the sunset, which was as red as the ground at the CCS.

'I found my unit on the 25th, in the middle of nowhere. There was hardly anyone there. "Where is everyone?" I asked. My friend

Davy Jacobson said: “Dead”. The staff-sergeant took a roll call. Out of 350 there were only 23 of us, though later we found some more, all over the place. We were a very sorry bedraggled lot.

‘They say you have a premonition when something bad is going to happen to you. I don’t know if that is true of other people. I certainly had no warning on the morning of the 28th that something was going to happen to me.

‘Dr Steenkamp came to me. “Reuby, the Dukes have got an Italian POW with a broken leg. Go and fetch him.” So off I went and put him in the ambulance. He was moaning terribly. I offloaded him and Steenkamp fixed him up. I was just standing there when all of a sudden someone screamed: “Look out, Stukas!” There they were, in lines of six, coming straight for us.

‘I heard their engines and firing and shouting and I ran. I fell down in the dust and said to myself, “Well, thank Christ, another raid is over.” Then I tried to get up, but I couldn’t. There was a lot of shouting and yelling and smoke everywhere, clouds of dust, and people coming through the smoke towards me. I couldn’t understand why I couldn’t get up. Then I saw this leg lying near to me. I looked at it and I thought vaguely, “That’s my leg. What’s it doing there?”

‘Everyone crowded round me. I looked up at them and I think I smiled. Davy Jacobson, who had been at school with me, looked very white. They picked me up and carried me to Dr Steenkamp. He gave me a shot and I went under. When I came round I was lying on the ground on a stretcher. Steenkamp said to me, ‘Reuby you were holding your Star of David so tightly in your hand we had to bend your fingers back to get it out.” I had bought that Star of David in Alexandria. I was lying there with a ticket round my neck and I knew that they would take me back to a CCS and then to a base hospital as soon as possible. I asked Davy for a cigarette, but he was shaking so much that he couldn’t find one, and there were tears running down his face.

‘I had been given morphia, so I didn’t feel anything, not even shock, and I didn’t feel much when they put me in the ambulance. All I wanted was a cigarette and water. When the ambulance doors were shut I lifted up the blanket and looked. There was plaster on the stump of my left leg and my right leg was all bandaged. There didn’t seem to be a foot on that leg. I lay back and thought, “Oh, bugger this.”

‘They gave me another injection at the CCS, so I was drowsy when they put me on a plane, a filthy old thing filled with cans and oil and rubbish, and then I was at Mersa Matruh. I woke to a scene from *Gone With the Wind.*

‘I was lying on the ground, on a stretcher, with nothing on but a jacket and a blanket. As far as the eye could see, wherever I looked, there were wounded men lying, with orderlies and doctors walking among them, bending down to look at the tags round their necks and sometimes pulling a blanket up over someone's face. And the noise … a low, low moaning. Some of the men had been blinded, they had bandages over their eyes, and they were feeling their blankets, looking dazed. We were all dazed.

'That night I was put on a hospital train. It was filled with wounded. There were no bunks, nothing. I was put on the floor and I was terrified, because the walking wounded, with their big boots, were walking all over me. I kept crying out "Hey, be careful, get off me," and I would try to move my stump to get out of the way, but I couldn't move. I was terrified lest one of them would tread on it. Eventually a New Zealander one-pipper came along and ordered everyone to get back from me, and he got me a medical orderly, who gave me an injection and I passed out, thank God.

'I woke up in an ambulance outside a British military hospital on the Suez Canal. As we drove in someone was playing a record in one of the wards: "Nobody knows the trouble I've seen …"

'It was there that I discovered that I had lost my right foot and that my leg, the one I still had, was badly mangled and broken, so they put it in plaster and on pulleys. The itching would get so bad that I would beg the doctor to help me and he would have me wheeled into the operating room, put me under, take the plaster off, clean up the leg, which had gone septic, and reset the plaster. I was there for about a month and a half.

'They told me that they wouldn't do anything for me there; they just wanted to get my weight up until I was sent back to Johannesburg, where they would sort me out properly, so I just lay and read. I got hold of a copy of *The Count of Monte Cristo* which I had loved at school and read it again.

'The other men in the hospital were good lads. They were Limies, Geordies, New Zealanders, Scots, and they died like flies. They arrived battered, battered to pieces. They died in the night, mostly, usually quietly; just an empty bed at dawn.

'On 17 January 1942 I was put on a hospital ship for South Africa. We were lifted on to the boat by a crane, put into a box with four stretchers on it and lifted off the quay on to the deck. The ship was full of terribly wounded men, blinded men, men with arms and legs missing, men who had been paralysed. But because we were all in the same boat, so to speak, there wasn't too much misery. I was beginning to suspect that I might lose my right leg too, and I prayed that if I did I would lose it below the knee. That would make all the difference to walking, and I was determined to walk.

'Before we got to South Africa a doctor came round to decide where we should get off: Durban or Port Elizabeth or Cape Town.

Although I was a Cape Town boy I begged them to put me off in Durban and to let me go to Johannesburg. I couldn't bear to face my parents. I was the baby of the family. I'd gone to war with two legs and I was coming home probably with none, and I didn't want to see them so soon. So I went to Johannesburg.

'I was in the Johannesburg General Hospital for two months, then I went to the Highfields Convalescent Home for a year. They tried hard to get my weight up, because I was just skin and bones. I weighed barely sixty lb, but I think I lost a lot of weight because of my addiction to morphia. When I had been wounded the ticket round my neck read 'Morphia on demand' and I was pumped full of the stuff. Eventually I simply had to have it.

'I would beg for it. Then when I got it I had to have a cup of tea and a slice of toast. I would go into a dream world, floating. I thought when I was dreaming that I was back in the desert with my mates. But it was a real nightmare. Two members of staff were pinching morphine for me because they felt so sorry for me. But when I realised what was happening I weaned myself off it. The doctors never knew what was happening.

'One day this doctor came to my bed. He and his students stood round me. "This is it," I thought. He gave me a pair of shears, big chrome shears. "Reuby, I want you to cut off the plaster on your leg. Then I want you to look at your leg. Then I want you to tell me that it must come off." I began to shake. I didn't want to lose my right leg. So I got hold of the shears and cut through the plaster. I couldn't believe what I saw.

'Was that thing a leg? Was that thing a part of me? That green and yellow pus-filled thing, just rotten flesh and, oh God, the stink ... it was too terrible. I gasped and lay back. I knew I would lose it. It was gangrenous. "What do you want to do, sir?" I asked. He said gently, "We're going to amputate it tomorrow."

'"Not above the knee, sir?"

'"No," he said, "we'll amputate below the knee and bring it to the same level as your left stump. Don't worry."

'After the operation I was lying there and the sister came up to me. She told me my parents were coming from Cape Town to see me. She could see that I was dreading their visit. I wasn't ready to see them.

'I wanted to be on my feet when I saw them. On the day when they were to visit me, Sister said to me, "Reuby, does your father pot a little?" And I said, "Funny you should say that, Sister, he does, all the time," so she arranged for a drop of medicinal brandy to be there when they came in.

'It was terrible. My mother came in and fell across my bed and sobbed and sobbed. It was an awful strain, and I felt exhausted when they

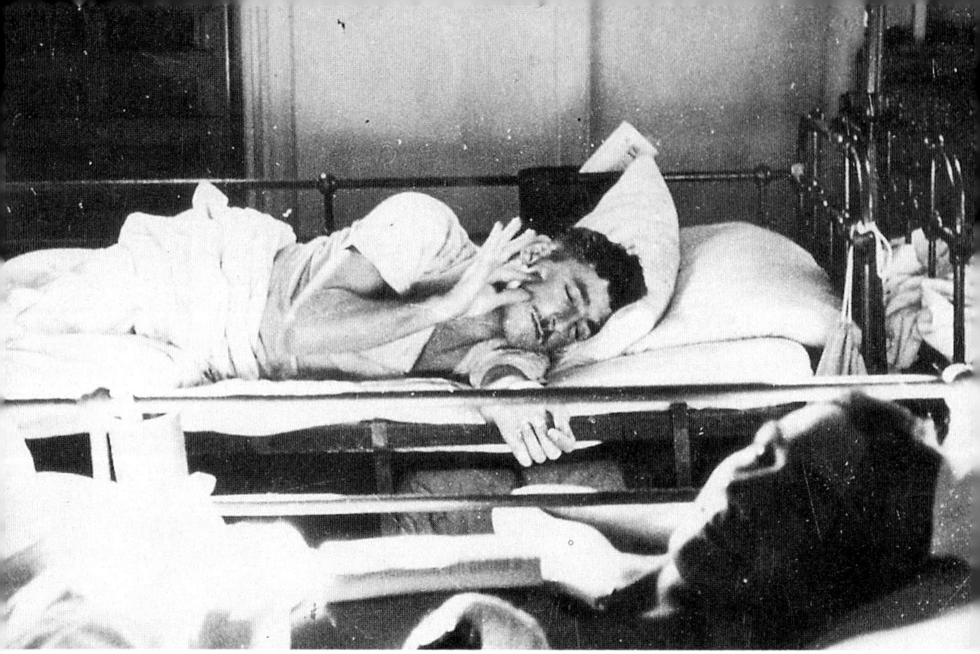

Reuby Cohen on the hospital ship taking him from Egypt to South Africa. He weighed only 60 lb at the time. At the Johannesburg General Hospital he lost his other leg. (Reuby Cohen)

A young soldier who lost a left arm and a right leg being fitted with a false leg; another legless man looks on. It took the men weeks or months to learn to live with their new limbs (South African National Museum of Military History)

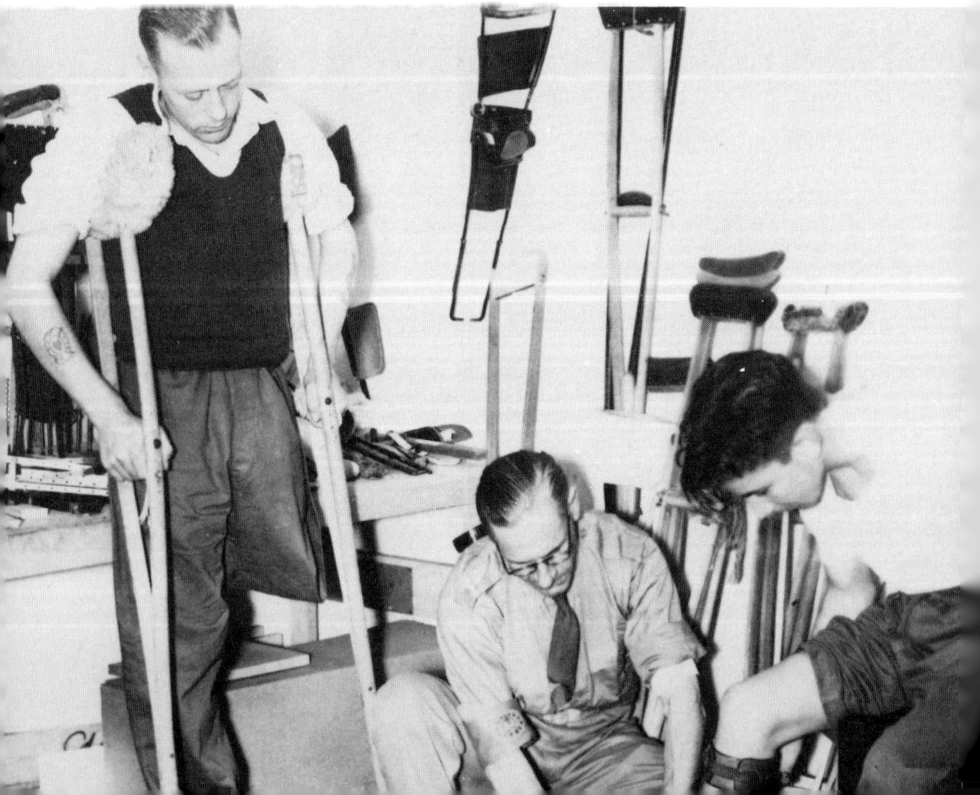

left. I was glad when they went away; at least I could concentrate on getting better.

'At Highfields I was given artificial legs. On the first day they were put on I fell flat on my face. "Get up or I'll kick you," yelled the orderly. "I can't," I yelled back, and I felt so helpless. But he kept yelling at me and eventually, in a sort of rage, I pulled myself up. From then on I progressed quite rapidly. Sometimes I felt sorry for myself. One day one of the sisters came to me and said: "Reuby, I'm taking you for a drive."

'She drove me to Brenthurst, the house that the Oppenheimers had given to Jack Penn for the war. It was a wonderful house. There was this man with bandages over his eyes. I put out my right hand to shake his hand and then I saw that he had no arms. Between us we had two eyes, two arms and two legs. His name was David Bell, and he came from Edinburgh. He was very brave, very cheerful, and I felt much better – even humble – when we left.

'I had 23 operations altogether. I was discharged from the army in 1943 on a hundred per cent disability pension. But, you know, life and living are for the able-bodied and the rich. I went to war with two legs and I came back with none, and all for £3.17 a month.* '

---

* Under the War Pensions Act of 1942, European male volunteers were awarded £200 per annum for 100% disability, black volunteers £50 per annum and (white) widows £48.

CHAPTER

33

'Pretty girls and high kicks'

Gordon Mulholland, entertaining the troops from Cape to Cairo and beyond

They were entertainers first and foremost, but they were also morale-raisers and ambassadors, a touch of normality in abnormal times. They made the men laugh and they reminded them of home, of something other than guns and sand and sweat.

They played on railway stations, in barns, on portable stages under the desert stars, in casualty clearing stations and hospitals, in bombed-out halls, in opera houses, in streets and on ships.

The men and women of the Union Defence Force Entertainment Unit (otherwise known as the 19th Reserve Motor Transport Company) literally played from the Cape to Cairo and beyond, in Italy and Austria, in Iran and Iraq, in Palestine, Syria, Greece and Malta. They played to men of all nationalities: to South Africans, of course, but also to the British, Poles, Canadians, Australians, New Zealanders and Americans.

The UDF Entertainment Unit was formed in Pretoria in January 1941, a motley bunch of professional and amateur entertainers. By the end of the war they had fifty-four variety shows to their credit: The Amuseliers, The Bandoliers, The Crazy Gang, The Ballyhoos, The Troopadours; and they had played to over three million men in the Union and over eight million in North Africa and elsewhere.

Names that South Africans have long been familiar with became familiar to the troops then: Larry Skikne (Laurence Harvey), Sid James, Leo Quayle, Muff Evans, Gordon Mulholland.

They trained as ordinary soldiers before they were allowed to set foot on a stage, and they were subject to military discipline. They learnt how to march and how to salute, how to drive three-tonner and ten-tonner trucks, how to change tyres and how to service them, how to get them out of mud and out of sand. They learnt that the show always went on, even if the rumble of guns shook the ground or if there was no applause because the audience had no hands to clap.

Staff Sergeant Gordon Mulholland, UDF Entertainment Unit, playing to the troops from 1941 to 1946. (Gordon Mulholland)

Gordon Mulholland, who volunteered in 1941 and was accepted because of his Tommy Trinder patter ('Good evening, ladies and gentlemen, my name is Tommy Trinder, T-R-I-N-D-E-R, pronounced Cholmondely'), was one of them. It was the best university he could have gone to:

'I suppose you could say it was a miniature Hollywood within the Defence Force. Our CO was Major Myles Bourke; the girls were looked after by Capt Sibyl Gaiger. The men in the unit were given the strictest instructions never to leave the girls on their own: we walked them in a body to their tents or barracks at night, we went shopping with them and we went to parties with them. It was important to do that in the Union, but even more so when we went Up North. We had some quite tricky situations with the troops, but nothing that we couldn't handle.

'Every person coming into the unit was auditioned: singing, dancing, comedy, whatever, and then assigned to a show. But it didn't end there. Lots of people, myself included, came in able to do one thing, say singing, and by the end of one year they could dance and tell jokes, even juggle. We had to be able to turn our hands to anything.

'We played all over South Africa before my unit went Up North, in camps outside funny little dorps all over the Union. We played to troops just before they were going Up North: they were tremendous audiences, because they were young and excited and nothing was impossible, although I suppose some of them must have been apprehensive.

'My first real encounter with war came when we played at Addington Hospital, Durban. I was the compère and the comedian in our shows, and I felt very out of my element standing in the middle of a ward with twenty men with no legs. We cut the show down, made it simpler, exchanged a piano for an accordion and cut out most of the dance routines. It was always the girls that the men wanted to see, and they would go and sit on the men's beds and chat to them and sing a song or two. We saw some terrible sights there. I felt so sorry for the men, some of them thousands of miles from their families and no one they knew to see them through that terrible time.

'I think that's when I realised that my job was an important one. My duty was to make them laugh, just as it was other men's jobs to go into the front line.

'Sometimes it was very hard to make them laugh, especially Up North. If I felt that they weren't enjoying themselves, then I would change the act halfway through. You always have four or five acts in your head, so you change them about as you go along. I had to make them laugh at all costs, even if I had to drop my pants. That's what they had come for. The key is to grab the audience's attention right at the beginning and not let it go. It was a sweat and sometimes it was anguish, but I had to leave them laughing and wanting more.

'We went Up North in 1941, just after Sidi Rezegh. We played to the troops on the ship going north – appalling conditions, all below decks, heat and hammocks. The girls had cabins.

'Helwan was our base, and from there, depending on where the fighting was, we went all over with the troops, just behind the fighting. Many a time we heard the guns or could feel the ground shiver when a bomb came down. But we were well organised when we were travelling.

'When we arrived at a camp, whether it was outside Alexandria or in the desert in places like Marble Arch,* it took us men two and a half hours to put up our stage, and that included the stage itself,† full lighting, dressing room and curtains. The girls would unpack the costumes (some of them, like the make-up, from Hollywood) and they would iron them all and set out all the make-up for the show.

'When we arrived in North Africa it was a desperate time for our chaps. Nothing seemed to be going right for them. They had left the Union convinced that they could take on the world. The whole of the Western Desert was a disaster. There was never any good news, and we kept getting pushed back and back. You could see the tension on the men's faces. They had a drained look; they were exhausted and with little hope.

'We kept getting messages from Pretoria: cheer up the men, chivvy them along, tell them they are wonderful, go to parties after the shows, put on more shows. And we did, of course. But it was always the girls who were the hits. They wore these saucy little satin skirts and kicked their legs high and the men loved them. So we put on more shows and we went to a party every night after the show. South Africans are a proud people. We don't like losing.

'The men went mad over the girls. They were all very pretty and, being in show-business they had that little bit of flair, and their make-

---

* A vast area, site of many tank battles.

† The portable stage, made by 61 Base Workshop of the Technical Services Corps, Cullinan, was in collapsible sections, easy to put up and easy to take down.

The Bandoliers with Larry Skikne (Laurence Harvey) dancing the jitterbug with Vivienne Broughton. To the right is the compère and comedian, Gordon Mulholland (Vivita Liss)

Also from The Bandoliers, a chorus line of 'pretty girls in short satin skirts' and Gordon Mulholland, with hat, spats and smile. (Muff Evans)

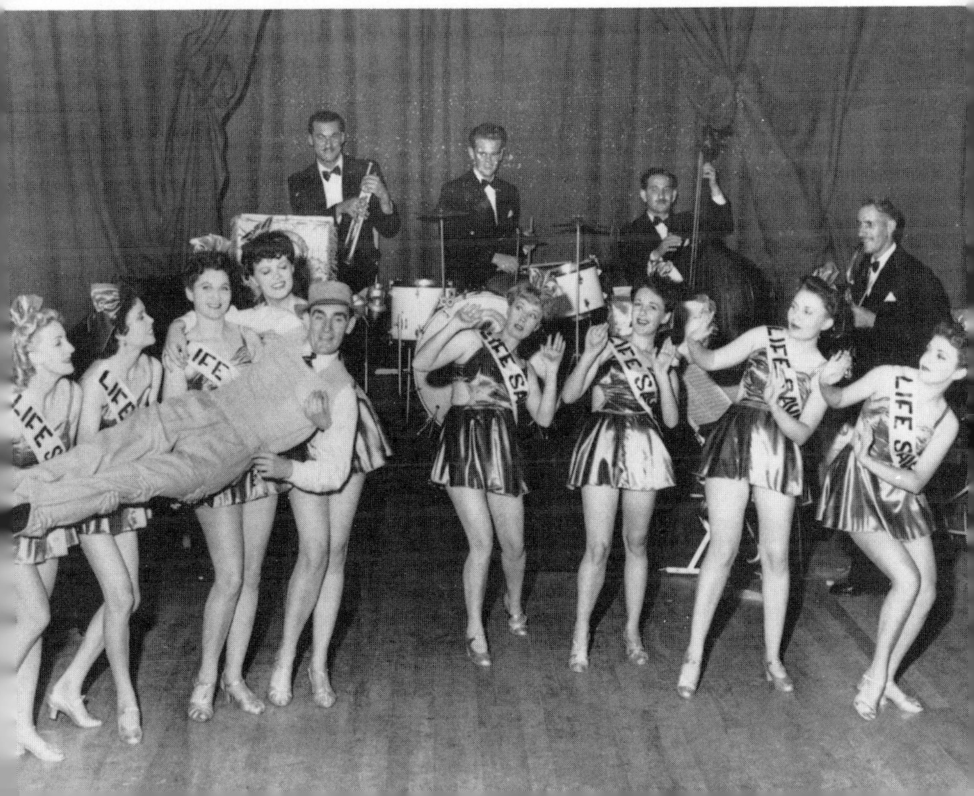

up and their hair were perfect, although I don't know how they did it. They had a rough time, changing in sandstorms, with sand in their ballet pumps, always having to look perfect.

'Of course there were lots of high jinks, especially in Helwan. They had to be in their barracks at ten every night, and it was like flies all over the walls, girls climbing out, men climbing in, like bloody cockroaches everywhere. It was very difficult to get into their barracks, but some managed. I did once, with two other chaps. We put on the girls' uniforms and got in, but once we were there we were so terrified of being caught that we went straight out again.

'The troops were sometimes a problem, but as we were on the move all the time nothing really bad ever happened. The SAAF and the RAF were the worst. They caused havoc. They were very glamorous. They all seemed to be good-looking and tanned, and the women went for them. But we had only one girl who went overboard. She was a human glory-bag; and she was a very busy girl. I think the soldiers were cabling each other: "She's on her way, get ready, line up." She was sent back to the Union.

'But the men weren't sex-starved, you know. There were army brothels. I went to one once. It was run by the army. I paid 2/6 and was given a flannel impregnated with disinfectant, a little cake of soap and a condom. There was this little Arab girl, about seventeen, and she was so utterly bored by the whole thing ... "Oh God, not *another* one," and I never bothered to go again. But the men were no monks.

'The best reception we ever received was at Leptis Magna, where we played in a Roman amphitheatre to an audience of thirty thousand. The acoustics were so perfect we didn't need a microphone. We hardly had to raise our voices. There were South Africans, Yanks, Canadians and British in that audience, and they went wild. They loved Larry's* jitterbug act and they liked my patter, but it was the girls who were the real stars.

'The jokes were terrible, unbelievably bad. Part of my act was to stand on stage and pretend I was phoning someone. "Hello, please may I speak to Oscar?"

'"I'm sorry, there's no one of that name here."

'You ring again. "Hello, may I speak to Oscar?"

'"That's funny, someone phoned me a minute ago and asked for Oscar. He doesn't live here."

'You phone again. "Hello, this is Oscar. Are there any messages for me?"

'Believe it or not, that brought the house down. We often had to accommodate visiting artists. We'd get a message from Cairo saying so

---

* Laurence Harvey

and so would take part in our act, and would we rearrange it to give them some time? One evening Josephine Baker turned up with her dresser. She took forty-five minutes of our act, but we didn't mind, she was so professional. I've never seen anyone dress and undress so rapidly. She had about twelve costume changes. She'd step off the stage, her dresser would unzip her, she would step into one of the dresses lying in a circle on the ground, her dresser would yank up the zip, and she was back on stage.

'In Italy things were different. There was a lot of hand-to-hand fighting, and the men would be suddenly pulled out of the line and there we would be, on the spot, entertaining them. Because the fighting was harder, in a personal way I think we were more needed in Italy than in North Africa. They really needed to see the pretty girls and the high kicks.

'We played in a lot of hospitals in Italy, and there the girls went in in mufti, not uniform, to brighten things up for the men. We also played to a lot of Americans, but they were very difficult. They had everything: big bands and Bob Hope, and then along came the South Africans with their potty little show. We went down well everywhere else.

'I don't think we ever had a "bad" audience, although we had a few difficult ones. We used to get lots of catcalls and shouts like: "Look at that moffie dancing with the girls," but it was all good-humoured. And in the end that's what it was all for: making them laugh, making them feel good, making them feel they could go out and do anything. I think we helped. ’

• Interview 1991

CHAPTER

34

'What the hell had happened?'

Private Vivian Rees-Bevan and the *San Sebastian*, 9 December 1941

What had happened to the three thousand men of the 5th Brigade taken prisoner at Sidi Rezegh? No one knew; all that the families in the Union knew was that the men were posted missing; which could mean anything.

South Africans prepared for Christmas with gloom. Many of the men were up north, many were missing, and the hospital trains filled with wounded and maimed were evidence that all was not well.*

All the same, in spite of shortages – fabric was one, so that men's suits were made without pocket flaps and dresses without frills anywhere and shorter skirts – consumers were urged to celebrate the festive season with a musical Christmas (accordions from ten guineas), to buy Meccano sets for boys, to drink Santy's brandy – 'its clean natural flavour acquired by distilling selected white wines in the French Cognac Way' – and by going to the movies to see *The Grapes of Wrath* (Henry Fonda, Jane Durwell and John Carradine), *Intermezzo* (Leslie Howard and Ingrid Bergman) and *Convoy,* a story of 'how the merchant marine brings home the bacon' with the help, of course, of the Royal Navy.

If attention needed to be diverted from Christmas and the scrawny chickens then on sale (turkeys were scarce), that opportunity came with a vengeance on 7 December when the main American naval base in the Pacific, Pearl Harbour, was attacked by Japanese aircraft. Eight US battleships were hit, one capsized, three were sunk. America declared war on Japan next day (so did Britain) and on 11 December

* The achievement of SAR during that time was astonishing. In 1940–1 the SAR served nearly two million meals, eight hundred thousand of them to servicemen. A thousand special Defence trains, including the War Train, which went as far north as the Congo, were operating in a single year. The Essential Services Protection Corps guarded railways, bridges and other vulnerable points against sabotage. All this was done with no new rolling stock and with fewer men than in peacetime, nine thousand white employees having been released for active service by the end of 1941.

Hitler declared war on the USA. The hard-pressed British, Commonwealth, Free French and Polish forces breathed a sigh of relief: with America in the war, the scales would be tipped inevitably in favour of the Allies.

Vivian Rees-Bevan of the 2nd Regiment Botha before he left the Union for Kenya. He returned home in 1945. (Vivian Rees-Bevan)

More was to come that December on the high seas. The British warships HMS *Prince of Wales* and *Repulse,* based in Singapore, were sunk by the Japanese. On 8 December 1941 the bedraggled and emaciated South African and British prisoners of war taken at Sidi Rezegh, many of them weakened by dysentery and wounds, were put on board a cargo ship, the *San Sebastian*, which left Benghazi that evening.

The Mediterranean was not a comfortable place. Above and below the waves a sinister game was played between British and Axis ships and submarines. British, Polish and Dutch submarines sank 270 000 tons between June and September. German reinforcements, mainly submarines, were sent to the Mediterranean. On 13 November, five days before Operation Crusader began, the British aircraft-carrier *Ark Royal* was torpedoed by a U-boat; she sank the next day 'like a sleepy child'.

The battleship HMS *Barham,* torpedoed by U-331, exploded, and in December, six Italian frogmen entered Alexandria harbour, fixed explosives to the *Queen Elizabeth* and *Valiant* and severely damaged both.

It was into this cockpit that the *San Sebastian* sailed. The crew were Italians, and the prisoners were stowed in the dark holds. In one of them was Private Vivian Rees-Bevan of the 2nd Regiment Botha. He was a Sabie man with a fine singing voice. He stood with his regiment at Sidi Rezegh, and on the afternoon of *Totensonntag,* 23 November, he was taken prisoner. Next day he set off on the hard Thirst March that ended in Benghazi. He sailed on the *San Sebastian* on the evening of 8 December 1941:

'It is impossible for a free and healthy man to understand what it is like to be taken prisoner of war. The sun still shines, the desert is still the colour of ochre, there's still pain when you hurt yourself. But nothing else is the same. It was not just the feeling that you are suddenly leaderless, that there is no order, but a sense of total demoralisation.

Men of the 2nd Regiment Botha taking it easy before they went through the wire into Libya and the Sidi Rezegh battle. (Vivian Rees-Bevan)

'Never in a thousand years would it ever have occurred to me that I would be taken prisoner. Even on the thirst march it had barely begun to sink in. You noticed things, but you didn't notice them. You lost all hope and all faith. You didn't know whom to talk to, you didn't know what to do, you didn't know where the devil you were going to; and when you are being herded along like a bunch of rabbits when you are used to being a free man and having some control over your life, it is indescribable. Total demoralisation only partly expresses what one feels.

'And I was terribly worried about my wife Hilda. Would the authorities know what had happened to me? Would they let her know? Would she think I had died? Would she be all right? I ached to get in touch with her, to let her know in some way that I wasn't dead. We got to Benghazi on 26 November, and a sorry sight we were, exhausted, emaciated, cold and hungry. Many of us had dysentery. We were housed in the local army headquarters, so many of us they didn't know what to do with us, so we mostly moped about. We were still so stunned we hadn't even thought of organising ourselves; but at least we had learned that there was such a thing as the Geneva Convention. None of us had heard of it before.

'I couldn't get out of my mind the wireless operator I had been working with on the day we were captured. He was a young chap from Durban. We heard we were to withdraw, and we made our way back to the 2nd Botha. I completely forgot the order to destroy the wireless set and the maps, and we had left them behind. So we went back to fetch them. On our way back he caught an anti-tank shell. His last words to me were: "Tell Mom I died."

'On Monday, 8 December bunches of men were rounded up by the Italians and driven away in trucks. When my turn came we drove down to the port with our issue of bread, biscuits and bully beef. There in front of us was a large grey ship, the *Sebastian Venier*, a cargo ship,* and we were being loaded on to it.

'As soon as we reached the deck we were hustled down into a hold. In the front of the ship were the Cape Corps. We climbed down into the hold, and when it was full the hatch covers were shut. When I looked about me there was just this cavernous hold full of men, some of them wounded, sitting or lying or standing on cold iron. I was so depressed that I didn't care what was happening to me; I didn't even pay attention to the chap over there with a broken leg.

'It was very dim in the hold. For a latrine we had a tin drum. Many of the men's dysentery had got worse, and it was very unpleasant for them and for us. We sailed into the Mediterranean about dusk. It never occurred to me to wonder how we would get out of the hold in a hurry if we had to, and it didn't cross my mind that we might be torpedoed. The chaps out there were British and we were allies, so why would they torpedo us?

'I slept uneasily that night – we all did – wondering where we were going. I didn't feel seasick. Down in our hold there was very little motion. The hours dragged on; and then there was a terrible explosion. The ship shuddered, but it was the shock rather than the noise that we felt. No one was standing in our hold when it happened, although we were thrown about.

'We knew we had to get out of that hold, but there were no doors, no ladder, and there were big wooden planks across the hatch. There was no fighting, just panic to get out. We knew that something serious had happened. The ship had stopped and there was a great noise, men screaming and shouting and pleading. Some had been hurt in the explosion. And there was the sound of feet running over the deck and Italians shouting.

'Even by standing a man on another's shoulders we couldn't reach the hatch. But someone wrenched the planks off from the deck, and they dropped a rope down, and one by one we hauled ourselves out of the hold. I must have got out that way too, but I can't remember it. The ship had been hit forward,† in the forward hold, where the

---

* 6 300 tons, with over two thousand prisoners on board when she was attacked on 9 December 1941.

† By a British submarine, HM *Porpoise,* commanded by Lt-Cdr E F Pizey. The *Sebastian Venier* was off Methoni Point, on the south-western tip of the Greek Peloponnes when she was torpedoed.

Cape Corps men were and there wasn't very much of them left. They had been blown apart, nearly 300 of them. The ones who were alive were screaming, but the hold was flooded and they were struggling in the water which was pushing and pulling them around.

'Although we didn't know it – how could we, battened down in the hold? – we were escorted by two Italian destroyers, which were now circling our ship and dropping depth-charges and ignoring the men who had jumped overboard and were trying to swim to the shore. If they dropped a depth charge and there were men in the water, it was just too bad; they were killed. They were damn fools to jump overboard, but we were in sight of land five miles away, and strong swimmers might make it there.

'The ship was down by the bow, with the screw and the propeller out of the water. A lifeboat full of men was sucked into it and chopped to pieces; there were bits of bodies floating on the surface. The Italians were running all over the place, shouting and cursing. We helped a few of them overboard without any qualms at all. Nobody seemed to be in charge. It was raining, and the deck was slippery.

'Then a German officer took control. He got what officers there were still on board together and told them he was taking command. Things quietened down a little after that. Some of the wounded were taken under shelter. I stood on the deck praying we wouldn't sink. The German officer managed to get the ship nearly to the shore, driving it hard against a reef about five hundred yards from a beach.* But five yards was a long way too for most of us.

'What saved the situation was this chap Friedlander, a champion swimmer from Cape Town.† He got hold of a lifeline and jumped overboard with it and then swam ashore through the grey sea. He secured the line and gave us a thumbs up and one by one we got ashore using the line. It wasn't the only one; once he had thought of it others did the same, and there was this network of lines stretching from the ship to the shore, with men slipping and sliding and clawing their way down them.

'By now we were pretty weak. We'd been prisoners for two weeks and most of us had gone through that thirst march and we had been physically tried. As we came ashore through sea covered in

---

* Remains of the keel can still be seen, stuck firmly on the reef.

† Lance Corporal Bernie 'Bull' Friedlander of the 3rd Transvaal Scottish stripped, tied the rope round his waist and jumped into the cold water. The wreck formed a buffer against the wind and heavy surf, but even so the weight of the rope wore him down. He was helped to shore by a young Greek and together they hauled the rope ashore, to cries of 'Thank God, he made it!' from the *Sebastian Venier*. The rescue of the men continued all night. On 13 May 1947, at Roberts Heights (now Voortrekkerhoogte), King George VI awarded Friedlander the George Medal.

diesel oil we were a bedraggled and shaken sight. But being covered in the oil helped a lot of us withstand pneumonia.

'When I reached shore I just stood shivering uncontrollably, not knowing what to do. Italian troops were standing on the shore to see that no one escaped. At least they were dry. We were soaked and miserably cold, and a lot of us were shocked, and we were not thinking straight. We were herded off the beach, and somehow we walked through Methoni and towards Pilos, where there was an old fort. Two Greek women tried to give us currants and raisins, but the Italians shot at them.

'By the time we got to Pilos we were in disarray. We filled the cells, the dungeons, the courtyards and the moat. I was in the dry moat. We slept outside, with no blankets, nothing, in that freezing weather, still in the clothes that we had been captured in, our only warmth the coat of diesel oil that the rain was washing off us. The walls round the castle were twenty feet high. I lay there shivering, wondering about Hilda and home. '

• Interview 1990

Private Vivian Rees-Bevan saw the war out as a prisoner in Italy and Germany, and he took part in the two-month 'death march' across Germany. When he arrived in England after the march his weight was down from sixty-five to forty-six kilograms.

CHAPTER

35

'A carefully prepared police plan'

The capture of Robey Leibbrandt, 24 December 1941

Throughout the war the Ossewabrandwag and other Afrikaner nationalists, were a painful thorn in the side of the government. Troublesome though that organisation was, in only a few quarters did it match the extreme fanaticism of the former light-heavyweight boxing champion of South Africa, Robey Leibbrandt and his followers.

Leibbrandt, who had been trained in sabotage in Germany and taken up the cause of National Socialism with a fervour that astonished even his teachers, was sent to South Africa with the general purpose of assassinating Field Marshal Smuts, overthrowing the government and establishing Nazi rule in the Union.

He was better known for his appearance, his temper and his arrogance than for his intelligence. He arrived off the coast of Namaqualand on 10 June 1941 (twelve days before Hitler launched the invasion of Russia) and made his way to Pretoria via Cape Town and Bloemfontein. He then set about plotting and recruiting. His followers swore a blood oath and were swept up not only by the cause but by the force of Leibbrandt's obsessions.

Although the government had a fairly efficient network of informers, the existence of Robey Leibbrandt within the borders of the Union escaped them until after a successful raid on the ISCOR site at Mooiplaas on 15 July, when five boxes of dynamite, sixteen hundred electric detonators and four hundred fuse detonators were stolen in a daring and well-planned raid.

At first the government reacted with incredulity to the leaked news that Leibbrandt was back, armed and dangerous, and that support for him was growing daily. Ironically, Leibbrandt was betrayed by the Ossewabrandwag itself, worried about losing members to the Nazi fanatic.

Even then the authorities kept it as quiet as possible. It was obviously in their (if not the country's) interests to do so. With Leibbrandt at large and new converts joining his cause, the spark that could set off a rebellion (the second in less than thirty years) was a real danger.

There was cause for more uneasiness in the country. As a year of bad news for the Allies drew towards its end, the Union was shaken by the débâcle at Sidi Rezegh. The U-Boat menace was far from over, and the country was desperately short of manpower for the Defence Force. Where would more men be found to put down a rebellion? Even the loyalty of the police was doubtful.

Furthermore, the Union, far from the real fighting, had earned a small but significant reputation as a haven for refugees of high rank. The Greek royal family had arrived on board a troopship in July,* the exiled King Constantine of Greece was a baby in arms.

The government was also giving hospitality to Prince and Princess Paul of Yugoslavia and their three children in a house in Wierda Valley in Johannesburg, and the Shah of Persia would soon arrive and take up residence in the Johannesburg suburb of Mountainview.†

A rebellion, even if it were put down and even if it had survived the national crisis that would undoubtedly have arisen if Leibbrandt's plans for the assassination of Smuts at his house in Irene had been successful, would have severely marred the reputation of South Africa in the eyes of the free world.

An undercover policeman, the indomitable Jan Taillard, insinuated himself within the Leibbrandt circle and arranged his arrest at Wierda Bridge, outside Pretoria.‡

Unaware of the danger that Leibbrandt might have become, the *Rand Daily Mail* reported his capture on Christmas Day 1941:

LEIBBRANDT ARRESTED

> Robey Leibbrandt was arrested by the police at Wierda Bridge, about seven and a half miles out of Pretoria, on the main Johannesburg-Pretoria road, just before 10 o'clock last night.
> Leibbrandt was accompanied by a man and a woman who have not yet been identified and are being detained by the police. Leibbrandt, although armed, put up no resistance.
> Leibbrandt's capture was part of a carefully prepared police plan which was carried out without a flaw last night. Leibbrandt was

---

* Smuts placed Westbrooke (which had also sheltered British child evacuees) in Cape Town at their disposal. Family jewels were stored in the vaults of the Board of Executors in Wale Street.

† He died there on 26 July 1944.

‡ Taillard was scandalously treated by the Nationalists when they came to power in 1948. He died poor and forgotten and in an old age home in Johannesburg in the 1980s.

apparently taken by surprise and had no opportunity of drawing his revolver before the police party pounced on him at the bridge.

The identity of the man and the woman found in his company will be ascertained today.

Leibbrandt and his companions were brought to Pretoria, where Leibbrandt was watched by special guards last night.

CHAPTER

36

1942

Shortages, blackouts, Marabi – and Tobruk

As a second full year of war began, South Africans were in a less jubilant mood. Things were changing, and none of them for the better. We were short of tea, petrol, hats, paper (stamps shrank to half their former size) short of silk stockings and fine wool for babies; and, worst of all, short of beer and whisky.

In February 1942, as the 1st SA Division was moved into the Gazala Line to help stem the advance of the Afrika Korps, and as the 2nd SA Division, with no premonition as to its fate, moved into the garrison of Tobruk, there was a squabble at home about the newly announced restrictions on the sale of tea. Panic buying – one woman spent the enormous sum of £75 on tea alone – enraged shoppers, their tempers hardly improved by the scarcity of petrol. After the ban on sales of petrol over weekends, coupons were issued to car-owners, permitting each car a limit of four hundred miles of travel a month.

No matter that Singapore, Britain's fortress in the Far East, had fallen (on 15 February) to the Japanese; what really concerned us in the opening months of the year was the change in the standard of living. The incredulous public were informed that, because of a shortage of corks and the obligation of the government to supply troops of visiting convoys with beer as well as to our troops in the desert, supplies of beer were to be cut by half to local South Africans.

But we were diverted (briefly) by the invasion of Madagascar by colonial and South African forces. Early morning commuters in central Johannesburg were bemused to see a horse-drawn buggy distributing copies of *The Star*;* there was a shortage of rubber as well

---

* Its nose seriously out of joint because, as part of The Argus Printing and Publishing Company, it had had the foresight to import newsprint before the outbreak of war, only to have its supplies taken over by the Paper Controller, who pooled all newsprint supplies and handed out Argus newsprint to anti-government papers as well as those loyal to the cause. The Controller also dictated the size of newspapers, and *The Sunday Express* was closed for the duration.

as fuel, and horses' hoofs, reasoned the distributors, lasted longer than car tyres.

At the end of May there was a real scare in the Union when, late on the afternoon of 30 May, an unidentified aircraft flew unchallenged over Durban. Almost certainly a Japanese spotter aircraft, it flew around for fifteen minutes and then headed out to sea. Five days later, also over Durban, sound locators picked up an aircraft high overhead. It took the anti-aircraft defence in Durban twenty-five minutes to report the aircraft, by which time it had disappeared.

Two hours later the sound of another unidentified aircraft was heard in the night sky over Durban, but even so, and with the threat of a midget submarine attack considered a real possibility, the town remained with its lights on until the captain of HMS *Valiant*, in harbour at the time, telephoned Fortress Durban's Headquarters to ask why there was no blackout.

On 16 June the blackout in Durban was made permanent. Three aircraft of 33 Flight failed to find the town at all and had to land elsewhere. It was all very confusing.

But the news that flashed round the world on 21 June eclipsed nearly everything else. Tobruk, occupied by the 2nd SA Division under the command of Maj-Gen H B Klopper, had surrendered after a savage blitzkrieg attack unexpectedly coming at its eastern perimeter and thrusting through to the town itself, neatly dividing the garrison in half.

Many of the men inside Tobruk, in wadis, on the hard and stony ground, in the shattered town itself, did not even get to fire a gun. Instead, readying themselves for battle and with radio communication with Headquarters severed the night before, word of the surrender was relayed from man to man.

Winston Churchill, who was under no illusions about the importance of Tobruk, was in Washington. In the Oval Office of the White House with President Roosevelt, Churchill was handed a telegram. 'Tobruk has surrendered with 25 000 men taken prisoner,'* it said. He was aghast. So was Smuts. Through all the confusion, Sapa's Middle East correspondent relayed a communiqué that simply said there was no news from Tobruk 'which must be presumed to have fallen'.

'It can be stated,' said Smuts, trying to put a brave face on the disaster and attempting to conceal how short the Union Defence Force was of fighting men, 'that the South African troops held to the last the

* An underestimate. The real figure was closer to 33 000, 19 000 of which were British, some 10 000 white South Africans and 4 000 black South Africans and the 2/5th Mahrattas (Indian) and the 2/7th Ghurka Rifles.

For six years women were the backbone of the country, and took over from men wherever possible. They manned anti-aircraft guns, coast defences drove buses, worked in factories and directed traffic. (South African National Museum of Military History)

The slight bespectacled figure of Ouma Smuts was seen everywhere. She did everything she could for her 'boys', including signing her name on caps. (South African National Museum of Military History)

defence in the Tobruk perimeter allocated to them. In this they upheld the fighting tradition of the South African Army.'*

The families of the men taken at Tobruk had no idea whether they were missing, dead or prisoners of war, and they waited long to find out what had happened to them. In July and August newspapers carried page after page of names, the names of men within Tobruk when it was surrendered (Klopper, the South African general who made the decision to surrender the garrison, did not take in the white flag himself: that unenviable task was given to another South African). Even then it was impossible to tell which of the men posted missing were prisoners. The Red Cross at last got word through, but it took many months.

In the Western Desert, a shaken and demoralised 8th Army retreated to the Alamein line – and waited.

Back home, the drift of black workers to the towns, principally Johannesburg, was turning into a flood. It was the birth of the squatter movement containing in embryo the grievances that exploded thirty years later (in 1946, the black population of Johannesburg was four hundred thousand). A severe housing crisis rapidly developed: only fifteen hundred units were built in 1941 and 1942 – and the Johannesburg City Council allowed householders to take in subtenants. Pimville (now a suburb of Soweto) for example, housed 150 000 people, served with sixty-three water outlets. But through it all beat Marabi, the music of the townships, played by legendary performers such as Todd 'Fingertips' Matshikiza on the piano and Vy Nkosi on the trombone and sung, of course, by the incomparable Snowy Radebe.

And then, amidst the acrimonious bus boycotts in Alexandria, came good news. On 23 October, along the length of the Alamein line running from Alamein on the coast south to the Qattara Depression, a thousand guns opened fire in a night assault on the Afrika Korps. By 4 November the Germans were in retreat, the SAAF had flown over three thousand sorties in seventeen days, and Tobruk had been partly avenged. On 13 November, with South African armoured cars in the lead, Tobruk was recaptured.

Few knew it then, but the tide of war had at last turned in favour of the Allies. But first South Africa had to bury one of its favourite sons, the much loved, quirky, prickly General Dan Pienaar, commander of the 1st SA Division, who was killed in an air crash on his way home. South Africans now looked to the next year with anticipation. There were to be no more Tobruks.

---

* The Kaffrarian Rifles, Die Middellandse Regiment, Natal Field Artillery, Native Military Corps and Royal Durban Light Infantry, the SA Police, Umvoti Mounted Rifles and the 2nd Transvaal Scottish were all there.

CHAPTER

37

'He was safe, he was alive'

Hilda Rees-Bevan, waiting for the news, 23 November 1941 – 28 January 1942

Hilda Rees-Bevan waved husband Vivian goodbye from her father's house in Sabie, Eastern Transvaal, in November 1940. How could she possibly have known that she would not see him for another five years?

Like thousands of other young wives, she busied herself at work, went out to dances, walked in the veld, listened endlessly to the radio and waited for his letters. They were few and far between, written hastily on small army issue air letter cards. But the longest wait of all was after the battle of Sidi Rezegh. Although she had no idea he had fought in that battle, it was natural that she should wonder – and worry about his well-being.

For two long months she heard nothing at all. Then, on 27 January 1942, an official letter lay in the postbox she unlocked every day for news of him:

'I didn't know for sure that Vivian had been at Sidi Rezegh. How could I? Of course, I'd had letters from him after he left in November 1940, but not many. A few from Mersa Matruh and then just silence.

'In a sense I was lucky, because I was living in a small community, I had a job at the mine and I stayed with my parents, who were very supportive. And we had no children.

'In fact, I was glad that Vivian was in the army: he was safer there, I thought, than being at home in uniform, because the Ossewabrandwag was very active in our area. After Vivian volunteered my father's garage door was painted with swastikas, and he received an anonymous letter. Viv was so angry he said that if anybody stopped him after dark he would just shoot him. I went to the magistrate to tell him about it.

'I collected his letters from a box we had at the post office – I cleared the mail every day and I would read them immediately, standing right there, and then again at home. During the time he was away I prayed for him often. We had only got married on 11 November, Armistice Day 1938, and I often felt that I was losing out. I prayed to God to give me triplets when he came back, just to make up for all that lost time.*

Hilda Rees-Bevan, without her husband for five years. (Vivian Rees-Bevan)

'When I read about Sidi Rezegh I wondered if he had been there. All I knew was that he was somewhere up north. Although I worried about him I never really thought of him being killed. Wounded, maybe. And I never thought of him being taken prisoner.

'It was nearly two months to the day after the battle of Sidi Rezegh that I received a letter. But not from Vivian. It was an official letter. I wasn't afraid to open it – simply had to know what had happened to him, to set my mind at rest. I tore the letter open at the post office. All it told me was that the army didn't know what had happened to him – he was missing. I knew that could mean anything. It also asked me to apply for an allowance or a pension until they knew what had happened to him, but I never did.

'Two days later a telegram came from the Red Cross. He was safe, he was alive and he was a prisoner of war in Italian hands. All that mattered to me was that he was safe. Now all I had to worry about was him coming home ... some time. When at last he got back, I hadn't seen him for five years. ’

• Interview 1990.

---

* Someone must have been listening. Hilda produced twins after Vivian returned from Germany in 1945.

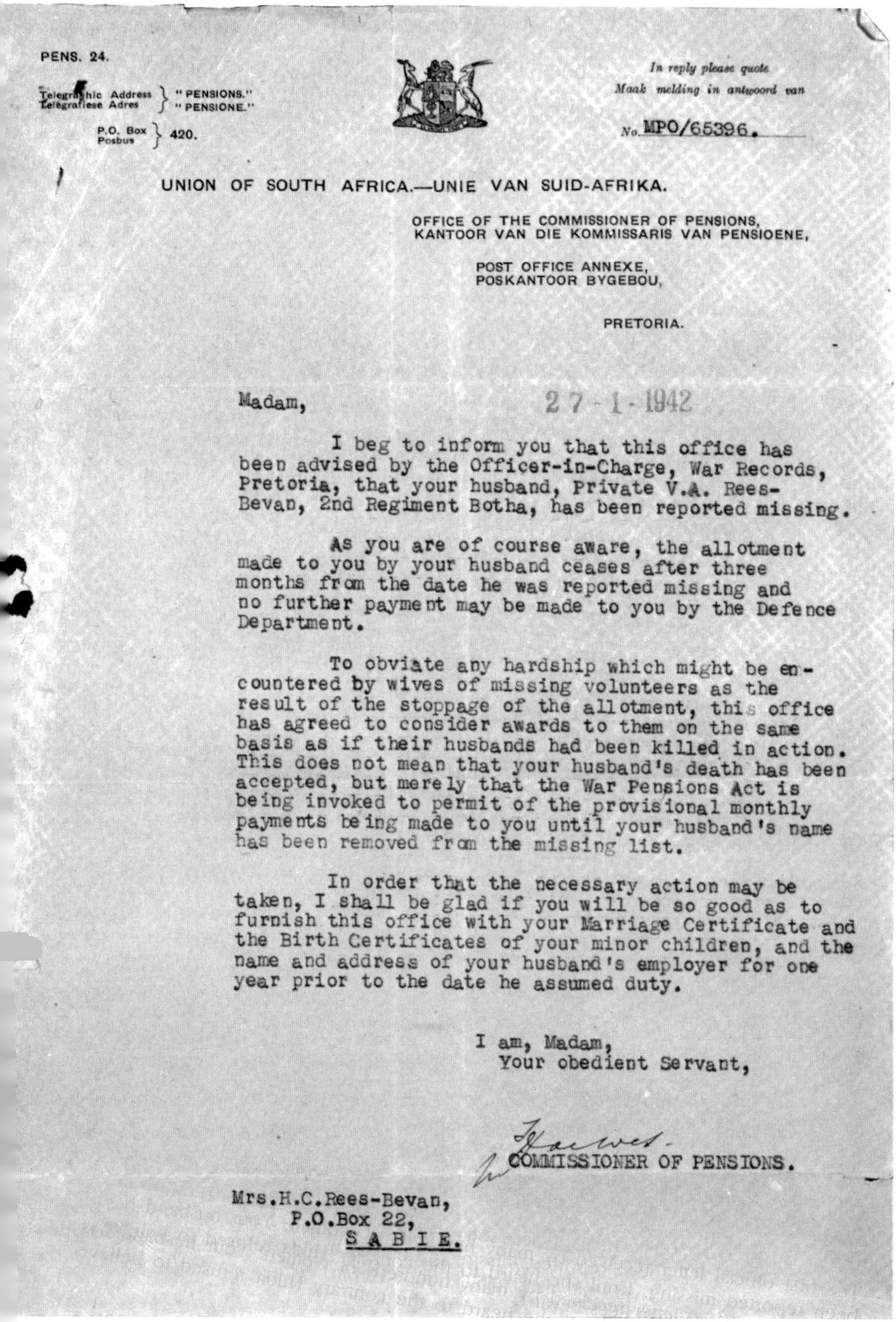

PENS. 24.

Telegraphic Address } "PENSIONS."
Telegrafiese Adres } "PENSIONE."

P.O. Box } 420.
Posbus }

In reply please quote
Maak melding in antwoord van

No. MPO/65396.

UNION OF SOUTH AFRICA.—UNIE VAN SUID-AFRIKA.

OFFICE OF THE COMMISSIONER OF PENSIONS,
KANTOOR VAN DIE KOMMISSARIS VAN PENSIOENE,

POST OFFICE ANNEXE,
POSKANTOOR BYGEBOU,

PRETORIA.

Madam, 27-1-1942

I beg to inform you that this office has been advised by the Officer-in-Charge, War Records, Pretoria, that your husband, Private V.A. Rees-Bevan, 2nd Regiment Botha, has been reported missing.

As you are of course aware, the allotment made to you by your husband ceases after three months from the date he was reported missing and no further payment may be made to you by the Defence Department.

To obviate any hardship which might be encountered by wives of missing volunteers as the result of the stoppage of the allotment, this office has agreed to consider awards to them on the same basis as if their husbands had been killed in action. This does not mean that your husband's death has been accepted, but merely that the War Pensions Act is being invoked to permit of the provisional monthly payments being made to you until your husband's name has been removed from the missing list.

In order that the necessary action may be taken, I shall be glad if you will be so good as to furnish this office with your Marriage Certificate and the Birth Certificates of your minor children, and the name and address of your husband's employer for one year prior to the date he assumed duty.

I am, Madam,
Your obedient Servant,

COMMISSIONER OF PENSIONS.

Mrs.H.C.Rees-Bevan,
P.O.Box 22,
S A B I E.

The first official letter received by many hundreds of women: Your husband has been reported missing. Until she heard to the contrary Hilda refused to believe Vivian was dead. (Vivian Rees-Bevan)

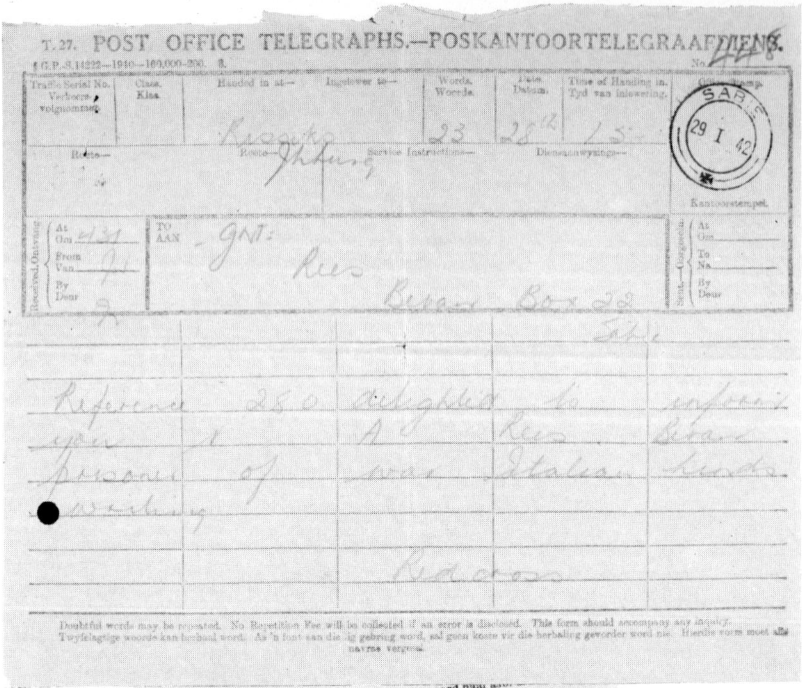

T. 27. POST OFFICE TELEGRAPHS.—POSKANTOORTELEGRAAFDIENS.

G.P.-S.14222—1940—100,000-200.

Handed in at— Ingelewer te— Kaapstad

Words. Woorde. 23

Date. Datum. 28/12

Time of Handing in. Tyd van Inlewering. 1.5

Office Stamp. SABIE 29 I 42

Route— Jhburg

Service Instructions— Diensaanwysings—

Kantoorstempel.

To Aan — GNT: Rees Bevan Box 22 Sabie

Reference 250 delighted to inform you A Rees Bevan prisoner of war Italian hands writing

Redcross

Doubtful words may be repeated. No Repetition Fee will be collected if an error is disclosed. This form should accompany any inquiry.
Twyfelagtige woorde kan herhaal word. As 'n fout aan die lig gebring word, sal geen koste vir die herhaling gevorder word nie. Hierdie vorm moet alle navrae vergesel.

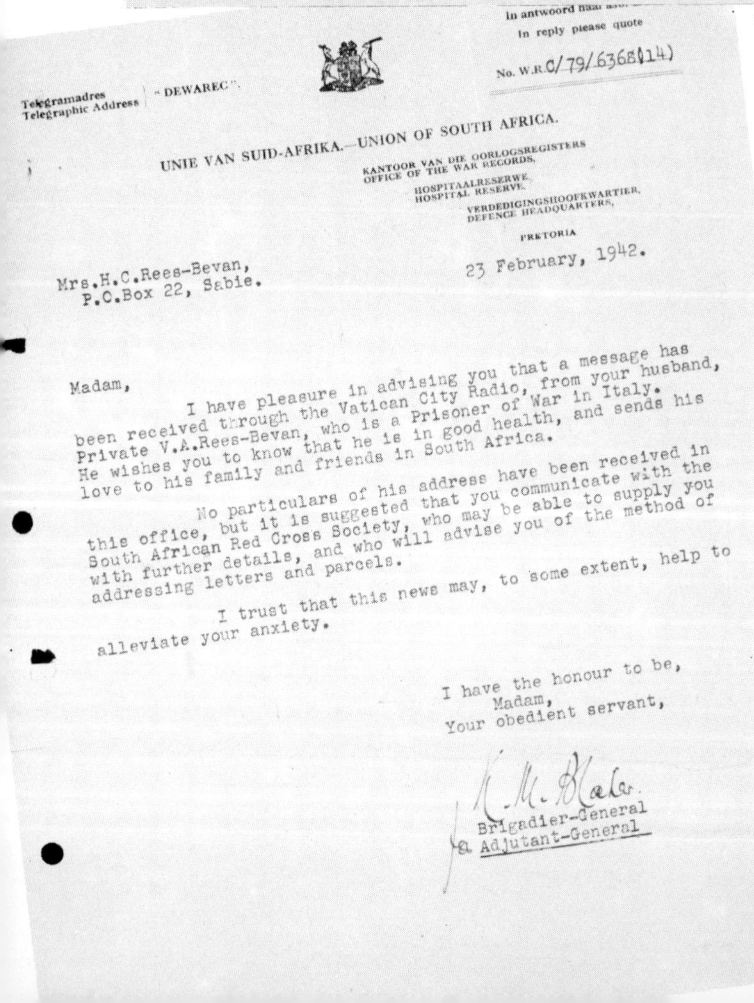

In antwoord haal aan:
In reply please quote
No. W.R.C/79/6368(14)

Telegramadres
Telegraphic Address "DEWAREC".

UNIE VAN SUID-AFRIKA.—UNION OF SOUTH AFRICA.

KANTOOR VAN DIE OORLOGSREGISTERS
OFFICE OF THE WAR RECORDS,
HOSPITAALRESERWE,
HOSPITAL RESERVE,
VERDEDIGINGSHOOFKWARTIER,
DEFENCE HEADQUARTERS,
PRETORIA

23 February, 1942.

Mrs.H.C.Rees-Bevan,
P.O.Box 22, Sabie.

Madam,

I have pleasure in advising you that a message has been received through the Vatican City Radio, from your husband, Private V.A.Rees-Bevan, who is a Prisoner of War in Italy. He wishes you to know that he is in good health, and sends his love to his family and friends in South Africa.

No particulars of his address have been received in this office, but it is suggested that you communicate with the South African Red Cross Society, who may be able to supply you with further details, and who will advise you of the method of addressing letters and parcels.

I trust that this news may, to some extent, help to alleviate your anxiety.

I have the honour to be,
Madam,
Your obedient servant,

K. M. Blake.
Brigadier-General
Adjutant-General

The telegram informing Hilda that her husband was no longer missing: he was a prisoner of war. This was followed by an official letter. The relief was enormous. But contact between prisoners of war and their families was at best tenuous. (Vivian Rees-Bevan)

CHAPTER

38

'The survivors were different'

Little Jenny Walters and the survivors

The Walters family lived in a large two-storied house in Montclair outside Durban. Taffy Walters ran a fertiliser factory, and, being classified as a key man, he could not join up. His wife Cecilie, a former nurse, brought up their two children, Owen and Jenny.

Like hundreds of other families in Durban and Cape Town, the Walters entertained troops. Sometimes they looked after survivors – Jenny called them 'revivers' – men whose ships had been sunk beneath them. One such ship was HMS *Dorsetshire*.

'We had an urgent call on the radio for people to take in sailors who had been rescued after the *Dorsetshire** was torpedoed,' Cecilie Walters recalled. 'I phoned and said we could take two. When I got to the camp "my" two couldn't be found, and I was asked to take three others; whereupon the first two appeared, and I ended up taking five. They were lonely boys, so tidy; they made their beds and rolled the few clothes they had into bundles in the cupboard. Neighbours helped by giving toothbrushes, shaving gear and other necessities.'

The poignancy of looking after these men, many of them shocked, made an indelible impression on Jenny. This is how she remembered the 'revivers' of HMS *Dorsetshire*:

'I was seven, and Durban was a long way from the war. We saw the horrible pictures of dead soldiers and bombed towns in the newspapers, of course, and there were recurrent rumours of German spies living in seaside cottages and signalling to enemy submarines at dead of night with powerful torches.

---

* HMS cruiser *Dorsetshire*, with HMS *Cornwall*, was part of the Eastern Fleet. On 4 April 1942 a Japanese fleet of four battleships, three cruisers and eleven destroyers was sighted 150 miles south-east of Ceylon. Next day both ships were sunk east of the Maldive Islands. 424 men lost their lives; but there were 1 122 survivors.

'But otherwise the war for us children meant minor discomforts like no chocolate and the car up on blocks because of petrol rationing. White bread was a sinful luxury, made surreptitiously for special occasions by sieving the coarse brown wartime flour and flushing the telltale bran down the lavatory for fear of being branded unpatriotic by quizzy neighbours. Sometimes there were weevils in the flour, and for a long time I thought of the enemy that everyone talked about as rather like weevils: nasty squirmy creatures eating away unseen at the fabric of our lives, a nuisance rather than a threat.

'Fathers who were not Up North rode bicycles to work and talked a lot about the Hun and put in long hours as black-out wardens or on guard duty down at the docks at night. Our mothers did voluntary work at the military canteens and hospitals, wearing square-shouldered linen suits and their hair anchored into long smooth sausages round their heads with special curling tongs and dozens of hairpins.

'I remember the black-out curtains that hung limply at every window, smelling stuffy and warm and metallic like the insides of old trunks. I remember the thrill of my first piece of chewing-gum, proudly smuggled into class in a sticky handkerchief tucked into the knickers of a friend whose father had been sent home wounded. You could make a precious piece of chewing-gum last for weeks by carrying it about in a matchbox full of sugar.

'Most vividly I remember waking up one night, flushed and feverish with measles, and being carried out on to the verandah wrapped in an eiderdown to see the searchlights practising over the harbour.

'They moved in random jerky arcs without pattern or form, a geometric dance of light, until one of the beams suddenly lit on the small biplane that was acting as a target. With chilling speed and precision the other beams converged on it and seemed to hold it suspended like a small black insect in a web of brilliant light. I saw the enemy, hunted and trapped, and he was far more frightening than the horrible newspaper pictures and the nasty little weevils had led me to believe. He was like me when I'd done something wrong and been caught.

'I began to cry, and they held me tight, shushing and soothing me and saying, Look! Look at the pretty lights! But the image of the prisoned plane hung desolately buzzing about my dreams for years, and I am still not sure who the enemy really is.

'During the war Durban was the last port of call for troopships going Up North, and later east. It was also the first port of call when they were sent home shocked and wounded, or fished out of the sea when their ships were torpedoed in the warm shark waters of the Indian Ocean.

'Durban people are proud of their reputation for hospitality. Like most families with large houses, ours took in as many servicemen as possible. They were exciting days. Often we came home from school to find men in blue or khaki uniforms sitting in the deck chairs on the verandah. If they were pale and chirpy, we knew they were on their way out. Those returning or convalescent were very tanned against their white bandages, spoke little, often limped, and sometimes cried silently when they thought no one was looking. Their eyes were like our old dog Leo's eyes, and they would sit very still, and flinch if you brushed past too close or let out a sudden shout.

'The survivors were different. They came to stay for days or weeks at a time while they were rested and refitted before being sent back to war again. I remember particularly the biggest party we ever had to stay, seven seamen who had been torpedoed in the Mozambique Channel. They arrived one afternoon in the hospital bus without caps or jackets or luggage, only the ill-fitting civilian shirts and trousers they stood up in, with the dazed look of men who don't know exactly where they are, but hope to find out before long.

'My brother rushed off to tell his friends. "They've got nothing, not even a *toothbrush!*" I heard him yelling through the hedge, and soon a row of boys came and stood, awed, to watch the survivors drinking tea on the verandah. I stood watching too, slightly apart as befitted my status of older sister.

'"Lovely cuppa, Missus," one of them said to my mother, grinning with discoloured teeth (maybe he had never had a toothbrush?). His name was Cocky Matthews, a stoker on the troopship and a plumber's mate in civilian life. It was only when I worked as a teacher in London years later that I recognised his accent as not just "funny" but pure Southwark.

'That first day he followed up his compliment to my mother by adding, "Wouldn't of minded a nice cuppa like this whilst we was treadin' the ole briny, eh?" And he made the loud snickering noise with his chin up and his eyes squeezed tight shut which we came to learn was Cocky's way of laughing. "Eh, Beezer, mate?" he wheezed.

'Effervescent with relief at being alive and unhurt, he could not understand why the rest of the men did not share his delight. "But yer still kickin', ain't yer?" I heard him say over and over to the others.

'Jim Beazley smiled uneasily and said nothing. In the ten days that the survivors stayed with us I saw Jim open his mouth only four times to speak, and the first two were to ask someone in a mumble to pass the salt.

'The other survivors remained subdued and lethargic, eating their meals in awkward silence and trooping back into the spare room afterwards to lie on their camp beds, smoking and staring at the ceiling. They didn't want to read or sit in the garden or go out to the cinema or the shops, and when our neighbour Mrs Andrews offered to take them to the beach for a swim, they refused vehemently.

Cecilie Walters (centre, seated) with the seven-year-old Jenny on her left and some of the 'revivers' they looked after during the war. Thousands of South African families played host to soldiers, sailors and airmen. (Jenny Hobbs)

'"Yer can't 'ardly blame 'em, Missus," Cocky said to my mother afterwards. "We was in the water for twenty-nine hours, and a lot of our mates was – "

'"Yes, I know," she said quickly, seeing me in the doorway. "It was tactless of Mrs Andrews."

'" – drowned." Oblivious of my mother's attempts to keep shielding us even from the filtered reality of war that reached us, Cocky threw up his chin and snickered. " 'Orrible noise a man makes, drowning. Never forget it once you've 'eard it."

'Mum put on her do-this-instantly face and said to me, "Lovey, run and call Gertrude. I need her to help me with the tea things. Now."

'As I dawdled along the passage, I heard Cocky say, "Beezer would of drowned too if I 'adn't of 'ung on to 'im. But I couldn't let me mate go, could I?"

'I heard him say it again the same evening when Mr Andrews brought over the last of his pre-war whisky to join my father and the survivors for a spot on the verandah before supper.

'Not noticing that I was sitting half-hidden by the dense Zimbabwe creeper that grew next to the steps, Dad and Mr Andrews led Cocky on to talk about the torpedoing.

‘He relived the nightmare of suffocating fumes and burning oil and flesh that sizzled when it hit the water, and of the shark that had begun to swim in smaller and smaller circles round the lifebelt that he and Jim were hanging on to before they were rescued.

‘I shivered, wondering if the same thought was running through their minds too. They were sitting very still in their deck chairs, a semicircle of dark monoliths round a sacred place, waiting.

‘Dad got up to fetch more beers, and Cocky began to talk about something else. But I was watching Jim’s tense silhouette slowly relax against the dim square of light from the open passage door. What had he said to Cocky? I wondered. “Thanks for saving my life?” Or had he just mumbled something under his breath that Cocky hadn’t considered sufficient thanks? How much gratitude should a person show towards someone whose efforts have staved off death?

‘Next day the survivors went off in the hospital bus to be refitted, and they came back in uniform. It was funny how the uniform changed them. Before they had been a group of oddly-assorted, rather surly men in second-hand clothes that didn’t fit; now they were sailors of the King, with the aura of heroes. They would be going back to war in two days.

‘My brother summoned his friends to bask in the reflected glory, and I found myself following the survivors round like an eager puppy, intrigued by the idea that these flesh-and-blood people who had been in my home would soon be facing Hitler’s guns again. Now that they were in uniform they spent more time on the verandah talking among themselves and watching people and cars go past on the road, and less on their beds. Or perhaps it was simply that the time had passed and the torpedo nightmare was beginning to recede.

‘Only Jim remained silent and brooding, his heavy-featured face turned away from his shipmates’ desultory talk. He seemed to be looking not at the vivid purple petrea that tumbled down the corner of the house or at the neatly mown lawn or the spreading feathery flamboyant tree whose comfortable branches were my favourite place to read, but somewhere inside himself.

‘Cocky kept trying to draw him out with endless speculation about their next billet. “Wonder where they’ll be sendin’ us next, Beeze-boy – India, maybe? Or Australia, likely. Some of them Sheilas isn’t ’arf bad, eh?”

‘“Never been a one for words much, ole Beezer,” he confided to me with a wink.

‘“Why not, Cocky?” I asked. “Is there something wrong with him?” I was thinking of the retarded girl who lived up the road, and whom we hardly ever saw because her parents kept her inside. I really wanted to know. The idea that grown-ups could have something wrong with them – wrong in the head like not being too good with words, I mean – was a novel one.

'He grinned at me, then threw up his chin with a loud snicker. "Kid wants ter know if there's anyfink wrong wiv yer, Beezer," he crowed.

'"I – I didn't mean that!" I blurted, feeling the blood rush to my face.

'Some of the survivors laughed. Jim began to turn his head towards me and I scrambled to my feet and knocked my glass over. But his eyes didn't stop at me. They moved on to where Cocky sat. "I'll thank yer not to call me Beezer no more," he said in a deep slow voice. "The name's Jim."

'Cocky's loud snicker stopped short. He was so surprised that his mouth fell open. It was the first time I had seen him at a loss for words.

'"But you're me *mate*, Beezer!" he said in a hoarse whisper. "We joined up togevver! We shared the same bunks! I 'ung on yer for a 'ole bleedin' night when yer kept wantin' ter slip orf! Remember the shark, Beeze-boy? Remember the way 'e swum closer and – "

'Jim Beazley launched himself out of his deck chair with the ponderous grace of one of the Sunderland flying boats that Dad had taken us to see as they took off near the Maydon Wharf graving dock. In two steps he was towering over the small man's chair, looking as though he would break it into matchwood. I shrank down as low as I could against the steps, my heart thumping. One of the survivors said in a warning voice, "Jim!"

'"I saved yer life," Cocky whined.

'Jim opened his mouth to speak for the fourth and last time in our house. The words were very quiet for such a big man. "I've done me penance now, Cock," he said. And he turned and went inside.

'Mum and I watched from the top of the verandah steps as they left next day on the hospital bus, jaunty in smart new uniforms, with their sailor's caps at rakish angles. They seemed very different from the dazed survivors who had arrived ten days earlier, and they were effusive in their thanks. Cocky was chosen to present Mum with the undreamed-of luxury of a box of Black Magic chocolates which they'd ferreted out and clubbed together to buy; my brother was too busy gloating over it even to come and say goodbye. Mum had tears in her eyes as she smiled and waved.

'The bus pulled away and they gathered in two knots at the windows, shouting, "Ta-ra!" and blowing kisses and laughing like schoolboys, as though war was the last thing on their minds. Perhaps it was at that moment.

'Jim was not with them. He sat alone at the back of the bus, and as it drew away from the steps he raised his hand to his forehead in a slow salute. We saw Cocky throw his arms over the shoulders of two others as they jostled for seats, and they began to sing "We'll Meet Again" very loudly as the bus turned under the fig-tree into the street.

'Mum had to dab her eyes with her handkerchief as the song faded away. I thought it was probably a good time to ask my questions. "What was wrong with Jim? Why didn't he want to stay friends with Cocky any more?"

'Mum looked down at me. "Jim is a proud man, and Cocky was asking more than a friend should ask," she said. "You'll understand one day, I hope."

'Then she went inside to put the chocolates away before my brother got any ideas about them. We wouldn't taste chocolate again till the end of the war. '

• Jenny Hobbs

There was a curious postscript to this story. Years after the war, Cecilie Walters called the service station for someone to repair her stove. The man looked at her strangely and said: 'Don't you remember me? I was one of your survivors.' He had married a Durban girl and had settled there.

CHAPTER

39

'Alone in the heart of Germany'

Sgt Donald 'Buzzer' Huntly and the Augsburg Raid, April 1942

Much was made in the Union's papers of the national heroes; and heroes there were aplenty: Ninety-two Air Force Crosses, eight George Medals, 451 Distinguished Flying Crosses, forty-two Distinguished Service Crosses, one Military Cross of Czechoslovakia;* and four Victoria Crosses.

The four South Africans who won the Victoria Cross in the Second World War were much lauded in the Union. Streets and schools were named after them; their parents were interviewed, their school records were dug out and much was made of their bravery. Two VCs were awarded to men serving in the Union Defence Force: Sgt Quentin Smythe and Sgt G R 'Toys' Norton. Capt Edwin Swales, of the SAAF was seconded to the RAF when he won his VC, and Sqn Ldr John Nettleton, the first South African to win the VC in the Second World War had joined the RAF in the autumn of 1938.

And we needed heroes in 1942, when nothing, it seemed, was going right. As we anxiously turned on the radio or skimmed through the slim newspapers, all the news seemed bad. The Japanese were running amok in the Far East; Singapore was gone, Java invaded, Rangoon and Batavia overrun. Malta was being pounded day and night by the *Luftwaffe;* in North Africa Axis forces faced British and Commonwealth forces across the Gazala line; Gen Dan Pienaar had succeeded 'Uncle' George Brink as Commander of the 1st SA Division in the line at Gazala.

In April 1942 three years of war stretched ahead. Service chiefs, and Churchill himself, knew that morale was low. What was needed was a raid on enemy territory that would show the world that although Britain was down, she was not out.†

---

* Won by the gallant 'Sailor' Malan, together with the DSO and Bar, and DFC and Bar and the Belgian Croix de Guerre.

† On 28 March British marine commandos raided the French port of St Nazaire; in August occupied France was again raided by Canadians and marine commandos. The Dieppe Raid resulted in heavy casualties; few of the men got off the beach.

RAF Bomber Command had a new Commander-in-Chief, Air Marshal Arthur 'Bomber' Harris. The Augsburg Raid was part of his offensive policy.

Two squadrons took part in the raid, 97 Squadron, RAF and 44 (Rhodesia) Squadron, the motto of which was *Fulmina Regis Justa* (The King's Thunderbolts are Righteous). It was also the first squadron in the RAF to be given the new, updated Avro Lancasters. Harris decided to use them in a low-level daylight raid on the M.A.N. Diesel Engine Works in Augsburg, Bavaria, which was estimated to supply about half the requirement of U-boat engines.

The raid was led by John Nettleton from Nongoma in Natal, with six Lancasters from each squadron and two more in reserve. To escape detection by German radar Harris decreed that the Lancasters should fly without fighter escort and at low level. The raid was determined for 17 April, to cross the coast of France at five hundred feet, with the attack also at low level using thousand-pound bombs with an eleven-second delay fuse.

One of darkly handsome Nettleton's crew was a twenty-year-old Rhodesian, Sgt Donald 'Buzzer' Huntly, the top-turret gunner. Unknown to Nettleton, Huntly kept a diary. He took it everywhere with him, including on the long and hazardous missions made by the squadron.

Training for what was described as a 'suicide' mission began five days before the raid. The Lancasters flew in formation over southern England, fresh with the new green of spring. Huntly's diary for this period is sparse: he was too busy to write it up. At 3.12 p.m. on 17 April twelve Lancasters took off from Selsey Bill on the south coast. The raid that won for Nettleton a Victoria Cross and Huntly the Distinguished Flying Medal (DFM) and much fame at home had begun.

Five minutes after Nettleton and his men crossed the French coast in daylight they were intercepted by about thirty German fighters. In the hour-long mêlée that ensued, Donald Huntly shot down an enemy fighter; but four of the Lancasters were lost.

Nettleton, in Avro Lancaster R5508 KM-B, pressed on, unaware that his top-turret gunner was jotting down impressions in his diary. By now the remaining eight Lancasters were flying so low they were virtually clipping the tops of trees.

The Lancasters achieved almost total surprise over Augsburg, which they reached in the dusk, at about 8 p.m. Flying through heavy flak (Huntly knocked out an anti-aircraft battery), seventeen bombs were dropped on the target;* but the flak brought down another two Lancasters.

---

* Five failed to explode.

Only five bombers, all severely damaged, returned after a flight of a thousand miles over enemy territory. Later the survivors learnt that only three per cent of the machine tools in the factory had been put out of action.

This is how Donald Huntly described the raid in his diary, written on the long and dangerous mission:

AUGSBURG
Friday, 17 April 1942

‘Took off from the Base at 1505 hrs in 2 formations of 3 in vic. Sighted French Coast at approximately 1650 – five mins later I saw about 15 Huns about 1 000 feet above – we went down to zero ft. Huns turned in behind the opened attack, on rear vic. We were attacked at almost same time by second formation of about 12 Huns. Rear gunners kept up considerable fire. I got in good burst at FW190 making port bow attack – saw tracers enter his belly – was then distracted by tracers fired from ground gunners in gun position in front. Got in good burst at them – they must have all been hit as fire stopped. Saw one starboard machine go down, hit by cannon. Fighters broke off. Rear formation of 3 – all down. Two of us left now! – and still 500 miles to go – kept at 20 feet – France very beautiful – many trees all in bloom – passed over many great forests – farmers and villagers all waved – in the distance there are mountains – we gradually climb – an hour and three-quarters and there below us is the Rhine – Up, up again – in front are high peaks – snow-capped – we are in the “Faderland” – scenery very beautiful – small villages all white with walls decorated in red – nestle in the valleys – sides of mountains terraced – and high among the snows is some great monument – Switzerland is heralded by Lake Constance – Swiss mountains in distance beautiful beyond words. We are near target. On again. There is Augsburg! Bomb doors open! – left – steady – right – steady – hold it – Then all hell is let loose.

‘Sheets of bullets of all sizes streak past with a white flash – over the target at chimney height! Bombs gone – direct hits! We weave – I see a heavy gun belching flame – spray it – it stops – the bombs go off – everything shakes and the whole area is covered with flying debris and smoke – Our mate is hit – he puts her down in the heart of Germany – we stay at naught ft flat out – waiting for the most welcome of all sights – the dark – at last after an eternity the sun sinks – we climb – it’s getting darker – what a relief – no further thrills, until hours later – that greatest thrill of all – there’s good old England. We’ve made it! But there is sadness among us – for many fell on the way.’

‘The Augsburg Raid shows what the men of the RAF can do,’ wrote the London *Sunday Times* in an editorial headlined ‘Glorious Enterprise’. ‘If

Some of the Augsburg heroes (in the middle of the photograph is Brendan Bracken, Britain's Minister of Information). Donald 'Buzzer' Huntly is second from the left, Sqn Ldr John Nettleton on the far right. Neither survived the war.

anybody is inclined to ask the usual question as to whether such an enterprise were worth while, the answer is that anything is worth while which so glorifies the human spirit, and sets an example to inspire the whole nation ...'

Shortly after the raid the newly decorated John Nettleton and 'Buzzer' Huntly left for the USA on a fund-raising and morale-building trip. They had a good time. On Saturday, 6 June Huntly wrote: 'For lunch I had steak – large – 2 fried eggs, peas, onions and mushrooms followed by strawberries and cream. Wonder what lads in England would say. Going out to Party – found an invitation under my door a few minutes ago. Don't know who she is ...'

On his return to England Huntly was offered the job of instructor by 44 Squadron. Walking in London just after this offer he saw a pitiful old woman bombed out of her house. He decided to turn down the instructor's job and return to flying. On 12 September 1942 he was reported missing over Holland (two months later, on 27 November, Huntly's elder brother was killed at El Alamein). John Nettleton was also short-lived. He was presumed dead after a raid on Turin on 12 July 1943.

The Augsburg Raid, while it produced a clutch of heroes and a brief glory, was deemed not worth while in losses and the modest results of the raid. Bomber Command now changed its policy to saturation bombing. Less than two months after the Augsburg Raid a thousand bombers set out from bases all over England. Destination: Cologne.

'Buzzer' Huntly signing an autograph album for a young admirer on the triumphant American trip after the Augsburg Raid. (Jeff Huntly)

The ticker-tape welcome for the heroes of the Augsburg Raid as they drove through New York. (Jeff Huntly)

CHAPTER

40

'I knew I could work with steel'

Airwoman Ethel Price and the art of building an engine

There were five full-time women's services during the war, of which the Women's Auxiliary Air Force (WAAF) was one. The Women's Aviation Association, forerunner of the WAAF, was gazetted as the WAAF on 10 May 1940, with the remarkable Miss Doreen Hooper as its head. It was formed in 1939, mainly for the training of female pilots.

By 1943 there were seven thousand women serving in the WAAF in a broad range of jobs: secretarial, ferrying or actually building aircraft. They practised more than forty different crafts. When she assumed command of the WAAF on 1 June 1940, one of the most urgent tasks facing Doreen Hooper was to encourage women to volunteer as artisans, who were desperately needed by the SAAF to replace male mechanics sent up north.

Her job was not made any the easier by low rates of pay or by the vast difference in pay between the sexes. A male flight mechanic got 8s 10d a day; during the three months' basic training the women got 3s 6d a day while the men got 5s a day.

To replace the men sent up to the Western Desert the WAAF needed to attract fifty women artisans a month, which was rarely achieved. All WAAFs, in whatever capacity, were sent to Valhalla outside Pretoria from July 1942 for basic training. They learned to march under the steely eyes and stentorian voice of the imposing-chested Miss N Edwards, the WAAF sergeant-major.

In spite of Doreen Hooper's fears that she would not attract enough women artisans, by March 1941 three hundred had volunteered for service. They were housed in Edward Street, Pretoria, a pleasant red-brick building formerly used as a domestic training school for girls, and they were trained at the Pretoria Technical College. To the chagrin of the men on the same course, the women were getting higher marks.

The women artisans were distinguished from other WAAFs by the badge of an airscrew worn high up on the left sleeve. They completed their training in a year and were then posted to air depots all over the country. They might find themselves calibrating and installing compasses, installing the electrical wiring in an aircraft, making new parts from scratch or putting in new cylinder-heads or winding armatures.

They were a tough breed these women (in June 1942 the WAAF disciplinary force was gazetted – the Women's Auxiliary Military Police Corps), working in a very rough and almost entirely male world. One of them was Ethel Price, a sturdy Free State girl who had always been more interested in working with her hands than the traditional feminine pursuits of cooking and sewing.

'I wanted to be where it all happened, not as an officer far from the coal-face.

'I first saw an aeroplane when my family was living at Waterval Boven. "How does it stick up in the sky?" I asked my mother.

'"It's got wings," she replied, and that was that. And from that moment I wanted to fly one. In 1940 I was only sixteen, and when my mother went to Johannesburg on a visit I volunteered for the Women's Volunteer Air Force.* I knew I couldn't fly, because my eyes weren't very good, but I could be a mechanic. I liked working with my hands.

'Besides I was very patriotic. South Africa was my country, and I was Jewish. I had a girlfriend who pasted up Hitler's portrait in the passage of her home and she told me she couldn't be friends with me any more because I was Jewish. I said to her: "You can do what you like, but South Africa's my country, and we're at war, and that means I'm at war."

'When my mother came back she told the authorities I was under age. I took it very badly, but there was nothing I could do. I wasn't quite eighteen in June 1942 when I signed on again, in Johannesburg. Because I wasn't twenty-one, I still had to get my parents' permission, but this time I was clever: I wrote to the Orange Free State Command Headquarters and asked them to help me get my father to sign. They went down to his shop and he had a major talking in one ear and a captain in another, and at last he signed. So I took the oath of allegiance and became an artisan airwoman. I wasn't interested in becoming an officer: I went in as an airwoman and I wanted to come out as an airwoman. I was good with my hands, they were very strong, and I knew I could work with steel.

'First came WAAF camp at Valhalla, then basic technical training at 77 Air School in Edward Street, Pretoria. We did woodwork, which I

* Later the Women's Auxiliary Air Force (WAAF).

wasn't interested in, and then the bit that I really liked, learning to dismantle and reassemble different types of aero engines; timing the camshaft and the crankshaft, timing the firing order of the pistons, timing the inlet and exhaust valves and adjusting and testing the various gaps: I learnt how to connect up the induction manifold and exhaust tubes and fit the magnetic harnesses.

'We also had to learn aerodrome procedures – windsocks, control tower, runways, signals, night flare-paths and general care and daily inspections on operational aircraft and engines. And I nearly got to pilot a plane, because part of our training was to start them up and taxi them about ready for take-off. We also learnt how to fit and make new parts. It was a very intensive course, learning in one year what you would normally do in five years. But it was wartime, and they needed the men up north, and we would be taking their place. A lot of women couldn't take the pace, but I was fine: I was doing what I loved.

'We lived in long barracks, and we airwomen had our own mess at Wonderboom. We had spare time, too. We'd walk the seven miles into Pretoria or catch a coal-lorry or the *Wag 'n Bietjie* train from 1 Air Depot to Pretoria.

'That was where my first position was after I had finished training – 1AD, Roberts Heights and then to 3AD [Brooklyn Air Station].* I worked on Cheetah 9 and 10 engines and also Ansons. You had to be tough to survive. I was on the assembly line, and I had to open the packing-cases sent on the Liberty Lend-Lease scheme, getting the engines out full of their grease protective covering and getting them cleaned up. I replaced or remade any broken parts and checked the engine and adjusted it if necessary. Then my mate and I got it over to the aircraft that was being built up by the airframe people. We all worked in teams of sixteen, each of us paired with another, usually a man. There were airframe teams, hydraulics, instruments, electricians, armourers, propellers and engine teams, which was me.

'It was hard work, but I loved it. It used to take us five days to put together a plane from beginning to end. We worked under incredible pressure. First of all, you knew that if you made a mistake, the pilot would go in. He might not always be dead, but let's say there would be a problem. So our work was always checked by a technical officer and then another, more senior. They checked not only to see if the work had been done properly but to see if there was any sabotage. And because of the sabotage thing, we had to go up in the plane that we had been working on with the pilot. If you've sabotaged a plane and it's likely to go in with you on board, you wouldn't be in a hurry to fly in it, would you?

---

* Now Ysterplaat Air Force Base.

Ethel Price, a WAAF aero-mechanic 1942–1945, doing a man's job and liking it. At the end of the war most of these women lost their jobs. (Ethel Price)

'We girls were as strong as oxen. I had biceps on me that I had to hide, not big muscles but rolling muscles. The Cheetah engine weighed seven hundred and fifty pounds and it had to be moved across the floor. We weren't supposed to push them on our own, but we did, often. I used to swing on the cranes like Tarzan. It was very heavy work, and you stood all day. And you had to hunker down on your heels when you worked on the bottom cylinders of a radial engine.

'I had calluses on my hands; they were pretty tough. Even if you weren't particularly strong at the beginning, you became strong. We were navvies. And you don't mess about with a navvy. I never really used my strength unless I had to. If I hit a bloke I knocked him out. I got out of a couple of situations by giving a good punch and leaving the chap out for the count.

'We girls wore plain khaki overalls when we were working, with green berets so that our hair didn't get caught in anything. It wasn't very prepossessing: the beret was a floppy thing and you could hardly see whether we had any hair. I used to wear a khaki shirt and a pair of trousers underneath because it was quite easy to get a rip if you got too close to an engine, and I didn't want to expose myself to anybody.

'The men found it very difficult to accept us, and it was particularly bad with us girls who were artisans. They sneered at us. But the chaps who worked with us eventually respected us. Anyway, we were expected to work like men. I found that when chaps came to us from other branches of the military or when they came back from Up North, they hadn't ever done anything serious. They had never built up an engine from the sump up to the prop shaft. They had only done replacements, plugs and cylinder-heads and running repairs. They had never done a proper overhaul. When they saw a woman working on an engine it really shook them.

'Eventually the men became protective. They teased the hell out of me. I had a hundred fathers. Every time I got myself a date it had to be vetted. They used to follow me, and if they didn't like what the man was doing, they'd collar him and say: "Don't you take Ethel out again!" There was a lot of camaraderie.

'One day we had a call from Lyttelton Air Station. There was a problem with an engine that needed a new cylinder-head. They asked for a mechanic to go down, because for some reason they couldn't have the engine removed and they needed the plane and the engine.

'The sergeant-major called me into his office and said: "I'm sending you down to Lyttleton."

'"Why me?" I asked.

'"First," he said, "your fingers are small enough; and secondly, you know what you are doing and I trust you to do the right thing." So I was taken down to Lyttelton with my tool box and my timing gear and all the rest of it and I was deposited outside the hangar.

'"You sent for a mechanic to replace a cylinder-head on an Anson. Can you show me where it is and what you want done?"

'And this chap says: "But you're a woman."

'"Yes," I said, stating the obvious.

'"But you're not an air mechanic?" he asked.

'"Oh, yes, I am an air mechanic. I'm an aero-engine artisan," I replied.

'"But you're a woman," he said again.

'"That cuts no ice," I said. "Let me telephone my superiors at 1AD Engine Repair Shop if you don't believe me." So I did, he spoke to the

Working on aircraft engines. The women had to be physically fit to handle the heavy machinery. All work was checked twice to prevent sabotage. (South African National Museum of Military History)

sergeant-major, and then without saying anything he took me to the working platform.

'I took off the cylinder-head and replaced it and retimed the engine. I was there for about an hour and a half with a whole crowd of spectators who couldn't believe their eyes. I was enjoying myself. I put new valves in and I tightened everything up and retimed the engine and valves that I had replaced. I put all the tubes back; and when I got down I said to no one in particular, "Please sign my chit." I laughed for days afterwards.

'Although I never had any difficulty with my work, I had problems with my partners. No sooner did I acquire a good partner than I lost him, because he would be sent Up North. Then I'd have to retrain. With one man, Du Plessis, we knew exactly what to do, and it took us half a day to do our work on the assembly line. Then he went off and I got this chap from the RAF, and it took us two days to do one plane. That held up the assembly line. Eventually I got him down to one day, but some men just never learnt.

'We women begged to be allowed to go Up North, but we weren't allowed to. It caused a lot of ill-feeling. Smuts told us that every woman working at home freed two men for Up North, so I suppose it was a compliment. Eventually we were told that we could go Up North in an administrative position, pushing pencils. Naturally we weren't interested.'

• Interview 1991

In 1945 Ethel married an RAF man and went to live with him in Britain as a British 'war bride'. He was reluctant for her to continue with her work as an aero-mechanic, and on her return to South Africa her application for employment with South African Airways was turned down.

CHAPTER

41

'Those are your orders'

Capt Patrick Maxwell, taking in the white flag, 21 June 1942

The Union looked anxiously to the north in the opening months of 1942. And with cause. Severely shaken by the losses at Sidi Rezegh and by the continuing ferocity of the stop-start desert war, plagued at home by an active 'fifth column' and hardly comforted by the information emerging from the trial of Robey Leibbrandt and his fellow conspirators and by the growing number of dead, evident almost daily in the roll of honour in newspapers, they wondered what was going to happen next.

All seemed dark. Japanese forces swept through Malaya and Java and captured Rangoon. Worse, Singapore fell and Malta was almost literally being blasted out of the water. We invaded Madagascar, but that was not enough to divert the grim news from anybody. On the Russian front the Germans invaded the Crimea, and in North Africa the 8th Army simply couldn't get the better of Rommel no matter how hard it tried.

The bitterly contested Gazala Line, running for forty miles from Gazala in the north to Bir Hakeim (defended by the 1st Free French Brigade) in the south had eventually fallen. Thirty-five miles to the west of Gazala along the Via Balbia the road ran past the Solaro Escarpment and through Fortress Tobruk before turning farther west by Bardia, Sidi Barrani, Mersa Matruh and El Alamein to Alexandria.

Tobruk was a symbol; besides, it had a good harbour, vast supplies of stores and a vital water-filtration plant. The 2nd SA Division under the command of 39-year-old Maj-Gen H B Klopper had been moved into Tobruk on 7 February. 'Tobruk must be held and the enemy must *not* be allowed to invest it,' signalled the C-in-C, Gen Claude Auchinleck, to Lt-Gen Ritchie, OC 8th Army. As the exhausted and defeated 8th Army poured westward, much of it went through Tobruk.* As the situation

* The Gazala Gallop. Surprisingly few men were lost, considering the exhaustion of the men, the speed with which they were retreating and their numbers. All the same, it was a rout.

deteriorated, Ritchie was reluctantly given permission to allow Tobruk to become 'isolated'.

Theoretically Tobruk might have survived the approaching storm. Within its thirty-mile perimeter there were more than thirty-five thousand men, two thousand vehicles, nearly a million and a half gallons of petrol, enough food for three months and 130 000 rounds of 25-pounder ammunition.

But the newly promoted commander, Maj-Gen Klopper also had to contend with an anti-tank ditch that had silted up, large gaps in the minefields, no support from the Desert Air Force (its bases, now far to the west, were beyond fighter range) and crucially no anti-tank guns. By 18 June the perimeter was invested and Tobruk was completely isolated.

At first light on 20 June Rommel attacked along the south-eastern perimeter, a ferocious attack that cleft right through the 2/5th Mahrattas, spread out and, bypassing 11th Indian Infantry Brigade Headquarters, made for the airfield, which it captured by 4 p.m., and Tobruk harbour itself three hours later.

As dusk fell Klopper, in the western part of Tobruk, was a shaken man. Hampered by his decision earlier that day to destroy signalling equipment, he nonetheless managed to get out a message to 8th Army in the early hours of the 21st. 'Am sending mobile troops out tonight. Not possible to hold tomorrow. Mobile troops nearly nought. Enemy captured vehicles. Will resist to last man and round.'

For the most part the men in the western part of the perimeter had not had a chance to fight. They readied themselves for battle. But as dawn came Klopper sent out the white flag.

History has ignored the man who bore the white flag. He was Capt Patrick Maxwell of the Umvoti Mounted Rifles, a regiment he had been associated with since 1924. At 6 a.m. on the morning of 21 June 1942 a telephone rang in his company HQ:

'We knew Tobruk was going to fall. We certainly knew we would be stranded because of the withdrawal from the Gazala Line. The regiment had various duties on defences and the mined areas. We were on the western edge of the perimeter with one of our platoons guarding "C" Gap near the sea.*

'We didn't get much news – there was little communication – but obviously we knew the Germans had penetrated the perimeter on the 20th. By that time we hadn't seen Gen Klopper for two weeks. We

* There were several gaps in the defences of Tobruk to allow the defenders to come and go without entering minefields.

really only heard snatches of what had happened early on the morning of the 21st.

'At 06h00 that morning, with smoke billowing from the town to our east, the telephone rang. The adjutant answered it. It was our commanding officer, Lt-Col Guy L'Estrange. John Crooks put down the phone and looked at me. The Colonel had instructed him to order me to take in the white flag on behalf of Maj-Gen Klopper.

'"What the hell has happened?" I asked. I was flabbergasted, and so was everyone round me. Then I said: "Why should I take in the flag and not a staff officer?" There were enough of them about.

'"Those are your orders," I was told, and I had to comply. It was the worst day of my life. I felt numb and angry at being given those orders.

Capt Patrick Maxwell, Umvoti Mounted Rifles, before leaving for North Africa in 1940. He carried the white flag at Tobruk and came home five and a half years after he went to war. (Patrick Maxwell)

'I had a couple of bedsheets with me. I took one and, with my orderly, I got into a staff car* and drove out through "C" Gap towards the Italians.† I was very tense; and after a few miles we came under heavy machine-gun fire. We stopped the car and got out. I took the white sheet and waved it. I was ashamed to do it, but I wouldn't have liked to have been killed at that stage.

'Two young Italian soldiers came running towards us. We held up our hands and I beckoned to them and told them I wanted to see one of their officers. They were somewhat bemused, but they got into the car and directed me to their company headquarters. I was greeted by a charming Italian officer, who expressed great surprise that I had come to surrender Tobruk. Naturally, he said, I would have to wait until more senior officers could get to his HQ.

'I waited about an hour. It was agonising. Then I saw a convoy of vehicles coming towards us with flags flying. I was taken and introduced to Gen Ascoli of the Trento Division. He too expressed surprise that I was surrendering Tobruk. "Where was the RAF?" he asked me. Then he questioned my authority to surrender Tobruk.

---

* Not a wireless van as previous reports have stated.
† The lines of Trento Division, XXI Italian Corps.

'"You must accept my bona fides as a British officer," I told him and then, at about 07h30* I formally surrendered Tobruk in Gen Klopper's name.

'There was nothing more to be done. Still feeling numb, I asked to be permitted to return to my old company headquarters and I was allowed to do so, accompanied by one Italian and one German officer.

'It was a sad scene when I got back, with most of the company gone. The few that were left came back with me to the Italian lines – I could not face being in the Fortress any longer with what I had had to do that day. My only comfort was that my sad duty had helped to save the lives of men who would have otherwise been senselessly sacrificed.'

- Interview 1991

Altogether Rommel suffered 3 360 German casualties between 26 May and 21 June. Winston Churchill was in Washington when he received the news. 'This was one of the heaviest blows I can recall during the war,' he wrote in his *History of the Second World War*. 'Not only were the military effects grim, but it affected the reputation of British arms ... Defeat is one thing, disgrace is another.' Capt Maxwell remained a prisoner of war until 26 March 1945, and returned to Durban two months later. His story has remained untold until now. 'I remained quiet about my part at the fall of Tobruk because I was ashamed,' he said. 'Some blamed the South Africans for the fall, but Gen Klopper was a sitting duck, as we all were.'

* Not 04h00, 05h45 or 08h00 as previously reported.

CHAPTER

42

'A miracle in the desert'

Lt Samler Gordon-Brown, Tobruk, 21 June 1942

The news that Tobruk had surrendered slowly filtered through to the men. Most of them had seen the columns of smoke rising from the battered town; few thought it was the end. As the morning of the 21st dawned, they checked their arms, deployed behind sangars and in the flat terrain and got ready for the battle they were sure they would fight that day.

But the battle was over for most of them before it had even begun. The news of the surrender passed from incredulous soldier to soldier. Ordered to break up their arms some men wept as they smashed their weapons on the stony ground. Then the rounding-up began. A few men escaped, like Sgt F J 'Paddy' Walker, who was rounded up with the others (he recalls hearing the skirl of pipes cutting a swathe through the still air: a British army Highland regiment, the last to lay down their arms, marching into the prison camp in perfect order with bagpipes playing). After four days they moved on to the camp at Derna, from which they escaped. Two months later they reached safety. His story appeared in the *Sunday Times* three months after the fall of Tobruk.

Most of the confused soldiers were rounded up during the day, winkled out of caves and off mine-strewn beaches, from wadis and in the open. Penned behind wire, some of the South African soldiers had to cope not only with the shock of the surrender and their new status as prisoners of war but with the gibes of British troops. The Aussies held Tobruk for months, they said; the South Africans under Klopper had simply given it away.

After some understandably confused reports of the disaster, more or less accurate stories on the fall of Tobruk filled the pages of every South African newspaper. The 2nd SA Division was gone and no one could quite appreciate the scale of the disaster. But the people whom the news most affected, of course, were the families of the men. Many

Lt Samler Gordon-Brown (left) with Capt Reg Tickton, ready to entrain for Durban in June 1941. (Samler Gordon-Brown)

didn't even know that their menfolk were in Tobruk; but all wondered what had happened to them. Captured, escaped, missing or dead – they had no way of knowing. It took nearly a month for the Defence Force to compile a grim four-page roll, and even then it was no indication of what had happened to the troops.

'The Department of Defence regrets to announce the casualties in the following list. Amendments to and reclassification of casualties appearing in this Roll will be notified by telegram to the next of kin immediately information is received from OFFICIAL sources … next of kin are … requested not to regard this Roll as containing the latest information. Official confirmation that a man is a Prisoner of War may be slow in some instances, but relatives will be notified as soon as possible … There is no special significance in the two classifications ie

"Missing, believed prisoner of war" and "Missing". In the one class the position is as stated, and in the other official or other information is awaited ...'

But while families waited in considerable anxiety for news of their men, the men themselves were dealing in different ways with the fact that they were no longer free men. One of these men was Lt Samler Gordon-Brown, attached to Rear Division. He was lying behind a sangar when news was passed down the line that Tobruk had surrendered and that the troops were to destroy their weapons. What happened after that was for him a little miracle in the desert; and it helped him to cope with the tribulations which lay ahead:

'The wadi became home. It was very narrow and with very steep sides, like a river that had spent itself out at sea, with sand at the bottom and a few trees and a strip of deep blue sky. When it opened out there was a nice sandy beach, mined, of course, but there was a path through to the sea if you wanted to bathe.

'The wadi was as near as could be to the middle of Tobruk, and on the whole it was a very safe place – if the Jerry planes came over they would have to be very accurate to hit us. We pitched tents and dug in, and it was as comfortable as it could be under the circumstances.

'Rear Div was sometimes as near to Advance Div as a mile, sometimes as far back as twenty, and it mostly consisted of staff officers who were more or less office wallahs. We also had the postmaster and the paymaster with us. The paymaster was never allowed to go in advance of Rear Div for obvious reasons. All the money was kept in a safe, so when it came to paying, I P de Villiers and officers at Advance Div, I carried the money out to them. There were two lieutenants in charge of the safe and the money. They had their own trucks and drivers but no other protection.

'The bombardment began in the early hours of the morning. We were fairly safe in the wadi. We saw lots of smoke, and there was a lot of noise, but no information came through to us. In fact no signals had been received since the previous evening. We knew that we had lost the Gazala battle and that Rommel might turn his attention on Tobruk, but I don't think it crossed anyone's mind that we wouldn't be able to hold out.

'Major Guy Nicholson was in charge of Rear Div. Because of the lack of signals, he did not believe the stories he was told later in the day. In the prison camp I was told that the signals were destroyed the night before. If this is so (and I have no personal knowledge of whether that was true or not) then it would seem that the signals were destroyed too early.

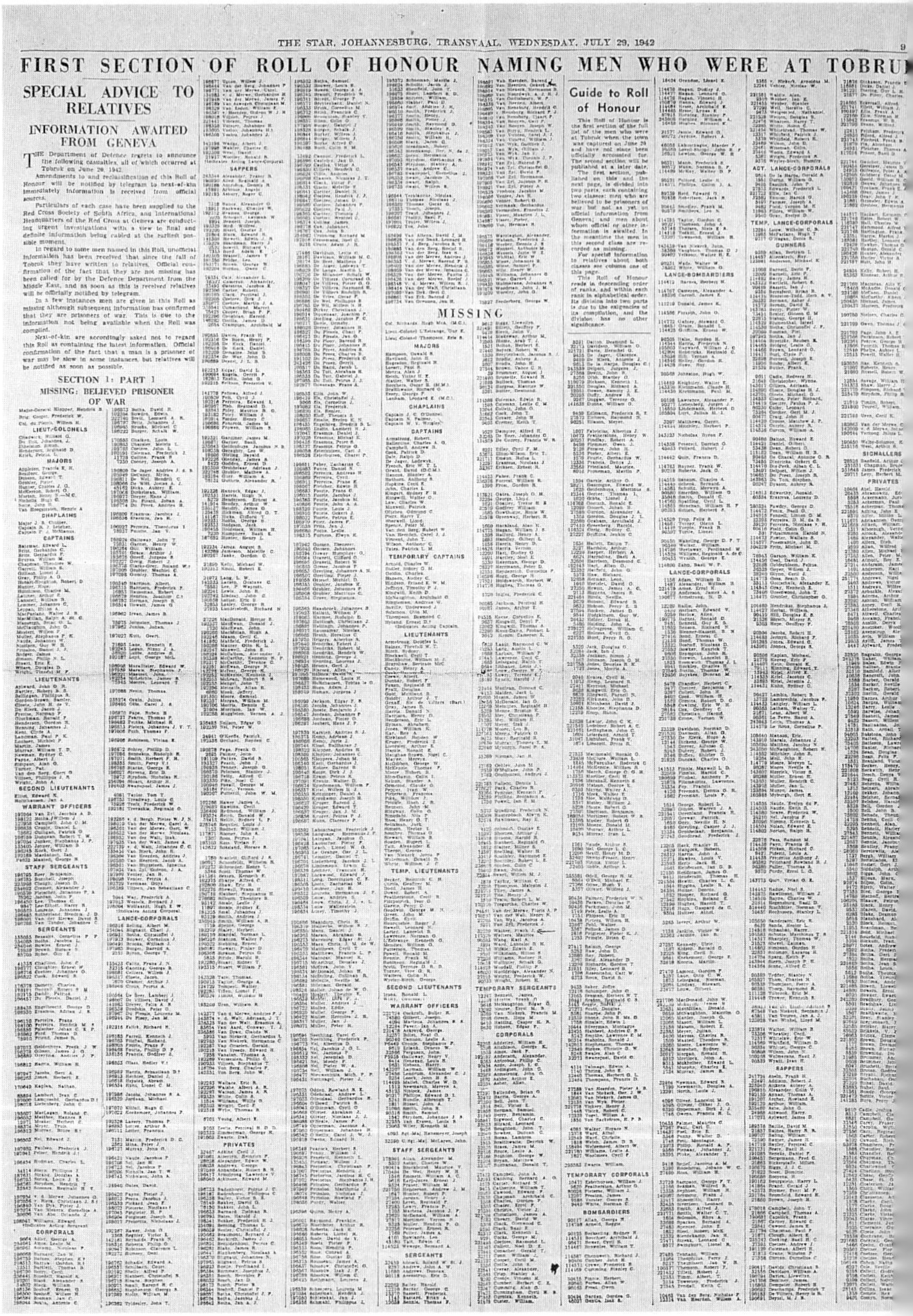

THE STAR, JOHANNESBURG, TRANSVAAL, WEDNESDAY, JULY 29, 1942

FIRST SECTION OF ROLL OF HONOUR NAMING MEN WHO WERE AT TOBRU[K]

SPECIAL ADVICE TO RELATIVES

INFORMATION AWAITED FROM GENEVA

THE Department of Defence regrets to announce the following casualties, all of which occurred at Tobruk on June 20, 1942.

Amendments to and reclassification of this Roll of Honour will be notified by telegram to next-of-kin immediately information is received from official sources.

Particulars of each case have been supplied to the Red Cross Society of South Africa, and International Headquarters of the Red Cross at Geneva are conducting urgent investigations with a view to final and definite information being cabled at the earliest possible moment.

In regard to some men named in this Roll, unofficial information has been received that since the fall of Tobruk they have written to relatives. Official confirmation of the fact that they are not missing has been called for by the Defence Department from the Middle East, and as soon as this is received relatives will be officially notified by telegram.

In a few instances men are given in this Roll as missing although subsequent information has confirmed that they are prisoners of war. This is due to the information not being available when the Roll was compiled.

Next-of-kin are accordingly asked not to regard this Roll as containing the latest information. Official confirmation of the fact that a man is a prisoner of war may be slow in some instances, but relatives will be notified as soon as possible.

SECTION 1: PART 1

MISSING: BELIEVED PRISONER OF WAR

Guide to Roll of Honour

This Roll of Honour is the first section of the full list of the men who were at Tobruk when the town was captured on June 20 and have not since been officially accounted for. The second section will be published at a later date.

The first section, published on this and the next page, is divided into two parts, each containing two classes: men who are believed to be prisoners of war but not as yet on official information from Geneva; and men about whom official or other information is awaited. In the meantime the men in this second class are recorded as missing.

For special information to relatives about both classes see column one of this page.

This Roll of Honour reads in descending order of ranks, and within each rank in alphabetical order. Its division into two parts is due to the exigencies of its compilation, and the division has no other significance.

MISSING

The Tobruk roll of honour – two pages out of four, filled with the names of missing men, a stern contrast to the first South African roll of honour of the Second World War that appeared on 28 February 1941, occupying two centimetres of space. The Tobruk roll of honour was printed in all the main newspapers in the Union on Wednesday, 29 July; the second list appeared nearly a month later, on 19 August 1942.

[TO]BRUK ROLL OF HONOUR: SECOND LIST

[The] Department of Defence regrets to announce the casual[ties in] the following list, which is the second and final list of the [casualti]es which occurred at Tobruk on June 20, 1942.

[Am]endments to and reclassification of casualties appearing [in this] Roll will be notified by telegram to the next-of-kin [immedi]ately information is received from OFFICIAL sources.

[Part]iculars of each case have been supplied to the Red Cross [Society] of South Africa and International Headquarters of the [Red Cro]ss at Geneva are conducting urgent investigations with a [view to] final and definite information being cabled at the earliest [possible] moment.

[In r]egard to some men named in this Roll information has [been r]eceived that since the fall of Tobruk they have written to [...]. Official confirmation in all such cases has been called [for].

[In a] few instances names of men appear as missing although [rece]nt information has confirmed that they are Prisoners of [War. Th]is is due to the information not being available when the [Roll was] compiled.

[Next]-of-kin are accordingly requested not to regard this Roll [as conta]ining the latest information. Official confirmation that [a man i]s a Prisoner of War may be slow in some instances but [they] will be notified as soon as possible.

[Ther]e is no special significance in the two classifications, i.e., ["...] believed prisoner of war" and "Missing." In the one [case the] position is as stated, and in the other official or other [informat]ion is awaited. Investigation and examination proceeds [urgently] and constantly with a view to final and definite classi[fication].

(Continued on next page)

'We certainly didn't know that the Germans had broken through. Smoke swept over Tobruk in a thick cloud and the noise of shooting and shelling grew louder and louder. No one seemed perturbed. But I felt that something was wrong. I went to Major Nicholson and asked if I could go out of the wadi and find out what was happening, but permission was refused. So, about 10 a.m. I sent a police corporal, a very fine man, to take a look, on the pretext of collecting rations. When he came back he was very shaken. His report was grim. The NAAFI was in flames and he couldn't get through to the South African food depot; his truck had come under shell fire. "I can't go back there, sir." That was the first real intimation we had that there was something seriously wrong.

'I went to Nicholson a second time, but again he refused me permission to leave the wadi, so this time I sent a sergeant. I had learnt early in my army career always to have extra food on hand, and I kept 48 hours' rations in my truck for everyone, but no one knew that. "Take no risks," I told the sergeant. "They won't believe what has happened. I want you to find out exactly what the situation is." He also came back a shaken man. There was fighting all over the place, he said; the Germans had broken through and he believed they were in Tobruk itself.

'I got into my car and was about to drive away when my driver came up to me. "You're taking my car, sir," he said. I shook his hand and he came with me. He didn't flinch. I took my field-glasses and we drove to the top of the wadi. The ground sloped down a bit there, and I could clearly see where the fighting had been. We could see a long way, although not the perimeter or where the Germans had broken through. Our previous camp had been on the area where the tanks were. They came in behind the smokescreen and were very difficult to see, but I could make out where they were because they were sending up white Very lights. The NAAFI was in full view of where I was, and it was very plain that it had been overrun. We drove up to the British food depot and the staff sergeant there said: "Sir, something's happened. The South African food depot has been overrun. Our colonel went off to see if he could find out what was happening and he's gone for two hours now."

'We must have spent an hour to an hour and a half there, sitting on bales of food, looking at everything through my field-glasses. There was smoke drifting over what had been an aerodrome, and I knew there was no defence there. There didn't seem to be any panic. The only people I had seen running the entire day had been down in the wadi. Two British soldiers came running down. They had no shirts on and they were very shaken, having been under artillery fire all day. I said to them: "If you go straight on, there's a minefield in front of you, and if you get through that and want to continue, you'll have to swim the Mediterranean." I took them to my orderly and told him to give them a cup of coffee and some food.

'We waited at the food depot until the sun was beginning to go down, packed up some food and returned to our headquarters. Major Nicholson had still not received any signals and still had difficulty in believing what I told him. Soon after I got back a Scottish major arrived to take control of the camp, there being no senior officers with us, only staff officers carrying out their duties, and they had no idea of what to do. One of the first orders he gave me was to destroy the money. I knew the men were prepared for that because a few days before the paymaster had assured me that he had everything ready to burn the money. He had applied to General Klopper, when it looked as if we were about to be invested to get the money out, but he had been told to keep the money where it was.

'The Scottish major told us to vacate the camp. That was the beginning of the very end for us. We moved to a line above another wadi. I spent most of that night collecting stragglers from the beaches. On the beach in front of our wadi I met a young British padre, no more than a boy, and ushered him off the beach too. We could clearly hear the MTBs going up and down near the coast, and I prayed to God we could get them, but it never happened, and all the boats were sunk. There was simply no escape.

'I took all the stragglers with me into the line at the top of the escarpment. The SA Police were lining the escarpment, and I was instructed to take over three sangars* – the only three on the skyline. I knew exactly where the first three shells would fall. Sangars are horrible things, and to my mind exceedingly dangerous. In the flat desert they stand out and make excellent targets. I passed one once, full of German and Italian dead. So I actually pulled the wall down a bit and said to the men: "Look, spread out, we're not going to be finished by a shell."

'The police were magnificent men. Each of them was lying down in line with a big stone in front of him clutching a tommy-gun. If the Germans had sent an aeroplane over they would have blotted the lot of us out. But as it turned out, it was very quiet, no shooting, no shelling. I only had one lot of ammunition on me, so I wouldn't have been very effective if a battle had taken place round me.

'Even as late as dawn it didn't occur to us that we had surrendered. We felt no fear, merely expectation of a battle we were sure would take place. The word "surrender" was never uttered.

---

* A stone breastwork.

'As I was lying on the ground waiting for action, a police officer near me told me that the white flag had gone in, and asked me to pass the message down the line. Nothing dramatic, just a message passed from man to man. I believe the white flag went in about 4 a.m. by Major Maxwell, a good chap who was desperately upset about it.

'It took some time for the surrender to sink in; there was a sense of disbelief, even of anti-climax, for we hadn't fired a shot. Then we were told to destroy our arms. I had a compass with me. With a compass I can go anywhere. I picked up a stone and I cried as I smashed it. That was my surrender, because without the compass I could go nowhere. Then I took my tommy-gun to pieces and threw them out into the desert and the rest I hurled down the wadi. There wasn't much else I could do.

'When we had finished with our weapons, we were told to clear off down into the wadi as quickly as possible. It was safer there, and when the Germans came there could be no accident with men wandering about above.

'It was very hot on top, and I had been up all night; suddenly I felt very tired, so I sat under some shade in the wadi. We waited. Eventually the Germans came and we were rounded up and taken in a truck to the top of the wadi and told to walk to the prisoner-of-war cage. I had no friends with me, and I decided to find myself a suitable place to sit down and wait for the Germans to take me to the cage in a truck. I was not going to walk there. As I crossed the Via Mussolini a German staff-car passed me and a head emerged from the window with much brass and a red band on the cap. It was Brigadier A A Hayton, Colonel of the Rand Light Infantry, a man I had always admired and liked. He was being taken off for interrogation. He greeted me, and I felt a little better.

'I shouted back to Brigadier Hayton and I stumbled blindly on into the desert. My brain wasn't working properly. There were no tracks and no shade, and I didn't know where I was going. I just walked straight on for about three hundred yards. It's a terrific shock when you're taken prisoner. I was extremely tired and extremely bloody-minded. They could damn well pick me up or I would stay there for ever. I had a heavy two-gallon can of dirty water, and eventually I said to myself: "For God's sake sit down and pull yourself together. Try and make your brain work."

'I sat down with the can of water and just waited. After about half an hour a British officer came up out of the wadi and wandered across the Via Mussolini. He saw me and walked towards me. When he got nearer I recognised him as the padre I had met on the beach.

'All I had with me when I was captured was a haversack with a toothbrush and a razor in it. I left it with the water and I walked over to meet him. I have never seen a man so upset as he was. He wasn't crying, he was utterly desolate.

'He kept saying: "I've been negligent, I have failed in my duty."

'"Come on," I said, "what's the trouble?"

'"I haven't got any equipment."

'I thought he meant his chalice and so on. So I said: "Don't worry, you can use a plate or an old mug, just make them as clean as you can, it doesn't matter. Hymn-books and prayer-books, they don't matter, hold your own service and make your own prayers." Nothing I said comforted him. He had no Bible, and without a Bible he was lost. I began to get worried, for time was passing and I was expecting to be picked up any minute. "What can one do with this man," I thought, "he's really in a very bad way."

'All the time we were talking I kept my eye on the desert, because I didn't want someone to come and machine-gun us. Then something in the sand caught my attention, and I bent down to see what it was. I wanted to give myself time to think of what to do as much as anything else. There was something small in the sand, between the padre's feet and about two inches in front of his toes. Without thinking I put my hand over it and saw it was the corner of a book. It had a mustard-coloured binding, and there was only one book of that kind: a soldier's New Testament.

'I handed it to the padre. The change in him was miraculous. He looked at me and said: "Now I'm armed, now I can do my duty." He went on his way rejoicing, and I never saw him again.

'It wasn't my prayer that brought us to the Bible. It was his: it led him to that point. It was only after a week that I began to understand that it had been a miracle in the desert. ’

• Interview 1990

CHAPTER

43

'Now presumed to have fallen'

Breaking the hard news, 22 June 1942

The day after the fall of Tobruk no one really knew what had happened; only the fact that Tobruk had fallen. Field Marshal Smuts, Prime Minister and Commander-in-Chief issued an official statement on 22 June:

> 'The fall of Tobruk has involved the capture by the enemy of substantial numbers of the South African forces in Egypt.
>
> 'The exact composition of the South African forces which formed part of the Tobruk garrison is not yet known. The general situation relating to the whereabouts of individual South African units as the result of the withdrawal of the Eighth Army is confused, and it may be some days before detailed information will be available. As soon as this more complete information is available I shall issue a further statement.
>
> 'In the meantime it can be stated that the South African troops in Tobruk held to the last the defences in the Tobruk perimeter allocated to them. In this they upheld the fighting tradition of the South African Army.
>
> 'While we should not minimise the seriousness of the losses the South Africans in the North have thus suffered, there remains in the field a strong and well-equipped and experienced fighting force and the larger part of the total South African forces sent to Egypt. These units, together with the reinforcements which South Africa will now provide, will play a vital part in the defence of Egypt and in the ultimate wresting of Libya from the control of the Axis.
>
> 'South Africa can take it and South Africa will seek retribution.'

This is what the people in the Union read when they opened their newspapers on 22 June 1942:

TOBRUK FALLS TO AXIS ASSAULT

DEFENCES PIERCED BY VIOLENT ATTACK

NUMBER OF SOUTH AFRICANS IN GARRISON

LARGER PART OF FORCE INTACT

THE CAPTURE OF TOBRUK by Axis Forces was announced in German and Italian communiques yesterday. They claimed the capture of more than 25,000 prisoners.

To-day's Middle East communique says there is no further news from Tobruk, "which must be presumed to have fallen."

From enemy accounts it appears that the fortress was stormed on Saturday by an overwhelming armoured force which broke through the defences from the east and south-east. With divisional headquarters and the town occupied, the garrison surrendered.

Field Marshal Smuts, Commander-in-Chief of the South African Forces, in a statement issued to-day, says "a substantial number of the South African Forces in Egypt" has been captured by the enemy in Tobruk.

There remains, however, "the larger part of the total South African Forces sent to Egypt," and these, he says, with reinforcements which the union will now provide, will continue to take part in the defence of Egypt.

Although commentators admit that the loss of Tobruk is a heavy blow, it is pointed out that powerful forces still bar the way to Suez, and the Eighth Army, in strong positions on the frontier, is prepared for Rommel's next blow.

ENEMY ACCOUNT OF ACTION

Sapa's war correspondent says it may now be revealed that a considerable body of South African troops was among the Tobruk garrison which is now presumed to have fallen. Their fate is unknown and in the absence of any account of yesterday's happenings the possibility that some escaped must not yet be abandoned.

Apart from the South Africans, the garrison was composed of various United Kingdom and Indian units.

There are no reports of the fighting which preceded the fall of Tobruk, but passing ships report heavy explosions which must indicate that the troops in the garrison were making every effort to destroy as much material as possible to prevent it falling into enemy hands.

There has been no direct contact with the garrison commander since 8 o'clock yesterday morning, but fighting all through yesterday has been reported.

Enemy claims of the number of prisoners taken must be treated cautiously.

The mobile British forces which have been operating south of Tobruk were apparently not in a position to engage the enemy forces which smashed through the perimeter defences.

GERMAN ACCOUNT

A German High Command communique yesterday announcing the capture of Tobruk says: "German and Italian troops acting on General Rommel's orders, yesterday stormed the greater part of the strongly fortified fortress of Tobruk. Thereupon this morning a British officer bearing a white flag of truce offered the surrender of the town to the staff of an Italian corps.

"So far more than 25 000 prisoners, including several generals, have been taken and quantities of arms, war materials and supplies which cannot yet be estimated."

The German Radio last night gave the following account of the battle for Tobruk:

"In most bitter fighting in torrid heat, the resistance of the British Eighth Army was broken and the advance of Axis troops against Via Balboa began.

"One part of the Eighth Army was encircled in the Tobruk area. An attempt by the British forces to break out of the ring which was supported by strong tank forces was repelled. German and Italian troops then began the assault of the fortress with decisive support from the air.

"The Luftwaffe played a large part in the capture of Tobruk. Numerous bombers in ceaseless attacks on the fortress wrought great destruction in fortifications and other military works in the port and town. The air above Tobruk was dominated by German fighters."

To-day's Italian communique states "the occupation of Tobruk has been completed and the Axis troops are marching towards the Egyptian frontier". It claims that booty taken includes several hundred guns, several hundred lorries, 100 tanks and large quantities of ammunition, food and fuel.

In the absence of details from Cairo it is perhaps too early to attempt to assess the causes which have cost Britain the loss of this citadel. Certain considerations are however fairly clear. The defences had been loosened to a certain extent to facilitate the flow of supplies to forward areas and it is doubtful if their efficiency could be fully restored in the brief interval allowed.

The attacks seem to have been made with an overwhelming weight of armour, which crashed right through the perimeter from the east and the south-east, where the lines are nearest to the fortress harbour.

The garrison, even after Axis claims which may be exaggerated seems to have been smaller than it was last year. A perimeter of more than 20 miles could not easily be held by 25 000 men, especially against such a massive blow concentrated in a limited space.

DEFENCES BREACHED

Sapa's war correspondent says the attack on Tobruk on Saturday, which was on a bigger scale than anything the enemy attempted last year, began with the aerial bombardment. Then Axis tanks made a breach in the perimeter in the El Adem area, through which infantry followed. Then the tanks attacked again. Rommel sent in two columns supported by tanks – one of them made for divisional headquarters which was established about four miles from the harbour, and the other attacked the town itself.

These points are now clear: Firstly, June 13 was the turning point in the armoured battle of Libya. On that fateful day the Eighth Army suffered a shattering blow when its main remaining armoured strength was trapped in a carefully-prepared enemy anti-tank ambush in the Acroma-El Adem-Knightsbridge triangle.

Secondly, the Eighth Army assembled planes, tanks and guns for the first time comparable in firepower to those of the enemy, but not in sufficient numbers. This was particularly the case regarding the General Grant tanks and six-pounder anti-tank guns compared with the German Mark III tanks and 88 milimetre dual-purpose anti-tank and anti-aircraft guns.

Thirdly, the enemy's advantage in manpower enabled him to use motorised infantry to press home any tactical success in the fairly even armoured battle.

CHAPTER

44

'It was all very hush-hush'

Lt-Col Alastair Macmillan and the Flail Tank, 1942

The army in North Africa was a depressed one. Its numbers had been depleted by attrition and the loss of prisoners, and the Desert Fox, Erwin Rommel, seemed invincible despite his setback at Alem Halfa. Now the British and Commonwealth troops regrouped on the Alamein line, and waited.

Clearly something was in the air. Precisely what it was only Bernard Montgomery and his immediate staff knew. South Africans at home scanned the papers daily for news of successes. There were none.

They were diverted by the constant subversion of the Ossewabrandwag: the main telephone cable to Johannesburg from Bloemfontein was damaged by acid, electricity to Vereeniging, Springs, Potchefstroom and Klerksdorp was disrupted, and in a well-planned and co-ordinated effort trains were held up in an attempt to blow up the power-station at Delmas (all disrupting vital war industry).

A succession of robberies and holdups also took place: £20 000 was stolen at Johannesburg station, £15 000 in Pretoria. The funds were used to pay for the subversion. Emergency Regulations were promulgated, providing for trial by special courts in cases of sabotage, and in June 1942 the Stormjaer Treason Trial opened in the Magistrate's Court in Johannesburg, with twenty-two policemen included among the fifty-one accused.

It was revealed that in the Transvaal alone there were over eight thousand Stormjaers organised in fifteen battalions. One battalion of six hundred men was recruited entirely from the South African, Railway and Traffic Police. They were determined to overthrow the government.

The Russian defence of Stalingrad began, and it was announced that eighty ships had been lost in South African waters in 1942 alone.

Up North in the workshops of 44 R&H Base Tank Workshop at Alexandria* a largely South African invention was about to make military history and to save lives in the forthcoming action.

Just before the battle of El Alamein, the workshop was asked to carry out a very unusual and highly secret task. Under the eyes of Major A H Macmillan 2nd I/C 44 R&H Base Tank Workshop Unit, it produced a weapon that confounded the enemy when it was first revealed:

'Early in August 1942 a major of a South African armoured car unit walked into my unit.† He took out a box of Springbok cigarettes from a pocket and showed me the back. On it were a series of straight-line sketches. "Do you think you can make this?" he asked me. It was a device for exploding mines: a forked attachment projecting from the front of a tank. Within the fork there was a revolving drum to which flails were attached. At the end of each flail there was a weight to beat the ground as the tank moved forward, exploding mines in front of it as it went through a minefield.

'I told the major that I thought it would work. It was a good idea, but of course it would have to be tested.

'We had been operational for only just over one year. The unit arrived in Egypt in May 1941 and was situated in a large empty warehouse in an outer section of Alexandria harbour. That was all there was: a large, empty warehouse with a splendid view of the *Luftwaffe* dropping bombs over Alexandria harbour. Before we began work, in conjunction with a small unit of the British Royal Electrical and Mechanical Engineers' [REME], we had to make equipment suitable for lifting tanks and scrounge tools and machinery necessary for repair work. We also had to explore sources of tank spare parts.

'There were hundreds of unserviceable tanks, Matildas and Crusaders, brought to us from the desert, most of them damaged in the retreat to the Alamein Line.‡ From the time we arrived at the warehouse until just after the battle of Alamein we worked seven days a week without a break. Each tank had to be taken to bits and entirely rebuilt. New engines from a pool of rebuilt engines would be put in, an undamaged turret from another tank, new gearboxes and transmission assemblies. An entirely new tank was made from overhauled parts from a common pool.

'We didn't need any more excitement than we already had, but it came our way anyway. HMS *Queen Elizabeth* and HMS *Warspite* were seriously damaged at their moorings in Alexandria harbour by miniature

---

* 44 R&H Base Tank Workshop was raised in the Union early in 1941, largely comprising railwaymen, 494 of whom were killed on active service with units that included the artillery and the tank workshop.

† 44 R&H Base Tank Workshop Unit.

‡ The Gazala Gallop.

Italian submarines. We were called in, together with a specialist welding team flown from South Africa, to weld large steel plate patches to the damaged bottoms of the two ships to make them seaworthy enough to sail round Africa and then to the USA for extensive repairs.

'Building something entirely new, such as the flail tank, was quite a challenge. We were ordered by GHQ Cairo to get on immediately with a prototype that would be used as a test machine. We were given all the material that we needed.

'First we needed a tank, and we were given a Matilda*. Then we needed lengths of angle-iron for the fork arms, a Ford engine with gear-box, propeller-shaft and differential (for a three-tonner troop-carrier), a specially made long steel drum about 10" in diameter with a short shaft at each end, bearings, and half-inch diameter lengths of steel wire cable with U-bolt attachments for securing the flails in staggered formation along the length and round the circumference of the drum.

'It was all very hush-hush. Although we knew nothing of the battle of Alamein it was obvious to everyone that something was in the air. So, in spite of air raids, which disrupted our work somewhat, and a few men injured by fragments, we built the prototype, besides repairing tanks and making them battleworthy.

'I discovered early that it was not practicable to power the revolving drum from the tank engine, which was needed to propel the tank itself. So the three-tonner Ford engine was housed in a small compartment suspended from the right hand side of the tank, opposite the turret. This compartment was also occupied by the driver who worked the engine turning the drum.

'Our camp was fifteen miles outside Alexandria in the direction of Tobruk, and it was there, in the middle of the desert, that we took the flail tank† for testing, with the help of minefield experts from the Sappers. It took place between high fences of hessian. For the first test "S" mines were buried at a shallow depth in the sand. We all held our breath as the tank moved forward, not least the chap in the compartment outside the tank. We used a short length of trek chain on the end of each flail for this test. To our delight the mines were effectively exploded.‡

---

* By 1942 the Infantry Mk 11 Matilda tank with its three-inch armour and two-pounder turret gun had been superseded by the infuriatingly unreliable Cruiser Mk 6 (the Crusader), by the Light Stuart Mk 1 (the Honey) and by the Infantry Mk 3 (the Valentine), the direct successor to the Matilda, but still not fast enough to match the speed of the German tanks.

† The tank was known at that time as the Durban Mk 11, after Mill Colman's home town.

‡ It later became known as the Scorpion Mk 11. When it was operational the Scorpion moved forward at the rate of 2 mph and the drum revolved at 72/80 revolutions a minute. On hearing of it, Gen Montgomery sent this message: 'My father hath chastised you with whips, but I shall chastise you with Scorpions.'

The 'flail' tank, made in the 44 R&H Base Tank Workshop at Alexandria just before the battle of El Alamein. The drum with flails can be clearly seen. To the rear (left) is the small compartment enclosing the Ford engine for the drum through a propeller-shaft. (Lt-Col A H Macmillan)

The beast in action, moving forward with the drum rotating and flails beating the ground ahead of the tank. (Lt-Col A H Macmillan)

Action over Alexandria harbour. The photograph was taken from the camp of 44 R&H Base Tank Workshop Unit. A continuous wall of ack-ack fire, in square formation, covered all sides of the harbour area. An Italian frogman, tired and hungry, was found outside the camp. (Lt-Col A H Macmillan)

A visit to the tank workshop (and the converted Matilda flail tank) shortly before the Battle of El Alamein by Field Marshal Smuts. On his right is Gen F H Theron, OC Middle East South African Forces, GHQ. On his left is Brig Tope, OC British Technical Unit (Middle East). (Lt-Col A H Macmillan)

The interior of the base tank workshop with the specially made tank lifting equipment in the background. A line of tank frames stands ready for the repair process. (Lt-Col A H Macmillan)

'We made some adjustments, such as replacing the trek chain with a heavy metal ball, and subsequent tests with this new arrangement detonated mines deeper under the sand.

'There was much elation when we were immediately ordered to convert six Matildas, and more if possible, into flail tanks. In fact we managed to convert eight tanks in time for the battle.

'A by-product of the flails beating the ground proved very helpful to the tank itself: dust. It was enveloped in a great cloud of dust that effectively concealed it. It was self-camouflaging.

'After the Alamein bombardment* the troops had to move through minefields. The flail tanks were sent in first to clear safe paths for them, which were immediately staked and taped with white tape and signboards bearing such names as Top Hat, Piccadilly and Churchill.

'Each of the flail-propelling engines fixed to the side of each tank was manned by a volunteer driver, mostly Aussies, in very lightly pro-

* It began at 9.25 p.m. in the 13th Corps sector (occupying the south of the line facing the Brescia, Folgore and Pavia Divisions, the 21st Panzer Division and the Ariete Division) and at 9.40 p.m. in the 30th Corps sector, of which the 1st SA Division was part. It faced its old enemy of Sidi Rezegh, the 15th Panzer Division and the Littorno and Trento Divisions, the Bologna Division slightly to the south of the Miteirya Ridge.

Fully repaired tanks, together with their repair crews, ready for a test run before delivery to fighting units. (Lt-Col A H Macmillan)

tected engine-boxes. The enemy could have had no idea of what was coming across the minefields through the clouds of dust. They directed their fire at these strange objects, and some of the Aussies were killed. But the tanks had helped to clear the way through the minefields, and the infantry, the tanks, the armoured cars and artillery were able to get through safely, thanks in part to the little drawings on the back of a packet of Springbok cigarettes. ’

• Interview 1990

The story of the flail tank (Baron) did not end there. They were used elsewhere in the desert, although by then the Germans knew what they were and the element of surprise was lost. They were also used in France in the landings (by then they were called Scorpions), but they failed to detonate mines buried in tough clay.

In July 1948 a Royal Commission of Awards to Inventors recommended grants totalling £20 000 to the men who had developed the flail tank. Of the eleven men concerned five were South Africans.

CHAPTER

45

'I was never a convinced Nazi'

Karl Heinz Glafke, interned for the duration

By August 1940 nearly four thousand men deemed by the authorities to be a risk to security were in internment camps in South Africa. Two years later, after the subjugation of most of Europe and a war that was still clearly in favour of Germany, the figure was much higher and the authorities were more determined than ever to suppress pro-German sentiment.

In the early days of the war selective internment where there was *prima facie* evidence of subversive activities was the rule. After Italy declared war and allied herself with Nazi Germany, the number of men in the camps rose sharply when the government automatically interned all Italians between the ages of eighteen and sixty living in South Africa. In the end, however, these were the most fortunate: they were released after the capitulation of Italy.

High on the list of suspects, although Russia was one of the Allies and there was a wave of pro-Russian sentiment in the country, were South African citizens who were also communists. They remained in internment camps until 1944/5.

There were five internment camps (as distinct from POW camps) in the country: at Koffiefontein, Jagersfontein, Ganspan, Leeuwkop near Johannesburg and Baviaanspoort outside Pretoria. South African citizens were interned in these camps, together with foreigners. The peak year for the internment of South Africans was in 1942 (it was in November that year that the trial of Leibbrandt began in the Supreme Court in Pretoria).

On the whole they were treated remarkably well, even with sympathy. In retrospect, some of the men interned should never have been there at all.

Responsibility for internments and the administration of the camps, a thankless task in view of the sensitive nature of such matters, first fell under the Minister of Justice, Dr Colin Steyn and from 1940 to 1943 under the Minister of the Interior, Mr H G (Harry) Lawrence.

The camps were regularly visited by officials of the Red Cross. Their job was not easy; for in spite of their efforts on behalf of the internees they were accused of being pro-British and therefore unsympathetic to the prisoners' plight.

One of those prisoners was Karl Glafke, a South African by birth but brought up in Germany. He was arrested in Windhoek in 1942 and spent three years in an internees' camp. He was staunchly pro-German and bitterly opposed to the participation of South Africa in the war; his story was like that of many other internees:

'I came from German stock, so naturally my sympathies were with Germany. But I was also South African by birth, although I had been brought up in Germany. When I came back to South Africa I had been in Germany for seventeen years. I was twenty-two, and I spoke very little English or Afrikaans. But it was rosy here compared with Germany between the wars.

'I had nothing against the Jews. I even worked for a Jew when I got back here, for a Cape Town company called Gesundheit & Gesundheit. On the other hand I worked for a German who had a big business in scrap iron, and he was undoubtedly a big Nazi. Every year he went to the Nazi celebrations at Nuremberg, and when we sent his copper pipes to Germany and Japan I had to sign the loading papers, so naturally people thought that I was a Nazi too.

'I was a member of the German Club (so was Oswald Pirow*) and I paid money every month for health insurance to the National Socialist Party, but I was never a convinced Nazi. We lost the First World War, and when the Second World War started I said to myself: "There are so many nations against Germany, how can we win?" All the same, when South Africa declared war, that was no good. That should not have happened. Many of us felt the same way.

'I moved with my wife and children to Windhoek which, after all, had once been German territory.† Germans living there were not permitted to have radio sets, but, because I was born in South Africa, I was allowed to have one. Naturally I tuned in to Germany. My sympathies were with Germany after all.

'As the war was going badly for Britain, things became tighter with the authorities. We were all watched. One day at the end of August 1942 the police gave me a list of thirty-two questions and told

---

* Former Defence Minister before the Smuts coalition government came in at the beginning of the war. He was an open admirer of the Nazis.

† Germany established a military base in South West Africa in 1884. In 1914 South African troops invaded the country. Less than a year later it was in South African hands. In 1919 the League of Nations gave South Africa a mandate to govern South West Africa. In 1990 South West Africa (Namibia) became independent.

me to answer them. Where were you born, that sort of thing. The last two questions were very difficult to answer. One was: "If you saw a German soldier on the road and he wanted water, would you give it to him?" Well, of course you would give him water, anybody would, so I said "yes".

'The last question was: "Do you want England to win the war or Germany?" My God, what could I say? I had to say Germany.

'Two weeks later, at 2 a.m. on 11 September 1942, the police knocked on my door. It wasn't a surprise: I had been expecting it. I knew both of the policemen who came to take me away. My wife was very upset, but what could she do? I was driven to the police station and taken into a room where a police officer, more English than Afrikaans, was sitting behind a desk. I was left to stand in front of it.

'"Good evening," I said. He did not reply.

"What's this?" he asked, pointing to a badge of the National Socialist Party [Nazi] with the swastika on it that lay on his desk.

'"It's the badge of the Nazi Party," I replied.

'"Ah," he said. Then: "Did you hear the news last night?" Of course I had to say yes, because they knew I had a radio. "What was the news?" he asked. So I told him what I had heard and that I had heard it from London. Of course, I heard it from Germany, but still.

'Then the officer, still sitting, says: "Look here, Glafke, I've got this paper that says you are a member of the German Men's Choir." Yes, I said, it was my hobby. "But the choir sings Nazi songs," he said. I replied that they were folk songs.

'"You are also a member of a German sick fund," he said. That was correct, I said, it was supported by the Nazi Party, but why not? He got to his feet and told me to stand facing the corner with my face to the wall. He told one of the policemen who had come to fetch me that I was to stand there like that until 4 a.m. As soon as he had gone they made me a nice cup of coffee and allowed me to sit down.

'But at 4 a.m. the police put me and eight other men into a van with darkened windows and drove us away. I was not even allowed to say goodbye to my wife.

'I was expecting to be interned, ja. But I was still very upset, being taken from my family and being driven to somewhere I didn't know. Two days later we arrived at Andalusia.*

'The first thing I had to do was fill in a form to let my wife know where I was. Since I was a South African I was entitled to ask why I had been interned. I was shown a piece of paper. "Although he is a

---

* This curiously named internment camp was on land formerly owned by a horse-breeder who imported his stock from Andalusia in Spain. Officially the camp was called Ganspan, near Warrenton, seventy kilometres north of Kimberley.

British subject by birth, all his sympathies are with Germany," it said. And it is also stated that I had supported the Japanese war effort by supplying metal to the Japanese government.

'Andalusia was a very big camp. There were nearly three thousand of us there, men from all over, from Kenya, from Rhodesia, from South West Africa and South Africa, Germans, men from the French Foreign Legion and, of course, a lot of Afrikaners. We became very well organised.

'We lived in pondoks, eight to eleven in a room. My pondok was of corrugated iron on the outside and inside hardboard or wood. There were two halls that could take about a thousand men each. Every morning we marched to keep fit, along a route we set ourselves. We also had our vegetable gardens. We ate three times a day, but most of the food came from our own gardens. Very often officers came from outside to buy our vegetables.

'Once a month we were checked. We had to be compared to our papers so that the authorities could see that each man matched his documents. They would ask us how many children we had, what was our name.

'Sometimes the wives used to come and visit, but that was terrible. It was no good: a small room divided by wife with a chair on either side and you couldn't even touch hands. That was very difficult. It was particularly difficult for my wife, because her father was also interned, in another camp.

'We were organised into groups. I was in *Gruppe Eins* (Group One). We would exercise in our groups, do everything in our groups. We were allowed to wire letters once a week, but they were censored. And I kept a diary, every day of my internment.

'The guards were not unsympathetic. One day a prominent Afrikaner came into the camp. The guards knew who he was. One of the officers said to one of the soldiers: "Take meneer's suitcase," which he did, carrying it to his pondok. In his hand meneer was holding a soccer ball. Inside the soccer ball was all the stuff necessary for a radio. So, with great secrecy, we were able to listen to the radio. We tuned in to Germany every night.

'Then the valves became weak. How were we to replace them? Every morning a man brought milk into the camp. He took it to the kitchen. We went into the kitchen one day.

'"Look, Johnny," we said to him, "here is an electric switch. And here is the water. If one of your hands was to hold the switch and your other hand was put into this bucket of water, do you know what would happen to you?" We explained it very carefully to him, very patiently. "We will do it if you don't bring us the valves." He brought them the next day.

'Two of our youngsters stored the radio in a pondok, between the corrugated iron and the wood. We could lift it up and down easily. The lieutenant in charge of us knew all the time that we had a radio and that we listened to it, but he ignored it. If he hadn't there would have been big trouble.

'The camp was surrounded by wire, but that didn't stop men from trying to escape. They were clever boys. One lot cut the wire and crawled through. Then they replaced the wire. Fifty metres away someone set fire to a heap of aluminium paper that they had collected. While the soldiers were trying to put out the fire, the men ran to a car standing on the other side of the sports field where the Ossewabrandwag were waiting. We had Ossewabrandwag men inside the camp, of course. We were all comrades together, don't forget that.

'A group of men also dug a tunnel and some of them got out, but one was nearly killed when the earth caved in and the thing was discovered. We were all given twenty-eight days. Things sometimes got quite tense. One day eight hundred youngsters decided to storm the gates. They charged at them shouting: "Down with Jannie, down with Jannie!"* But the men on guard† said they would open fire, and the demonstrators backed down. Next day policemen in blue uniforms came from Pretoria. They were all boereseuns, and they all had pickhandles, and when we came for our food at 12.30 we were knocked about with the pickhandles, even the old men.

'In our spare time we made all sorts of things. Beautiful puppets, really beautiful works of art. Once a month we had entertainment. Once we put on *Dr Faustus*. That was a really grand show. We printed programmes in Gothic lettering, every letter carved out of bone. We held it in the Staat Theatre in Andalusia. It was a *Puppenspiel* show, and all the officers came to it. It was very clever.

'We were also allowed to study. I studied Afrikaans. But a lot of the men in the camp shouldn't have been there at all. For example, a whole class of boys from South West Africa, I think, when they wrote matric they scrawled "Heil Hitler" on their examination papers. Two weeks later they were in the camp.

'Of course there were Nazis in the camp. Some of them were double Nazis, very extreme. Even now. They were not loyal to South Africa. Some of them tried to put pressure on us to become more Nazi, but in the end they more or less kept to themselves. There were three religions: Protestant, Catholics and Rhenish Andalusia, which was mostly the Nazis, but after two years that died out.

---

* Jan Smuts.

† The men were guarded by the First City Regiment, mobilised in September 1940 under the command of Lt-Col W D Wood for camp guard duties.

In their leisure time internees produced some beautiful objects. Here are hand-printed programmes for some of the entertainment staged in the Andalusia camp. Each letter was made from a piece of carved bone.

'When Mussolini fell we heard it on the radio. Then we saw a picture of him hanging. The picture was pinned up but the next day it was gone. And of course we knew what was happening to Hitler. The camp was stunned when we learned what had happened to him, just stunned. And for some of the men it was a real tragedy because their homes were now overrun by the Russians. When Germany surrendered, not one man said a word. It was, after all, a camp in German hands.

'Because I was South African I was released eight days after the end of the war. Some of the men, the real Nazis, were never allowed back into South Africa. I was told that I could send a telegram to my wife of not more than two words. I sent just one: "Released".

'Twelve of us went back to Windhoek by train. We stayed one night in a hotel. The man running the hotel was Jewish, but because we had been warned not to make any propaganda there was no Heil Hitler.

'When I got home … how can I explain how I felt? My wife wasn't there – she was visiting her mother in Swakopmund. My little girl was there. She was very polite. She called me "sie", the polite form for a stranger. That was terrible for me, terrible. I had been in prison for three years and my daughter called me "sie". ’

• Interview 1990

CHAPTER

46

'Don't worry South Africa'

Sgt Quentin Smythe, VC, and the horrors of broadcasting

On 5 June 1942, in the area of Alem Hamza in the Western Desert, a sergeant in the 1st Royal Natal Carbineers won the first Victoria Cross of the Union Forces.*

Sergeant Quentin George Murray Smythe's citation appeared in the *London Gazette,* 11 September 1942: 'During an attack on an enemy strongpoint, in which his officer was severely wounded, Sergeant Smythe took command of a platoon although himself suffering from a shrapnel wound in the forehead. The strongpoint having been overrun, our troops came under enfilade fire from an enemy machine-gun nest. Realising the threat to his position, Sergeant Smythe himself stalked and destroyed the nest with hand grenades, capturing the crew.

'Although weak from loss of blood, he continued to lead the advance and, on encountering an enemy anti-tank position, captured the crew. He was directly responsible for killing several of the enemy, shooting some and bayoneting another as they withdrew. After consolidating the position, he successfully defeated an enemy attempt at encirclement.

'Throughout the engagement Sergeant Smythe displayed leadership which was an inspiration to those who followed him.'

When news of the newly promoted Sgt Smythe's VC got to South Africa, it was front-page news. And it was good news for a change. With the best will in the world, it could not be said that the war was going well for the Allies (although the tide was on the turn. By the end of the year, after the El Alamein offensive, the Afrika Korps was in retreat, Tobruk had been recaptured by the Allies, and the German attempt to relieve Stalingrad had failed).

---

* But he was not the first South African to win the VC in the 1939–45 war. That honour went to Sqn-Ldr J D Nettleton of the RAF for the Augsburg Raid (see 'Alone in the heart of Germany.')

The disaster at Sidi Rezegh in November 1941 had been followed by the 'Gazala Gallop' and the withdrawal of Commonwealth forces back to the Alamein line, where they stood at bay expecting the worst.*

At roughly the same time, from 7 March to 9 July, Robey Leibbrandt and seventeen other defendants were appearing at the preparatory examination to allegations of high treason in the Pretoria Magistrate's Court. Although the full details of how near the Prime Minister, Field Marshal Smuts, had come to assassination and of a planned armed seizure of the country emerged only at Leibbrandt's trial for treason later in the year, South Africans who supported the war were understandably horrified at how near the country had been to the precipice.

Sgt Smythe's VC, then, came as a much-needed tonic; and the Defence Force exploited it as much as possible, from the time when he received his VC in the Western Desert to the time when he returned home on a special trip in September 1942.

Soon after he received his VC Smythe was congratulated by war correspondents. 'My mum and dad will be simply overwhelmed,' he said.

'Well,' said a correspondent, 'you will have to broadcast a message to them.' Smythe was horrified. A bayonet was one thing, a microphone quite another.

But in the end Smythe succumbed. Hauled in front of a microphone the moment he stepped off the aeroplane in South Africa, his speech lasting two and a half minutes was delivered in a state of panic. He stumbled and fumbled with his words, and endeared himself to all who heard him:

'When I climbed out of the plane which brought me down from Egypt yesterday, I ran smack into a barrage of questions, but it wasn't until late yesterday afternoon that I met the question, the answer to which gives the clue to how I am feeling at the moment.

'Somebody said to me: "Tell me, Sergeant Smythe, how does it feel when you go into action?" My answer was: "Just plain scared," but after a while when one has something to do, there is always plenty to do in the show in the Western Desert [sic]. The scare wears off and one gets on with the job.

'That's exactly how I felt when I was asked to broadcast: plain scared. I'm not exaggerating when I say the scare hasn't worn off this time. So I hope you will forgive me, ladies and gentlemen, if I don't put up too good a show in this broadcast.

---

* If the Alamein line had been breached the gateway to Egypt would have been wide open. Instead, ten days after Smythe won his VC in bitter hand-to-hand fighting, Tobruk fell, and with it over ten thousand South Africans became prisoners of war. But the Alamein line held.

ABOVE: Sgt Quentin Smythe, VC, being painted for his portrait by Neville Lewis. (South African National Museum of Military History)

LEFT: The finished portrait: Sgt Quentin Smythe, VC. (South African National Museum of Military History)

‘I’m a farmer, I’ve been a farmer ever since I left school.* Farmers don’t use a lot of words. Neither do soldiers. I’m a soldier second because I honestly believe this war is fought for the things I think worth while. My farm, for instance, and my right to run that farm as I think best.

‘Most soldiers up in Egypt think this way. They haven’t a lot to say, fighting being more important than talk up there, but if they had my chance to come on the air they would say much the same thing. It means something to be a South African soldier and to serve under men like Field Marshal Smuts and Maj-Gen Dan Pienaar. They are fighting South Africans and their example has done more than anything else to make South Africans out of all of us.

‘Whether we speak English or Afrikaans, or whether we come from Natal or the Cape, the Free State or the Transvaal, I’m proud that my decoration means acknowledgement of the fighting qualities of the 1st Division, General Dan’s Division. We’ve been in some pretty tough shows up there, but we’ve always stuck together because we have the inspiration of a first-class leader.

‘It came as a pleasant surprise to me, this home leave to the Union. I had been ordered out of the El Alamein line to spend a few days in Cairo and then visit the press camp. My orders were to report back to my unit and then suddenly I was told I was coming home.

‘The excitement of that news, coupled with all the fuss of interviews and the rest of it, and quite honestly I would rather face Jerry’s strongpoint than a reporter or camera made it difficult for me to think clearly [sic].

‘I should have collected a message for South Africa but I didn’t, so you will have to be satisfied with one that comes out of my own head.

‘“Don’t worry, South Africa, the men in Egypt, clerks, businessmen, professional men, youngsters straight out of school, and farmers like me, though they are very tired, they’re getting on with the job. If you give them all the support you are capable of, they will make a good job of it.”

‘I have only broadcast once before. That was a message to my parents. I wasn’t very pleased with the way I put it over, so if you will excuse me I’ll push off now and I’ll deliver my message in person. ’

- SABC Archives

---

* In the Natal midlands. He was born at Nottingham Road.

CHAPTER

47

'A bar their battle zone'

The provenance of this little poem, written in the Western Desert before the battle of El Alamein, is unknown. It illustrates two points: that soldiers enjoy doggerel, not necessarily of a high standard, and that the ill-will towards the men who stayed at home was not confined to the families of the volunteers who did their bit.

'My Pals Who Stayed at Home' was copied and circulated among the South African troops in the Western Desert and then at home.

Nothing to write home about to the pals who stayed at home?

" I wish I could think of something to write home about."

MY PALS WHO STAYED AT HOME

I'm pulling off my colours
I've thrown my webbing away
And I'm going down to Cairo
To draw some blinking pay
I'm tired of chewing biscuits
Of eating bread and jam
And trying to find out
Just whereabouts I am
And fighting blinking Jerries
Up here on my own
Especially when I think of the Union
And my pals who stayed at home
I bet they're walking down the street
Their cheeks puffed out with pride
And telling all their girlfriends
How they saved their yellow hides
Whilst here's me in the desert
Afraid to raise my head
For fear some blinking Jerry
Will fill it full of lead
And when I told my pals at home
I'd volunteer to fight
They up and said God Bless you mate
And bring you back all right
They called me a chocolate soldier
A five-bob-a-day airman too
They said you'll never see the front
Or even get a view
They said you'll have a picnic
A trip across the foam
But they weren't game to try it
My pals who stayed at home

They weren't such bad pals either
When on the hunting track
But there, there ain't no danger
For small game don't shoot back
They shine before the ladies
The brag across the bar
In summer on the beaches
It's where they always are

A billiard cue their rifle
A bar their battle zone
But there ain't no bullets flying
For my pals who stayed at home

So I'll up my old Lee-Enfield
Buckle my webbing about
Tho' I'm only a Springbok airman
I'll see this darn job out
And if I stop a bullet
I'll die without a moan
Tho' 'tis for their sakes I did it
My pals who stayed at home.

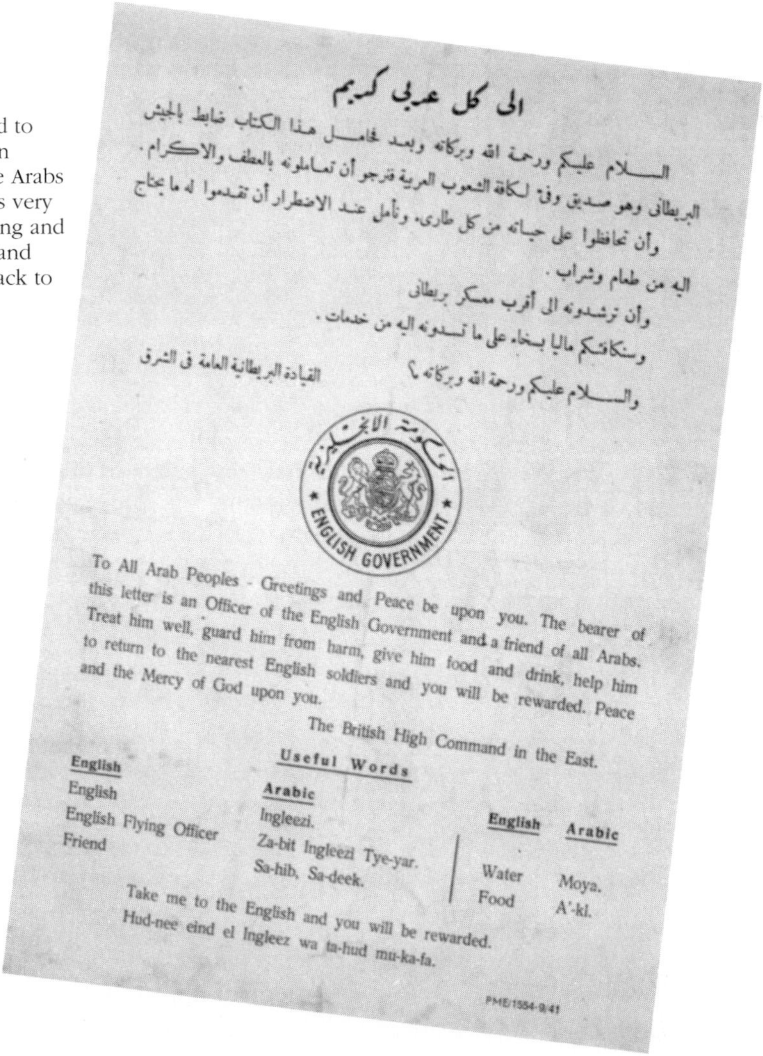

الى كل عربي كريم

السلام عليكم ورحمة الله وبركاته وبعد فحامل هذا الكتاب ضابط بالجيش البريطاني وهو صديق وفي لكافة الشعوب العربية فنرجو أن تعاملوه بالعطف والاكرام.
وأن تحافظوا على حياته من كل طارىء. ونأمل عند الاضطرار أن تقدموا له ما يحتاج اليه من طعام وشراب.
وأن ترشدوه الى أقرب معسكر بريطاني
وسنكافئكم ماليا بسخاء على ما تسدونه اليه من خدمات.
والسلام عليكم ورحمة الله وبركاته
القيادة البريطانية العامة في الشرق

الحكومة الانجليزية
ENGLISH GOVERNMENT

To All Arab Peoples - Greetings and Peace be upon you. The bearer of this letter is an Officer of the English Government and a friend of all Arabs. Treat him well, guard him from harm, give him food and drink, help him to return to the nearest English soldiers and you will be rewarded. Peace and the Mercy of God upon you.

The British High Command in the East.

Useful Words

English	Arabic
English	Ingleezi.
English Flying Officer	Za-bit Ingleezi Tye-yar.
Friend	Sa-hib, Sa-deek.

English	Arabic
Water	Moya.
Food	A'-kl.

Take me to the English and you will be rewarded.
Hud-nee eind el Ingleez wa ta-hud mu-ka-fa.

PME/1554-9/41

A leaflet handed to troops for use in emergency. The Arabs were sometimes very helpful, sheltering and feeding troops and leading them back to safety.

CHAPTER

48

'A piece of cake'

Lt Chris Kavanagh, SAAF, and the art of writing home

Throughout the war letters to the Union from the front were censored, sometimes heavily, depending on the indiscretions of the writer. But at no time was censorship stricter than in the months before the second, decisive, battle of El Alamein.

Few servicemen other than the most senior knew what Lt-Gen Bernard Montgomery, who took command of the 8th Army in August 1942, was planning. Austere, religious, resolute, Montgomery planned methodically for the offensive demanded by Winston Churchill* – the offensive that would turn the tide in North Africa for the British and Commonwealth forces who had fought there so long and till then to so little effect.

After the fall of Tobruk and the Gazala Gallop, Sir Gen Claude Auchinleck stemmed the German advance in the first battle of Alamein, fought by a still demoralised 8th Army, smarting from its losses, between 1–9 July from Alamein in the north to the Qattara Depression in the south.

Part of the first battle of Alamein had been centred on Ruweisat Ridge, defended on its western face by the 1st SA Division, now reduced by attrition to about three thousand fighting infantry. Between 2 and 4 July the South Africans twice repulsed their old adversaries, the 15th and 21st Panzer Divisions. By 21 July Rommel knew that he had lost, and heavily. He retreated behind a broad swathe of minefields; and Montgomery in the meantime settled down to plan the greatest artillery barrage of the war.†

* By insisting on an offensive in September Churchill in effect sacked Gen Claude Auchinleck, who refused to move before 15 September. Auchinleck's reputation, oddly enough, was redeemed by Rommel himself. 'Although the British losses in the Alamein fighting (1–17 July) had been higher than ours, yet the price of Auchinleck had not been excessive, for the one thing that had mattered to him was to halt our advance, and that unfortunately he had done … Auchinleck was a very good leader …'

† According to military experts, exceeded only by the Allied barrages against the Iraqis in the Gulf War of 1991.

By 6 October his plans had been completed. In the seventeen days between the completion of his plans and the opening of the spectacular thousand-gun barrage the 8th Army was moved into position, leave was cancelled and a strict security blanket covered the entire operation.

In the preparations for Alamein the Desert Air Force played a crucial part, especially in air reconnaissance. One of the squadrons was South African: 40 Squadron (Fighter Recce), an army co-operation squadron, whose job was photographic reconnaissance, photographic surveying, ground surveying, ground reconnaissance, escort duties and even on occasion bombing.

Lt Chris Kavanagh was one of the pilots of 40 Squadron. Before the war he had been a journalist with the *Daily News* in Durban. Although he was a skilled pilot (Kavanagh went down in SAAF history in December 1943 for an act of bravado: he took a plane on New Year's Eve and dropped a greetings card on Rommel's headquarters. 'All the worst for a really bad New Year!' it read, in German), Kavanagh yearned to become a war correspondent. He never did.

But he wrote many letters to his wife, whom he called 'Mysti' or 'Fishy', warm, affectionate letters, vivid with descriptions of his air war. He wrote on air-letter cards, odd scraps of paper and air-mail paper, in ink with a favourite pen or, irritably, in pencil. He wrote from Cairo, from Alexandria, from advanced landing grounds in the desert, in time snatched between sorties.

40 Squadron aircrew working out strategy. They often flew from advanced landing grounds in the desert. Conditions were hard and dangerous. (South African National Museum of Military History)

In the edited letters that follow, all written about the time of Alamein, the excitement of that time, and the events that bound together those magnificent men in their flying machines are brought to life:

‘Lieut C Kavanagh
40 Squadron SAA UDF
Middle East
APO, DURBAN
Sept 16 1942

My darling old fishy-cat, how are you?

Well here I sit in the desert again. Not a very dangerous desert, it's true, but it is quite strange to have to start economising with water again, strange to have new kites, new tents, new flying kit and a new colonel, and our spirits are quite high. The moon is waxing and fairly soon now our pals the Jerries will be paying visits to this district, I suppose. Luckily there are more important targets round here than ourselves, so don't worry. Judging by the latest papers things seem to be getting rather bleak in the Union, no silk stockings, few matches, no drinks after 8.30 and blackouts everywhere. As far as supplies go things seem to be a damn sight better up here. Matches, cigarettes, razor-blades and so on are plentiful, and every woman seems to wear stockings, so I suppose they are to be had. A good score of the Kaap Korps are in the VD hospital as a result of visits to the Ismailia red-light district, and also their frequent contacts with the wife of a wog [sic]. He used to bring her to the outskirts of the camp and offer her services at five akkers a time.
Cherrio, my love, till next mail.

October 22 1942

My Darling old fishy-cat

That was a lovely letter you wrote me on October 10th and it arrived at a time when I needed it – as a sort of reward for a long day.

Since I last wrote there's been never a dull moment. Jack Freemantle did a sortie at dawn the next day and I was briefed for another to be done later, with a fighter escort. I was to weave with a fellow from the RAF squadron.

Next day: Delays occurred and we didn't take off until 2.30. First the upper cover took off, made a wide sweep while we and the close cover formed up. As the top cover came over we all took off together – grand feeling. It had been a lovely day up to then – the fighter boys had been scrambled once or twice, and there had been a dash raid by bomb-carrying 109s followed by a dog-fight right over the camp. We expected trouble, because our route took us just a few miles from one of their fighter dromes. That is why we had the escort. The escort weren't too happy, nor was I, but I felt all right in the air when I looked backwards and saw all those kites weaving above us.

These fighter boys don't mind the 109s if they're all together (the fighter boys), but they hate ack-ack. We don't mind ack-ack quite so much, but are very wary of 109s, because we don't often see them and when we do we're by ourselves with no escort to protect us. On a TAC/R* escort the fighters say we lead them low over all the ack-ack, they've got to keep an eye on us, and at the same time search the sky to make sure they don't get jumped themselves.

As we crossed the coast I looked up and saw the heavy ack-ack – fat white puffs bursting among the fighters. They were ignoring us for the moment, but soon it was bursting around us too. I twisted and weaved, furiously trying to keep my man in sight all the time.

Then over the R/T came the first warning of trouble. It was the voice of our control station commander. 'They're taking off – watch out – watch out.' I switched my sights on, squinted through them and turned the guns on to Fire. The lower cover came closer.

The ack-ack was still pretty heavy, and from the small puffs below it seemed as if every infantryman was shooting at us too, but we were a bit too high for them. It didn't seem too hard to avoid the heavy stuff – sooty black puffs the size of a flamboyant tree that followed our tracks and occasionally burst on the side. (Some ack-ack puffs are white, others, the worst, are black.)

Suddenly the voice of the control station came through again. 'Fifteen plus snappers at five thousand going south-east.' I didn't fancy that. We were at 5 000 and they were clearly out to intercept us. However, we kept on still weaving away from the ack-ack. After about two minutes I saw a black speck far away going like hell in the opposite direction to ours. A moment later I saw the close cover wheeling and turning far behind and the voice of the squadron-leader came through directing the pilots of his formation.

We were clear of most of the ack-ack by now, but the fighters were still getting it hard and strong as they were circling. They were too far behind for us to return and get among them, so we kept on with our reconnaissance by ourselves, helped and screened by quite a lot of cloud. We flew just under the base of the cloud, and if anything had jumped us we would have pulled up and hid in it.

Eventually we turned to home clear of the ack-ack, but the dog-fight was still going on a few miles back above the clouds. I was so excited by listening to the squadron leader's orders that I forgot to be scared. He had marvellous control of his formation. This sort of thing: 'There they

* Tactical reconnaissance.

are now, three o'clock, climbing into the sun. Watch 'em, watch 'em. Now! There they are, right overhead! Turn right! Turn right! You squirt him Johnny, you squirt him. Good boy! Watch him, watch him. Tommy, Tommy, come closer, form up again' – and so on. It was magnificent; the only part of actual operations that I have found pleasantly exciting so far.

We didn't see our escort after the dog-fight. We weren't attacked, and the two of us got home safely with our news. Quite valuable news too. Later we went to see the fighter boys. One of their kites had been a bit shot-up, but the pilot was untouched. We got a 109 that was trying to get away along the deck. Of the 'fifteen-plus' only four had attacked the escort. The others stayed up in the sun, followed us part of the way home, then buzzed off.

I flew back to our drome late again and put down another dusk landing. As I entered the mess, tired as hell but feeling fairly satisfied with the day's work, someone who'd come up from base handed me your letter of October 12th. That was a good end to a bloody good day.

Don't worry about VD among the cooks, honey, the whole of the Cape Corps is now examined every fortnight and there have been no more discoveries.

I love you. You and Pat hold thumbs for me and I'll be all right. I'm holding thumbs for you both always.
Love Chris.

October 25 1942

My darling: You'll probably get this at the same time as the letter describing my escorted sortie because I think that one missed the post at base. The post truck is going back again today and here I am waiting to go on my next sortie.

By now the news of the battle* will have broken and you will have grasped what I have been trying to hint at in my letters for some time past.

Zero hour was 10 p.m. on Friday† and as the time approached everyone became all tense and excited. A few minutes before the hour we went out into the moonlight and looked expectantly to the west. The front was thirty miles away, yet when the barrage of artillery started it roared like thunder close at hand. It was like thunder except that it kept on with hardly a lull for ten hours! Under cover of the shells the infantry were fighting their way through the minefields, clearing a passage for the tanks. We'd seen those tanks, scores of them, moving up at night two days before. They had been a thrilling sight in

---

* El Alamein.
† Not really. The barrage began in the 13th Corps Sector at 9.25 p.m.

the moonlight, roaring up the dusty track, nose-to-tail with silent overcoated figures in the turret. Darling, why weren't you there to nudge me and get all excited? All the pilots crowded around calling 'Go, Joe, Go!' The little Pommie in the turret waved and said: 'I think we're going to give them f---- 'ell this time, mate.'

Ho! ho! German radio announced last night that their kites bombed ------ with good effect on the 23rd. We are at ---- and there wasn't a Jerry kite in the neighbourhood all night. I see they haven't said a word about the battle yet either. Hope that's a good sign.
All my love to both of you.
Chris.

7 November 1942

Mysti my love, sorry for this sort of letter, but I know you'll want to hear from me and I don't know when we'll settle down long enough for me to get out my kit and write a proper letter. Have tons to tell about the big advance, I was the first Allied pilot to set foot on what was previously enemy territory. Only I came by land, hot on the heels of the Jerries. I was in charge of our advance party, and as we drove down the crammed desert tracks, spitting out dust and lurching over bomb craters, we saw Jerry and Iti tanks still smouldering on the roadside and prisoners were still coming in from their dugouts.

Spent the night of the 5th with the HQ of an Army Corps and were pretty busily bombed and strafed all night. Nothing came near us. Next morning we came to the landing ground from where I'm writing this. Our kites arrived from the old ALG* refuelled and took off on sorties at once. This was the drome from which the Jerry fighters used to try to intercept our TRE/Rs, and everywhere you look there are 109s, some badly pranged and shot-up, but many in almost perfect condition. We got a complete field kitchen, a Volkswagen [motor car], motor bike, rifles, machine guns, and all kinds of loot. The Jerries here must have just dropped everything and run. We knocked hell out of their transport, and every hundred yards or so along the main road there is a burned or smashed truck, with suitcases, clothes and rifles littered all over the place.

I started off on a sortie yesterday, but we had to turn back because of rain and mist right down to the deck.

I don't seem to have washed or changed my clothes for ages. We're living on tinned stuff and biscuits, never sleeping in one place more than one night, landing at strange aerodromes every day, refuelling and taking off again, with our convoy, with special rations, kit, etc. always along behind in the pursuit. I don't mind it, it's rather fun and

* Advanced Landing Ground.

Distinguished visitors in the officers' mess tent of 40 Squadron. The photograph was taken over tea and sandwiches at Garba Tulla. With Smuts was Maj-Gen Cunningham and Maj-Gen Godwin-Austen. The squadron flew virtually non-stop before the battle of El Alamein in October 1942. (*The Star*)

I'm making sure that my bedroll goes where I go. You have to live as a self-contained unit, looking after your own kit, your flying things and your aircraft. The ole war-bird is doing well.

So my dearest old Fishy-cat, if you don't hear regularly from me for a bit, don't fuss, see. Sorties now are quick affairs over a pretty demoralised enemy. He's being helped by the rain, the lucky bugger, but I think we've pretty well won. Huge kiss to Pat.
All my love, Chris.

November 16 1942

Mysti my dear,

Hello, old darling. At last I've got another chance to write to you again and I'm all the more pleased because some good Samaritan flew up from base with our letters yesterday morning.

By the time you get this we should have moved on a good few hundred miles, and I expect that before the end of the week we'll have Benghazi.* After that (the end of the week) I and the rest of A flight will have a bit of a rest for a fortnight. We won't do any sorties, but we'll just keep flying the base aircraft up as the BLG moves westward.

It would be boring to give you a stage-by-stage account of our progress here in Alamein. Every day pretty much the same thing would happen. We'd get an hour's notice to get away. We'd pack madly, climb into out kites and take off while our ground convoy filed off below us and sandwiches itself among the stream of traffic on the

---

* Benghazi was recaptured on 21 December.

main road. Over the new landing ground we'd circle until the advance bloke has lit a fire or fired a signal showing us where to land, for the Jerries had wired a lot of the landing grounds and we could only land where it was clear. The landing strip isn't always into wind, and it is no wider than Moore Road,* and with a big hill in the middle, but on all the seven landing grounds we used in the first eight days there was only one mishap, and that was just a scraped wingtip.

We've lost two pilots since the push started, but there's good reason to think they are both safe, though prisoners of war. First to go was Jackie Webb, my new flight commander. The ack-ack got him in the engine at Alamein, and he wasn't able to glide as far as our lines. For a time we were afraid that he'd come down in a minefield and been blown up, because that did happen to a South African pilot about the same time that day. The guy lived though very badly smashed up, and we've now discovered that Jackie hasn't been through any of the hospitals, so it couldn't have been him.

Chris Beith is missing too. He and Jack Orpen were coming back from a sortie near Halfaya Pass.

18 November 4.30 p.m. – Yes, as I was saying, Chris Beith and Jack were dived on by two kites, which might or might not have been 109s. They didn't fire, Jack lost sight of Beith in the confusion and didn't see him again. Next day we passed the place and found Beith's aircraft. He'd belly-landed, and the cockpit wasn't broken up at all. Prisoner of war, I guess. They usually whisk pilots away pretty quick and don't allow them a chance to be rescued. The 109s others of us bumped didn't seem very skilful and were very wary about pressing home their attacks. I didn't bump any 109s (that I saw!), but on the sortie I did. That sortie was the longest I've ever done. We took off in the dark with long-range tanks and flew for an hour out to sea right down low, about twenty feet above the water. I didn't like it a bit. It was dark, and I had a terrible kite, and one of the cocks on it was in such an awkward position that I'd have to discard my Mae West to be able to reach it. Had a rubber dinghy on my 'chute though. After a while I altered course, climbed steeply and eventually crossed the coast well behind enemy lines, and going like hell. The sun was rising, and the Jerry convoys that had been camping along the main road were just beginning to stir for the day's gallop. Here and there a guy was boiling tea over a fire. The whole area round Bardia was crammed with stuff, and it made me almost weep to think of it all there asking to be bombed. I'd just happened to come over at the right minute. In another hour the stuff would all be on the move westward. I lost a good bit of height in my dive towards Capuzzo, and I couldn't have been at much more than 800 feet as I turned to come out

* One of the main roads in Durban.

over Sollum. Luckily I was weaving like hell by instinct because one big lot of transport all opened up on me at once, too bloody close for my liking. I looked for Lategan, but he'd got through all right, and we beat it quickly.

Flying back across a bay a few minutes later I saw some broken water about ten miles from the coast. As I looked at it I saw a parachute descending close by. I saw the bloke hit the water and the parachute floating on the water. At first I thought of throwing him my dinghy, but realised that if I threw it out not inflated it would sink, and I was buggered if I was going to inflate it in the cockpit. Also I reckoned that whatever shot the boy down was up above watching so I just about bent the throttle over, pushing it forward and went home, flat out. Landed quickly and got a flash message sent, giving the details of where and when I'd seen him got out on the strength of my message. He'd been 18 hours in the water. His name is Alan White, a South African fighter pilot. Way up above us the fighter boys were climbing with twelve Stukas escorted by 109s. They shot down eight Stukas, and the Yank fighters got the other four just as they were circling to land on their home drome.

It was near the place where the guy hit the water that Lategan afterwards told me he'd seen two suspicious-looking kites. My radio wasn't working properly, and I couldn't hear him at the time.

Eighteen hours is a bloody long time to be in the water, but the chap wasn't much worse for it and is back flying now. He had a Mae West on luckily. At a drome near Tobruk some days later and only a day after the Jerries abandoned the town I met a Canadian observer-navigator who'd just come out of a hiding-place. He'd had a hell of a time during the previous four days.

He was in a huge bomber over Tobruk on the night of the 10th when ack-ack hit them in the bomb compartment. They had a few small bombs left, and they went off killing the rear gunner and setting the kite on fire. The pilot was wounded, and this bloke put his parachute on – these bomber boys don't wear them all the time – and pushed him out, but he couldn't swim, and he's probably had it by now. ’

The history of 40 Squadron was an illustrious one. It was formed in the Union on 30 May 1940, and its first sortie was to intercept two Italian ships off Durban. At that time the pilots flew Hartebees. In East Africa they flew Fairy Battles, sometimes as low as 500 feet, through gorges and well below the level of the hilltops, where the enemy waited with machine guns on what was known as 'offensive reconnaissance'. It was there that the squadron lost its first aircraft, flown by Capt Dick Lemmer of A Flight. Forced down during the El Wak assault, Lemmer's air gunner, Sgt S Lewis of Parow, was shot dead as he tried to hold off approaching Banda with his machine gun.

For the rest of the war the squadron flew Hawker Furies, Tomahawks, Hurricanes and, in Italy, the Spitfire IX, which could carry bombs. It operated continuously throughout the Italian campaign and was moved to Austria after the cessation of hostilities in 1945.

Kavanagh returned home at the end of the war and resumed a career in journalism.

CHAPTER

49

'Wer wird bei der laterne stehn mit dir, Lili Marleen?'

World War II's most popular song

'Tuxedo Junction', 'Chatanooga Choo-Choo', 'The White Cliffs of Dover': which was the most popular song of World War II? None of them. It was the haunting German song broadcast to the Afrika Korps in the Western Desert: 'Lili Marleen'.

At 9.57 each night German radio broadcast 'Lili Marleen', sung by the throaty-voiced Lala Andersen. But it didn't remain the sole property of the Afrika Korps for long. British soldiers took it, translated it and made the English version of 'Lili Marlene' uniquely their own. The song was everywhere, heard in the lines on both sides and sung by German prisoners of war as they were marched into prison cages.

The song was forged out of war. It was written by Hans Liep, a German private in the 1914–18 war, for his two girlfriends, Lili and Marleen, both of whom waited for him (at different times) underneath the lamplight across the barrack square. Norbert Schuter set it to music, but it was rejected by over thirty German record and music publishers. Then Lala Andersen rediscovered it.

Legends have grown about the song. One has it that German and British troops met each other in battle in the desert, each side singing 'Lili Marleen'/'Lili Marlene'. At El Alamein, according to German legend, so determined were the 51st Highland Division to get hold of a copy of the record that they attacked a section of the German line. And (again according to martial legend) both sides would occasionally cease fire just before Lala Andersen came on the air and resume firing after the last notes died away.

The story of 'Lili Marlene' didn't end there, however. Troops embarking to and from Vietnam from Travis Air Force base in San Francisco did so to the strains of 'Lili Marlene'; it has been adopted by the Canadian infantry as its official marching song; and in 1971 it was top of the Japanese hit parade. Even in the 1991 Gulf War, British troops listened to Vera Lynn's 'White Cliffs of Dover' and to their grandfather's favourite wartime song, 'Lili Marlene'.

An Australian version by courtesy of 450 Fighter-Bomber Squadron, 239 Wing, as a two-finger sign to Nazi propagandist 'Lord Haw-Haw's' smarmy 'regrets' for the 'dreadful losses they [the Allies] have suffered' is given here:

THE DIVE BOMBERS' SONG
(To the tune of 'Lili Marlene')

Get the right deflection,
Check reflector sight,
Give your speed correction,
And see your range is right.
Then you can press the tit, old son,
And blow the Hun to kingdom come,
Poor Marlene's boyfriend will
Never see Marlene.

Half a thousand pounds of
Anti-personnel,
Half a dozen rounds of
The stuff that gives them hell.
Finish your bomb dive, zoom away,
And live to fight another day.
But poor Marlene's boyfriend will
Never see Marlene.

CHAPTER

50

'Such ghastly wounds'

Allan Bird, Regimental Medical Officer

During the second half of 1942, as war production reached its peak, so that munitions could be exported, two factors dominated the Union: the shortage of volunteers, aggravated by the losses at Tobruk, and the U-boat menace off the coast.

The Japanese were still unchallenged in the Far East, and the Union, it was believed, was a tempting target for them with the heavy increase in shipping caused by the fall of Singapore. Unidentified aircraft were sighted off St Helena Bay, and so were submarines. Orders were given for all submarines to be treated as hostile unless notification had been received to the contrary.

The minelayer *Levern Bank* (previously the *Dogger Bank*) was sighted off the Cape with a dummy cargo on deck marked 'General Motors New York'. Challenged by an Anson of the Coastal Air Force – itself undermanned – the *Levern Bank* signalled 'Levernbank from New York via Pernambuco for Cape Town' and the aircraft flew off. That night the ship, within clear sight of Cape Town, laid sixty mines in groups twenty miles west of Table Bay Harbour. By May Bofors anti-aircraft guns and searchlights had been installed in Durban and Cape Town. But the Coastal Air Force was weakened at this critical time by having to supply men and aircraft for the Madagascar operation.

Ships were going down all the time off the South African coast, and the British Ports Defence Committee allocated more defensive guns for Simonstown, Llandudno, Robben Island, East London and Durban. German surface raiders sank ships off St Helena and mines were seen off Cape Town (in July). Plans were made for a minesweeping flotilla.

Only three days after the fall of Tobruk a new recruiting drive was begun. Field Marshal Smuts made an appeal at the July Handicap in Durban. A squadron of armoured cars went round the race course bearing placards reading: 'Avenge Tobruk'. So desperate were the infantry and artillery for men that volunteers with hernias and sight defects were snapped up, provided they accepted medical treatment.

Doctors straight out of medical school were also accepted and posted to North Africa to serve as regimental medical officers.

The South African Medical Corps was raised as the Cape Medical Volunteer Staff Corps in 1887. By 1914 it was the South African Medical Corps. It sent field ambulance units abroad and to German South West Africa in the 1914 war. In 1939 the SAMC numbered only twelve hundred. By the end of the war it was over six thousand.

Under the able command of Brig A J Orenstein the Corps, helped by the SA Red Cross and the St John's Ambulance Association, served in the East African, the desert and the Italian campaigns and provided eight thousand beds in the Union for Imperial forces.

SAMC volunteers served in the front line with the troops. Often working in arduous conditions and under fire, doctors, stretcher-bearers, first-aid men and ambulance drivers worked heroically to save the lives of over eight thousand wounded men who passed through their hands during the five years of war.* Regimental medical officers, many of them young and fresh from medical school, were among the first to reach the wounded. One of them, Dr Allan Bird, tells his story:

'When war broke out I was still studying medicine at Wits.† One of the first things that happened was that practically every GP in the country volunteered for service. That was fine, but the result was a terrible shortage of GPs in South Africa. The men who stayed behind could barely cope, so the army had to find a way round this. It was very simple: they asked for recent graduates, like myself – I graduated in 1940 – to volunteer.

'I was quite happy to volunteer, and I went up north with twelve other recent graduates. Not one of us had even done our internship. It was made quite clear to us that we would not be practising particularly "sophisticated" medicine or surgery: we were to be RMOs, in the front line, dealing with men who had been wounded and then sending them down the line for more difficult treatment.

'We were all posted to various regiments. Mine was the Duke of Edinburgh's Own Rifles, a Cape Town regiment, located at Mersa Matruh at that time. I must confess that I didn't know what to expect or how I would behave under fire, or whether there would be cases that I couldn't deal with; but I reasoned that if other men could manage then I could too.

'Mersa Matruh was huge, a fortress we South Africans took over from the Poles. They had bitter memories of Hitler's invasion of their country, and they had built extensive underground shelters, which I

* Of course the SAMC treated many more than the eight thousand South Africans wounded; they treated men of all nationalities, including Germans, brought to them.
† The University of the Witwatersrand.

hated. I preferred to be above ground day and night, and I learnt to dig little foxholes, like little graves, which put you below the level of the surrounding desert, and if there was a Stuka raid, of which we had many, you were safe unless you got a direct hit.

Allan Bird, a Regimental Medical Officer with the Dukes. Like other young RMOs he volunteered straight from medical school and served in the battlefields with the men.

'The first cases I dealt with at Mersa Matruh were mostly cases like pneumonia or malaria or skin troubles, and I simply sent the men off to one of the base hospitals. My first "military" case was a young Australian who looked quite fit when I first saw him. He had taken a machine gun off a Messerschmitt that had been shot down and mounted the gun on a tripod. He used to shoot at enemy planes when they came over. It sounded like a good idea, but it wasn't, not for him, anyway, because when he fired it the first time a percussion cap from one of the bullets came off and hit him in the middle of his forehead.

'He walked into the surgery and said he thought there might be something wrong, but he wasn't sure. I had a look at him. There was almost no blood, but I could see a little external mark, and I sterilised a probe to see how deep this thing was. I probed around and suddenly the probe just disappeared into his head for about an inch and a half. God knows what was happening inside his head. I got him into hospital really quickly, and later I learnt that the missile hadn't struck any part of the brain. It had been slowed down by going through the skull and found its way to the base of the brain, where it just sat. Because it wasn't presenting any symptoms, the surgeons decided to leave the thing where it was.

'Then came the order to go through the wire between Egypt and into Libya.* The men were champing at the bit to get into action. They wanted to relieve Tobruk, which had become a kind of mission for the troops. The men had been practising desert manoeuvres and were eager to get to grips with the real thing.

---

* 18 November 1941, as part of Operation Crusader.

'We RMOs had our own little trucks and our own equipment; very elementary, but adequate to deal with casualties as they happened: morphine, bandages, plasma. I first came under fire as we went through the wire, a very elaborate structure that had been breached by the engineers so we could get through. Unfortunately we were new to the game, and everyone bunched up as they went through the openings, an irresistible target for the dive-bombers.

'What had been an organised advance suddenly turned chaotic, with people scattering all over the place. Three or four of our men were killed outright. I was rushing around in my four-wheel-drive Dodge truck, seeing to the casualties and getting them into ambulances and back down the line as quick as possible. I saw a man sitting next to his anti-aircraft gun. He looked very distressed, so I leapt out of my truck and rushed up to him. I was about to start examining him when a more experienced colleague came up to me and said "You can't do anything for him. He's dead." As he was firing his Bofors gun he had been hit and killed without even being knocked over. He was just sitting at his gun.

'The duty of getting wounded men out of the field fell to the Director-General of Medical Services, Brigadier A J Orenstein.* It worked something like this: a field ambulance would consist of about eight doctors who dealt with the casualties in the front line. The wounded would then be carried by hand-stretcher if they couldn't walk to the RAP, where more first aid, such as putting on splints, giving morphine, blood transfusions and nursing if their blood-pressure was low, until they could be transferred to an ambulance, which would take them to the casualty collecting station, four or five miles from the front lines and usually near Brigade headquarters. The men would receive rather more care than the first aid that we were able to give them in the front line and at the RAP, and then they would be sent to the Main Dressing Station [MDS].

'This was where they would receive emergency surgery: an amputation, perhaps, of a limb that we at the RAP thought might have been saved, and then the men would be nursed until they could be sent further. Evacuation by air was almost unheard of. We had ambulance trains from Mersa Matruh to take the wounded to the big hospitals in Cairo or Alexandria, or even Tobruk when it was operational. It was only at the big base hospitals that the men first saw female nurses.

---

* As Col Orenstein, he had been appointed Director-General of Medical Services in 1939 and assumed command of all medical services in East Africa on 30 June 1940. By 1941 this talented and highly efficient man had been promoted Brigadier and was Senior Liaison Officer of the UDF, shuttling between DHQ in Pretoria, the Middle East and Nairobi. Part of his duties was to provide eight thousand beds for British and Allied troops in South Africa.

'In the RAPs we had men trained in first aid. Only in very rare circumstances did we carry the wounded with us. We weren't equipped for anything but emergency treatment. An exception was when we crossed through the wire into Libya and the Dukes were severely bombed and we had to keep the wounded with us for a while. But it was terribly uncomfortable for them, being carted around in the back of an ambulance or, even worse, an open truck.

'Sometimes you would get a man who simply refused to go down the line. Duggie Ovenstone was one of them: he was in an armoured car when a bullet hit the turret, splintered and went into him. He was wounded in his calf, not very badly, but badly enough to justify being sent away. "I don't want to leave," he told me; and he was so emphatic about not leaving his little group, who all came from Bishop's, that I carried him about in my Dodge. He had to lie down and bear it, but the wound gradually mended, and about a month later, when things had settled down, I sent him to hospital, where they dug out a piece of explosive bullet.

'After Tobruk had been relieved* we could, in theory, send the wounded to hospital there, but the place had a dreadful reputation because it was bombed so often, and the men didn't like being sent there. Some of them had had harrowing experiences there, and it was more sensible to send them elsewhere. My batman, Aaron, came from the Transkei. He had been preparing a simple meal for me. We cut British four-gallon petrol cans in half, threw in sand and poured on half a gallon of petrol. It burnt with a rather sooty flame, but at least we could heat up our food.

'Aaron decided to put more petrol on, because the fire was burning poorly; so he threw a cup of petrol on to the fire. Of course the petrol caught fire on its way from his hand, and he was badly burnt, badly enough to need a skin graft. But he refused point-blank to go to Tobruk. He'd heard about it, he said, and he wouldn't set foot in it. So I kept him, and without any special sterilising his hand healed up.

'Although I was used by now to seeing dead men, I must confess that when I went over the battlefield at Sidi Rezegh I found it very difficult to stomach. It was a dreadful experience seeing so many of our boys dying, dead, and mutilated. There had been no chance to bury them. One man on an anti-tank gun had had a flame-thrower turned on him, and there he was, like a Giacometti statue, totally charred. I couldn't bear to look. I found the body of a fellow doctor, Gerald Kraudis, who had been shot in the forehead. From the way he had fallen I believe he had been trying to stop a German tank – there were tracks that suggested that – from approaching his wounded men. One

---

* On 27 November 1941, only to be recaptured by Rommel on 21 June 1942.

of the Germans shot him in the head with a Luger. In the heat of battle you can't say they fired on the Red Cross; it's battle, and terrible things can happen in a battle.

'Because the desert campaign was so mobile, we RMOs rarely had time to dig in properly. Most of the time we would simply quickly dig down as far as we could go, stretch, a piece of canvas across from my truck to keep the sun off, and deal with the men there and then. If I had casualties at night, which was rare, since most of the action was in daylight we would rig up a twelve-volt battery from a truck with a lamp slung about where I was working.

'There were no sterile conditions. We just washed our hands. But we knew about infections, and every man carried a first-aid dressing, a little packet containing an acriflavine pad and bandage, and if he couldn't put it on himself a first-aid man or an ambulance corps man would slap it on. We carried sterile dressings in sealed tins.

'The important thing was to get the men out as quickly as possible. To save time I would get a man into the ambulance and examine him there, stop the bleeding and make him comfortable so that he could go out of the line. If I had a lot of casualties I had to make very difficult decisions about who should go in the ambulance. An ambulance could carry four men, and I would have to decide who would go and who would wait for the next run. For example, I had to choose between a man with a terrible abdominal wound and a man who had been blinded. In the end I sent the man with the abdominal wound off first, because I thought he might be saved (he died in the ambulance), whereas the man who had been blinded was, very simply, blind.

'If we were going to stay in a place for a while, as at El Alamein, the engineers would come and dig down four or five feet and make us a neat little dug-out with sandbags all round. At El Alamein I even had a corrugated-iron roof. Our position there was right on the ridge with the 1st SA Division, fairly near to Sanyet el Miteiriya. We knew that a battle was imminent, but it was only at the very last minute that we were told tonight was the night.* I was all prepared, with my instruments ready and dressings and splints on hand. Although I knew there was going to be a barrage, when it began I got a terrible fright. It was mighty, there was no other word for it. The hairs on your arms stood up. It wasn't frightening, because the guns were shooting over our heads, but the barrage was almost continuous, just an endless boom boom boom boom, and as far as we could see flashing against the night sky.

'After the barrage the infantry and the tanks went in, and we began to get casualties. For me, they were the worst casualties of the war, terrible things. They were such ghastly wounds. One poor boy

---

* 23 October 1942.

A stretcher-bearer waiting for the gun barrage at El Alamein. (South African National Museum of Military History)

was brought in with his arm blown off. A shell had passed through his chest, dismembering his arm. He had his paybook in his pocket with a photograph of his wife, and half of it had been sliced away, just as if it had been cut by scissors, by the shell. There was nothing I could do for him.

'The padre was always there, to comfort the wounded and help the dying on their way and to bury them. One didn't have time to think when one was under fire, but the sights I saw during those years are sights I never want to see again as long as I live. ’

• Interview 1990

CHAPTER

51

'Some little comfort'

The Rev Stanley Pitts, the Northern Desert and El Alamein, October 1942

As a small boy in south-west London Stanley Pitts was snatched from his bed by his mother and carried in her arms, as she sought shelter in a cellar to escape a Zeppelin bombing raid in the First World War. He came under fire again in the second, in the northern desert.

He was twenty-two when he arrived in South Africa as a candidate for the Methodist Church, and he was a probationer minister in Claremont in Cape Town when the war broke out. Pitts, a blunt-speaking, warm-hearted man, didn't hesitate to offer his services as a chaplain. 'The very thought of sitting back when other men were going away to fight was anathema to me.' He became one of the Chaplains' Branch of the Union Defence Force, which had been formed at Roberts Heights in 1914, and served with the 1st and 6th SA Divisions' Artillery Regiments in North Africa and Italy. He ended the war as Senior Chaplain of the Free Churches with the Middle East and Central Mediterranean South African Forces.

He tells his own story from the time of his arrival in North Africa (November 1941) until his brief return to South Africa after the battle of El Alamein.

'I first came under fire at a place called Timimi, out in the desert. One minute all was calm and the next the ground was shaking and there was dust everywhere, and the muffled whine as the shells came over. I was terrified – I wanted to run, to save myself. I had a tin hat, but it seemed very small protection at the time. I can remember the perspiration and a kind of animal fear. Then I said to myself: "Look, old boy, if you run now, you'll never face anything in the future," and of course I stayed. How could I have looked my God in the face if I had run?

'When I packed to go Up North I took very little with me. A Bible and some clothes. We chaplains wore uniforms, like everybody else, but we had a special badge, a star, with the insignia "In this sign conquer." Sometimes I wore a dog-collar and sometimes I didn't, but I always wore one when I held a service in a gun-pit, which I did frequently, and I also always wore a special lightweight cassock I had made for me, and that was an enormous help. When you are in a gun-pit there's not much space for reverence and awe, so you did what you could, and I think the cassock helped.

'Every chaplain was given a truck and I used to drive all over the place to see the men, who as artillery were very scattered, and I visited the headquarters of the unit, which might be a little distance behind the front. For services I would get into the gun-pit with the men, put up a collapsible table with a cloth on it for an altar, and put a cross on that. That cross was very special: one of the men in the transport section made it for me from driftwood that landed on a beach. It was very useful, too, because it was collapsible and I could assemble it quickly. The services would be quite brief when there were shells flying overhead, but there was a responsiveness on the part of people you don't find in civilian life. It was partly camaraderie and partly coming face to face with the fact that when the men were under fire it might be their turn to go next.

'No one in the 4th Field ever asked me for help when they were under fire; they were much too busy for that. But I know that my ability to face fire was a result of my faith; and the same was true for many of the men.

'I didn't only say services, though, nor was my ministry confined to being with the wounded and the dying or with counselling. I used to see that the men, especially in the long training periods, had literature to read. I ran a sort of library from the back of the truck. I would pitch up in the middle of the desert and let the tailgate down, and the chaps would come and exchange their books.

'Our headquarters were in Cairo, and we chaplains held conferences there from time to time when we could be freed and things were quiet.* There was a great camaraderie amongst us, with great co-operation between the chaplains of all faiths. When you were assigned to a unit you were the padre of that unit, no matter what your denomination and no matter what the religious affiliations of the boys were. But if a boy had a particularly strong denominational feeling a chaplain who represented faiths that were smaller in number were usually at headquarters, and they would move around to see the boys rather than have a unit of their own.

'We lived with the men, going backwards and forwards across North Africa. When you came to a place a hole would be dug and your

---

* The Chaplains' Branch of the UDF made appointments for the Anglican, Catholic, Dutch, Jewish and Free Church faiths from 1940. In 1942 there were 159 full-time chaplains. Three of them were killed and fifteen taken prisoner.

A church service in a gun-pit at Gazala in the Western Desert. Padres went everywhere with a collapsible altar and a Bible. They comforted the wounded, said the last rites and buried the dead. (The Rev Stanley Pitts)

A Heath-Robinson system of bells in the desert, calling the men to a service. (The Rev Stanley Pitts)

tent would go over that. You would make yourself comfortable; and it's an incredible thing, how comfortable you could be and how quickly you settled in, especially if we were going to be in one place for some time, as at Gazala. Not that they were always safe: an Anglican chaplain called Wheeler got a shell all to himself when he was in his hole.

'I arrived at Port Tewfik in November 1941, just after Sidi Rezegh. It was shocking, going over that battlefield. The place was littered with burnt-out tanks, and corpses everywhere, lying under the sun. Sidi Rezegh was fought over a wide area, but no matter where you looked you saw death. Burnt-out tanks with charred corpses – a grim business. I was very shaken. I stood there and wondered about man's inhumanity to man; but of course you are caught up in something bigger than individual responses. The utter shockingness of war struck me particularly there. It was terrible that fellows should be caught in a tank and roasted; terrible.

'Each unit had a doctor. If the battle was static there would be a tent and the wounded would be brought there, tended to as quickly as possible and then moved out. But if a man was dying you went to him. At Gazala, where there was a lot shelling, the doctor and I were called out to a young signaller who had been hit very badly.

'He was about twenty, with blondish hair, lying on his own. There wasn't much blood. He had been hit by a shell splinter. The doctor examined him, but there was nothing he could do. The boy had been trying to mend a cable on the surface when he was hit. I am not even sure he was conscious, but I prayed with the fellow and stayed with him until he died. I wrote the letter home. I didn't pray for boys who had died. They are in the hands of God and I believe they will be ministered to. But I prayed for the living, for the families.

An ecumenical conference of churchmen in Cairo, discussing problems common to padres whatever their denomination might be. (The Rev Stanley Pitts)

'The morale of the boys was sometimes very low, but when Monty came there was a great change. He never moved until he was ready, and that gave the fellows confidence. It seemed to us astonishing that each time Rommel attacked he did it in much the same way, and each time we were virtually in the bag. No one seemed to learn from his tactics, and of course we South Africans had been greatly shaken by Sidi Rezegh and Tobruk. But Monty changed all that.

'We were at Alamein for a fairly long period before the battle. Roads were carved and the armour he had demanded arrived; but when the attack was launched there was no doubt about the outcome.

'The unit at El Alamein was part of a much bigger and grander thing. It happened suddenly. The sky was suddenly lit up and the ground opened up – it was tremendous. When that moment came there was never a doubt that we would go through. There was a lot of work for me to do, very sad. It was also the occasion when I had to write the saddest letter I have ever written.

'There was this family living in the Wilderness, with five sons. One had been killed in a motor accident just before the war. The second died of the 'flu in the early part of the war at Premier Mine. The third was killed in the SAAF. Both remaining sons were in our regiment. One was an officer, the other, the youngest, was a despatch rider.

'We used to send out armed patrols in an armoured car. This young artillery officer was sent to reconnoitre. It was a place where Jerry shelled every day, at irregular intervals. He went to this spot, a shell landed, and he was killed. Just like that. I wrote to his parents. Because of this terrible family tragedy, we applied at once to send the remaining youngster back to base. The night before his transfer came through there was a critical situation, and a message had to be delivered to a neighbouring unit – there were no telephone lines and communications had been cut. And the only despatch rider was this fellow, so he had to go.

'He ran into a minefield, his leg was blown off and he died, he died out there, the last of the sons. I sat in my tent, and I had to write to the family … again … five sons … nothing left. It was the most terrible thing. With one lost, well, all right; but five sons, and then nothing. My heart bled for those parents, their five sons, gone, gone. Perhaps my letter brought some little comfort.

'It didn't shake my faith. My faith is not that everything is going right, that all will be well. What we are called upon to do is to make a better world. Our Lord was quite clear: in this world you will have trouble, and He was right. I prayed for those poor, dear parents. ’

• Interview 1990

CHAPTER

52

'Now it's your time to come forward to help'

Maj-Gen Dan Pienaar asking for men, November 1942

The first phase of the battle of El Alamein had been successfully concluded. At last there was good news at home. The battle, which began at 9.25 p.m. on 23 October with a thousand gun artillery bombardment, was fought by British and Commonwealth troops with a clear superiority.* By 4 November the enemy troops had begun their long, hard retreat which finally ended in their capitulation on 12 May 1943.

For Britain and the loyal Commonwealth troops the El Alamein battles clearly signalled the turning of the tide in their favour.

In North Africa, a tired but delighted Maj-Gen Dan Pienaar, OC 1st SA Division, allowed himself a brief moment of triumph after the battle by speaking to South Africans at home. Pienaar was by far the most popular of all the senior wartime South African commanders; he spoke fluent English and Afrikaans and good Zulu, all with a rapid delivery.

His message to South Africans was simple and direct: we've won a great battle, but don't allow yourselves to become complacent; and please, we desperately need more men. Pienaar's message on 21 November 1942 from 'somewhere Up North' was heard by hundreds of thousands of listeners at home:

'I am sending this message to you from all of us serving in the north, and especially from those of us who are serving in the 1st SA Division. As you all know, this Division has played its part in the battle across Africa, from Kenya through Somaliland, Abyssinia and Egypt.

---

* 195 000 British and Commonwealth troops to 104 000 Germans and Italians; 489 German tanks to the British 1 029; 1 219 German guns to 2 311 British and Commonwealth and 350 serviceable German and Italian aircraft to the 530 serviceable aircraft of the Desert Air Force.

'During this long war the Division has had its ups and downs, but it has never been broken or defeated. The Division has been involved in heavy fighting for the past twelve months. This terminated with the recent resounding victory at El Alamein. There, on that narrow stretch of desert between El Alamein and the Qattara Depression, one of the greatest battles in history was fought, from 23 October to 7 November.

'During this period, twelve enemy Divisions were completely destroyed as fighting entities. These included Rommel's mighty panzer army. We fought against a well-trained and resolute, determined enemy, but notwithstanding his high morale, arrogance and excellent fortifications, his defences were completely smashed at an unbelievably low cost of human lives to ourselves.

'South Africa can be more than proud of the magnificent conduct of her sons. I have never known morale to be higher than during this great and historical battle. I have never known such success to be achieved in so short a time in an onslaught of this description. It can be truly said that all troops who took part in this battle reacted magnificently to every task which they were called upon to do.

'In this great battle South Africans fought shoulder to shoulder with Australians, Highlanders and New Zealanders. In fact, the whole of the Commonwealth and the United States of America were represented, either on land, in the air, or both. And I feel it was a great honour to have played our part in this great and historic battle, conjointly with all our friends of the United Nations.

'There are many who view the war as won and over. Any ideas that all is over bar the shouting is absurd. A glimpse at the map, I think, will convince students of strategy that the Axis powers will make every endeavour to use every force at their disposal to prevent the Mediterranean being reopened to Allied shipping. It therefore follows they will do all in their power to retain a foothold on the north coast of Africa.

'I would therefore like to warn everybody against complacency and smug satisfaction. There is a lot of hard fighting to be done before we can even think of resting. During the last year's fighting our ranks were depleted by normal wastage and battle casualties. These losses have made reinforcements urgently necessary to ensure the maintenance of our units at full battle strength.

'Further serious efforts will be made by the Axis powers to get hold of the Suez Canal and the fertile Nile Delta in order to link up with their eastern partners through the Red Sea and so cut our vital lifeline across our main sea-routes.

'I feel that the Axis sun is past its zenith, but it would be premature to say that it is immediately setting. A great deal has been done, but much more will have to be done before this war is won.

'I therefore call on every able-bodied man in South Africa who is capable of carrying arms to come forward and join the services now. Recruits are particularly needed for our armoured formations, which include infantry, artillery, tank personnel, signallers and workshop personnel. Your fellow-countrymen in the north have faced the music for a long time. Now it's your time to come forward to help them in order to be ready to go forward to meet the enemy during the next phases in which the South African troops will take part.

'There are many armchair critics who have no knowledge of the components needed to fight a modern battle. They say that the day of the infantryman and the artilleryman is past. I can give you the assurance that this is as much a war of guns and bayonets plus the other arms with which our modern infantry is equipped as in previous wars.

'The great battle in the north, which has now passed to its second phase, again demonstrated the destructive power of artillery and the necessity of infantry and engineers to create the necessary bridgeheads, lift mines etc, in order to allow armoured formations to pass through. No army can be complete without the full establishments of those most important arms, and no armoured formation can fight without adequate infantry and artillery support.

'South Africa has played a magnificent part in this war so far. We must continue that contribution until the day of final victory. Every fit man is needed. Men and women of South Africa, I leave the rest to you.'

• SABC Archives

CHAPTER

53

'He was so deeply loved'

Norma Pienaar on her husband, Maj-Gen Dan Pienaar

He was a prickly customer, was Dan Pienaar. Temperamental, obstinate, suspicious of authority, a heavy drinker. He was also a patriot, a brilliant tactician, a family man, utterly devoted to his men, informal, dashing, courageous; and from the time when he went Up North, a teetotaller.

When he died in an aeroplane crash at Kisumu *en route* for South Africa the country lost one of its legends. The mourning at Pienaar's funeral in the military cemetery at Roberts Heights was exceeded only by that given to Smuts in September 1950.

Pienaar was a man of the people – that was part of his appeal. By the time war broke out he had had an extraordinarily varied military career; he had held the position of Officer Commanding Wits Command, and at the end of 1939 he was promoted full colonel.

With a new and young wife of only one year,* getting ready for war could have not been easy for him.

With his strong Afrikaans accent, fluent English and fluent Zulu, Pienaar embarked on an intensive recruiting campaign. His theme was a simple one: unity for the country on a common front to defend South Africa against a 'fierce and dangerous enemy'. Reviewing the Botha Regiment in Pietersburg, Pienaar gave voice to his own thoughts. 'Patriotism is useless for the man who merely talks … The worst soldier that ever lived is one hundred times better than the best man out of uniform.'

He was appointed Brigade Commander 1st SA Infantry Brigade. He stood on the Durban docks watching the first South African troops boarding a troopship. 'Well,' he said to a padre standing beside him, 'I've just had my last drink.'

---

* Pienaar married Norma Klerck, his second wife, on 29 November 1938. His first wife and the mother of his three children, Eileen Leffler, died in January 1937.

Two days after Dan Pienaar died cartoons appeared in newspapers all over the country. This one, which appeared in the *Natal Mercury* on 21 December 1942, was one of the most effective. (*Natal Mercury*)

'What do you mean?' asked the padre, J A Robertson.

'I'm on the water-cart for the rest of the war. I have got to set an example to my boys,' replied Pienaar. And indeed he stayed on the water-waggon for the rest of his life.

He was awarded the first DSO to a South African in the Second World War, and after sweeping through Abyssinia and Somalia he joined his men in Egypt. It was there in the arid sands of the desert that the love affair between Pienaar and his men was forged, and the legend took firm root. He described the Springboks as 'the finest youngsters who ever drew God's air'; and they responded in kind.

'Two points struck everybody who met Dan Pienaar,' wrote Samuel Brewer, war correspondent to the *Chicago Tribune*: 'first, a disregard for personal danger; second, his solicitude for his men.' Pienaar wanted the war to be over quickly. He intended to go into parliament, and he was in a hurry to get his men back home safely and get on with his life. 'There's far too much talk of striking the enemy in 1944 or 1945,' he once snapped. 'The time to strike him is right now, and the place to strike him is right where he is.'

After Sidi Rezegh Pienaar and the 1st SA Brigade held the line at Gazala, fifty miles north of Bir Hakeim. After the withdrawal of the 1st SA Brigade and the 50th British Division through McDougall Pass, Pienaar's energies were directed towards the coming battle at Alamein.

He worked feverishly. 'As he grew smaller and thinner, the steel within him seemed to gather strength and spring', Maj-Gen Godwin

Austen described him at the time. 'Get after them, get their tail-feathers,' he urged his men, refusing the 1st Division the traditional tot of rum before battle because 'my boys need no synthetic courage'.

After El Alamein Pienaar went home for the last time. On the day he left, 15 November 1942, he was admitted to the military division of the Most Honourable Order of the Bath. He stayed at home for eleven days, tired and tense, and arrived back in the Middle East on 28 November. He wrote his last letter home on 12 December.

A few days later, on 17 November the man whom Peterborough of the *Daily Telegraph* described as 'one of the most brilliant tacticians in the Middle East ... a born leader whom men will follow anywhere', was on board a Lockheed Lodestar *en route* for South Africa. Its captain, Douglas Mail, fifty-one, had logged fifteen thousand flying hours, or one and a half million miles. He was tired, and Pienaar, eager to get home, was urging him on. On 18 December the Lodestar flew from Luxor to Kisumu, a distance of about two thousand miles. 'Duggie looks done-in,' said someone of the pilot.

Early the following morning the plane fell from the sky soon after take-off. No one survived.

Back home Norma Pienaar, Dan's young wife, was readying the house for his return. This is her story:

'The car came slowly down Magazine Road. The moment it stopped outside our house I knew something was wrong. I just stood there, rooted to the spot. Then Pierre van Ryneveld* and George Brink got out of the car and walked towards me. I knew then something terrible had happened to Dan.

'He was a charismatic man, I knew that the moment he walked into my flat four years before. He asked me to go to Pretoria and have dinner with him at the Union Hotel, where he was staying at the time. I suppose it was love at first sight. Everyone except my parents, who had indirectly introduced us, thought I was crazy to be marrying a man twenty years older than myself, with three very naughty children, the eldest of whom was only ten years younger than I was.

'We were married on 28 November 1938. Almost from the day we were married there was talk of war. He was a very gregarious man, and the house was always filled with his friends, and I often used to hear him say that some day soon we would be going to war. On Sunday, 3 September 1939 we had a lunch party in our home at Roberts Heights.

---

* General Sir Pierre van Ryneveld, Chief of the SA General Staff and Maj-Gen George Brink, former GOC 1st SA Division and now GOC Inland Area.

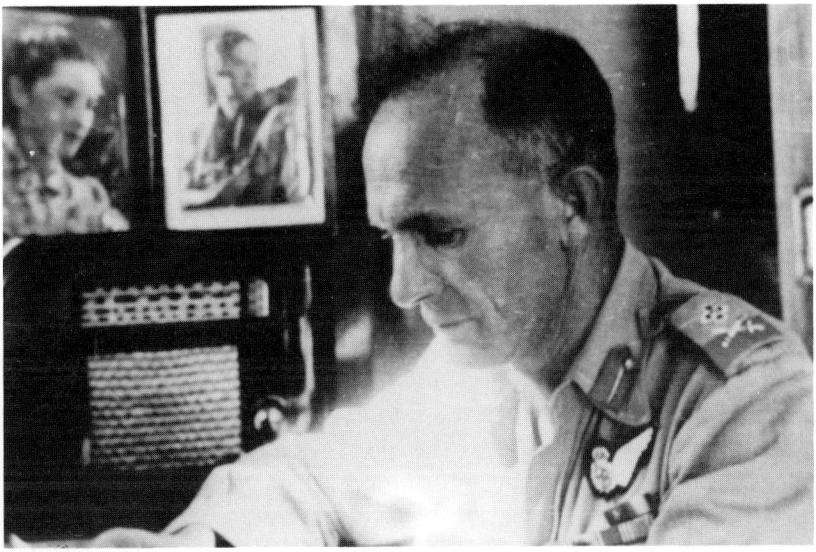

Dan Pienaar in reflective mood. He took a photograph of his second wife, Norma, with him everywhere. (South African National Museum of Military History)

Pienaar was informal with his men, and they responded with warmth and loyalty. He was much missed. (South African National Museum of Military History)

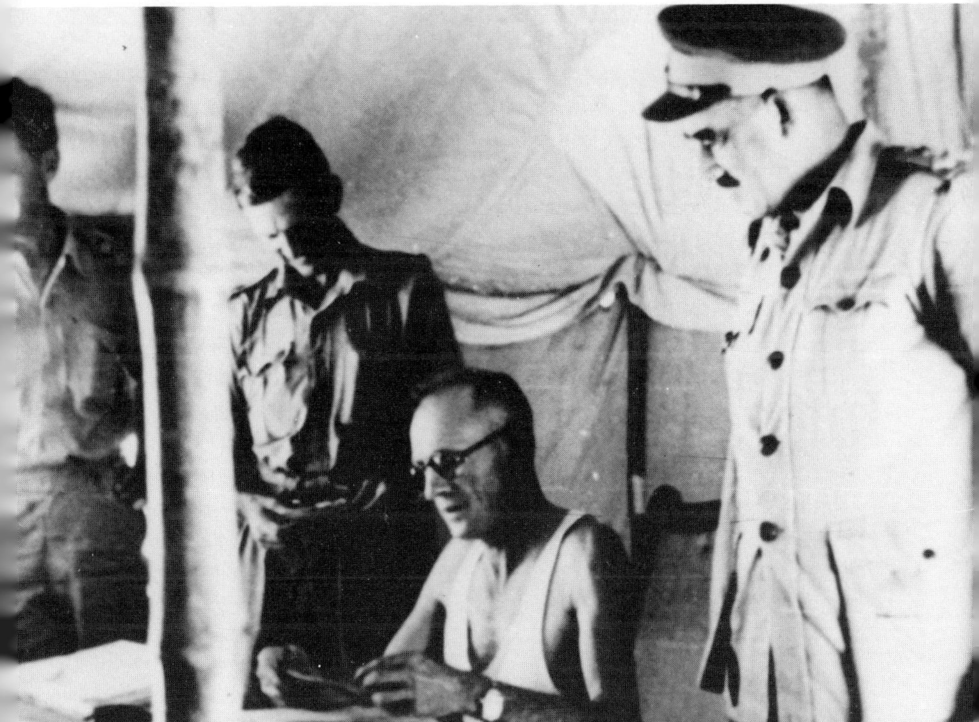

'My parents and some friends were there. Dan turned the radio on, and we all sat and listened to Neville Chamberlain telling the world that Britain was at war with Germany.

'I went cold. I realised that he and I had to part. I knew he would go. It never occurred to him not to serve, not to volunteer. He had it in his blood, and he loved South Africa. He was a soldier ready to serve his country, and a soldier should have no politics. When Chamberlain finished talking there was a hush. Then Dan got up and took out a bottle. "Let's drink champagne together," he said.

'South Africa had to raise a volunteer army, and right from the beginning Dan was involved in recruitment. He went to hundreds of meetings. Sometimes he went alone, sometimes I went with him. One night we went together to Brits, which was very National Party and anti-war. There were only two men in the audience wearing the red flashes. The police warned Dan that there was a great deal of agitation and unrest. They put us into a room on our own and fetched us out at the appropriate time.

'Dan climbed on to the platform and looked at the men in front of him. "I know you want to shoot me tonight," he said, "but I also know that no one here has the guts to do so." With that sort of bravado the crowd was stunned. Nobody did anything. I was so proud of him. Police escorted us home that night and told us to sleep with our windows shut.

'He was terribly busy at that time, very much under pressure. He used to come home very late at night. He didn't talk much about what he had been doing, but he did talk about the volunteer army. He was enormously proud of it, and he felt a great sense of responsibility towards the men who had volunteered. He used to say that he had to look after his men. "General Haig* said that his men must all die for their country. But what is the good of a dead man to his country? They have to live to fight." He was always very sparing of men.

'He remembered old comrades from years before. We would go to military dances and functions and I would suddenly find myself without a husband. I would retrace my steps to the front door and find him talking to the doorman whom he had known years before. He always had that warmth.

'Dan was very bothered about the Italians as a threat to us, of their moving into Kenya, and he believed that the first thing the South Africans had to do was to push them out of Africa. He knew the volunteer army would be going Up North soon, and he felt very much for me because I was very young and there were the three children whom

---

* Sir Douglas Haig, C-in-C British forces, was an austere Scot and responsible for the strategy of attrition in the 1914–18 war. He believed that it was possible to break through German trenches with cavalry charges in mass tactics. He died in 1928.

he had to leave behind, but we didn't talk about it much. We simply accepted it.

'Before he went Up North* we discussed what would happen if he died. I didn't really relish talking about it, and I didn't encourage it very much. He told me his pension would be very small, but that in addition to his army pension he qualified for a pension from the Natal Police in which he had served before he joined the army. It didn't bother me at all, looking after the children. What bothered me was the growing hysteria about men going north.

'Many of the wives became rather hysterical, and I was asked to go and calm them, many of them considerably older than I was. Most of the women were living either in Roberts Heights or Pretoria. Somehow it seemed natural for me to do these things. Everybody finds me very placid. And Dan expected it of me.

'Whenever Dan went to mess dinner and came home to change, he expected me to lay his clothes out for him and chat while he was dressing, even if I had friends in the house at the time. So when the time came for him to go I did his packing. He put what he wanted out and I packed it. He took a photograph of me, and it went with him wherever he went, right to the end. I said goodbye to him at Roberts Heights, and I was very calm as he drove away.

'But instead of getting straight on to a train he went to Premier Mine. A message came through asking me to gather all the girls and wives together and bring them out for a farewell dance on the evening before they went. We danced all night, but it was all terribly nostalgic, and there were a lot of tears. It's hard saying goodbye and then having to do it all over again. When I said goodbye the second time I was very controlled, but my feelings were very deep. It was so much to give up, and I knew I had enormous responsibilities ahead of me with the minimum of happiness and married life.

'He wrote to me regularly, and of course I wrote to him often.

'I kept a scrapbook of all the newspaper cuttings of all the battles that were going on. He didn't write much about his problems, either in Abyssinia or in the desert, but he did find the British commanders, who were all trained at Sandhurst, to be textbook men who were somewhat at a loss when they got on to a battlefield and had to apply their knowledge in reality. Dan was very much an artillery man, and he had precious little military education, but he was well read, and he had a very natural flair for tactics. His boys could improvise, he said, and they understood terrain because they understood the veld.

'He came home only once before El Alamein, and we went on a motoring holiday. I drove the car all the way: he was thoroughly

* With the 1st SA Infantry Brigade, which left for East Africa on 16 July 1941.

exhausted. He didn't want to talk of his experiences, of Sidi Rezegh or Tobruk or Gazala. He couldn't sit still, and we had to be on the move all the time. There was one little incident that was very telling, I thought. We stayed at a little hotel in Knysna. The garden was full of daffodils, and I said "Look at those lovely yellow daffodils." Dan shuddered.

'"Yellow is cowardice," he said. We spoke no more of the daffodils.

'Dan came home for the last time just after the battle of El Alamein. He was with us for five or six days to make arrangements for the troops to come back home.

'He told me that after the battle he had been offered the command of a British army. At that time South Africa had only two divisions and a British army had three, so it was a great honour. It was offered to him privately, and he was thinking about it, no more than that. I don't know whether he would have accepted it or not.

'"It's a great honour," he said, "but if I accept I shall have to desert my own." I thought that it was a feather in the cap of any South African, something the country could be proud of.

'It wasn't a premonition, I think; but this time I couldn't keep my feelings under control. It was very dark when I saw him out to the car. I stood at the door as he got in, and I was still begging. "Please take me with you," I kept saying. He just looked at me and said "No." The car drew away, and I went back into the house to the three children. I cried myself to sleep. I knew I was being irrational, because I would be seeing him again fairly soon.

'The days passed until the day when I was expecting him home again, this time for a long stay. It was a Saturday, and I went to the market and bought a great many flowers and I filled the house with them, from top to bottom. There were no yellow flowers. I was supposed to go to a big society wedding in Pretoria that afternoon, but I just wanted to be at home, getting things ready.

'The children were out. I went to the letter box, and lying in it there was a letter from Dan. I began to open it as I walked back. That was when I saw the car. I stood there as Sir Pierre and George Brink came up to me. We were still outside when they told me Dan had been killed.* I don't remember walking into the house, and I have no idea how I got up to our bedroom. I don't even remember telling the children that he was dead, but I suppose I must have.

'My parents came and stayed with me, and every day I had hordes of visitors, all the cabinet ministers and their wives, diplomats,

* Col Frederick Theron, Lt-Col Eric Frykberg, Lt-Col Eric MacKenzie, Maj Frank Rawlins, Maj John Bell, Capt Peter Bairnsfather Cloete, Capt James Mail, Lt William Lloyd, Air Sgt Cecil Flush, Sgt Archibald Weldon and Air Corporal L B Lafayette were killed at the same time.

soldiers, and people from Johannesburg and Pretoria came in droves. At half past twelve each day my father would say: "Now, no more until two-thirty," and a friend, Vivia Steenkamp,* took me upstairs to the bathroom and undressed me and sponged me down from top to bottom with cool water and wrapped me in a dressing-gown; and I would rest for a while until the people came again.

'The funeral was two days after Christmas. There were so many people who wanted to come that no church could hold them, so the service was held on the sports ground at Roberts Heights. There was a huge crowd. Field Marshal Smuts gave the funeral oration; and the bodies of those who had died with him were buried together. When that was over and the soldiers marched away the band played "It's a Long Way to Tipperary", and everyone sang, to break the tension. I think I joined in. I was emotionally drained.

'Even though he had been dead for such a short time, people kept asking me to come to this or that reception, they expected me to make speeches. My father helped me to write them, and I would take the speech with me and go riding; and as I rode I would make the speech so that I could get used to the sound of my voice. But there is only one speech that I remember.

'When the 1st Division landed at Durban I went down to welcome them home. "In the absence of my husband I have come to greet you," I said. Many of them had tears in their eyes.

'I remember him as probably the finest leader of men there has ever been in South Africa. He was so deeply loved, and not the least by me. '

• Interview 1990

The funeral of Maj-Gen Pienaar and the men who died with him was at the military cemetery in Roberts Heights. Thousands of men and women of all ages, colours and persuasions lined the roads leading to the cemetery in a spontaneous display of respect and affection.

Every unit of the SADF was represented, land, sea and air. Diplomats and service chiefs stood beside the Pienaar family. Standing in front of the gun carriages, Field Marshal Smuts described the dead as 'clean, strong, lion-hearted men'. Pienaar, he said, 'first conquered himself and his own weakness … it will be universally admitted that he was the finest tactical general – *Veggeneraal* – whom South Africa has so far produced in this war … he literally exhaled dash and bravery and the atmosphere of victory.'

---

* The sister of Dr Willem Steenkamp. (See: 'Not above the knee, sir?')

Pienaar's funeral at Roberts Heights. With him were buried all the men who died in the crash at Kisumu. (South African National Museum of Military History).

At the same time, in the Western Desert that he knew so well, men with tears running down their faces lined up to pay tribute to Dan. They stood silently as the prayers were said in English and in Afrikaans. Then the buglers played the Last Post and the flag was hoisted again.

Norma Pienaar served in the army until the end of the war. She opened a small dress shop in Pretoria, and after two years she remarried and went to live in Britain. The three children were educated by the Dan Pienaar Memorial Fund.

CHAPTER

54

1943

Black militancy, the khaki election and the baby boom

Two and a half years of unbroken warfare lay before the Union at the beginning of 1943. But times were changing, and for the better.

The success of El Alamein in October 1942, a meticulously planned and executed set-piece battle, had given heart not only to South Africa but to the other hard-pressed Allies too. The defeat of the Axis forces in North Africa was now inevitable (on 8 April Rommel was recalled to Germany), and attention could be turned to new theatres of war.

On New Year's Day advance units of 1st SA Division came home. Two weeks later the bulk of the Division sailed into Durban harbour on board the *Nieuw Amsterdam.* Twenty thousand people gathered in Johannesburg to welcome them home after two years' fighting. Amidst the banners and the bunting Gen George Brink, now Officer Commanding Inland Command, told the men that there was still a lot of hard work to be done. 'I know that whatever the Oubaas asks of you in the future, you will respond, as the 1st Division has always responded in the past.'

Next day, in Casablanca, the historic conference to determine the future conduct of the war took place between Churchill, Roosevelt and De Gaulle. Nothing other than total surrender would be accepted by the Allies.

Since it was obvious that the North African campaign had only a limited course to run, a motion was introduced in the House of Assembly for voluntary service anywhere in the world (the General Service Oath) – but many soldiers, dissatisfied with conditions and indifferent leadership, refused to take the oath.

In spite of the increasing difficulty of obtaining volunteers for the UDF and the disturbing information that many Afrikaners serving with the UDF were also 'serving' with the Ossewabrandwag, the 6th

Armoured Division, under the command of Maj-Gen W H E Poole, was formed on 1 February. Desperately short of men as it was, the UDF was heartened by news from Salisbury on 23 March that all Rhodesians serving with the UDF would be general service personnel. But the dissolution without justifiable reason of the proud SA Tank Corps emphasized the dissatisfaction.

There was serious inflation on the local property market, in spite of the Fixed Property Profits Tax. Estate agents on the Witwatersrand, ever ready for a quick buck, offered profits of £1 000 as an inducement for property owners to sell their houses. On 11 March amidst dramatic scenes at the Pretoria Supreme Court, Robey Leibbrandt was given the death sentence, and retired behind bars for the rest of the war.

By the beginning of April the battle of the Atlantic had reached its peak. Two hundred and forty U-Boats sank over six hundred thousand tons of vital shipping, some of it destined for the Union. The enemy forces, at the end of their tether, retreated into northern Tunisia, and on 19 April the 6th SA Armoured Division, with its complement of Rhodesians, sailed for the Middle East and a long period of training. But they knew they were going to places further afield than the Middle East. Trains *en route* for Durban were covered with graffiti: 'Destination Berchtesgaden' said one optimistically.

As the first part of a consignment of ten thousand half-litre bottles of blood serum destined for the Russian Army donated by six thousand South Africans left South Africa, news came on 12 May that the once invincible Afrika Korps had surrendered.

It was suddenly fashionable to be, if not a communist, at least pro-Russian as the titanic struggle between the Russian and German forces developed. The membership of the South African Communist Party (SACP), as low as three hundred in 1939, rose to several thousand in 1943. 'Defend South Africa' rallies held by the SACP took place all over the country, together with a mischievous campaign to give UDF 'natives' arms. The SABC even allowed the singing of the 'Internationale' over the air.

The brief moratorium on the Pass Laws ended in 1943 and the charismatic thirty-three-year-old Anton Muziwakhe Lembede, newly arrived in Johannesburg, preached an aggressive message to his black countrymen: Africans are one; Africa belongs to Africans; they must work together for national liberation and adopt a militant attitude, fight for black rights.

Dr Alfred Xuma was president of the African National Congress (ANC), and his council of five had abolished the House of Chiefs, given equal rights to women in the organisation, and, even more significantly, permitted the founding of an ANC Youth League (CYL), the first meeting of which was held the following year, with membership open to all blacks between the ages of twelve and forty and with Anton Lembede as its first president. The Congress Youth League had a handful of young men at its core: Walter Sisulu, Peter Mda, Jordan Ngubane, William Nkomo, and Nelson Mandela.

The founding of the CYL, whose Young Turks were unimpressed by the then ANC policy of appeasing whites, the birth of the squatter movement, the establishment of the African Mineworkers' Union (in 1941), a series of work stoppages on the mines and the subsequent appointment of the Lansdowne Commission to investigate the working conditions and wages of black miners, all demonstrated the growing militancy of black nationalists.

When bus fares from Alexandra to central Johannesburg were raised the workers boycotted the buses; twenty thousand men and women walked the ten miles to and from town every day. The ten-day protest was marked by support of black workers by white liberals, members of the SACP, police and traffic department officials, and by the Department of Native Affairs.

Amid this embryonic militancy white South Africans went to the polls in the October 1943 'Khaki' election, which returned Smuts's United Party with eighty-nine seats and the National Party with forty-three, with the sixteen remaining seats shared between the Dominion Party and the Labour Party. Although it failed to win a seat, seven thousand whites voted for the SACP. The National Party, flushed with its success, wondered aloud whether it would take power by 1953.

Prescient café owners on the Witwatersrand may have known the answer: several were prosecuted under an ordinance of 1904 for reading fortunes with tea-leaves. This storm in a teacup came shortly before a new theatre of war opened, with the invasion by American and British Forces (and a handful of South Africans, mostly of the SAAF) of Sicily on 10 July.

Mussolini was deposed, and Gen Badoglio took his place; but his time as head of the state was brief. After the British (Messina) and American (Salerno) invasions of the Italian mainland, Italy capitulated unconditionally on 8 September. Meanwhile the 6th Armoured Division, thoroughly fed up and missing the show, was still in training in North Africa.

The 6th Div needn't have worried about missing anything: in a Roman volte-face Italy declared war on Germany. The enraged Hitler, keeping a weather eye upon the coast of France, where the main invasion must surely come, threw extra forces into Italy. The battles there, which lasted almost until the end of the war, were ferocious.

The capitulation of Italy had a direct effect on our prisoners of war languishing there. Warned by the BBC to remain within their camps until relieved by Allied soldiers, a few of the less trusting souls took to the hills, some fighting with partisans, some regaining Allied lines and coming home (like the ill-starred Maj-Gen Klopper, who reached Allied lines after a 150-mile walk through German held territory. In spite of support from local newspapers, Klopper's never very brilliant reputation did not recover from the surrender of Tobruk). But most of the prisoners of war were seized by German troops and sent to Germany or other German-held territory before Allied forces could reach them.

We protested about the shortage of meat. What was the country coming to? In Johannesburg a scrawny fowl was sold for 6s, and its triumphant purchaser was immediately offered 10s for it as she left the butcher's shop. Women in the Peninsula who, after all, had survived the Aussie convoys, queued for meat from 8 a.m. and cried piteously when they couldn't get any. A few of the more truculent shoppers threatened to break up butchers' shops if the situation didn't improve. The price of pork soared to 1s 4d a pound wholesale, higher than it had been for ten years.

By the end of the year petrol was rationed, with no sales permitted at all at the weekend. The number of white wartime babies reached its peak of 58 765 births in 1943. We rocked the cradle and listened to heart-throb crooner Frank Sinatra, we watched Ingrid Bergman and Gary Cooper in *For Whom the Bells Toll* and, at the end of the year, as Robey Leibbrandt languished in gaol and women knitted furiously for Ouma Smuts, we read an announcement that signalled the beginning of the end of the war: the appointment of the commanders of the proposed Allied invasion of mainland Europe.

The Supreme Allied Commander, we were told, would be Gen Dwight D Eisenhower. We were at the beginning of a roll, and we knew it.

CHAPTER

55

'Dearest Mom and Dad'

POW Corporal Robert Eckhardt's letters home, 1943

Nearly thirty-three thousand men were taken at Tobruk: nineteen thousand British troops, thirteen thousand South Africans and a few Indians for the loss of little more than three thousand German casualties between 26 May and 21 June. With the exception of four thousand black and Coloured South African troops, who were kept at Tobruk, the rest of the prisoners were sent to camps in Italy.

One of them was a young corporal, Robert C Eckhardt, serving in the headquarters of the 4th South African Infantry Brigade.* He was reported missing in June 1942 and the fact that he was prisoner of war was confirmed by a broadcast from Vatican City four months later.

Eckhardt was sent to *Campo Concentramento 85* PM 3450, the southernmost POW camp in Italy, not far from Taranto and facing the Adriatic. From there he wrote short postcards and letters to his parents, Mr and Mrs H R C Eckhardt of Calvinia. Often using only the stub of a pencil, his early letters illustrate one of the main preoccupations of prisoners of war: getting enough food. Eckhardt returned to South Africa via Germany and Britain in September 1945 after nearly five years' service, three years of it as a prisoner of war:

'**CAMPO PG 85 PM 3450**
ITALY
January 19 1943

Dearest Mom and Dad,
I am still fit and well and hope you are too. In my postcard of January 17 1943 I gave you a brief description of our meals, so now I want to tell you of my experiences since I was captured, starting from the time

* 2nd Royal Durban Light Infantry, 2nd Natal Mounted Rifles, Kaffrarian Rifles.

that the German officer collected us. I won't tell you about the battle on the Saturday or my feelings on Saturday and Sunday 20th and 21st of June. I was with my truck about 14 miles from the town on Saturday evening with the rest of our section. Bill Tyler and myself slept on solid rock about ten feet from the water's edge. Fortunately we had half a bottle of brandy with us, and as soon as it got dark the two of us had a stiff tot and I can assure you we needed it. Later on some Tommies joined us and we finished off the bottle and crept into our blanket. We pushed our heads under a piece of overhanging rock for protection against shrapnel. Anyway we slept like logs and never heard a sound until daylight on Sunday.

Everything was dead quiet, not a shot or anything else. This meant one of two things: they were beaten off, or were close. About 8.30 a.m. pillars of smoke were seen all over the place, and then fellows round us started burning their trucks. We destroyed ours about 9.30, and I had just broken my rifle when the German officer came to us. My last meal was on Friday evening, although I had had a few bites in between but I simply couldn't eat on Sunday. Anyway we had to march into town. We were not hurried by the Germans. We hadn't gone far when thirst got us. I'll never forget it. As we neared the town I asked a German in a truck for some water. He gave me a tin of milk and that saved Cecil and myself. Next week I will tell you about the water-point in town and of the following 4–5 days at Tobruk. Many happy returns on 18 April and 30 May, Dad and Mom. I hope we will be together for the next. DON'T FORGET TUCKBOX.
Love, Bob

February 10 1943

Dearest Mom and Dad,
Today has been a real Red Letter Day for me, so to complete it I am writing to you. It started off with news that parcels would be issued at the rate of one per man per week. Then I had first choice on bread and ration cheese. The next good thing was to hear that I draw my parcel today. Following on this, I had a good helping of soup at lunch. Next on the list came our cigarette ration, then the Italians issued us with two sheets each and then this letter card. So you can see it has been a terrific day. Owing to a shortage of milk everyone got a quarter of a 13½ oz of Nestle's coffee and milk. My supper in the evening started with soup. I drank the soup, separated my cabbage and macaroni, put some margarine on the hot cabbage and ate. My macaroni I mashed up with half of a 7-oz tin of salmon and half an onion I had scrounged. Next I ate an 8-oz tin of sausage (pork) and followed up with a bit of bread, margarine and jam. Next I mixed a little coffee and

LEFT: POW tags worn in Italian camps. (Property of Vivian Rees-Bevan)

BELOW: A German POW tag, with number and the name of the camp: *Stalag XIIIA*. (Property of Vivian Rees-Bevan)

ABOVE: Spending money for POWs, German style. The men were paid a small amount each week according to rank. (Property of Vivian Rees-Bevan)

RIGHT: A home-made purse made by Corporal Vivian Rees-Bevan. (Property of Vivian Rees-Bevan)

milk and water and finished up with 'iced coffee'. This was followed by a Players cigarette and half a $\frac{1}{4}$ lb slab of chocolate..I had a break of about an hour when I had a few biscuits, using the remainder of my coffee and milk as a spread. (The latter reminded me very much of Mom's coffee biscuits.) I then lay back and smoked half my cigar. To say I have fared sumptuously is putting it mildly. I don't think any meal has tasted better. I still have a meat roll, cheese, jam, margarine, and a few biscuits left for tomorrow. Cecil Tyler and myself share parcels and his comes up on Saturday. If you can please send me some cigarette papers (not allowed), I roll my own smokes out of 'entjies' now. Hoping to hear from you soon.
Love, Bob

June 27 1943

Dearest Mom and Dad,
I hope you are all well. Thanks ever so much for the parcel you sent off. I have written to thank Izak's dad for his gift. I've now turned farmer. We go out by cart in the morning and sleep in camp. The hours aren't very long and the farmer is quite good to us. Please include slippers (9).
Tons of love, Bob

July 28 1943

Dearest Mom and Dad,
I hope you are all keeping as well as I am. I have been farming for the past seven weeks but unfortunately it has come to an end now. I am sorry it has ended because it really was a very enjoyable diversion from camp routine. I've spent the whole day playing bridge – contract. I'm getting on famously but rather inclined to overcall sometimes. 'They' beat 'We' by 2200 on about 12 rubbers and every hand was crammed with interest. I wonder if you included a pipe in any of my parcels. My present one has been eaten away so much that the bowl squats right under my nose and I have to squint to see. I really don't know why I don't discard it, because there are plenty in the canteen. I think POW life must be making me a trifle sentimental. We just bought a good few 'spunspeks' and intend having a bit of a feast later on. We're rather flush at present, having received our farm pay. I'm dropping Frank Reid a line tonight, so I hope he gets it.
Tons of love, Bob.

• Africana Library, Kimberley

CHAPTER

56

'We kept loyalty to our flag and to our government'

Duilio de Francheschi, Italian prisoner of war

In 1943 there were about sixty thousand Italian, two thousand German and sixteen hundred French prisoners of war in South Africa.

The Germans, the Vichy French and a few Italians were repatriated, but most stayed in South Africa until after the end of the war.

By far the largest of the eighteen known Italian prisoner of war camps was Zonderwater, twenty miles from Pretoria, near the Cullinan Diamond Mine. The first Italian prisoners arrived in South Africa in April 1941, and they were accommodated all over the country. Zonderwater itself was opened in 1943 under the benevolent command of Col Hendrik Prinsloo (whose father, Cmdt H F Prinsloo, led the charge of the Carolina Commando at Spioenkop).

The Italians were treated, if not royally, at least with great generosity by their South African hosts. The Geneva Convention of 1929 (since then superseded) was signed by South Africa on 23 June 1931, and its provisions on the treatment of prisoners of war were scrupulously observed. Zonderwater, which was in fact a small town, held nearly a hundred thousand prisoners of war before it closed down on 1 January 1947.

The Italians who arrived in this country during the years of war were mostly captured in the East and North African campaigns. Many of them were illiterate, many of them were untrained for any trade. By the time less than a thousand prisoners had been repatriated, Zonderwater alone had taught nine thousand to read and write, and five thousand trained tradesmen took their skills back with them to Italy.

One of the men captured in Abyssinia was a sergeant-major, Duilio de Francheschi. Like every other prisoner he longed for food, good treatment, and contact with his motherland:

'My regiment was a proud one, the Alpine Regiment. My army number was 41917(96). Later I was to have another number, one I

Thousands of Italian prisoners of war were taught a trade while they were at Zonderwater.

The prisoners put on elaborate plays. Everything was made in the camp. (South African National Museum of Military History)

A home-made Christmas card made by Zonderwater Italian POWs and sent to officers and staff at the camp.

could have done without: 53813. It was a sad day for me, a former amateur champion boxer of Italy and a sergeant-major, to be taken prisoner by the British. My freedom ended on the banks of the Jima River in Abyssinia in 1941.

'The only thing you want to do when you have been taken prisoner is to escape, and I escaped after three days. I put a red cross on my arm, and I escaped detection for months. But then I was recaptured and taken to a camp in Diri Dawa. It was there that I had a brainwave: I would make a radio receiver. With the help of fellow prisoners I got all the parts smuggled into the camp and assembled the radio.

'We were moved from camp to camp by the British, and I took the radio with me. It was a simple matter to conceal it from them. We men of the Alpine Regiment were issued with aluminium water flasks bigger than those of the other regiments because Alpine men like to drink a lot of wine. That is due to the cold and snow and the altitude. I cut the flask in half and put in a false bottom. The radio was taken to pieces and some parts were put in my flask and some in other flasks. We had false tops welded on.

'I was taken to Naivasha in Kenya, where the British gave me a very hard time. In the first place, because I was an NCO, I refused to work, and in consequence I received bad treatment. In the second place they suspected that there was a radio in the camp. I buried it a few miles from the camp. Five of us were charged with having a radio, although there was no proof. The British tied our hands behind our backs and told us we would be sentenced to death. But the commandant of the camp had just received news that his son had escaped from a prison camp in Italy and was being looked after by an Italian family, and this softened his heart, and instead of having us shot he sent us to a punishment camp seventy miles from Naivasha. Naturally this meant I was cut off from the rest of the world, and I decided I must retrieve the radio. It was the custom in the camp for the prisoners to be sent out with axes to chop wood.

'I went out with a working party and hid in the bush until it was dark. When a train went past in the direction of Naivasha I hid in one of the trucks and in the dark of the night jumped off near the camp and got the radio. The next morning I hid until the Naivasha prisoners emerged to cut wood, and I joined them, then hid again and jumped back on the train to the camp.

'But next morning, when I was back in camp, the British took me away and put me in confinement for thirty days. Every night at midnight they woke me up and put me under a cold shower.

'It was in this camp that a soldier who read palms took my hand. He said to me: "Duilio, in a few months you are going to travel by ship. And you are going to arrive at a certain place in a strange country, and there you will find wine and spaghetti."

'"You're talking nonsense," I said. He had TB, and one day he was taken from the camp and I didn't see him again for a long time. When the British wanted to punish us, they would take a crowd of three hundred and tell us they were going to send us to a terrible island in the Pacific, Snake Island, and there we would all die of starvation.

'Imagine our feelings when we were told to get on to a train to Mombasa. That meant a ship and Snake Island. When we got into the train we could not see out of the windows. They had been painted black. The journey was terrible. We had Kikuyus looking after us. I cannot adequately describe how terrible they were. Men were sick with dysentery, all the way to Mombasa. They were being sick in their laps. The smell was dreadful. It was one person after another in the lavatory, no food and very little water.

'Then we were put on to a ship in Mombasa, and no sooner were we at sea than the ship was torpedoed. We were rescued in little boats and taken back to that terrible camp at Naivasha. After three months we repeated the train journey and went back to Mombasa, where we boarded the *Piedmonte,* an Italian ship that the Allies had taken. Of course we had no idea where we were going.

'I still want to cry when I remember that ship. We were in the holds where they used to put the mules and other animals. There were no windows, no ventilation, nothing. We were all naked because the heat was so intense we couldn't bear to have any clothes on. The sweat on the floor was fully one centimetre deep, and we had to sleep in that.

'Again our guards were Kikuyus from Kenya. They are cannibals, a terrible race. They would not allow us to go to lavatories. We had pots in the hold, and at least thirty per cent of us had dysentery. They gave us something called soup, with potatoes in it, unpeeled. They also put in corks from wine-bottles. They cut them into pieces and put them in the soup.

'One day the ship stopped. We asked the sailors where we were. They said "Durban". We had never heard of Durban.

'We were taken out on deck. It was night, and we could see all the lights, and we said to ourselves: "This is not an island in the Pacific."

'Can you imagine what we looked like when we emerged from the hold? Can you imagine our clothes? We were stinking, because we had no water to bathe or even wash. We had long beards. We were in a very bad condition. They put us on to a train and again we could not see out of the windows, but the guards were very polite.

'They gave us bully-beef and some things called biscuits, which we appreciated. We were starving, thin and dirty. Anything was appreciated. We were taken to a transit camp in Pietermaritzburg, under canvas. I stayed there for three years, with three thousand other men.

'As soon as we arrived we were put into the showers. Everyone had to go through. Then we had to see the doctors, and all our stinking clothes were taken away and we were given uniforms. I was put into Block 2. The first meal we had was spaghetti. Spaghetti! The South Africans were too wonderful to us. They treated us like human beings.

'Next day I saw prisoners run to the kitchen. I took my food container and ran too. Outside the kitchen they had little drums like petrol drums and in it there was this yellow stuff. I filled up my container and went back to my tent, and all of a sudden I realised I couldn't swallow, but I forced myself to, and I got terrible pains in my stomach and had to spend three days in hospital. I later learned that it was peanut butter.

'Between the two wire fences there was a small infirmary. When I was leaving the hospital I heard someone calling my name. I turned round. It was the man who had read my palm all those months ago. He threw me a flask of wine. So his prediction had come true in all respects.

'It was necessary to build a new receiver because the old one was not powerful enough to get Germany or Italy. But where would we get the parts we needed? I heard that in a nearby hospital there were radios, and I decided I would become ill and would be taken there. Two of my comrades also fell sick. On the second night in hospital we found the radios and removed the parts that we needed from them. When we returned to the camp we built a new receiver and were able to hear the news from Germany and Italy.

'I built a room 3m x 3m under my tent. Each night I would dig, with picks and shovels made from waste pieces of steel, and after three months there was this room. The soil was brought to the surface, and during the night we smoothed it over and planted vegetables. So in the morning there was nothing but a vegetable garden.

'We dug a tunnel too, which allowed us to connect the receiver to the underground electricity of the camp kitchens. Another tunnel was dug to another part of the camp so that people didn't keep coming into my tent all the time. We placed large pieces of slasto on the floor of my tent where the entrance to the room was and in front of the tent we put up a board: "School of Language". When the guards investigated the men appeared to be studying. In reality they were translating news bulletins from Germany into Italian.

'My days were spent translating. I filled ten volumes of news broadcasts with my translations, which I would read to the prisoners every evening. Again I was asked to work; but how could I with the translations to do? I dedicated myself to keeping the Geneva Convention. If you want to give me food, that's fine, I told them, if you don't, that's fine too. But I am not working.

'Our stonemasons and bricklayers built a church and a priest came to say mass every Sunday.

'Suddenly one day the prison guards made a search in the camp for the receiver. All the prisoners were taken to one side of the camp while they searched, but they could not find it. While they were looking for it, two operators were down in the room listening to the news, unaware of the danger. At last, the operators intercepted a telegram from the Reich High Command* to Mussolini, and after two days there was no more communication from the Germans to Mussolini. It was then that we realised that the end of the war was in sight.

'At the end of 1944 I was taken from Pietermaritzburg to Zonderwater. The rest of the prisoners arrived later.† I was shocked at the size. Zonderwater was a city, a city of barracks with beds. It had everything.‡

'The commandant of Zonderwater was Col 'Hennie' F Prinsloo.** He wasn't a commandant, he was a father to us.

---

* Italy capitulated on 3 September 1943.

† On 27 April 1945.

‡ It had indeed. For the hundred thousand prisoners of war Zonderwater had fourteen sections, fifty sub-sections, eighteen miles of roads, three thousand hospital beds, seventeen theatres, sixteen soccer fields with tracks and grandstands, six tennis courts, eighty bowling alleys, seven fencing halls, volleyball fields, basketball fields, boxing rings and gymnasiums, sports clubs, sports committees and committees promoting the arts, besides the church.

** Col Prinsloo won the affection of his prisoners. So outstanding was his service that he was awarded the Order of the British Empire, the Bene Merenti (by the Vatican) and the Star of Honour (Italian).

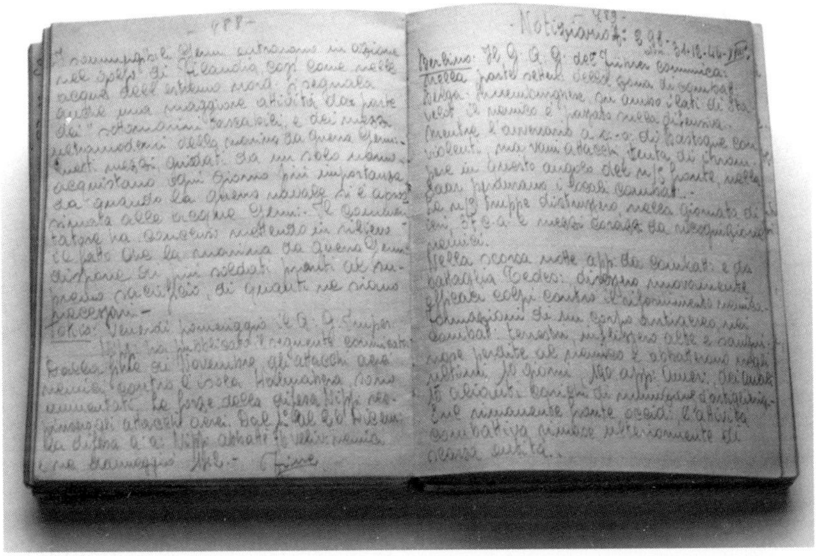

Duilio de Francheschi filled eleven diaries while he was a prisoner in South Africa.

'The food at Zonderwater wasn't very good, so we protested, and it became better. We had canteens where we could buy food. We were paid 30/- a month, so we could buy and cook spaghetti. Five or six of the deaths at Zonderwater were due to overeating.* The men used to wait until the end of the month when they were paid and they would buy food and eat like camels. They died of indigestion.

'Many tried to escape. I did. Two prisoners had a pass, and I asked them to give a taxi-driver from Pretoria by the name of Rossi a message from me. We arranged to meet on a certain night at a certain place beyond the wire. Two of us crawled under the wire and we found the taxi because it flicked its lights. Rossi took us to the house of an Italian family in Pretoria. They gave us civilian clothes, and we were able to get to Johannesburg, to a good benefactor called Cosani, a builder who helped to lay the foundations of the Voortrekker Monument. He had been put in Koffiefontein, and he had escaped because he had so many business commitments and needed to be at home.

'When I heard that, I knew the police would come to his house and I was afraid. After two days I decided to go back to Zonderwater. I just walked in through the gates, and for punishment I spent thirty days in a small room. During the day I was made to work and sweat.

* Two hundred and fifty-six Italian prisoners of war died at Zonderwater.

'We knew by the beginning of April 1945 that the war was lost, that everything was finished. Col Prinsloo told us that Germany had capitulated. What can you say, what can you do? Some of the men were crying, some took their lives. One man hung himself in my barracks; I took him down myself. But we kept loyalty to our flag and to our government.'

• Interview 1990

Duilio de Francheschi was one of about a thousand former Italian prisoners of war who were permitted to remain in South Africa after the war. His ten volumes of translated news broadcasts can be seen in the small museum at Zonderwater, with other artefacts from the eighteen Italian prisoner-of-war camps in South Africa during the war.

CHAPTER

57

'This is bloody awful, just waiting'

Captain Arthur Pearce, CSO 7 Wing, waiting for the baby

58 765 babies were born in South Africa in 1943. Many were born to men serving outside the country. Most of the women had an elaborate back-up system of aunts, brothers, sisters and mothers to get them to the hospital on time.

The men went through the agony of waiting. In spite of anguished daily letters home, and in spite of the excellent speedy despatch of telegrams, few of the men serving Up North heard about the birth for days afterwards. When they learnt that the baby had been safely delivered, what was there to do but have a few drinks and get on with the war?

One of these men, a father for the first time, was Captain Arthur Pearce, late of 64 Air School,* and posted to Egypt as Chief Signals Officer 7 Wing, SAAF.† He left the Union on Friday, 8 January 1943 on a SAAF Lodestar one month and ten days before his baby was due.

---

* 64 Air School (motto: Audeo), established before the end of 1940 under Lt-Col F C Elliot-Wilson at Bloemfontein, assembled some of the foremost engineers in the country to work on wireless communications and direction-finding. Experts trained radio mechanics, morse code operators (who left the air school with a minimum of thirty words a minute), air-gunners and electricians. Communications played an essential part in both land and air battles.

† 7 Wing, consisting of 2, 4 and 5 Squadron, SAAF, was formed in August 1942 as part of the Desert Air Force. It operated in the Western Desert until the fall of Tunis and then embarked for Sicily and the Italian campaign. Its service was honourable and dashing. Its most notable achievement was probably in 1943, when the support given to the New Zealanders resulted in the outflanking of the Mareth Line and the interception of large formations of JU52s on 19 April and ME323s on 22 April, when 24 Me323s, 12 Ju52s and four other aircraft were shot down. During this time (see diary) the ground staff endured heavy bombing and strafing.

Capt Arthur Pearce just before he went Up North. He left on his first wedding anniversary and a month before his first child was born. (Mrs P Pearce)

He left things as well organised as he could. His cousin Denys Morton was deputed to take his twenty-two-year-old wife Pat to the nursing home and the family was mustered.

'Many times today I've taken your picture from its frame,' he wrote miserably in his diary between Pretoria and Ndola, 'and read and reread the beautiful words you wrote.'

Pearce was convinced his first child, due on 18 February, would be a boy, Michael. Like many a man before him, Pearce learnt that nature does not always oblige: Michael turned out to be a girl.

He began his war diary in his flight Up North. But although there were vivid descriptions of his work in North Africa, Sicily and Italy, the diary was really an extension of the letters he wrote home to Pat.

Cut off in the midst of the North African war, he was by turns worried, frantic, numb and finally elated. His thoughts must have echoed many another new father's in the year of 1943:

'ZVARA, EGYPT

Sunday 14 February, 1943

Once again the wind is howling through the date palms, and each gust brings with it pounds of fine sand that not only gets in my eyes and mouth but clogs the hair, so that I'm now missing several teeth off my comb! Such is life – but what wonderful consolation to receive three more letter-cards from you.

Not much work today, followed by an early evening filled by thoughts of our wee family as I lay snuggled in my bed with the wind howling round the tent.

Wednesday 17 February, 1943

The day before Mike is due to arrive, darling – in fact you are probably in the nursing-home now waiting – my thoughts and love will be more completely with you than ever.

Our move was cancelled at 2am today as Jerry had rendered the drome unserviceable – but we didn't know until we had risen at crack of dawn, packed our kit and heaved it all outside the tent.

No less than 21 dead and exceedingly bloated Itis have been washed up on the beach near Zuara harbour, and the doc reckons they have been washed up from a torpedoed troopship, probably trying to escape from Tripoli harbour.

Thursday February 18, 1943

How are you, angel wee? This is bloody awful just waiting and being completely in the dark – not knowing where you are or what you are going through – I'll get no rest now until your cable arrives to tell me you are well and Mike is Mike or Jennifer Jennifer!

I went with friends to see the old Roman ruins at Sabrata this morning and took twelve photographs, as it was exceptionally interesting – particularly from a hygiene point of view!

Have you ever sat in a dentist's waiting-room with an empty feeling in the pit of your tummy? – well, that's how I've felt all day – I haven't been able to think or worry about anything else but you, angel pie. Heaven knows how much I wish I could be with you.

Friday 19 February, 1943

What it is to wake in a howling gale with the tent flapping like a lame bird trying to take off – the worst problem is shaving, as the door has to be kept closed on account of the dust with the result that the illumination is about zero – the best thing is to scrape away and feel!

So the day went on – wind and dust and dust and wind. I inspected the section pretty thoroughly, investigated the battery-charging position, studied the 32RB circuit diagram and generally tried to occupy my time intelligently, which was exceptionally difficult – not for the reason you are about to say – but because my mind is trying to cover seven thousand miles to find out how you are.

The CO brought post with him at dinner time, and I felt less gloomy when I found your letters of the 8th, 9th and 10th to cheer me up.

Saturday 20 February, 1943

Today has been much more satisfactory from the worry point of view and a sort of calm confidence that all is well has been with me the whole time –

Major Von Ginkel went shopping and bought the officers' mess a pig for £ 3.15.0, so great preparations were made for the evening meal – fresh peas were shelled, and after some consultation (in view of the lack of apples) pear sauce was manufactured. The whole outfit went down well, particularly with the large quantities of Iti wine on tap.

We heard bombs falling about 6 p.m. some distance from camp, but we're not paid the same compliment ourselves, for which Jerry many thanks!

MEDININ, TUNISIA

Wednesday 3 March 1943

My darling, – what can I say? This signal arrived just after I had sealed my last letter to you, and I don't know what to say – I'm just choked up inside. I know I love you with all my heart and soul and that a great weight has been lifted from my mind, but as yet words just won't come.

Friday 5 March 1943

Today began promisingly with warm sunlight streaming into the tent, but as the sun rose so the wind rose with it, until sand and more sand was deposited everywhere.

Several important matters had to be cleared up today, so I have been pretty busy, and I only finished work at 6.15 – even then I had to return. Anyway, it's grand to have a real job too, and it helps the time to fly.

I have just been thinking that eleven days have passed since our first baby's birthday wee, so you are probably either nearly ready to leave the home or else just getting things sorted out on your return – I wish I could have been there to welcome you home!

Saturday 6 March 1943

I don't quite know how to describe the events of today, for a lifetime has been crowded into a few short hours. During the night gunfire had become louder and we understood from ALO sources that the Jerries had launched an offensive to cut us off from our base here at Tripoli. However, I slept well, and we breakfasted to the constant rumble of the guns over the hill – our misgivings we kept to ourselves, though it would have been a relief to have told someone. At 11 a.m. we were paraded and told 'Jupiter', the code word for 'pack up and on your way' – but no sooner were those words spoken than high up in the blue, slinking from cloud to cloud, we saw nine Messerschmitts. I watched them peel off one by one and hurtle towards us before I had sense enough to drop to the ground. For fifteen minutes there was hell, bombs falling, AA thundering, the whine of engines as Jerry dived – then it was over. We gathered together where our mess had been, but within ten minutes we were in our slit trenches while JU88s and 109s blasted hell out of everything in sight. We had pulled into convoy

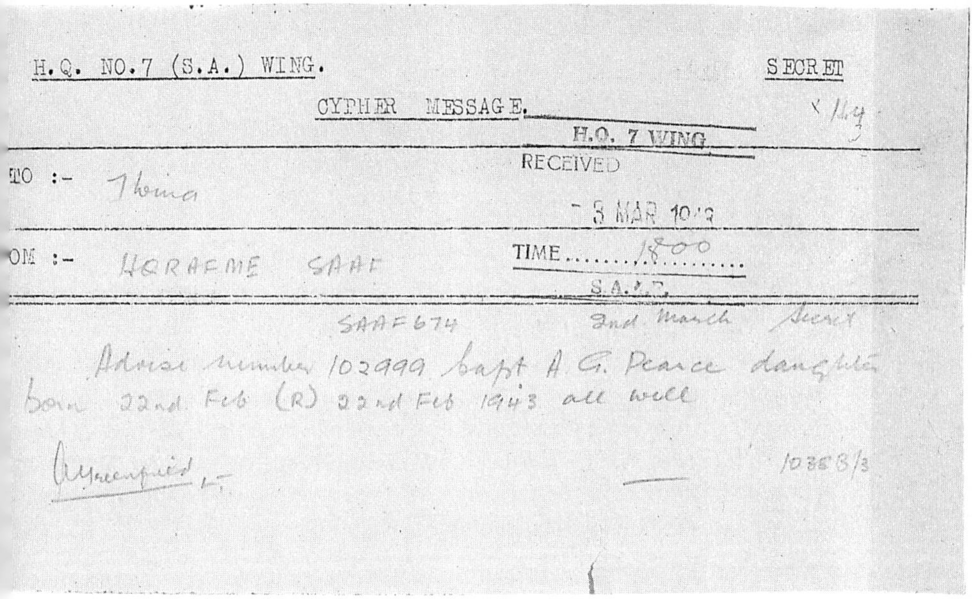

H.Q. NO.7 (S.A.) WING. SECRET

CYPHER MESSAGE.

H.Q. 7 WING RECEIVED 3 MAR 1943

TO :- Thima

FROM :- HQRAFME SAAF

TIME 1800

S.A.A.F.

SAAF 674 2nd March Secret

Advise number 102999 Capt A. G. Pearce daughter born 22nd Feb (R) 22nd Feb 1943 all well

10358/3

In spite of the speed of Forces mail, it was ten days before Capt Pearce learnt that he had a daughter.

Telling the new father what he wanted to hear – that the baby looked like him. Although signed by his wife it was actually sent by his aunt. Families rallied round young mothers whose husbands were away fighting.

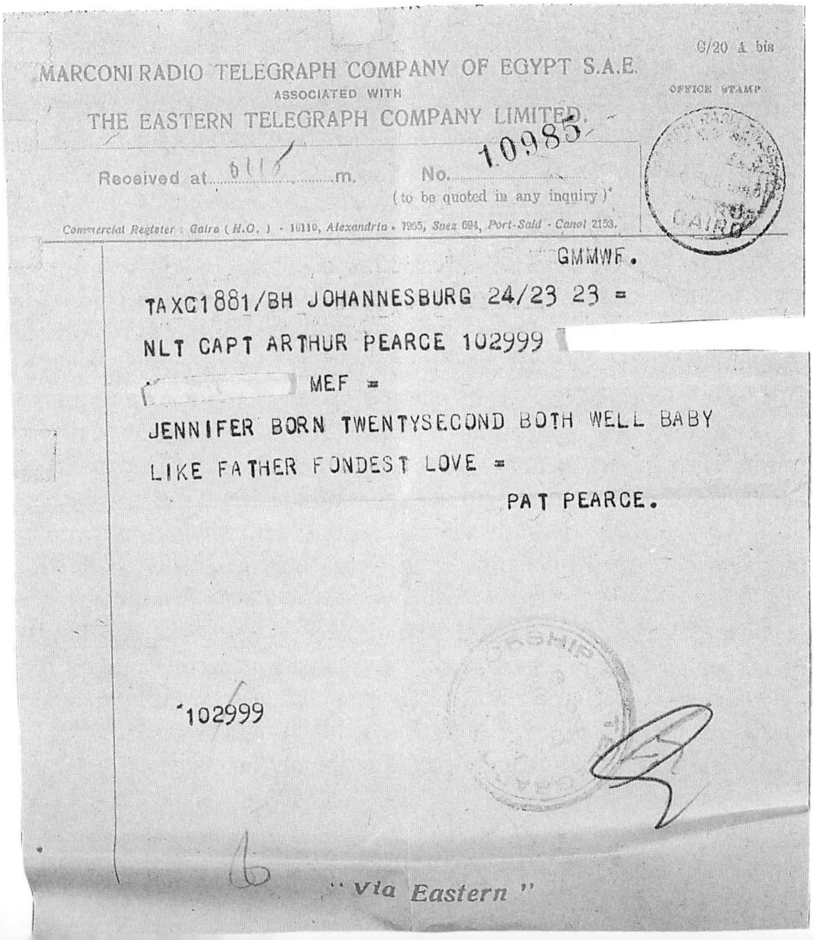

C/20 A bis

MARCONI RADIO TELEGRAPH COMPANY OF EGYPT S.A.E.
ASSOCIATED WITH
THE EASTERN TELEGRAPH COMPANY LIMITED.

OFFICE STAMP

Received at ....m. No. 10985
(to be quoted in any inquiry)

Commercial Register : Cairo (H.O.) - 10110, Alexandria - 7955, Suez 694, Port-Said - Canal 2153.

GMMWF.

TAXC1881/BH JOHANNESBURG 24/23 23 =
NLT CAPT ARTHUR PEARCE 102999
MEF =
JENNIFER BORN TWENTYSECOND BOTH WELL BABY
LIKE FATHER FONDEST LOVE =
PAT PEARCE.

102999

"Via Eastern"

– Maj Aap and I stayed to the last for orders, and at 12.15 they came through – pull out! I left the convoy at the main drome to see how B party had fared – what a mess – two killed by a direct hit not fifty yards from the mess, another near ops who had taken shelter under a garri – things looked pretty grim. Shelley had a narrow escape when a 500-pounder fell eighteen yards away (I paced it out) and our receiver garri had bomb splinters in both doors – everyone was shaken.

Nobody had much sleep, as we were all expecting to have to do a midnight evacuation – besides Jerry was out looking for us, as we could see from the flares he was dropping all round. However, after a desultory stooge round he buzzed off and left us in peace.

Two letters arrived from Mum – one telling me you had gone to the nursing-home, the other that you were well and Jennifer, a sweet young thing weighing 7 lbs! I wonder if you ever imagined I'd be reading letters with one ear listening for tanks, the other for JU88s!

1943

Sunday 7 March 1943

I slept well – although a bit cramped in the back of the garri, though I was rudely disturbed by Bets at 1.30 who thought my charging plant was a Jerry tank.

It was a glorious day and seemed very peaceful as I got forth to visit 'B' party and the only things that reminded me there was a war on were the newly dug graves, bomb craters, and roped off areas round unexploded bombs. About 12 I left on my return journey feeling as carefree as a bird on the wing, but as I stopped the garri at Wing I saw everyone scatter, and at the same time I heard the now familiar whistle of bombs – I flung myself to the ground and said a little prayer as the earth trembled to the explosions of a stick about 75 yards away. Jerry did a circuit and came back with a cannon fire and anti-personnel that made the air alive with vicious cracks and whistles – I think I sweated more during those fifteen minutes than ever before in my life.

Our next do came twenty minutes later, when we were in the middle of lunch – the only thing to do was run like hell and drop to the ground clear of the garris as the fine 109s did their circuit. This time the runways collected the lot, and it was a relief to see the bombs bursting no less than three hundred yards away. We were just getting out of our trenches when we heard the drone of 88s and just had time to get under cover when the north drome AA opened up – but what a different story this time, for as the Jerries peeled off out of the sun the Spits of 1 Squadron came – I was so excited that I forgot the raid and stood up to watch the fight above us as the 109s and 88s tried to get away.

I heard a roar just above my head and there was a 109 with smoke pouring from his engine and a Spit on his tail. As I looked the

Spit got into position and opened up. With the first shot a piece about as big as a chair-seat fell off, and in half a second the 109 had broken in two and was hurtling to the ground. It hit about 400 yards from our camp and exploded with a terrific spout of flame at least 300 feet high, and I almost felt sorry for the Hun inside – but no, there he was, floating gently to earth with the victorious Spit circling round him.

Meanwhile the raid had finished, and apart from the burning kits and columns of dust from the bombs all was peace again. No doubt, my love, if you heard the Daventry news you would have heard something like this:

'109s and JU88s of the *Luftwaffe* attempted to raid our airfields in the forward areas but were turned back by RAF fighters. From these and other operations in Tunisia, eleven German planes have been destroyed, six are probables and eleven damaged.'

Actually No 1 Squadron (SA) destroyed three of the Hun.

The German pilot was entertained in our mess that evening and apart from the fact that he was a typical Hun – fair, square-headed, twenty years old and insultingly arrogant – proved quite entertaining; rather, I should say, he relieved the monotony.

Go to sleep peacefully now, my darling, for this will soon be over and I'll be back to live in peace with my darling wife and sweet baby!

Thursday 11 March 1943

At last your letters have come and for the first time really in my heart I feel that Jennifer has really come.

Capt Pearce's wife, Pat, at the christening of their first born. (Mrs P Pearce)

I have been so busy today that I haven't had time to settle down and talk to you – but now at last I can relax and think of you and Jennifer without interruption.

Today I saw one of the most thrilling and heartening sights I have yet seen – eighteen Bostons escorted by twenty-eight of our fighters going west to bomb the Mareth positions – the beginning of the end, Adolf, if you only knew it!

All my love, darling, and to our baby too. ’

Capt Arthur Pearce (Mentioned in Despatches) went on to Sicily and Italy with the SAAF. When he returned to the Union his daughter was nearly two. Some men, especially those taken prisoner, did not see their children for five years.

CHAPTER

58

'Die Vierkleur Hoog'

The day of judgment: the Leibbrandt treason trial, March 1943

'I find it a joke,' said Leibbrandt at the beginning of a trial which would make South African legal history. From 16 November 1942 until 11 March 1943 Sidney Robey Leibbrandt and six other men stood in the dock of the Pretoria Supreme Court listening to argument and counter-argument.

It became the longest criminal trial in the legal history of the country; by the end of it the record filled two thousand pages, nearly two hundred witnesses (many reluctant) had been called and the judgment, delivered by Mr Justice Schreiner, took fifty thousand words and six and a half hours to deliver.

Through it all Leibbrandt, who never doubted the rightness of his cause, remained silent. He glared and grimaced, but for most of the time he sat in the dock with what reporters of the time described as a smirk.

On the morning of 11 March, the court was crammed with people who had queued for places for hours. Outside the Supreme Court hundreds of people stood waiting in silence for the sentence. It was a scene uncannily reminiscent of another treason trial in the same Supreme Court twenty years later, although that would have far more serious repercussions for the government of the day.

Before sentence was passed on Leibbrandt and the other six accused, Leibbrandt stood to make a statement; and then, although he was rebuked by Mr Justice Schreiner, to address 'the Afrikaner volk'.

When Leibbrandt had ended his impassioned speech, Schreiner passed sentence of death on him. Leibbrandt stood impassively, and the people in the public gallery gasped. This is what the South African public read in the *Rand Daily Mail* next morning:

LEIBBRANDT SENTENCED TO DEATH FOR HIGH TREASON

Five Years' Gaol for Le Roux and Olwagen

SIDNEY ROBEY LEIBBRANDT was sentenced to death in Pretoria yesterday for high treason by a special criminal court consisting of Mr. Justice Schreiner, Mr. Justice Ramsbottom and Mr. Justice De Beer.

Two of his fellow accused, Dr. Lodewikus Jacobus le Roux and Frans Joseph Olwagen, were each sentenced to five years' imprisonment for high treason. The other four accused, Hendrik van Cittert, Frans Maartens, Johan van der Walt, Adriaan Johannes Stadler and Ernst Hendrik Annandale, were acquitted.

Before sentence was passed, Leibbrandt, in an atmosphere charged with dramatic intensity, addressed the court in Afrikaans and said that he rejected the idea of mercy and demanded that right be done.

He saluted the three judges with his right arm raised and called out "Die Vierkleur hoog" (The Vierkleur high).

When Mr. Justice Schreiner passed the sentence of death, Leibbrandt flushed slightly, gritted his teeth and then smiled.

Leibbrandt's Address

Leibbrandt's counsel, Mr. J. F. Ludorf, did not address the court when the time came to pass sentence, but Leibbrandt himself did so. Speaking in a harsh voice, which he sometimes raised until it became a shout, he declared that he alone bore the responsibility for what he had done and was doing.

Turning to the rear of the court, Leibbrandt then began. "Kamerade and kameradinne," but Mr. Justice Schreiner interrupted him and said that he could not address the public. If he did not address his remarks to the bench, he would be removed and the trial would proceed in his absence.

"We are not guilty of high treason, unless it is a crime to love your people," continued Leibbrandt. "Democracy remains the pestilential young brother of Bolshevism and its ally, Judaism . . ."

Mr. Justice Schreiner interrupted: "This is not an address to the court. The court does not wish to interfere with your rights, but you must not use the occasion for a propagandist speech."

Read from Notes

Leibbrandt, who was reading from notes, went on to express his pride in his Afrikaner blood and said that his most cherished possession was his past. For nearly

19 months he had implored the German authorities to allow him to return to his land and people.

"I knew," he said, "that it would probably cost me my life to return but that did not deter me, for I love my fellow Afrikaners. I came here not to win cheap leadership, but to implant the idea of Adolf Hitler in the hearts of all Afrikaners."

Raising his voice, Leibbrandt exclaimed. "Our hope and future do not lie in democratic cross-making but in deeds and sacrifices – in him who was sent here by the Almighty to save the suffering peoples of this planet, in Adolf Hitler. Communism can never destroy National Socialism. (Here Leibbrandt banged his fist on the dock). The sword of Adolf Hitler must triumph in this great struggle.

"To hell with mercy. I demand that right be done. Long live Afrikanerdom. Long live national socialist South Africa. God be with me, comrades."

Nazi Salute

Turning to the public, who crammed the court and sat in utter silence, Leibbrandt gave the Nazi salute and shouted "Die Vierkleur hoog."

Mr. Justice Schreiner then passed sentence of death on Leibbrandt.

Passing sentence on Le Roux and Olwagen: Mr. Justice Schreiner pointed out that their crime had not been as serious as that of Leibbrandt. Nevertheless, high treason was a grave offence, and the lightest sentence the court could pass on each would be five years' imprisonment.

At this point Stadler, who had been acquitted, asked leave to address the court, but this was refused.

The court then adjourned for a few minutes and women crowded round the accused, weeping and congratulating them. Leibbrandt embraced his sister and then went down into the cells, smiling and saying, "Die Vierkleur hoog."

The court rose at 6.30 p.m. Mr. Justice Schreiner had delivered a 50,000-word judgment, reading mostly from notes, in about six-and-a-half hours. For hour after hour he read on, delivering one of the longest criminal judgments in South African legal history.

CHAPTER

59

'We arrived with nothing'

Irena Dolinska and her long journey to South Africa

It is not only men in uniforms who become casualties of war. Ordinary people living ordinary lives are swept up in the conflict and become perhaps the saddest of all victims. Among the victims of the Second World War was the Dolinska family. They were forcibly uprooted from their home in eastern Poland and taken to Siberia, to Uzbekistan, to Persia and finally to South Africa. Irena Dolinska was ten years old when her long journey from Poland to Oudtshoorn began.

'It took us three years and two months to reach South Africa, our new home. The road there was not taken by choice: it was thrust upon us by war.

'My sister Eleonora and I began our journey to South Africa early on the morning of 10 February 1940. There were six of us in my family: my parents, my eldest brother Leon, Eleonora, my brother Tadeusz and myself. We were living in a settlement called Antonin in the east of Poland, and we were prosperous. We had horses and pigs and cows and a nice house.

'Czechoslovakia had already gone* and Poland was invaded next.† We were far from the fighting, but it affected us all. There were many Ukrainians living round us. When the Russians invaded‡ our area

---

* On 15 March 1939 German troops marched into Prague. Next day Hitler declared that 'Czechoslovakia has ceased to exist.' It was a shameful hour for Britain and France and the appeasers.

† At 4.45 a.m. on 1 September 1939 the German *Luftwaffe* crossed the frontier. One hour later, under cover of darkness, the *Blitzkrieg* was unleashed upon Poland. The defence by the Polish army was heroic but futile. Horses and ill-equipped men were no match for the might of the Panzers and trained and determined troops. By 6 October it was all over.

‡ Before dawn on 17 September the Red Army crossed into Poland along an 800-mile front in accordance with a secret clause in the Nazi-Soviet agreement which effectively divided the country between the two powers. People living beneath the Russian yoke saw an immediate redistribution of wealth, the abolition of Polish currency, food shortages and the introduction of Russian language and ideology in schools. Thousands simply disappeared. Thousands of Polish officers were murdered in Katyn forest.

the Ukrainians built a welcoming arch for them. But the first time we saw the Russian soldiers was when they came to our farm and took all our stock. They left us with one horse, one cow and one pig, and they took my father away; but he came back after a few days.

'It was bitterly cold on that morning of 10 February. They came before dawn, without any warning, banging on the door. One soldier asked my father if he had any weapons. He said no, he had nothing. Then they told us: no matter, we were leaving Poland anyway, and we should pack food, to last us for a month and take some clothes and bedding. I was only ten years old, and it was very frightening. My sister Eleonora was crying and trying to find some photographs to take with her. One of the soldiers told her not to cry, that it was to our advantage that we were going to Russia. "Where you are going you will have everything," he said. We took sugar and meat and flour with us. We had to leave everything else behind.

'We were loaded into cattle trucks. They had no windows, just small barred openings high up and a lavatory that was an opening in a corner of the truck with a blanket hung in front. We were in that truck for a whole month, freezing, getting deeper and deeper into Russia.

'Then the train stopped. It was the end of the railway line. All round us was heavy snow, stretching for ever. We were told that we were going to Siberia, to the Arkhangelsk Region in Siberia, and that the rest of the journey would have to be done on sledges. We travelled on the sledges by day and stopped as night began to fall. We stayed with Russian families. Then we saw that the soldier had lied, that in fact they had nothing at all.

'The camp was a small one. The only Russians there were the camp officials. There was nowhere to escape to. We were in the middle of Siberia, huge flat plains covered with snow and dark forest and nothing else. The nearest railway station was 150 kilometres away.

'We children had to learn Russian. Sometimes the teacher let us sing Polish songs. But we had no food, no doctors and no medicine. My eldest brother Leon died of pneumonia. There was nothing anyone could do to help him.

'Our only food was porridge and flour. Once a donkey died and we wanted to eat it, but we were told that its meat would be bad for us. But we found a way to catch a hen. We sprinkled some porridge on the ground near the door of our hut, on the step and inside. The fowl came in, pecking at the porridge. When it was inside we killed it. It was delicious. We buried the bones and the feathers.

'We had no salt. There were heaps of salt, but we were not allowed to touch it. In the summer we collected sorrel and berries in the forests. My mother went into the forest to try to find some food, and she got lost. When she didn't come back we went to look for her.

We found her wandering about dazed. The forests were very dark and frightening. We were in Siberia for two years.

'Then the Russians and the British became friends* and we were allowed to leave Siberia. During the summer the pine trees were cut down and brought to the river along a sledge-track, which my mother had to keep clean. They were allowed to make a raft out of the logs. My parents lashed the logs together until we had a raft four square metres. My father built sides on it and a big rudder. We put what little we had on it and pushed it out into the Dvina. Each night we pulled the raft in to the shore and stayed there until dawn, when we set out again.

'I hated that raft. It used to get stuck on sandbanks, and I thought it would sink, so I walked along the bank rather than travel on it, about twenty kilometres a day. We went to the south, to Uzbekistan.

'We stayed in a little place, in clay huts, with no windows and no beds – and no food. We were always hungry. There were cotton fields near us, and my parents went into the fields to collect balls of cotton to make beds for us. Their hands were bleeding, but we had something to sleep on. We had no milk, no eggs, no meat. I used to go down to the river with my sister. We would put a sheet in the water and catch tiny fish, as small as sardines. I squeezed the insides out with my thumb and we ate them with porridge and a teaspoon of oil in the porridge.

'Then people began to go down with typhoid. There were thirty of us in this village, and one after another they died. There was a Jewish family of seven, and five of them died. Then my mother got ill. We knew that she had typhoid, but there were no doctors. We knelt down round her bed and prayed for her, but still she died. Two weeks later my father died. Now there were only three of us left, my sister Eleonora, my brother Tadeusz and me.

'One day I was out in the fields collecting cotton sticks for a fire when I felt terribly ill. My head was so sore. Then I remembered nothing at all until I woke up. My sister, who had also had typhoid, had prepared a dress for me to be buried in. When we were better we were allowed to leave Russia altogether. My brother had been taken away to fight the Germans, but he was so weak that he came back again. With a lot of Polish people, mostly children, we were taken to Persia, to Teheran.

'I didn't know it then, but we were getting nearer to South Africa. People were still dying, most of starvation. We were terribly thin, but for the first time since we left Poland we had enough to eat, only we

---

* The Anglo-Soviet Alliance was signed on 26 May 1942. For the time being they were indeed friends, if not particularly good ones.

had been hungry for so long that our stomachs revolted and we were all very sick. Eleonora and Tadeusz stayed in Teheran, but I was taken by a holy father with a hundred younger boys and girls to a convent, the Ispahan Convent. It was run by French nuns, and we were very well looked after. I could hardly believe it.

'We were in Persia for about a year; then we were told that we had to go. Where to? We were told that we could go to South Africa if we wanted, so we chose South Africa rather than another country. I never saw Tadeusz again. He joined the cadets and left for Palestine, but Eleonora and I got on board the French ship *Dunera* in March 1943, and we sailed from the Persian Gulf to South Africa. We were told that it was going to be our home.*

'We stopped for a time in Durban, but we weren't allowed to get off the ship there, and we sailed on to Port Elizabeth. For two weeks we stayed on board because of quarantine, and then three hundred Polish girls and two hundred boys were allowed off the ship. I remember being amazed at the black faces. And there was a Polish priest standing at the bottom of the gangway waving to us.

'A train was waiting. We were very excited because we knew that the next stop would be our last, our new home; no more being pushed from one place to another. I sat on the top bunk. It had beautifully clean sheets on it. It was like being in heaven.

'We arrived at a place called Oudtshoorn. Army trucks and soldiers were there to help us, and soon we came to the camp. It had barrack-rooms, and each one had twenty-one children and a teacher or supervisor. The youngest of us was a little girl of four.

'Most of us were orphans. Some had parents, others only a mother or a father in the army. The children with parents received letters and sometimes money, but the orphans like my sister and me had no one to help us, and we had no letters. But the people were kind to us.

'We arrived with nothing. The South Africans knew that we were coming, and they had filled two barrack-rooms with clothes and toys for us. A few of us at a time went in to try on a dress. A new dress! Mine was a lovely pink smocked dress with little flowers. Boxes of shoes arrived from a local factory.

'The weather was very cold, and after lunch we mostly sat on our beds wrapped up in blankets. Later in summer it was very hot, and we poured water on the cement floors to keep it cool. In the evenings we went out in groups for walks after supper.

---

* In addition to the 500 Polish children given refuge in South Africa, nearly 350 English and Scottish children were being educated at schools and colleges under the legal guardianship of the Minister of Social Welfare. (See: 'They Sang "There'll Always be an England")

First Communion in the Ispahan Convent in Teheran for some of the hundred Polish girls taken in by the nuns. Soon after the photograph was taken they were taken to the Persian Gulf and South Africa.

Irena Dolinska (standing, third from left, middle row) with girls and a supervisor outside their barrack-room at Oudtshoorn, soon after the war ended. Many girls were sent to convents for their education.

'For pocket-money we embroidered articles, and when these were sold we were given the money. Another teacher taught us Polish dances, which we had almost forgotten. We made our costumes and held our first concert in the camp, with the girls and boys dancing together. Then we took our show to Johannesburg and Cape Town, together with the tablecloths, tray-cloths and cushion-covers that we had made. It was like saying Thank you to South Africa.

'I wanted so much to buy a suitcase to keep my things in. I saved my pocket-money, and one day I went into Oudtshoorn to buy a suitcase. But before I went into the shop I saw some sweets in a café, and I spent 5d on them. Then I went to buy the suitcase, and to my horror I was 5d short. The man behind the counter saw the disappointment on my face and said I could have the suitcase for whatever money I had. I was so grateful. It was my first suitcase, and I was so proud of it.

'Our day began with prayers in the chapel and ended with the evening prayer. Each Saturday we had to change our sheets and wash the windows and the floors. The wind would blow clouds of red dust on to the clean floors. I was doing the floor once and the supervisor came in and saw me washing the floor wearing my smocked dress. "How can you dress like this for cleaning the floor?" she asked me. But I had no choice, for I had only two dresses, the one that I was wearing and the one that was clean for church next day.

'For our first Christmas in South Africa the soldiers in the camp next to us organised a party, our first. I didn't understand what was being said, but the clown outfits and the movements made me laugh, and they gave us nice food and sweets and cool drinks. I was still very thin and undernourished, so I was sent off with a few of the other girls to a holiday farm, "Eight Bells" near Mossel Bay.

'One day we were all taken to an ostrich farm. When I got back my sister was crying, but she wouldn't tell me why. A friend of hers took me outside the barracks and told me that Eleonora had received a letter with a photograph informing that our brother Tadeusz had been killed on 3 November 1942 in an accident during military training in Palestine. There were only two of us left of our family.

'In spite of all the kindness round us, they were still sad times for us. Many of us received letters, often with the news that someone had been killed in action. That loss was a loss to us all. We were one big family. We hoped and believed that when the war was over we would all go back to a free Poland; but Poland didn't become free.*

'It took a long time before I realised that South Africa was truly my home and that I wouldn't be moved on elsewhere. I still have nightmares.

---

* Not until the end of 1989, when the Eastern bloc crumbled.

A small monument built in 1947 in remembrance of the Polish children sheltered in the army camp at Oudtshoorn from 1943 to 1947.

'I dream that I am packing my things or that I am running away from something. Memories of Poland will be with me for ever. I am thankful to God and to the people of South Africa that I am alive; that we orphans were taken in and given a home and allowed to remain here. I pray that our children and their children will never have to go through what we did.'

• Interview 1990

Irena Dolinska stayed in South Africa. In June 1952 she married Stawek 'Jimmy' Banach who also survived Siberia and joined the Royal Air Force. They live in Port Elizabeth. Eleonora Dolinska married an apple farmer in George and died in 1983. Irena is the last member of her family of six.

CHAPTER

60

'Cairo stinks, every inch of it'

David Grice and Abe Berry on Cairo, the town that South Africans loved and hated

Cairo and Alexandria were the main places of recreation for thousands of South Africans on leave. Wives and girlfriends in the Union got to know Cairo at second-hand through letters and gifts sent to them: filigree necklaces, brooches of lapis lazuli and fretted silver, 'rubies' bought at astonishingly low prices (though not so astonishing considering that they were bogus), silk scarves, vibrant swatches of fabric.

Sprawling, noisy, vibrant, filthy, filled with cafés, dubious restaurants, nightclubs and brothels (some of them run by the British authorities) and the more high-class haven of Shepheard's Hotel, Cairo was both loved and loathed by the troops; (but mostly the latter).

One of the hundreds of thousands of fighting men who passed through Cairo during the war was David Martindale Grice, a sergeant in No 2 Coy, South African Army Signals. He wrote regularly to his childhood friend in the Union, Beryl Newman, and his letters were redolent of the smells and colours of Cairo.

MUSEUM PIECES, CAIRO.

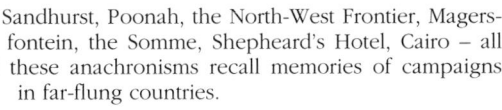

Sandhurst, Poonah, the North-West Frontier, Magersfontein, the Somme, Shepheard's Hotel, Cairo – all these anachronisms recall memories of campaigns in far-flung countries.

In Cairo at much the same time there was another South African, Sgt Abe Berry, who served with the Mobile Map Printing Coy. Before the war Berry had been a freelance cartoonist; during the war he drew cartoons for *Springbok* magazine. Berry, as his cartoons show, loved Cairo, specially 'the dichotomy between wealthy whites and the absolute squalor of the Egyptians'.

Together they gave a vivid picture of a town that so many South Africans knew so well, most of whom resolved never to set foot in the place again.

'No 576296
Sgt Grice, DM
6th SA Armd Div Sig Sqn,
UDF MEF
C/o APO, DURBAN

Dear Beryl,

My first trip to Cairo (which you have already in detail) followed what is termed the 'Barrage Road' in contra-distinction to the 'Desert Road', the main civilian route between Cairo and Alexandria. The latter is less pleasing, since it passes through unrelieved wastes of sands stretching on either hand to the horizon: a straight shimmering band of earth and sky; for their junction is indistinguishable in the heat of the day.

I have a theory to account for the vice of the Wog [sic]. It is that, having practically no country holiday resorts nor scenic spots he is compelled to find his pleasures and recreation within the City itself; and city-dwellers the world over are notoriously more open to vice than the country born and bred. Visitors to Egypt are no more fortunate and are subject to the same restrictions. This is a necessary digression to show why Cairo, the epitome of a desert town, is just like it is.

We travelled along the desert road for some hours, straight as a die for miles, the road and telegraph poles tapering ahead and behind, forming a perfect example of perspective which would make all the art-teachers in you leap for joy.

"PSSST . . . RAZOR BLADES – WHITE MARKET ! "

As a result of wartime shortages there was an enormous trade 'under the counter' in Cairo. The traders were loathed by the troops.

Then we approached a line of foothills (large dunes, really, but having the appearance of mountains in the surrounding flatness) which cut across our path. Above and beyond these two triangular shapes become discernable – my first sight of the Pyramids of Gizeh [Giza]. It was not long before we had wound through the foothills (which I now found to be the rather higher outline of a plateau on which the Pyramids stand) when, for a second time I experienced the queer thrill evoked by a sudden glimpse of green fields after the monotony of sand. First, a large palm plantation running into vegetable gardens, and citrus, mango and guava orchards.

The road continues in this fashion for two miles, then turns left (almost at the base of the Pyramids) and strikes out straight as a saint for Gizeh proper and Cairo. On either side of the road the land is given up to cultivation. Small fields, again, neatly clipped together without an inch of soil wasted. This careful thriftiness gives the earth the appearance of being tightly tied together lest a little should stray away. However many times one may pass by, the first intense feeling of constriction never loses its effect. You may think this is an exaggeration, but I tell you that, after seeing only the large ragged farms at home, open fields and grassland, the feeling cannot be escaped.

And no one can blame the fellah for clutching on to his little plot of earth; for the city is spreading and encroaching on his demesne. Already a number of expensive mansions have been erected near the road as private dwellings (which by their size must eventually deteriorate into tenements and roadhouses and cabarets to while away the wanton's weary, idle hour).

Cairo has always been an attraction to tourists, but ten years of tourists did not bring to Cairo a tenth of the money that has flowed in during the war. Remember that there are no holiday resorts, no pleasant driving nor picnic spots, there is nothing in fact that man may do except what he has contrived for himself.

Hence: cabarets – hundreds of them from the oldest and lowest to the newest and less low; cafés, bars, chophouses and restaurants, on every corner and five or six between, all licensed to sell liquor. And so the cunning Wog [sic] smiles while he panders to the whims and desires of his guests and takes their money while they glut themselves. Each looks upon the other with suspicion and contempt, but however much it may hurt race-pride to say so, the Wog [sic] in his filth and dolour can stand them better, and his contempt is better founded.

The streets are still only dimly lit at night, but the shops, bars and cafés are all ablaze. The Cairo streets are rarely parallel and cross each other at right angles; hence there are numerous odd corners and open circles (Midans) which they call squares, where six or seven streets meet or split up. The rule of the road is keep right which can be

ABE BERRY
CAIRO
"POST-WAR PLANS, GEORGE? VERY CHEAP. VERY HYGIENIC!"

Which South African serving Up North can forget the blandishments of the Cairo street hawkers – either extolling the quality of their merchandise or the virtue and hygiene of their sisters?

extended to 'keep-right-on-till-you-hit-something-then-just-go-on'. Taxis, buses, trams, cars, gharries, cycles, delivery vans and lorries all drive on their brakes and their hooters. To cross a road is an achievement, a successful co-operation of drivers and Allah.

Somehow during my first night I managed to dodge all the taxis and hawkers and reach the cabarets tucked away in a street called Emad el Dine. Between 9 and 10.30 I visited four of the worst. They were crowded with soldiers of every 'United Nations' in various stages of intoxication, and a bunch of scabrous prostitutes whose English vocabulary started and stopped at obscenities. When they are not practising trade these beauties are employed by the cabaret owners on commission to lure the soldiers in to drink. They attach themselves and order in rapid succession till their companion is either drunk or cleaned out. Then they drop them and take on some more. I reached the last of these places just before closing time. The bars had been emptied of liquor, so those who weren't lumbering about on the dance floor and could still stand were amusing themselves by throwing bottles and chairs over the dancers' heads to smash against the wall.

A very third rate band was blaring discordantly in an upper gallery, and the lights blazed garishly on old paint from an imitation coloured candelabra, which twitched and swayed to register every hit scored by a bottle or a chair-leg. The whole atmosphere had the stupid quality of delirium, bright lights, fast-tempo music and slow-moving figures. A hot, sweaty crowd milled aimlessly in the entrance. Then one Maori hit another.

A fight started.

A couple of Red-Caps popped in, and popped out again. One hero tried to butt in, but was slung out and went screaming into the night like a haunted dervish. Eventually the two Red Caps returned with a large number of their kind, and the victim was carted off to hospital or the morgue. The whole evening didn't cost me a piastre, and it may be recorded that I have had Cairo Cabarets!

Blake and I went into the Mousky or Bazaar quarter one morning.

On the fringe of the Mousky there are some meat, fish and poultry stalls. Except for the excessive filth and stench, they are not unlike our own Indian Market in Durban. The rest of the bazaars cover acres of ground; room leads into room, alleyway into alleyway, all constructed of reeds and daub like a vast human ant heap.

First a number of junk stalls. Each is as if you had turned out your tool shed or lumber room and packed every item: rusty nut, nail, door-handle, curtain rod, scrap metal, broken lock – everything – into trays, and built a three-wall daub hut around the lot. A whole row of these with several silent Wogs [sic] sitting in the dirt at the entrance of each.

Next, a group offering for sale a weird collection of gaudy baubles, trinkets and the like, gleaming dully through layers of dust. Filigree and bracelet makers, leatherworkers, vase turners, metallurgists, spinners and weavers – all using the crudest methods imaginable, but turning out some excellent work for all that.

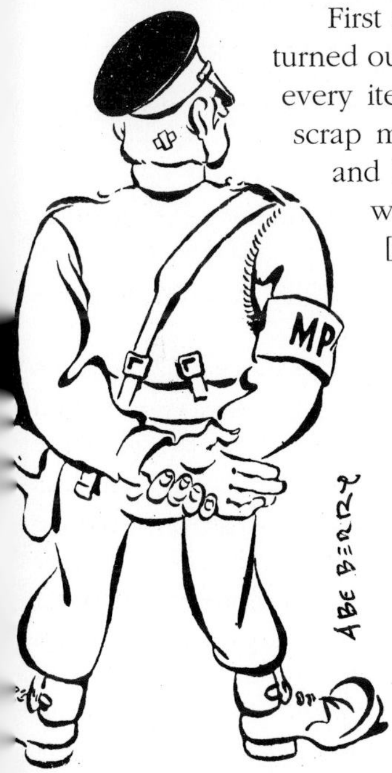

A military policeman (redcap) watches for trouble. He often found it. They patrolled in pairs and pounced on any breaches of military discipline. (All cartoons by Abe Berry)

The rich tapestry of a Cairo street.

The spinners and weavers are perhaps the most garrulous of the lot. Their fingers play nimbly with their shuttles while they squirm their bodies to add gesture to their conversation. Yards of fine-woven cloth, all shades of all colours, drape from the rafters, while their fingers go on twitching out yards more.

Cairo stinks, every inch of it. Only some parts stink more than others and the Mousky is perhaps the worst. Dirt everywhere at your feet, on the walls, pools of foul liquid in the alleys and the pervasive stench of decaying matter, dry dung and old urine. Disease on every face: mouth sores, ophthalmic maladies, and syphilitic distortions on almost every person.

You will appreciate the relief, then, when suddenly one's nostrils detect a new scent battling against the others. It grows stronger till one enters a low room, dim-lit and heavy with perfume. An old Mohammedan was sitting cross-legged on a mat, pulling languidly on a hookah while his son was explaining the peculiar merits of each perfume to a bewildered soldier. The prices are colossal; so Mohammed is willing to spread himself, coffee, spiced, in small cups, long, long, stories which he loves because he can exercise his voice, which he loves even more – one or two sales a day.

In a large, daub hall the spice merchants are gathered together. Sacks, boxes, tins, string-boxes, sacks of spices, all giving forth their odours, which are almost overpowering. I should have liked to have remained longer, but we had to hurry away to duty.

This is Old Cairo, on the fringe of Older Cairo represented by the mosques and gares, walls and fortifications erected originally by the Roman conquerors, and destroyed and partly rebuilt several times since.

There is such a conglomeration of architectural types that it is impossible to generalise about them. One feature common to them all, however, is that, whether allowance has been made in the foundations on the first floor, or no, each is almost invariably added to, story by story, as occasion or whim demands.

Apart from Arabic, which is spoken by all Egyptians, the most commonly spoken languages are French, English and Greek, in about that order.

Berry's impression of the entrance to one of the toughest districts of Cairo, the Berka, notorious for its brothels, pimps and dives. It was out of bounds to all Allied servicemen, as can be seen by the notice which spanned the width of the street. It was, of course, widely ignored.

A trip from Gizeh to Mena, where the pyramids stand, is not very unlike a trip through any new Estate Area near Durban or Johannesburg, Jacaranda and flamboyants (both in bloom now) alternately down both sides of the street.

This will allow me for now. There is a lot more to be seen and a lot of time in which to recount it – in time to come when I have only the sand for inspiration.

Yours, David. ❜

CHAPTER

61

'A sea of khaki'

Joyce Kuenzi, Cape Town, 1940–43

Joyce Kuenzi was fourteen when war broke out. She went to school in Cape Town and grew up in a town, darkened at night, a sea of khaki during the day. In spite of the war and shortages of petrol, food and clothing (mild by British and European standards) and in spite of the often depressing war bulletins, hers was a relatively carefree youth. There were after all plenty of men from which to choose (under mother's supervision), visiting Tommies to entertain and the challenge of baking a cake with no eggs. And of course there was knitting: socks, balaclavas, sweaters, gloves, for the boys who had gone Up North.

'We lived in a house below Lion's Peak with the whole of Cape Town at our feet. Before the black-out was enforced* the lights seemed to go on for ever. After that it was very dark, and you could see very little. The black-out was very strict: we put up hideous black curtains, which were drawn at dusk. If even a chink of light was showing a warden would hammer at the door and tell us to see to it, and quick. If we had to go anywhere at night, especially in a thick fog, I was terrified, because we had hoods over the headlights and you could see nothing in front of you.

'The black-out made the evenings very long, especially in winter. The radio would be the focal point of the room. I always wanted to listen to Mafeking Radio because of all the dance music. "A Nightingale Sang in Berkley Square" was one of my favourites. When the news came on it began with the morse code for V for Victory and Alvan Liddle or Richard Dimbleby always seemed to read it. At the end of the news there was a minute's silence.

'My father and my grandfather played cribbage and whist in the evening. I would do my homework in front of the sitting-room

---

* The first trial black-out in Cape Town was on 3 July 1942. Later in the year all vehicles were treated for black-out.

fire or knit. Everyone knitted, no matter where they were, on buses, waiting for buses, on park benches, everywhere. We knitted endless socks, scarves, gloves, balaclavas and sweaters, all khaki, of course. The wool came in skeins, not balls, and we had to hold it for each other while we rolled it into balls. It wasn't easy to get wool, so when we were tired of a garment, we'd unravel it, join all the wool together, wash it and wind it round two verandah chairs till it dried and roll it into balls. It was somehow very companionable.

'I was fourteen when war was declared. I was on my way to visit a girl boarding at St Cyprian's, and as I got off the trolley in St George's Street that Sunday, thousands of leaflets were raining down. I don't know where they came from. They all said "We are at War". I wondered whether my life would change, but it didn't.

'One summer morning I saw the first convoy come in. Eight gorgeous big grey ships nosing into the harbour. It was such a stunning sight that my uncle and I tore through the gum plantation to see them more clearly. We knew them all: the *Queen Elizabeth*, the *Queen Mary*, the *Empress of Britain*, the *Dominion Monarch*. In peacetime, when a ship left the harbour, my mother would run into my grandmother's bedroom, unhook her dressing-table mirror and stand on the verandah until she caught the light of the sun on the mirror, and she would flash the ships goodbye. She saw no reason to stop doing that in wartime, and every time a convoy went out she would flash the mirror at them. One day two senior men in army uniform came and asked her what she was doing. Who was she sending messages to? Did she know how dangerous it was to flash anything at ships during a war? It took some talking to convince them that it was all harmless; but she didn't do it again.

'I got used to seeing the convoys coming in and going out. Cape Town would be just a sea of khaki. You even got to know who the troops were, Canadian or New Zealand or British. The Senior Service was always very dashing, terribly glamorous in their summer whites and navy in winter. My parents were very careful with me. Sometimes the town was painted red, mostly by the Australians. They went into Stuttafords and cowed the girls so much that they were able to take two or three boxes of stockings and not pay for anything. They were dreadful.

'We used to entertain the soldiers often. They'd come for meals or tea or we'd go for a drive. My mother had coupons for the soldiers, so petrol was no problem. We'd drive to Franschhoek, stop on the way to drink some wine, take a picnic basket for lunch, wander about Paarl and then come home to dinner. We always had to get them back to the docks quite early. The Tommies were astonished at how much food we had.

'Sometimes I would get a telephone call from one of my mother's friends saying: "I've got three men here, please come and help to entertain them," and I would put on a long skirt and go round and have supper, then we'd put on the 78 records and have a little dance. I loved dancing to "I'll be Loving You Always". After the dancing we'd be taken home, and mother would be waiting in bed with the light on. It was terribly proper.

'None of my boyfriends was killed or even wounded. But sometimes you would hear of a convoy being torpedoed, and you would wonder if any of the soldiers you had met had been killed. It used to tear my heart out to go and see somebody off at the station; the farewells were heartbreaking, just heartbreaking. I often saw Just Nuisance at the station.

'It was terribly important to look right. If you had long hair, which I had, you simply couldn't be seen outside your house without one or two rows of sausage curls. We all went to bed with Queen Bess curlers in our hair, lead things covered with material, and each curl had to be just the way the curler set it. At school we had to wear dreadful elastic nets over our hair.

'Then there were the stockings – lisle, black or beige. We only read about nylon stockings. All my clothes were made by Malay dressmakers. Our laundry-maid used to tell us when a shop in District Six had received a load of material or underclothes or nighties. We would go down and pick up a few yards. Often these goods were illegally brought in by sailors and exchanged for favours.

'In January 1942 I had to do the catering for the month. We had sixteen people in our household that month, family from up country, my four brothers and sisters and the servants. I was given £5 on a Friday and told to go and do the shopping. For £20 a month I fed everybody, and we still had a jam cake and a dessert with cream on Saturday and Sunday.

'Of course there were economies. If a convoy had been in, there were shortages, but these were never really serious. The butcher and the grocer called at the kitchen door and you'd write your orders in the book. The baker came with a basket covered in hessian, which he would sweep aside to let you choose the bread. Then he'd go away with the order and deliver it by bicycle. Bananas were 1/6d for fifty.*

'To make butter go further you softened it and beat gelatine into it. Making cakes was sometimes a problem if butter was short.

---

* In 1940 butter was 1/8d a lb, bacon 1/4d, tea 2/11d, cooking oil 1/6d a bottle, 10 lbs mealie-meal 1/- and ham was 2/2d a lb. Fifty C to C cigarettes cost 1/6d. A six-seater Peugot cost £330, three-quarters of an acre of land in Dunkeld in Johannesburg cost £885 and the fees at Michaelhouse were £150 a year.

Hats in 1940 became smaller than the big brims of the 1930s. Tilted forward or over one eye, the shape was to stay essentially the same for the rest of the war, but as shortages of fabrics became the rule the flowers and netting disappeared.

Neat little padded-shoulder dresses, skirts just over the knee were the order of the day. Gloves were worn more often than not. A tailored suit cost roughly 42/-, blouses 7/6d and hats between 5/- and 7/6d. Prices could go higher for big spenders: twelve guineas for a stunning evening dress and five to six guineas for a top-of-the-range day dress. As the war progressed women rolled their hair up and off their faces, either in one long sausage curl right round the head or in a frivolous mop of curls piled on top of the head and held in place by combs. Veronica Lake, with her long side-parted blonde hair in her films was the bane of factory managers, who insisted that female employees should wear their hair pinned up or in a snood. Snoods became more elaborate and eventually found their way into evening wear, together with full-length capes.

We substituted vinegar for eggs, which were also sometimes hard to come by. And we had boere meal, which was brown. We weren't supposed to sift it, but of course we did, in sieves with wooden sides. Coffee was ersatz, not very nice, but at least it was hot. We ate a lot of fish, but a luxury meal would be a big roast chicken on a Sunday. Meat was rationed, but we stretched it by making stews with dumplings. Puddings were mostly stewed fruit, and we had a lot of spotted dick.

'But when you went out you could still have fun. Every Friday I would go down to the Waldorf and have a banana split, and sometimes if an officer took me out we would go dancing at Kelvin Grove. Tickets were 10/6d, and the suppers were wonderful. It was the only place in Cape Town where you got trifle with real cream. We danced to the music of Vera Lynn, Victor Sylvester, Joe Loss, George Formby, Gracie Fields, Judy Garland and, of course, Glenn Miller.

'I was allowed to wear lipstick in the evening. It was very difficult to get. I used to trudge up and down Wynberg looking for lipstick. When you got it it was never the right colour, so you'd take it home, melt it over the stove and blend it with another colour. Then you'd pour it into a tin and let it set. It was a frightful mess. Powder was also hard to come by; and powder was *essential.*

'We spent a lot of time making up parcels for the troops and sending them privately. We'd pack the parcels with razor-blades, shoe-laces, jerseys, Du Maurier cigarettes, gloves, biscuits and tins of sweets, as many sweets as we could squeeze in. These were packed with so much love and so much care. The men up north were always on our minds. ’

• Interview 1990

CHAPTER

62

'I'll leave it to you, Dr Jack'

Dr Jack Penn, reconstructive surgeon

Thousands of men now living all over the world owe their faces or noses or hands to the work of one man. Jack Penn, a major in the Active Citizen Force, became the only South African reconstructive surgeon during the war. He was thirty when Lady Oppenheimer allowed him to use the family house, Brenthurst, as a hospital for reconstructive surgery. The Brenthurst Red Cross Military Hospital for Plastic Surgery received the burnt and disfigured men from the East African, North African, Desert, Italian and Mediterranean theatres of war.

'It was a bright and sunny day early in 1941. I was sitting on the verandah of Sir Ernest and Lady Oppenheimer's home, looking out on the beautiful gardens. I had made an appointment to see her for one thing only: to persuade her to let me take over Brenthurst as a plastic surgery hospital.

'I told her about plastic surgery and how vital it was, but she had never heard of it and had difficulty in understanding me. "Now sit here," I told her. "I'm going to fetch some photographs to show you what it is about;" and I got into my car and drove to the Johannesburg General, got the photographs and came back. I spread them in front of her, showing her the terrible befores and the near-miraculous afters.

'"Right," she said, "you've got your hospital and anything you want in it."

'"Thank you," I replied. Later she said to me, "You know, Jack, you persuaded me to give you that hospital," and I said: "Of course, how else would I have got it?" She shook her head and said, "Yes, but not in the way you think you got it. When you told me to sit there and you went off and left me, I thought: What an impertinent young man; and then I thought: But he knows what he wants. So when you came back you had already persuaded me; even though I hadn't seen the photographs."

'The house had to be extensively altered and operating equipment had to be bought and installed and staff assembled before I could begin work. The Matron, Janet Ford, was thirty, the same age as me.

'This hospital was very important, because it is psychologically much better for deformed and maimed men to be kept apart from simple amputees and chaps with bullet wounds. Psychologically deformed people, burnt or whatever, feel inferior when they are with other people, but together they are very supportive.

'It was a war of crash, crush, and burn. We took them all in, men with deep and bizarre burns they received in tanks (if they weren't incinerated) and men burnt in planes who arrived with what we called "airman's burns". Most of the patients who came to Brenthurst needed skin grafts, and some were terribly deformed or disfigured.

'One of those men was Neville Fisher. I first saw him in a military hospital in Nairobi. I had been receiving large numbers of burnt pilots; British and South African, and when they got to Brenthurst many were blind. But they were blind only because their eyelids had been burnt, and their eyes were then destroyed by infection. I insisted that if pilots with burnt faces were brought to Nairobi I should be notified; and I would fly there and put on their eyelids; and when these had taken and they could close them I would bring them down to Brenthurst.

'I received an urgent call to come up for a particularly bad case. When I first saw Neville Fisher he had the most extensive area of burns that I had come across in the war, including the Battle of Britain cases that I had seen in Britain. His entire face and neck, body, arms and legs were all burnt: eighty per cent of his body. He had crashed in Somaliland and had been thrown from his plane with a compound fracture of the tibia.

'He crawled back into the plane, which was burning, and pulled out his observer, who unfortunately was dead. While he was pulling him out he got severely burnt. When he was found he was unconscious. He was taken to Nairobi, where he survived, but only just.

'He was a skeleton, weighing 88 lbs, half his normal weight, and he looked like a hunk of boiled beef because of the burns. His fractured leg was in plaster, he had a bedsore the size of a soup-plate, and he was blind, because he had lost his eyelids, and he had developed corneal ulcerations of his eyes. The first thing I did was graft eyelids, but the only area of skin available on his entire body was the inner part of one arm, the rest being a mass of scar and bone. I used the skin to create his lower lids and ten days later, when the skin on his inner arm had healed, I used the new skin to graft his upper lids.

'After five days Fisher's eyelids had taken and he was able to close them, and his corneal ulcers had healed and he was able to see. Together with sixteen other men I had him flown down to Johannesburg. He was with me for two and a half years, and he had thirty-five operations. Every bit of his face was regrafted, including his nose and his eyebrows, but fortunately not his ears, which had been protected by his flying helmet.

'Fisher's hands were like claws. As we gradually built him up I let his normal skin grow again, and then I would take it off, let it grow again and take it off again, because he had so little skin to give. He insisted on eating eggs. He ate eggs all day. Forty years later we discovered the one thing you must give a burnt person is protein, and he was doing what his body told him to do. It was a great day when at last he left us.*

'We could accommodate fifty patients at Brenthurst. The library and the sitting-room took a number of patients, but there were so many I had to take over five large houses that had been given to the army as convalescent homes. After I had operated on them and they had recovered they would go to one of those beautiful houses and rest there till they came back for the next operation.

'It was very important to have a sense of humour. There was a wonderful relationship between the staff and the patients. They could say anything, there were no holds barred. No matter how bad the men were, they laughed; and that was very important for morale. The psychological side was as important as the surgical. It was vital for the men to understand that I was on their side, that I was not doing it for the money. When all the men are deformed in one way or another they become a team.

'My anaesthetist, Lt H "Speedy" Bentel, organised some of the men into a band. Speedy played a sort of mandolin and sang appallingly. A long-term patient with half his face blown off was able to make strange noises through his exposed antrum like a trombone and a bass cello. Another patient whose fingers of both hands had been blown off by a booby trap played the drums by holding the sticks in the forks made for him between the meta-

---

* Lt Neville Fisher returned to the SAAF and flew Spitfires into Italy during the invasion. He was shot down over enemy territory. He walked thirty miles to the Allied lines. After the war he completed his BSc in geology and then took up medicine. He became a Fellow of the Royal College of Surgeons, a tribute to both Penn's skilful surgery and his own strength of will. In spite of his obvious bravery Neville Fisher was not decorated.

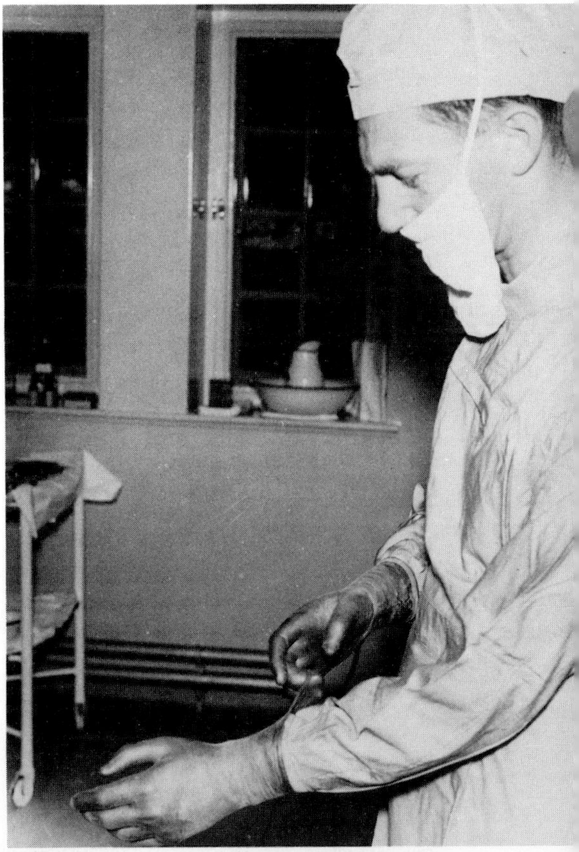

Dr Jack Penn, the only South African reconstructive surgeon during the war. 'To be successful in this field you need the talents of sympathy, simplicity and integrity.' (South African National Museum of Military History)

Brenthurst, turned over to Jack Penn by Sir Ernest and Lady Oppenheimer as a hospital for the duration of the war. The men were able to relax in the beautiful gardens as they recuperated. (South African National Museum of Military History)

carpal bones; and he sang well. Speedy made music and made men happy with the flotsam and jetsam of the battlefronts.

'The work was hard, twelve hours at a stretch, doing operations right through the day, and then ward rounds; but I was young and fit, and I did it because I wanted to do it. I always kept in mind what Dr Will Mayo of the Mayo Clinic in Minnesota said to me when I told him that I wanted to get home for the coming war and do reconstructive surgery. "It is the divine right of every man to look human;" and I have borne that with me all my life.

'And of course I was a fortunate man. I was the only reconstructive surgeon in the country; I had "my" own hospital, and because I had no one telling me what I could or couldn't do I developed all sorts of new techniques that were practised as far afield as Russia and the USA. I am an individualist, and I like to do things in my own way. I thrived on challenge.

'One of the most challenging cases was an airman who had crashed. His skull was smashed and he had pulverised the whole of the left frontal lobe of his brain. That and the bone over it were removed, and although he was alive he looked monstrous because he had no forehead and about three inches above his eyebrow was flat. The blood-vessels of his brain under his scalp were visibly pulsating.

'Something had to be done not only to restore the man's appearance but to protect his brain. A plaster cast was made of the deformity. It was plain to me that there wasn't enough of his own bone to use without causing severe deformity. I asked the dental mechanics to make me a large plaster "graft" perforated with numerous small holes, which made it lighter and allowed the healing fibrous tissue to grow through the holes and keep the graft in place.

'After the operation, to my astonishment and pleasure, there was no reaction to the plastic graft. He left the hospital a fit man, and although he had only half the amount of thinking brain that he had before he later passed his BA LLB examinations and became a successful lawyer.

'Throughout the war the Straits of Gibraltar were cut off, and we received all the long-term casualties needing plastic surgery from the Mediterranean and Near East zones. We had South Africans from Abyssinia, Egypt and Italy, British from the armies in Egypt, Syria, Greece and Italy and from the Air Force and the Navy and the "free" soldiers of the Greeks, French and Poles and even a few Americans. More than half the time spent in the operating theatre was for reconstruction of burn cases, an experience that helped me when I was invited after the war to help with the burn cases of Hiroshima and Nagasaki. Until the middle of 1944 the pressure of work increased progressively. New convoys kept arriving, and with the accumulation of long-term cases my operating periods became more and more concentrated. I tried to keep everyone in the operating theatre relaxed by playing music, but the pressure of work was intense, and the number of cases ran from the hundreds into the thousands. Sometimes I was so tired I would lie down on a bed fully dressed and wake up in the same position in which I went to sleep.

'I was never depressed or daunted by any of the cases I dealt with. It was my job to make these men whole again, and I worked in an atmosphere of warm friendship and challenge: when you work out a new idea you become very satisfied if it is right, like thinking up a different way to make a nose or developing an artificial eye.

'To be a successful reconstructive surgeon you have to have an artistic sense and you have to have taste. Artistry means good taste. When I have to build a man's nose, or change his nose, if I did them all the same I would make a mess of the man's face. They all have to be different, to fit in with the man himself and his features.

'You need an artistic sense for that. Not one of the men ever differed with me. "I'll leave it to you, Dr Jack," they would say, and that was incredible confidence from those shattered men.

'When they left Brenthurst the men often asked me if they could have something to remind them of their stay there. I gave them a badge: a phoenix rising from the flames and flying again.*

'They paid the price in pain and courage for megalomania and political stupidity. It was my privilege to be able to help them. ❜

• Interview 1990

---

* The badge later became the symbol of the Brenthurst Clinic built by Dr Penn in 1948. It has also been adopted as the official symbol of the South African Association of Plastic and Reconstructive Surgeons. After the war Jack Penn became Professor of Reconstructive Surgery at the University of the Witwatersrand and Visiting Professor at Oxford, Harvard, Ann Arbor, UCLA, Edinburgh, Jerusalem, Hiroshima, Tokyo, Taiwan and Iran. Over thirty years he has helped and taught in Israel on the rehabilitation of the wounded, and in Hiroshima he dealt with the victims of the atomic bomb and trained Japanese surgeons. In his career as a reconstructive surgeon, sculptor and philosopher he also helped Dr Albert Schweitzer in the reconstruction of patients with leprosy. He retired in 1978.

CHAPTER

63

1944

'A lightness of spirit'

Tobruk, Cairo, Alexandria, Alem Halfa, Sidi Rezegh, Marble Arch were household names in South Africa by the time the Western Desert campaign came to its victorious end. Now South Africans had to learn another set of names: Taranto, Bari, Cassino, Cellano, Chiusi, Bologna, Castiglione, Monte Salvaro, Florence. For on 20 April 1944 the 6th Armoured Division* under Maj-Gen W H E Poole landed at Taranto in Italy.

The year had begun with a little reassurance and a reminder that South Africans had not always been as safe as they had thought. Naval authorities in Cape Town announced that, unbeknown to the public, German raiders had laid two minefields off the South African coast: the first, off Cape Agulhas before May 1940, the second in March 1943 in the approaches to Table Bay and within five miles of Mouille Point. So near had been the minelayer to Mouille Point that the captain would have been able to see the lights in the centre of Cape Town.

The RAF and the USAF announced that production had begun on a new kind of aircraft, one without propellers and driven by the 'expulsion of a steady stream or streams of gases or compressed air' – Frank Whittle's British Gloster Meteor, the first jet plane on the Allied side to fly.

A lightness of spirit entered the Union from the beginning of the year, minefields or no. Most of the fighting troops were at home. Only the SAAF and the engineers were still abroad.

While Berlin and other German towns were pounded by the British and Americans and Hitler stood defiantly looking out from citadel Germany, the world was still largely unaware of the Third Reich's death camps in Germany and Poland.

---

* Formed in the Union on 1 February 1943.

The war in South Africa was winding down. By November 1943 the threat to the coasts had receded and all operations by the Civilian Protective Services (with the exception of the Civil Guard) were suspended beyond twenty miles from the coast. With the Italian surrender (on 8 September 1943), Italians living in South Africa, with the exception of prisoners of war, now for the most part concentrated at Zonderwater, were freed from restrictions. Food control was in full force and would continue long after the war in what was in effect a controlled economy.

Fifth column activities had more or less petered out, although feelings still ran high. It was estimated that there were thirty thousand members of the Ossewabrandwag in the country, although its commandant in chief, Dr J F J van Rensburg put the figure at nearer a hundred thousand; and as late as the day before the D-Day landings in Normandy on 6 June he was still confident that Germany would win the war.

Production of armoured cars ended in April 1944 (nearly six thousand had been made) and the output of small-arms ammunition in 1944–45 fell sharply from its peak of 240 786 132 rounds in 1943. Total expenditure by the government on the manufacture of munitions and war stores also fell from the 1943 figure of £26 904 928 to £8 607 742. By December 1944 shipping routed round the Cape had also fallen off. Up to then we had played host to 49 241 ships.

In early autumn the debonair Noël Coward arrived in Durban. He was greeted by an excited crowd of three thousand. He performed in Durban, gave South Africans a pep talk and gave endless interviews on the radio. It was a change from the next news to dominate the airwaves and newspaper pages, the news everyone had been waiting for: the invasion.

A few people who tuned in to European stations before the SABC came on the air had already heard a warning directed by the BBC to Holland advising civilians near the coast to leave the area. But most heard the news just after 7 a.m., when the morning physical jerks programme was dramatically interrupted. Later came a message from General Eisenhower via the BBC: 'People of Western Europe: a landing was made this morning on the coast of France by troops of the Allied Expeditionary Force. This landing is part of a concerted United Nations plan for the liberation of Europe, made in conjunction with our great Russian allies.

'I have this message for all of you: Though the initial assault may not have been made in your country, the hour of liberation is approaching. Do not needlessly endanger your lives. Wait until I give you the signal to rise and strike the enemy ... Be patient. Prepare ...'

The fighting in Italy was equally fierce, and the Germans resisted every step of the way. After the bloody battles at Cassino Rome was liberated on 4 June, and the 6th SA Armoured Division, at first entranced by the sight of olive groves and vineyards, settled down to the close-contact fight that characterised the Italian campaign. On 19 August, the South Africans entered a delirious Florence only six days after a second largely airborne invasion force, setting out from Rome, landed in the south of France. On 24 August Paris was liberated and Gen de Gaulle came home.

Now under the command of the US 4th Corps, the 6th SA Armoured Division began its advance towards Bologna through the Apennines. By 6 October, at Castiglione, the Division pushed forward to Monte Salvaro.

By the end of 1944 the end was in sight: advances in the Far East, the port of Antwerp re-opened, the *Tirpitz* sunk and President Roosevelt elected President of the United States for a fourth though short-lived term. And at home, as we looked towards 1945? A total ban on white flour because of a poor wheat harvest.

CHAPTER

64

'Just crumpled ruins'

Frank Watson and the barrage at Monte Cassino, May 1944

Little did the men of the 6th SA Armoured Division, under the command of Maj-Gen W H Evered Poole, think that in little over a year from when it was founded in the Union in February 1943 it would be taking part in the Allied offensive against Monte Cassino.

The division was a mixture of soldiers who had never seen battle and of men who had been through both Abyssinia and the Western Desert. It left for Egypt amid scenes by now familiar to South Africans: troop trains to Durban, embarkation on grey ships, the Lady in White singing them out of the harbour.

On 20 April 1944, after nearly a year's intensive training in the desert, the men of the 6th SA Armoured Division landed at Taranto on the heel of Italy. They were deployed under the 1st Canadian Corps and with the 24th (British) Guards Brigade under its command. They were immediately moved to a few miles south of Monte Cassino.

Among the men of the Division there were a few hundred Rhodesians, now incorporated in the South African forces. Great care was taken to retain their individuality and *esprit*. One of them was a young gunner, Frank Watson.

On 6 May 1944 Watson, fresh from King George VI Barracks in Salisbury, noted in the diary that he had kept since 1936, when he was at public school in Britain, that as the troop train *en route* for Durban arrived in Johannesburg there was 'a maze of lights as if the heavens were being reflected in a mirror'.

Now, a year later, he and his fellow Rhodesians in the 6th Armoured Division were beside themselves with excitement when they learned that they were to relieve a Canadian Brigade, man for man, in the Cassino line.

The battle for the town and the monastery of Cassino has been called the Italian Stalingrad. It raged for more than five months and saw some of the fiercest and most heroic fighting of the war.

The medieval Benedictine monastery, sheltering behind almost impregnable walls, stood solidly on top of Monte Cassino. Below it, cradled within vineyards, stood the village of Cassino. It was the tragedy of both the monastery and the village that they lay almost on the Gustav Line, a strongly fortified defensive line built by the Germans. Cassino also stood at the entrance to the Liri Valley, the gateway to Rome.

There were two main battles for Cassino. The first began on 17 January 1944, when the British artillery of the 10th Corps opened fire, and ended on 18 February, when the battle was broken off; but not before the monastery, which was believed to be harbouring German troops (later emphatically denied by the Germans), was bombed on the night of 15 February by 142 B-17 Flying Fortresses that dropped 350 tons of high explosive and incendiary bombs, shattered the basilica and the buildings inside the walls, but left the great walls intact. The second battle for Cassino which, by then was front-page news in South Africa and elsewhere, began on the night of 14 March and ended in pyrrhic victory on 18 May, when the Polish 12th Podolski Regiment stormed the ruins.

When Frank Watson and the gun crew of which he was a member was led, in the dark of night, into their position in the vacated Canadian line, none of their families in the Union or Rhodesia had the faintest idea of where their menfolk were. They thought they were still in North Africa, although some of the more percipient may have wondered why their boys should be in North Africa when the fighting was in Italy.

At this time of the war the Allies were understandably nervous about security. The bloody American and British landings at Salerno (on 8 September 1943, the day Italy capitulated) had been successfully concluded, while the even bloodier landings at Anzio still continued. Then there was the big one: the Allied landings in Normandy in June, followed by another landing in the south of France in August 1944.

The sector of the Allied line the South Africans took over from the battered Canadians ran under the nose of the enemy, from the end of the New Zealand line on the South Africans' left flank right up to the Colle Pietrobove, where British troops were in position. The sector was about five thousand yards wide from east to west.

Watson, dug in with his gun crew, still managed to write home at least once a week. He had also kept a diary since 1936, never missing a day, even on 11 May which, he noted, was the 1 713th day of the war.

Frank Watson's gun position near Cassino, May 1944 (Frank Watson)

On that night the might of the Allied 15th Army Group – twenty-one full-strength divisions with equipment to spare, together with eleven brigade-strength formations faced fourteen battle-weary German divisions, helped by three more brigade-strength units.

At a sign broadcast from London by the BBC the Allied artillery, of which the South African guns were part (and which would have pleased Dan Pienaar enormously), opened fire with two thousand guns at 11 p.m. An hour later the men of the 5th and 8th Armies began to advance. This is how Frank Watson recalled his battle of Monte Cassino:

'Friday 28 April 1944
(1700th Day)
The weather had been much finer today and there was no rain. It was still very muddy, but by the end of the day quite a lot of it had dried up. We were again busy all day, getting everything ready, the ammo into the limber, the final touches to the Quad and other sundry items. I am on duty tomorrow as orderly bombardier, so will not be able to give the sub a hand. We are all wondering when and where we are going into action; some say it will be very soon. I am inclined to believe it. I hope so, in a way, because the bullshit about guards etc, is getting beyond human endurance and imagination.

Tuesday 2 May 1944
(1704th Day)
Today is the eve of our going into battle, for tomorrow night we are relieving a Canadian regiment. We were up very early and on our way by six as we had 120 miles to do. The first part was along the plain towards Foggia, with its wavy cornfields. All day the weather was fine and the scenery was magnificent, especially after we struck inland to the Apennines. In the distance there was snow on the hills, air lovely and crisp.

Wednesday 3 May 1944
(1705th Day)
We did not have to get up this morning, and it was lovely to lie in bed and listen to the birds singing, and everything seemed so peaceful that war was unimaginable. We arrived at the assembly point near Acquafondata and waited for the Canadians to come out; then we went in about seven with that empty feeling of nervousness and fear. We have an amazing gun position, two guns in the hollow and two in the side of the hill (we are one of them). Dugouts all over, heavy artillery (5,5 in.) behind us – helluva noise. We are working in shifts and our shift got to bed about midnight. Heavy mist over mountains.

Thursday 4 May 1944
(1706th Day)
We are in the bulge near Cassino, but we do not know disposition of troops, but they belong to many of the Allied Nations.* The weather has improved, the mud is drying up and the snow is melting. There has been intermittent fire from us and the mediums.

Saturday 6 May 1944
(1708th Day)
We did not do much firing during the morning, but after lunch we fired at twelve thousand yards and so had to use super charge. Our gun is the first to fire that charge; it has a terrific bang. After the second shot one of the gun-pit walls fell in, so we spent all afternoon fixing it up. At first we used to jump when the 5.5 went off behind us, but we are now getting used to it, and the noise rings in waves as the shell passes over the many valleys. It is my night duty, and it is expected that we shall have harassing fire tasks to do.

---

* For security reasons troops did not know which countries made up the front line.

Sunday 7 May 1944
(1709th Day)
For a long time to our left the noise was like continuous thunder. This morning has been more peaceful, but it was the calm before the storm, because soon after two Jerrys, began ranging with air-burst on a nearby crest. Then the fun started. Our mediums opened up, but it did not stop Jerry, and the crest under heavy fire was switched over to the front of us. The padre held a nice service on the gun position, and just as he was giving the blessing our guns opened up – the challenge for the advent of victory. The jeep-head for supplying all forward areas got a terrific hammering. A medium behind us had a premature and all the crew were injured, one seriously.

Tuesday 9 May 1944
(1711th Day)
During the afternoon Jerry started air-burst shelling to our right. At once our mediums opened up, and we had a battery shoot on a hostile battery. This continued all afternoon. I went up a little rise and could see Mount Cairo, Monastery Hill etc. The Jerries look on this bulge from all sides. This evening we did a lot of effective shooting on targets pointed out by the infantry. It was so successful that later tasks were cancelled.

Wednesday 10 May 1944
(1712th Day)
It was expected that we were going to fire a barrage tonight, so we had to carry a lot of ammo up the short, steep climb to our gun-pit. Tomorrow night the greatest onslaught in history takes place when there will be a general offensive all along the Italian front, the Russian front and without doubt the second front, where 44 divisions are waiting for the first landings. The Poles have been given the task of breaking through Cassino and Mount Cairo. We are supporting the Kiwis in a side show feint attack.

Thursday 11 May 1944
(1713th Day)
Today has been quite peaceful as regards artillery duels, but very busy getting ammo ready for the barrage tonight. There is to be a general attack on all fronts in Italy, Yugoslavia, Russia and the 2nd front. A message from Lt-Gen Sir Oliver Lease, Commander of the 8th Army, was read to us; it was quite inspiring. Our intention now is not to drive the Boche out but to kill him, so the Poles and the Indians have been given that task. The first objective is Rome, and

already the Germans are falling back on the Adriatic sector. The first barrage starts at 11 p.m., and in our sector there are fifteen hundred guns, many of them of large calibre. These next few days will be a stern test for our infantry.

Friday 12 May 1944
(1714th Day)
The barrage last night was terrific. On the stroke of 11 p.m. the whole front was lit up by hundreds of flashes, and a few seconds later the noise was tremendous. As the large shells passed over us on their way to the enemy lines it was like an express train in a tunnel. It was amazing, almost incredible to those of us to whom this was all a new experience. Our barrage – rather a series of concentrations – lasted 38 minutes, and between them and the next barrage, at 2 a.m. we engaged other targets. The mediums and heavies boomed all night and throughout today. This afternoon was spent replenishing our ammo etc. We have heard no news about the attack. This evening we got one beer, and there was also some mail. Tonight I am on night-shift – have only had five hours' sleep in two days.

Saturday 13 May 1944
(1715th Day)
Night-shift was very tiring, for we had to fire at irregular intervals on given targets. Then at 4.30 a.m. there were two Regimental alerts. The fellows on beat loaded and fired the guns by themselves. I was so tired that I slept through the whole morning; it was lovely, only to be woken up at lunch by a Jerry plane dropping bombs close by. Later in the evening another plane swooped low over the front. Ack-Ack gave him a hot reception. There is another barrage of forty minutes tonight at 2 a.m., but as it is simple the three men on duty are going to manage. I've prepared the ammo for them. News of the battle for the Gustav Line is very good.

Sunday 14 May 1944
(1716th Day)
Last night there was plenty of artillery fire, which included a small barrage. Our front-line troops are having a few casualties from mortar fire, booby-traps and a patrol. Gradually, against stiff opposition, the Poles, Indians, British and Canadians are straightening the line from Cassino to the coast. This afternoon the Major gave us a short chat about things in general. Tonight is our night on duty, but there seems not to be much on the go. It may be a quiet night.

Monday 15 May 1944
(1717th Day)
I said yesterday that it might be a quiet night. Between midnight and 1 a.m. we were subjected to air-burst shelling from the enemy. It was a horrible sensation, especially in the middle of the night, a blinding flash and a great explosion. It seemed as if the shell burst right above us. We found refuge in our bunk-holes until we thought it was over, then we went to sleep in the gun-pit. Between 3.30 and 4.30 a.m. we fired twenty rounds on a working-party. Many pieces of shrapnel have been found from last night's episode. It certainly makes the war a little less one-sided than before.

Thursday 18 May 1944
(1720th Day)
The weather has been fine and cool all day. We heard the grand news that Monastery Hill had been captured by the Poles, whose flag is now flying nobly from its summit. The pincer movement round Cassino has worked, for the Germans were now evacuating this much-battered village. It has been very quiet all today, with hardly any artillery fire, except for a few rounds this afternoon. 16th Battery put up a big smokescreen for an advance by the Poles. Everything is going according to plan: it may seem slow, but the going is rugged and hilly.

The 25-pounder in action in Italy in 1944, after Cassino (Frank Watson)

The winter of 1944 in Italy: a German prisoner, wearing the Iron Cross, is brought in through the South African lines. (Frank Watson)

Sunday 28 May 1944
(1730th Day)
I am writing this near Cassino, just off the famous Highway 6. In front, looming majestically against the sky, is Mount Cairo, which overlooked all the Allied positions here before the new offensive. Then no one could move in daylight; now the front is twenty miles away. The journey here – Div dispersal area – was beautiful, along good roads over which there was tremendous traffic. We are quite near the position – as the crow flies – that we were in over a week ago, having travelled over a hundred miles to get here. We are camped in an old vineyard full of shell-holes and bomb-craters, with poppies trying bravely to add some colour to this war-scarred area. The villages are shattered ruins, the trees torn fragments of trunks and branches.

Monday 29 May 1944
(1731st Day)
There was tremendous traffic along Highway 6 today, with many tanks going forward. This morning our troop commander gave us an interesting talk on the present battle situation in our sector. Everything was going according to plan, even better in some places. The Fifth Army are nearing Valmontone on Highway 6, and if they capture it the main German road of retreat is barred. But the

ultimate intention is the same. I went for a lovely walk towards Cassino and saw Monastery Hill, taken by tanks; much of the Monastery is a battered remnant silhouetted by the setting sun, and the villages are complete ruins and the trees mere stumps and matchwood. ’

In the war annals of the German armies in the 1939–45 war there must surely be a place of honour for the parachute troops who defended Cassino. General Alexander paid them handsome tribute: he doubted whether any other body of men could have survived and fought with such doggedness as the *Fallschirmjäger* at Cassino.

The fighting was vicious on both sides. When the 15th Carpathian Brigade of the Polish 3rd Division lost Peak 593 (Mount Calvary), north-west of Monte Cassino to a German parachute regiment on 12 May, the Germans found one officer and seven men out of the whole battalion capable of resistance. And when the Poles stormed and took Monte Cassino on 18 May they found not one effective man left: only a handful of wounded.

The approximate figures (the real ones will probably never be known) stand at 107 144 for American dead, wounded and missing from 15 January 1944 to 4 June, when Rome fell, 7 835 men of the British 8th Army, including the Poles, and 20 002 Germans. The German figures include those lost at Salerno.

Nineteen days after the fall of Monte Cassino the Allies landed on the beaches of Normandy on 6 June. To South Africans at home, listening with the rest of the world, the landings meant not only the beginning of the end but also the return of their men from prison camps.

CHAPTER

65

'They were so afraid of going home broken'

Capt Madeleine van Straaten, nursing the boys

The UDF was formed when the Union of South Africa came into being in 1910. It needed a military nursing service; so, under Section 21 of the South African Defence Act of 1912, the South African Military Nursing Service (SAMNS) was created.

In the 1914–18 war the nurses accompanied the soldiers. Fourteen of them died during the hostilities.

At the peak of World War II there were 3 691 nurses (of whom three hundred were Canadians seconded to the SAMNS), their uniforms bore distinctive cherry-coloured epaulets and a badge with the springbok facing left within a circle and the letters SAMNS (SAMVD in Afrikaans).

Many of these women were sent to Kenya, Abyssinia and Somalia, the Western Desert and Italy. They went wherever the men went. They were mostly kept well back from the fighting, although some nurses were actually in first-aid posts immediately behind the lines and were sometimes caught up in the fighting, so mobile was the desert campaign. Most of them were in base hospitals.

One of these nursing sisters was Madeleine van Straaten. She nursed the men, jollied them up when they were down, wrote letters for them and sat with them as they died:

'The wounded usually came in at night. Each man had a tag with his name on it and the nature of his injury. If they had had morphia or a tourniquet they had a red cross on their foreheads. You look at them hopelessly at first, all these boys coming in. You look at them and think poor things; and then you get stuck in. That's your job.

'Our first big influx was after Sidi Rezegh. At a base hospital we usually had twenty-four hours' notice that the men were coming, but with the wounded from Sidi Rezegh it was much less than that.

Capt Madeleine van Straaten at the South African Military Hospital outside Cairo. (Madeleine van Straaten)

'I was having tea with my sister, who was based in Cairo, when the warning arrived. We quickly put up a ward to cope with the numbers. I put the tea aside and threw some sheets at her and said: "Here, make some beds."

'They came at lunchtime; and they came and they came and they came. They had wounds on arms and legs, the body, the head, the odd amputation. You show compassion by the way you handle your patients. When they arrive they are usually shocked, even though they have been in a field hospital, and they are exhausted. All they want is a cup of very hot tea and a sleep. We wanted to treat the Sidi Rezegh boys and so we gave them Christmas pudding; they loved that.

Christmas in Ward 20, No 5 (SA) General Hospital, Helmieh, Cairo, in 1943. After the photograph was taken Capt Van Straaten went to Italy. (Madeleine van Straaten)

'Some of them were terribly wounded. One boy called Marais, was blind, he had no nose, his arms were in a saline solution in a basin and his legs were in plaster. I went to him and said hello. "How are you?" I asked. I didn't want him to know how shocked I was.

'"Well, Sister," he said, "under the circumstances I'm very well."

'There was a boy from Bredasdorp called Van Breda. A tall boy, in great pain, and he wouldn't have morphia He simply refused it. Eventually I had to give it to him, and he went off very easily after that. It doesn't matter when or how it is; a death is always distressing.

'Nursing wasn't easy. One day when I came into the ward it was under two feet of water. We had to dig holes in the floor to let it out. And then there was the khamsin: you would go into the ward in the morning and find the patients' faces outlined on the pillows. You just couldn't stop the sand coming in. The men slept under nets because of the sandfly, nets much finer than mosquito nets, and they were terribly hot and everybody hated them.

'One night we heard the guns of El Alamein. The floor shook, and all the men woke up. "It's started," they said to each other, and there wasn't a man in the hospital who didn't want to rejoin his unit and take part in the battle.

'In April 1944 I was posted to No 102 General Hospital at Bari in Italy. The "hospital" was an unfinished building, three storeys high with no window-panes, because a bomb in the harbour had shattered them all. The walls hadn't been plastered, the floor was rough, there was no hot water, and we had to clean this place from top to bottom to receive our patients. We arrived there on a Wednesday and we were told a convoy of wounded would be coming in on Saturday.

'We were given brooms with no handles. We just got stuck in. We scrubbed and washed until we had blisters on our hands. Then we carried in the beds and the bedding and the lockers. When we had finished the matron told us she wanted us all in uniform to receive the wounded.

'The convoy that Saturday wasn't too bad, but later ones were, with wounded and shocked men. One convoy consisted entirely of partisans from Yugoslavia. They were in a state. Wounded, terribly.

'They had been fighting and hiding in the hills of Yugoslavia, and their clothes were in rags. They had to be deloused, their hair cut and everything. One lad came to me and said: "Sister, please come here." I went over to him, but it wasn't a lad, it was a lassie. She had been fighting and had been wounded. We had to open a separate ward for women partisans.

Nursing sisters at 102 South African Combined General Hospital. In Italy Germans were nursed along with Allied troops. From Italy Madeleine van Straaten went to Brighton in England to nurse South African former prisoners of war. (Madeleine van Straaten)

'Their wounds were so bad, and the smell, the pus, the suppuration was terrible. These poor people had had no water for a long time. The boys walked to the showers and they cleaned themselves again and again, wounds or no wounds, and of course that got rid of a lot of the poison. But I can never forget that smell. And then we had a hospital ship full of Germans.

'I admitted a hundred patients that night. Some were very young, but most were in their thirties. They were sick, wounded, exhausted. At one point the nursing staff were up in arms at having to nurse Germans, but they were told very firmly when a man came into the hospital his nationality or his rank mattered nothing but that he was a human being and he needed help.

'I shall never forget giving those Germans water. They kissed the basin. "We haven't had water for a long, long time," one little lad told me. "Please, Sister, if you find one of us with lice, please forgive us – we haven't had any water for so long." But they were clean, clean, in spite of having no water. I liked nursing them.

'We called one of them Bambino because he was so young. He was in plaster from his armpits to his thighs. On the night we admitted him I heard groaning, so I walked into the ward. Not a word, not a sound. I did that twice.

'The third time I heard the groaning I stood at the door and when it came again I went straight to the bed. It was this little Bambino. I asked what was the matter, but he turned his face away from me. There were two SS men in the ward, and one of them was in the bed next to the boy.

'"Sister," he said to me, "he's got a very bad tummy ache." What with the plaster and the aperient he had been given during the day – well, he hadn't had a motion for three weeks. He was in agony. So I gave him an enema and he filled two bedpans. I finished off that night giving seven enemas in that ward. When men are in that state, an aperient doesn't help much. The relief on that poor little devil's face – he was so grateful.

'One of the Germans there was such a charming man, a real gentleman, a true German, not the Nazi type. He had been amputated at the thigh, and we were worried that he might haemorrhage. He was in great pain. I said to him: "I'm going to give you some morphia."

'"No, Sister."

'"I'm going to give you morphia," I repeated.

'"No, Sister."

'"Why not?"

'"You need the morphia for your own people."

'He was in agony. I said: "Look, morphia has been ordered for you. You are my patient in my ward, and you are going to get your morphia." Without any further ado I gave him the morphia and he sank back on the pillows. He was a very brave man.

'Some of the men were terribly worried about going home with their wounds. They were afraid that their families would reject them. They longed to go home, but they were afraid.

'There was a married man, a pilot, who had had a bad crash. His legs were broken, his pelvis was broken and his arms in a bad state. When the plaster was taken off he was able to walk on crutches. The hospital ship *Amra* was leaving, and he was due to go on it. They day before he left he said to me: "Sister, I don't want to go home."

'"Why not?" I asked.

'He said: "What am I going to do if my little girl says 'Daddy, pick me up' and I can't pick her up?" They were so afraid of going home broken. It nearly broke my heart sometimes. ❜

• Interview 1990

When Capt Madeleine van Straaten came home it was on a ship filled with worn, thin and excited former prisoners of war. The first thing she did when she got off the ship was to eat a banana. She had been away for over five years.

CHAPTER

66

'I just said "yes"'

Joan Lee, war bride, war widow

Joan Lee (née Tissiman) was one of the 121 606 women who got married during the war. Many of the weddings, which reached their peak of 28 387 in 1940 as South African servicemen went north were 'three-week specials': impromptu weddings that took three weeks to arrange while the banns were called. Joan's wedding took a little longer: four months. Then her husband, Sergeant Philip Lee, went back to the war. Like 4 307 other South African men, he never came back. He died in a field outside Florence in July 1944. Joan tells the story of a war bride and a marriage cut tragically short:

'When we got married I thought it would last for ever. Of course there was a war on, but somehow you never think anything bad will happen to you and yours.

'There were lots of marriages in wartime. There was an urgency, a need to pledge yourself, to belong. A lot of the marriages were silly – men coming off convoys, ready for anything, and they would marry one of the Durban girls within a week and get back on another convoy, and she'd never hear from him again. One girl I knew, a very nice girl from White River, married a Greek sailor. They got married within two weeks. Then he sailed away and she never heard from him again. He could have been killed, he could have had another wife, or he could simply have forgotten her.

'Our marriage wasn't like that. I met Philip Lee in a little village in Zululand called Hlabisa. I was running a farm school for the children, and he was the agricultural officer. He had been to Michaelhouse and Cedara, and he loved the country and farming.

'It was a good life in 1939. We all used to play tennis on Saturdays and there would be dances in Mtubatuba or Vryheid; we'd all pile into a car and go together.

'Philip was tall, about six foot, slightly bow-legged, a marvellous dancer and tennis player. He was rather shy, and I liked

Philip Lee (second from left, bottom row) with men of the Royal Natal Carbineers in the Western Desert, 1941.

Joan Tissiman shortly before she married Philip Lee in May 1943.

that. We became such good friends. When war was declared he enlisted almost immediately. He was with the Royal Natal Carbineers, and with the rest of the 1st SA Infantry Brigade he sailed for Mombasa on 16 July 1940.

'I wasn't sure whether I was in love with him then, but as the months passed and his letters came through I suppose I became surer of my feelings. He was away for a long time, from 1940 to 1943.* His ship arrived on 13 January. When I saw him again – he was very brown and lean – I knew that I loved him, so when he proposed I didn't hesitate. I just said "yes".

'We were married in May 1943, less than four months after he got back from North Africa. It was an awful rush. It wasn't a big wedding, because it was wartime and we had decided not to get married in Durban, where I was working for Lever Brothers, but in Vryheid, because that was where his father, Bishop Lee, was.

'It was almost impossible to buy a wedding dress, and I didn't try very hard. I bought a dress and jacket, which I thought would be sensible in wartime, but both our families thought we wouldn't really be married unless I wore a proper old-fashioned white wedding dress.

'There was a little dress shop in Glencoe, of all places; and believe it or not, they had a wedding dress hanging there, very pretty, with lace and tulle. It cost £10 – that was a fortune. But I was marched in by Philip's sister Molly and I bought it. It had no veil, so there was a frantic scrabble for that, and at last I found a simple veil and borrowed it.

'We were married on a Saturday afternoon, a fine, cool Natal day, in the church next to the bishop's house. Philip was in uniform, and he looked so fine. The reception was simple, more like a tea than a sit-down meal; but we had a wedding-cake in spite of butter rationing.

'But our families were happy about the marriage: we both came from good solid stock. I was so proud of him. We had to catch the train for Estcourt at 5 p.m., so we left before the reception was over.

---

* On New Year's Day 1943, 6 400 men of the 1st SA Division embarked from Egypt on the *Nieuw Amsterdam* for Durban arriving to an ecstatic welcome – and greetings from Perla Siedle Gibson ('The Lady in White') singing through a megaphone on the dockside. During the war she sang to more than 1 000 troopships and 350 hospital ships. But when the 1st SA Infantry Brigade left for East Africa in July 1940, this gallant fifty-year-old mother of three stood silently at the docks. On board the *Delwara* were her two sons, Roy (21) and Barrie (20) with the 1st Transvaal Scottish. 'I was afraid to sing,' she said. 'I would have broken down.' Roy was killed in Italy.

'We went to Cathkin Peak Hotel. We were supposed to stay there for about two weeks but after one week we'd had enough. Philip had worked on a farm not far away, with an old farmhouse on the banks of a river, and we thought it would be fun to do our own housekeeping for a bit, we hadn't got much time together, so we just moved in.

'It *was* fun. We lit a fire at night and wandered in the fields during the day, and one day Philip shot a guinea-fowl for us. But time was marching on and Philip had to report back to Pietermaritzburg.

'We stayed with Philip's Aunt Cora for a month in Pietermaritzburg. I found a boarding-house, Faylands, and took a room there. It was only a room, but it was our home, and we were happy. Every now and then I'd open a newspaper and read about the fighting and my stomach would give a little lurch; but I didn't think about it much. I was sure he would be safe.

'One afternoon in September a messenger came to tell him to report to headquarters for embarkation that night. It wasn't a surprise because were expecting him to go. I watched him as he packed and I thought "I'm going to be alone, without him, in an hour or two." Saying goodbye was terribly hard ... we had only been married for four months. We had hardly begun our life together. Then he left, very quickly, and I went up to the room feeling stunned.

'That evening the door burst open, and there was Philip. There had been some mix-up and a delay, and he had a few more hours. He left at 2 a.m. It was heartbreaking to say goodbye for the second time in one day. It was pitch-black outside. He waved. I never saw him again.

'They went to Italy. He wrote to me whenever he could. I couldn't stay in Pietermaritzburg with nothing to do, so I went back to Durban, took a room in the YWCA with my sister Kay and went back to work for Lever Brothers.

'Ten months after he left, not long after our first wedding anniversary, I woke in the middle of the night. It was 21 July 1944. I had a dream – I think – and there was Philip, standing at the bottom of my bed in a bright light. He was stark naked. He looked at me and said "I've come to say goodbye. I'm going on a long journey."

'Three days later, on 24 July, I was at work, just after lunch. My Uncle Chick, who worked in the same department, sent someone to call me to him in the corridor. He was drawn and shaking. He had a telegram in his hand. He put his hands on my shoulders and said, "I've got bad news for you. Philip was killed three days ago."

'Philip was dead ... the firm provided a car and a friend took me back to the YWCA. My sister Kay was with me. At first I was numb, then I was distraught. I couldn't take it in. My sister-in-law Molly drove from Vryheid and took me to a friend's flat in Pietermaritzburg for a few days, just to get me away. They were terrible, dark days. All I could think was how little time we had had together and how happy we had been in that farmhouse – only a week – and then in the boarding-house. I felt as if there was nothing left for me.

'Philip's friends sent me a photograph of his grave. It seemed a very little grave to me, just a white cross with his name on it in a field with lots of other white crosses. He was buried near where he was killed, outside Florence, with a shell splinter in his chest. He didn't even get to hospital … he was killed at once. I don't suppose he knew much about it.

'A few years later I remarried. My daughter's middle name is Lee.'

• Interview 1990

Sergeant Philip Lee's grave in the Military Cemetery at Florence, Italy, plot 11, row B, grave 7. He was killed on 21 July 1944. (All photographs: Mrs J Horning)

CHAPTER

67

'I wish my mother could see me now'

Capt 'Ossie' Baker, parachuting into France, August 1944

It's just as well Ossie Baker's mother *didn't* see him falling with the soil of France coming up hard and fast towards him.

By August 1944 victory was unmistakably in the air. It could almost be felt, like the last notes of a Glenn Miller tune, a galloping jitterbug towards the bells of peace. No matter that there were a good nine months of the war to run, the Rhine had yet to be crossed, there was still hard fighting in Italy, and in the Far East Japan had still to be beaten. We knew that the war was won.

Nylon stockings were beginning to appear, quinine was being synthetised and audiences were flocking to see Olivier's timely propaganda film version of Shakespeare's *Henry V*, triumphant against the odds at Agincourt.

Agincourt still inspired men six centuries later. They wanted to be in at the kill. The difficulty was that after Tobruk the Union Defence Force was stripped of private soldiers, but had an embarrassing number of young officers with no men to command.

There followed a sometimes amusing scramble to find jobs – real jobs in the field and not behind a desk in South Africa. South African officers were allowed to serve in one of the British forces. Nearly three thousand South Africans were seconded to the Royal Navy, the Royal Air Force and the British army. They still proudly wore their red tabs.

One of the men who found himself without a 'job' was nineteen-year-old 'Ossie' Baker. Fresh home from Egypt and determined not to stay put in spite of the entreaties of his family, Baker, and many others in the same position, volunteered for the newly formed Parachute Squadron of the equally newly formed South African Air Force Regiment.

After undergoing training at the Premier Mine Battle School, Baker found himself without a job: the 6th SA Armoured Division was so short of men that the SAAF Regiment was abandoned, with some 750 men transferred into an amalgamation with the Natal Mounted Rifles.

Two officers from the short-lived Parachute Squadron joined the British Parachute Regiment, together with twenty other South African officers, all of whom stayed with the regiment until after VJ Day.

They found serving with the British very different. Hierarchical, well-disciplined and much less prone to questioning orders than the South Africans, serving with British troops was, as Baker found out in the last full year of war, both novel and exciting – and not at all like serving in the 1st SA Division:

‘The sea looked sinister as we flew over it, a dark, still, pewter grey. When we crossed the coast of France the land below looked very inhospitable, a deep smudge of green just before dawn. I was number one in the stick. As I dropped I shouted to my batman, who was just behind me: “Eaton, where are you?” But he didn’t hear me because the wind was wafting men all over the place.

‘We jumped from three hundred feet, and it took us only twenty-five seconds to get down. You drop fifty feet before the parachute opens – that prevents the spreading out of the troops. As I fell I thought (while worrying about the tracers coming up towards me): I wish my mother could see me now.

‘It was 15 August 1944, the second D-Day.* We were dropped some ten kilometres inland from the south coast of France, near Cannes and St Tropez. We were there to prevent German reinforcements getting down to the coast where the main invasion, by the Americans and the Free French† was coming by sea, and to stop the Germans from retiring inland along the main road going up to Toulon and Avignon and, of course, back to Paris.

‘It had been a long night for us, the men of 5 Battalion, the Parachute Regiment, Anti-Tank (No 2) Platoon, before we dropped. When I heard about the D-Day landings all I could think was: Why aren’t we there too? We hung about for two months because there weren’t enough Dakotas. Our last instructions were given on D-Day minus one [14 August], the day when we were taken to Rome aerodrome.

‘The airfield was an amazing sight: endless Dakotas lined up for us, first for the line drop, then to tow the gliders. On the even-

---

* The first, of course, was the D-Day landing on the coast of Normandy on 6 June 1944.

† The US 7th Army and the French 1st Army. By 23 August the French had occupied Marseilles. Gen de Gaulle entered Paris on 24 August 1944.

ing of the 15th we had a special supper. Take-off was to be about 1 a.m. We hung about drinking coffee from tin mugs, joking to ease the tension. We had a last light meal and then got into our Dakotas, each of us carrying more than 150 lbs of equipment.

'The flight was supposed to take three hours. We took off about 2 a.m. and the Dakotas circled about Rome because the armada was getting bigger and bigger and all the planes had to go in one long taxi-rank. After sitting in the plane for an hour on the ground we had to stooge about over Rome for another hour and a half until everyone was airborne. The tension began to build up.

'None of us had dropped in wooded or built-up country before. Would the Germans be there to meet us in force? Would the natives be friendly? None of us knew. No smoking was allowed, and we were in complete darkness with the door open and the wind howling round us, and although it was summer it was bitterly cold. One of the men puked and the floor was slippery when we moved.

'At last we reached land – Vichy France – blacked out and with searchlights criss-crossing the sky, but far from us. We had

Capt 'Ossie' Baker (right) with Lt Denis Erwin, both senior instructors at the Battle School at Premier Mine. The SAAF Regiment Parachute Squadron underwent strenuous training there in 1943. Both men later joined the Parachute Squadron. (Ossie Baker)

Major Craig Anderson, OC SAAF Regiment (in truck) with Major Kat Ferreira, Second-in-Command. The Parachute Regiment insignia and the red berets can be seen. Men received half a crown a day danger money on top of their ordinary pay. The training at Premier Mine was said to be more arduous than that of British parachute troops. (Ossie Baker)

already been given the twenty-minute warning: 'Stand to the door', and the stick was lined up behind me at the open door, all hooked up. The battalion padre was in our stick, unarmed of course.

'Then the landing light was on and I was in the air, falling madly before my parachute* opened. It was twenty minutes before first light, and to my horror I fell through the curving tracers into a wood and was caught in a tree with my feet three feet off the ground. And Eaton was nowhere in sight.

'Strapped up like a dummy I couldn't even get to the release box to get my harness off, let alone my fighting knife or my pistol

---

* The canopy was tied to 'static line', a long webbing strap, that pulled the parachute out of its pack.

or my tommy gun. I just dangled helplessly. It was a parachutist's nightmare. There was a bit of a battle going on round me. As usual in an airborne landing there is a lot of confusion. When you land among the opposition they are as scared as you are. Everybody was shooting – in fact, more of us were killed by our own side than by the Germans. You couldn't see who was who.

'The gliders were coming in now, getting smashed themselves on the asparagus sticks* that the Germans had put up in all the fields.

'Then, to my horror, along came a young German troopie – I later learned he was a Russian – only fourteen or fifteen years old. He just stared at me and I just stared at him. Then he said words to the effect that for me the war was over. But over his shoulder, thank God, I could see Eaton creeping along behind him. He came up and put his tommy gun in the Russian's back and said: "No, for *you* the war is over!"

'Eaton came and cut me down. I now had to organise my platoon. We were all over the place, some already fighting. My platoon sergeant landed on the roof of a two-storey building which had housed the pay offices of the German army, and he was up there for over an hour fighting them.† Our weapons had been dropped separately in containers, and we had to find them – quickly.‡ It was chaos.

'The chaos was made worse by the inexperience of the American sprog pilots, so that our brigade was spread out between ten and fifteen miles. Fortunately for us the Germans were as confused as we were. We had troops all over the place, Americans, French, British. We all wore identification on our arms, the Union Jack or the stars and stripes, but in the dark it didn't help much.

'We carried crickets, little toys you clicked. If you found someone behind a hedge and you didn't know if he was ours or theirs, you gave two clicks and he answered with three clicks. If there was no answer you fired. To add even more to the confusion, dummies ("dummenpoppen") had been pushed out of the planes before we jumped. They had a cracker arrangement, like jumping-jacks, so it sounded like machine-gun fire. But instead of landing farther away as a diversion, they had landed on our DZ** and announced our arrival to everybody.

---

* Asparagus sticks, rather like telephone poles, were put up to prevent gliders from landing. The pilots put the nose of the glider between poles and brought the craft to an abrupt stop.

† 'Ossie' Baker recommended him for a Military Medal, which he later received.

‡ The parachute troops carried a Sten gun – with seven magazines, a Colt automatic pistol with two magazines and grenades, and enough equipment and food to make each man self-sufficient for forty-eight hours.

** Dropping zone.

'We had to take two or three villages near the DZ; not only my platoon but the whole formation, nearly two divisions of parachute troops. We had secured the landing fields for the gliders, and now we were ready to move. By now it was broad daylight. We had to take a village, and two platoons went forward from the flanks with one platoon in reserve. It was close fighting because it was so heavily wooded. This took us about four hours, and when we went into the village we were astonished at our reception.

'To say the villagers were unenthusiastic was an understatement. They were spitting at us, and some of the chaps got really browned off at this. It was Vichy France, and those people had not had a difficult war. Certainly no flowers were thrown at our feet. It was the same at Cannes and Nice.

'Now we had to set up roadblocks to prevent the Germans from going either inland or to the sea. We saw a convoy of German trucks, and the only way we could stop them (since we still had no heavy equipment) was to climb into the trees over the road. Fifteen of us were up there, more or less concealed by the leaves, with another fifteen on the ground.

'As the trucks passed below the men dropped Gammon bombs* and the whole lot went up. For me that was the most frightening part of our very long day, for if we had been seen we were sitting ducks. '

• Interview 1990

Capt 'Ossie' Baker made thirty jumps, each of them, as he says, an unnatural act. After three weeks in France, he returned to Rome to prepare for the invasion of Greece. Baker's platoon was ordered to take the Parthenon where German snipers were lurking. The platoon hid in the bushes during the night and stormed the Acropolis at first light. There wasn't much of a fight, but the parachutists had to use grenades, with the result that 'there were a few more bullet holes on the Parthenon than before'.

---

* The ingenious Gammon grenade was first introduced in 1942, the invention of Capt R S Gammon, MC, one of the first volunteers of the 1st (British) Parachute Battalion. It was a lump of plastic explosive with a seven-second fuse in it contained by a stretchable stockinette 'sock'. It could be slapped on to the side of a vehicle or tank. A useful weapon in the right conditions.

CHAPTER

68

'Very good batmen, sir'

Private Nelson Koza, 1944

With the end of the war in sight nearly fifteen thousand South Africans were prisoners of war. It was through the Red Cross that their families in the Union knew where they were, communicated with them, sent them food parcels* and sometimes passed on messages over the Vatican radio.

The International Red Cross also inspected conditions in the camps. Although many of the visits to prisoner-of-war camps in Germany and Italy were arranged beforehand (in South Africa, too), some visits by Red Cross officials were unannounced. The International Red Cross persuaded the German government to allow fifty-word messages (the usual was twenty-five) from prisoners to their families. The letters sometimes took three months and longer to get to the Union, but at least it was a communication.

The prisoners' health was also checked, weekly medical reports sent to the protecting power and to Geneva. Deaths and serious illnesses were reported. Some seriously ill patients were sometimes sent home.

But the work of the Red Cross did not end there. Some South African prisoners of war, like the Australians, Canadians, British and New Zealanders, were able to educate themselves. Some began law degrees, others learnt French; some took matric courses, others were lectured in literature or mathematics or astronomy by qualified prisoners. Much of this educational material came through a branch of the South African Red Cross in South Africa House in London.†

---

* But only until 1943. After that, the prisoners received the British and Canadian Red Cross parcel which literally saved lives. The shortage of food in South Africa made it necessary for parcels to be sent by the British Red Cross. £1 million was donated for the purpose. The parcels were made up carefully so as to give 'the maximum food value in the limited weight allowed'.

† It was run by a South African, Helen Caddell, trapped in Britain when war broke out.

Particularly poignant were the black prisoners of war, mostly captured at Sidi Rezegh and Tobruk.* Many of them spoke little English, fewer still could write, and some were undoubtedly discriminated against, by both the enemy and fellow prisoners.

One of these men was Private Nelson Koza, a twenty-year-old Shangaan, one of 77 239 who served in the Native Military Corps (NMC) in non-combatant capacities† both in South Africa and elsewhere. Koza, like thousands of others, was recruited through a network of tribal chiefs. He lived in Mamitwa's location in the lowveld east of Tzaneen with his wife Rosie and a baby son, Booysen.

A recruiting officer came to the village in 1940. Chief Mamitwa listened attentively and then conferred with the tribal elders. He strode to the old tribal war drum and beat it while the men shouted and stamped their feet and the women stood silent. Mamitwa's men were now at war with the Germans, of whom they had heard, largely because of the German missionaries who worked there, and the Italians, of whom they knew nothing.

When Koza and fourteen other men from his village had finished their training they were shipped to Mombasa as part of a unit of 250 men for service with the officers of the 5th South African Brigade.

Standing on the parade ground at Gilgil in Kenya, waiting for selection by brigade officers, Koza was astonished to see Maj Harry Klein,‡ whom Chief Mamitwa and his men had known before the war. Koza broke ranks. 'My baas, my baas, I know the baas from Tzaneen. Me and the boys of Mamitwa very good batmen, sir.' Klein chose all fourteen of Mamitwa's men to serve with his armoured car company.

Koza was a loyal batman, stealing chickens from villages to ensure that Klein was well fed. But he longed to show that he was a real soldier, armed and ready to fight, not merely a batman. Klein gave him a Banda rifle recovered from the scene of an ambush at Garba Turbi. Bent and rusty as it was, Koza oiled and cleaned it and secretly laid up a supply of ammunition. One day he took pot-shots at the enemy, for which he was severely reprimanded. Koza could not understand why South African troops could fight alongside other black troops (the 22nd East African and the 24th Gold Coast Brigades) while he could only be a servant.

---

* Altogether 123 131 non-whites served with the Union Defence Force.

† They were not allowed to carry arms; but some served with artillery units in South Africa and five hundred Zulus guarded vital military points, including the naval base at Simonstown, incongruously armed with assegais and knobkerries. Rates of pay for the lowest white rank began at 3/6 a day; that of a black private was 1/- a day, with no allowances for dependants.

‡ See 'The renaissance of extreme Afrikaner political nationalism'.

As they fought through Abyssinia and Somalia and the Western Desert a warm friendship grew between the two men. Klein was posted back to the Union without Koza, who remained to be taken prisoner at Sidi Rezegh in November 1941.

He was one of 1 655 members of the NMC to be taken prisoner, and one of the 381 men who died in captivity. All that remains of this engaging and gallant man is a bundle of letters from his prison camp in Italy:

'Nelson Koza 1797
Campo No 22,
Roma.
18.8.42

Dear Major Klein,

I am so very much glad to have this time of dropping you this few lines letting you know that I am still well. I hope to hear the same from you and all yours. Your (letter) was well written and understood. I am so very glad that you are still alife. Will you please kindly send me your scrap. I will be very glad if you can do so and as for the thing you said you have sent me, I didn't find it yet. I will write to you if I have got it. Please kindly also write me a letter to Chief Mamitwa and let him know I am still alife. I am also thanking Mrs Klein for the parcel she sent to me so far. With best wishes to all there,
yours, N. Koza.

From Chief Mamitwa:

Mamitwa Pte Bag,
P O Letaba,
19th June 1944.

Dear Mrs Klein,

Your letter was well received and we thank very much about your kind information.

Rosie received one letter last week from Nelson saying that he is now under the supervision of the German Commandant. Surely Rosie was very pleased to receive that letter from him.

He said that Rosie will get the address from you. If the address is sent to you Rosie will be very glad to get it.

Pass on our best regards to Major Klein when writing to him. We all hope for the best.
With kind regards,
Chief Mamitwa.

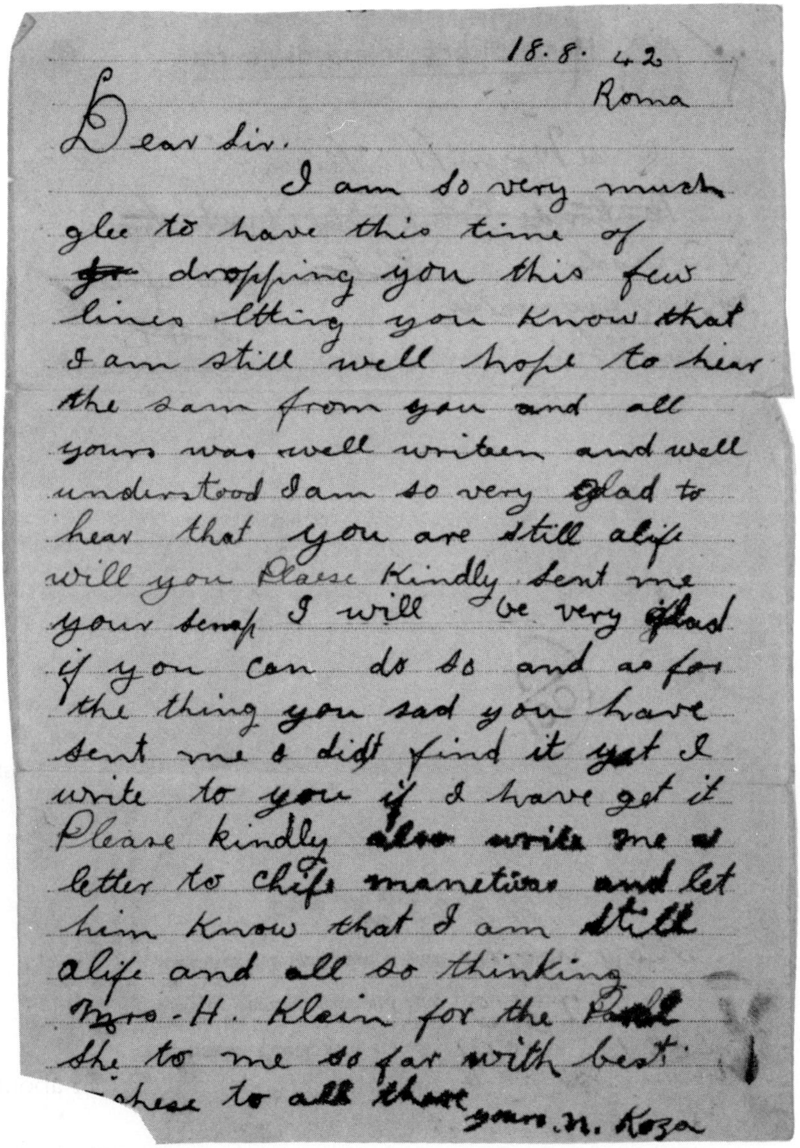

18.8.42
Roma

Dear Sir.

I am so very much glee to have this time of dropping you this few lines ltting you know that I am still well hope to hear the sam from you and all yours was well writeen and well understood I am so very glad to hear that you are still alife will you Please Kindly sent me your senap I will be very glad if you can do so and as for the thing you sad you have sent me I didt find it yet I write to you if I have get it Please kindly also write me a letter to Chifs manetiwa and let him know that I am still alife and all so thinking Mrs. H. Klein for the Pall She to me so far with best wishese to all those

yours N. Koza

Nelson Koza's last letter home.

From Rosie Koza:

Mamitwa Pte Bag,
PO Letaba,
15th August 1944.

Dear Mrs Klein,

Thanks every so much for the news which were in the letter of Fofoza Mamitwa about my husband Nelson Koza.

I kindly ask to send me my husband's address as soon as you get it. Nelson wrote me a letter saying that he is fit and well and that I have to ask you for his address, for there was no address on his letter. I shall be glad if you can happen to send his address to me ere long.

It gives me pleasure to learn that you like my husband thought he left long.

Booysen and I are still well.

With kind regards to be sent to Major Klein in Italy.

We hope to see our husbands before long.

Yours very truly,
Rose Nelson Koza
(signed) Fofoza Mamitwa.

From Mrs Klein:

c/o Bureau of Information
214 Escombe House
Johannesburg

Dear Rose,

Thank you for your letter of the 15th August, written on your behalf by Fofoza Mamitwa.

Since that date you must have had news of the death of your husband, Nelson Koza, of tuberculosis, whilst a prisoner of war. Dear Rose, I was deeply grieved to hear this news, and I know that Major Klein, too, will feel it very deeply. He was very fond of Nelson, who worked for him so faithfully and well for a long time, and he looked forward to meeting him again when the war was over. But, alas, the gods have decreed it otherwise. There is so little I can say to help you in this time of sadness, Rose, but I want you to know that my husband and I will always be your friends, and Booysen's also, and that we will always be ready to help you if at any time you want our aid.

Nelson has given his life for his country as much in a prisoner-of-war camp as if he had died on the battlefield. He was a good soldier and we honour him.

Please let me know at once if there is anything you would like me to do for you. I myself am due to go to Egypt within the next two weeks.

We await news from the International Red Cross at Geneva of the date and place of Nelson's death. You will be informed as soon as this news arrives.

I salute the soldiers of Chief Mamitwa's Location and I salute you, the wife of one of the best of them.

Yours sincerely,
Your friend, H. Klein ❜

THE SOUTH AFRICAN RED CROSS SOCIETY

CENTRAL EXECUTIVE COMMITTEE

TELEGRAMS: "REDCROSS."
P.O. BOX 8726.
TELEPHONES 33-3421/2/3/4.

President:
THE HON. JUSTICE O. D. SCHREINER.

In reply please quote
PW/SA/N
4

OFFICES:
HIS MAJESTY'S BUILDING,
ELOFF STREET,
JOHANNESBURG, SOUTH AFRICA.

ALL COMMUNICATIONS TO BE ADDRESSED TO THE
GENERAL SECRETARY.

16th August, 1944.

Mrs. H. Klein,
c/o Bureau of Information,
214 Escombe House,
JOHANNESBURG.

Pte. Nelson Koza.

Dear Mrs. Klein,

It is with regret that we advise you of the receipt of a cable from our International Committee in Geneva, which states that No. 1797, Private Nelson Koza, has died of tuberculosis of the lungs whilst a prisoner of war.

No further details are given, and we pass out this information to you in view of the kindly interest you and your husband have taken in this man.

Assuring you of our desire to be of every assistance,

Yours sincerely,

p.p. Clara Urquhart

for GENERAL SECRETARY.

/DR

The letter from the Red Cross informing the Kleins of Nelson's death. Mrs Klein and her husband immediately wrote to Rose.

CHAPTER

69

1945

'The footsteps of the messengers of peace'

This was the year of defeat and the year of surrender, the year of victory and victory parades, the year the men came home and the guns fell silent across the scarred face of Europe and the Far East.

Before they did there still was hard fighting to be done. As the Union Defence Force began to make preparations to bring the men home the Russians were driving the Germans back across devastated Poland, the *Tirpitz* was sunk by RAF bombers, and bombs rained down on Germany. They were being softened up for the Allied advance.

In December 1944 the Germans attacked the American 1st Army through the hilly Ardennes and pushed them back towards the Channel. The Battle of the Bulge was fought in bitterly cold weather. By January it was all over, and the Germans were retreating. There was little to stop the Allies now.

As they advanced towards the Rhine, Germany lay devastated before them. The soldiers knew what they would find in the Fatherland: towns in ruins, a hungry people, a retreating army, a collapsed leadership. By 27 January they also knew that among the rubble of a beaten people they would find some of the worst horrors of the twentieth century: the death camps.

On that day, in the bleakness of a Polish winter, Russian troops opened the gates of Auschwitz. As death camp after death camp was relieved, appalled war correspondents attempted to put into words and on to film what they found in the camps, but nothing could describe the stench of genocide.

On 13 March the Americans had crossed the Rhine. Amid the ruin, the death camps and the shattered people the Allies found their own men, prisoners of war with gaunt faces and wary eyes.

Many had survived their last trial, the infamous Death March, when hundreds of thousands of prisoners of war had been marched in the bitter snows of a European winter eastward away from the British and Americans and westward from the Russians.

In London the V2 bombardment ended as suddenly as it had begun, and in April with spring pushing through new green, the final collapse began. The Americans took Hanover on the 10th; two days later, less than a month before the German capitulation, President Roosevelt died and was succeeded by Harry Truman; on the 15th, the 6th SA Division took Monte Sole in Italy, and on the same day the Allies liberated Bergen-Belsen. By the 20th the Russians were in the outskirts of Berlin. Hitler was underground, in his bunker. His days were numbered.

As the London blackout was lifted and the lights blazed once more, as Berlin echoed with the sounds of destruction, as Genoa, Verona and Venice were taken, Hitler was still issuing absurd orders to non-existent divisions, Mussolini and his mistress were killed by Italian partisans and their bodies hung head down for all to see.

On 29 April the SA 6th Division crossed the Brenta River and went on to Milan in northern Italy. Its days of battle were almost over.* Next day the gates of Dachau were opened.

Shortly after 11 p.m. on 30 April 1945 an announcement was read over the German radio. 'It is reported from the Führer's headquarters that our Führer, Adolf Hitler, has fallen this afternoon at his command post in the Reich Chancellery, fighting to the last breath against Bolshevism and for Germany ...' It was a nice story, a Wagnerian ending, if it had been true. In fact Hitler had shot himself and his new wife and their bodies had been carried out of the bunker and burned as the guns thundered in Berlin.

On 30 April the German forces in Italy surrendered. On 7 May 1945 the Germans under Field Marshal Jodl surrendered to General Eisenhower and, on 8 May, the last German forces under arms surrendered to the Russians.

8 May was VE Day. The world rejoiced at the coming of peace. In London crowds gathered outside Buckingham Palace; in Johannesburg, a 21-gun salute from the guns on the *Berea* was fired off, flags fluttered everywhere, people ran through the streets and cinemas and theatres stayed open long after their usual closing times. In Cape Town, to salvoes from ships in the harbour, crowds took over Adderley Street.

'How beautiful upon the mountains,' wrote Alice Duer Miller in her book *The White Cliffs*†, 'how beautiful upon the downs, how beau-

---

* Seven hundred and thirty-three South Africans died in the Italian campaign; 4 443 were injured.

† Published in 1941 and rivalled in popularity only by Paul Gallico's *The Snow Goose.*

The 8th Army service of thanksgiving at the end of the war began with 'God Save the King' and ended with the Blessing. There was a special prayer for the peacemakers: '… we pray for the representatives of the nations who are called to the task of laying the foundations of peace and settling the affairs of this distracted and embittered world … raise the minds of men everywhere above the mists of suspicion and hatred into the pure light of justice and goodwill, that justice and freedom may be established among all nations …'

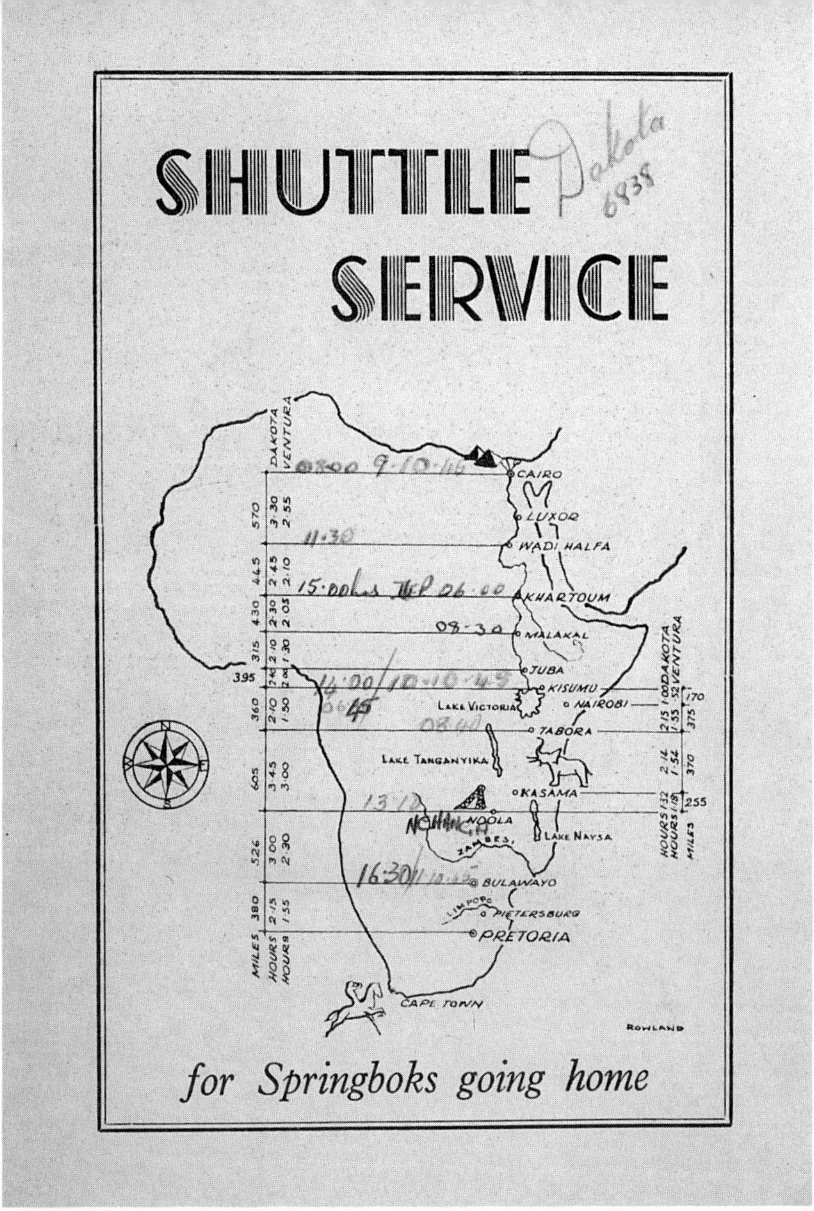

Coming home: the pamphlet handed to Springboks coming home by air from Cairo to Pretoria in Dakotas and Venturas. It contained homely advice: 'It is inadvisable to go on the "spree" if you night-stop anywhere. A hang-over in mid-air is a terrible thing.' This pamphlet belongs to Paddy Walker, who timed each step of his journey home in Dakota 6838.

tiful in the village post office, on the pavements of towns – how beautiful in the huge print of newspapers, beautiful white telegraph wires hum, while telephone bells wildly jingle, the news that peace has come – that peace has come at last – that all wars cease. How beautiful upon the mountains are the footsteps of the messengers of peace.'

CHAPTER

70

'Thank God we are no longer prisoners of war'

Sgt Herbert Cawood-Meaker and the long march to freedom, 1945

It was high summer in South Africa. The children were back at school after the Christmas holidays. Six pounds of No 1 sugar cost 2/-, Australian steak-and-kidney puddings in a pound tin cost 1/10d, a dining-room suite and sideboard cost £29.5s and a house in Parkwood cost £3 000.

As 1944 slipped into 1945 there was a growing sense of excitement in the Union among the people who had supported the war for over five years. Although the 6th Division was in Italy, together with large numbers of the SAAF, Ouma Smuts's Gifts and Comforts Fund was still churning out glory-bags for the boys, but the war was obviously coming to an end.

Plans were already in existence to bring thousands of troops home by air, and to bring back the ten thousand South African prisoners of war. Although most families knew where their men were, thanks to the Red Cross, – anywhere in Poland or Germany – they had no immediate knowledge of them. It took three months and more for a letter from South Africa to reach a POW, if it arrived at all.

And as the Russians approached the Vistula the euphoria of getting the men back in South Africa was tempered by growing concern about their safety.

It was fortunate for the families anxiously reading about the progress of the war in newspapers, crammed with news of the Allied and Russian advances, that they did not know what was happening to the men from South Africa.

A few had already made the long journey home: prisoners who had escaped from Italian camps after the capitulation of Italy and before the Germans moved in and took them to Germany (and from there to Poland, Lithuania, Czechoslovakia and Austria), and prisoners who had been repatriated through the International Red Cross on medical grounds.

Most of them remained in their *Stalags* and *Oflags* eagerly awaiting the infrequent letters from home, their Red Cross food parcels and the BBC news relayed on hidden hand-made radios.

On the pretext of Article Seven of the Geneva Convention, which states that prisoners of war should be removed from fighting zones, the Germans decided to vacate the prison camps in Poland and eastern Germany when it appeared that the rapidly advancing Russians would relieve them.

By January 1945, however, German transport was in chaos. Although it was impossible to move large numbers of prisoners of war by truck or by rail, plans were made to march everyone on foot westward, in spite of the malnutrition many of the men were showing.

In most cases the men were given only a few hours' notice. They packed clothes, Red Cross food-parcels, a precious book, perhaps, a few letters from home, nearly all of which had to be abandoned as the rigours of the long march intensified.

With no indication of where they were going, other than westward (nor had their guards much idea either), with the rumble of the Russian guns audible from some of the camps, with no bedding and precious little food, the prisoners walked out of the camps and into a countryside full of the panic of war. The conquerors were about to become the conquered.

On country roads the men jostled with hundreds of thousands of civilians fleeing the Russian advance. German military transport was also moving west, much of it horse-drawn. The weather was bitterly cold, with thick snow and more to come. Sledges were improvised by some men to carry their food and belongings. Many of them had to be abandoned or, at the expense of personal belongings, given over to men who could no longer walk.

By the end of February a vast and seemingly endless trek west by prisoners of war was under way. There were three main columns marching westward: about a hundred thousand on the northern route from Poland and East Prussia in the direction of Bremen, Hamburg and Lübeck; sixty thousand marching from *Stalag Luft VII* near Bankau and *Stalag 344* near Lamsdorf through central Germany, an area bounded by Berlin, Dresden and Leipzig (not far from *Oflag IVC,* the notorious Colditz) as far west as Duderstadt; and eighty thousand making for Bohemia by Brunswick, Karlsbad and thence to *Stalag XIIIC* outside Hammelburg.

At night the men were packed into barns with leaking roofs after a day's march of twenty miles through deep snow. With blistered and frostbitten feet, their Red Cross food exhausted and German rations reduced from 1 200 calories at the end of February to 800 and less in March, the seven-week ordeal reduced the men to walking skeletons. Some of them lost up to sixty pounds. They were forbidden to accept food from civilians (who had very little themselves) and they were weakened by stomach disorders, pneumonia and the usual results of malnutrition.

Some died on the march (some through Allied bombing), although most made it through a crumbling and devastated Germany to eventual freedom. The men thought of nothing but food, survival and their families at home.

Some of them even managed to keep diaries. One South African among the seven thousand on what became known as the Death March was Sgt Herbert Cawood-Meaker. He had been captured in Tobruk while serving in the Intelligence Corps (working with cyphers). He wrote up his diary almost compulsively, often two or three times a day, buoyed up by the knowledge that every step he took westward was a step nearer to freedom and his wife and seven-year-old daughter in South Africa. He left *Stalag 344* near Lamsdorf in eastern Germany on Monday, 22 January 1945:

Sergeant Herbert Cawood-Meaker with his wife Joy and his daughter Sydney-Anne. With thousands of other South African prisoners of war he took part in the arduous 'Death March' across Germany towards the end of the war. (Herbert Cawood-Meaker)

‘**Monday 22 January**
It is 10 to 12 a.m. and a very cold day. The loudspeakers have just ordered everybody back to their blocks for a very important message. Here it is: Blocks 2, 3, 4 and 5 will leave at 2 p.m. Here we go!!

Wednesday 24 January
It is 9.30 a.m. and we are in a barn, sitting on some straw in some God-forsaken village about 45 km from *Stalag 344*. And those 45 km represent absolute HELL. The tale from the beginning. We left *Stalag* at a quarter to six on Monday night and each drew a Red Cross Christmas Parcel and half a loaf of bread and some margarine. At about 7 we started the march. The snow was thick everywhere and the roads were like glass, which made marching very difficult. The moon was brilliant and everywhere was white, gleaming snow. The first few kms were not too bad, and then the pack started feeling heavy. I was far too heavily laden, and it wasn't long before I began dumping things. I now carry all the clothes I own on my body, 2 vests, 2 sweaters, shirt, long underpants and pyjamas. All the way we could hear intermittent gun-fire from behind us, our general bearing being west. We were on our way again at 9 a.m. and I will gloss over the 20 km march yesterday. Thank God I made it this time. I was very nearly dead at the end.

All the way along – all the villages we passed through (about one to every 3 or 4 km) we found Gerries evacuating – walking, riding, pulling sledges etc., all heavily laden. We were thankful that we have our *Stalag* guards guarding us and not fresh ones or fighting troops.

January 28, 3.15 p.m.
Very cold indeed. Managed to scrounge some milk from pigswill. Had some biscuits and honey. We were indeed grateful to the Red Cross on this day. If it had not been for them we would have had to exist on four small biscuits a day.

Monday 29 January
In the last three days the Germans have given us one pkt. biscuits (4") and about 4 spuds, and we don't know where anything more is coming from. We have had a blizzard all the way (15 km) and it has been hell pushing and pulling the sledge. The roads were as glassy as ever, and some of the byways we took were rough and narrow. The snow was falling hard nearly all day. The country was flat and devoid of any shelter. The wind was almost at gale strength and whipped off the loose snow from the open fields, blowing in our faces. This was the nearest thing to a real blizzard I should like to experience. One of the most uncomfortable results of the intense cold was one's nose was inclined to run and the water froze in our nostrils. The balaclavas froze

into stiff boards round our faces and our eight days' growth of beard stuck out like quills. We occasionally came across cans of milk by the roadside and, if we were slick enough, we could whip off the lid and collect a beaker full of milk. This was generally in or outside villages. Gerry shot at one or two chaps after a while, so the game is up.

Tuesday 30 January

We have at last got our promised day of rest. And we got spuds. We are high up on the platform of a thresher. Have had my right foot (arch) bandaged – swollen up to the heel. Lots of fellows with frost-bitten hands and feet. My right little toe is also frostbitten. When I went on sick parade I saw some terrible cases of frostbite. Black fingers and toes; toes swollen to bursting. I learned later that certain amputations had to be performed.

Saturday 10 February

We are very weak, all of us, wondering how far we can make. Gerry has taken out a working party of 200 – Heaven knows where. Terrific crowd in here at present. Don't like the look of this walk at all. Our rations were: 1 loaf to 2 men and a tin of meat (about 1kg) to 10 men. This is for 2 days. The pack feels damn heavy already. Heaven knows when we will reach our resting place for tonight. There are approximately 3 000 on this march. Civvie guards as well as soldiers. There was a column of about 1 000 Russians in our contingent.

We were not very well shod, but those poor blighters walked in clogs and rags – anything they could find to cover their feet. Up to Görlitz, we had little organisation on the road and men straggled along and rested when they were fagged.

Sunday 11 February

The Gerries on this march are bad. A fair amount of stuff was stolen last night and the *Hauptman* in charge has formed a District Court Martial. Anyone violating the laws will be shot within half an hour: we are not to attempt to escape; we are not to light fires nor smoke in the barns; we are not to steal anything. We hear that we are going to Dresden, about 100 km from here. We did 20 yesterday and at least 14 km today.

Monday 12 February

This morning I sustained the biggest loss of my life. My watch-strap broke and I lost my watch in the straw. It breaks my heart. We are on the road now; it is our first pause. It is about $\frac{1}{4}$ to 10. We have another 16 km to do to Bautzen. We left Weissenburg at about 9. Rations issued: $\frac{1}{2}$ a cup of coffee last night and this morning; $\frac{1}{2}$ a loaf; 1 tin of meat for 16 men. One day's ration.

Tuesday 20 February

A sunny day and ¼ to 11 now. We left Döbeln at 9.15, after having drawn another three day's rations – 14 loaves and 7 tins of meat for 20 men. We were billeted in the attic of the three-storey building. The room had a wooden floor. Our hip bones were so prominent that they hurt like blazes. We had a really thick barley soup last night and coffee this morning. We are heading for Leisnig, about 17 km. This is our 24th day on the road; our 22nd march. Must have done about 500 km, heading for *Stalag IVF,* according to Padre Welchman. *2nd pause.* And about time. Those German swine have made us do 5½ km in the last bit. We are very weak; three days' rations to carry too. Smoking leaves now; picked up at Döbeln.

Friday 23 February

A distance of 28 km today. This is our second pause; an air raid is on. AA is bursting overhead. We can hear the bombing – overcast, we can see nothing. Left at 8.30 a.m. – early, thank Heaven. Everyone is very weak; so far I have noticed seven chaps fallen out on the side of the road. *About 12.30 p.m.* Our 3rd pause, and we must have done half-way. I am a lot weaker – so are we all. More chaps falling out. And these swine have just made us march for 1½ hours before this pause. A bastard of a guard had the energy to kick one of our chaps this morning for going to the left side of the road. The brave German swine, kicking a tired and worn-out POW. There's another air raid on and I hope that thousands of Nazis are killed.

Saturday 24 February

I have been eating raw sugar beet and mangel-wurzels and find them good. Have just looked at my face again – first time since Sunday. Have put on some years on this trip.

Sunday 25 February

We are weaker than ever now and the pace is very slow. Rations issued this morning were: 16 loaves to 40 men and one day's meat. We left Zeitz at about 9.30, having risen at 6.30. We drew coffee and bread on the road. We are very hungry and can't afford more bread. More chaps are falling out along the road. Please God we may get some more food.

Tuesday 27 February

Waiting to move off – 9.15 a.m. and so far no rations. Gerry tells us that we are doing 16 km. Yesterday we finished off our rations: reserve and all. We *may* get rations later. The sick increase – everyone is weak. I hope and pray that I can make the 16 km today. We rested at a small village, Serba, 9 km outside Eisenberg. This is the first time we have been laughed at by adults and children. The Germans are worse down here – the natives are hostile! It hurts to be laughed at when you are tired and nearly dead. *12.15 p.m.* Second pause. Everyone is very much weaker and still weakening. No rations today so far. We've had nothing but a little lukewarm coffee. Dozens of chaps have dropped out along the roadside – nothing *we* can do.

Friday 2 March

5.15 p.m. Sydney-Anne's birthday.* I pray to God that she is having as happy a time as mine has been unhappy! She is seven. We are resting and are about 11 km away from our destination, having eaten 1½ slices of bread all day. Our rations this morning: 7 loaves and 4 tins of meat to 40 men. Too much snow … I hope my baby had such a happy day. Very miserable out in a big field. Tried to brew but they wouldn't let us have fires. The air raid kept us under the trees for a couple of hours.

Monday 12 March

About 1.10 p.m. We are resting in a road about 20 km from where we started. We are in sight of *Stalag IXA,* we hope, at last!! The last signpost said 'Ziegenhain: 6 km'. So this should be our destination, after more than 500 miles from *Stalag 344,* Lamsdorf. Pray God this is the end.

Tuesday 13 March

It is nearly 4 p.m. and I am sitting up in 'bed'. I have only just worked up enough energy to write this up. WE ARE IN STALAG IXA, Tent No 1. 300 of us in the tent. We entered the Stalag at 2.45 p.m. yesterday, thank God. There are only a few British troops here: those from Breslau. We were bunged into these tents – 967 of us – three tents.

Sunday 18 March

It is 5-ish and our *dolmetscher* [interpreter] has just read out an extract from a pamphlet dropped over Germany by the RAF. Finland declared war on Germany on 1st March. Big cut in food rations on 28th February. Feeling pretty weak today. News is great all round: we have advanced all over the place; 10 ton bombs being dropped now. Yesterday afternoon we heard of an answer from the Red Cross man who was acting on behalf of the Protecting Power: He would 'phone Berlin for parcels. There are millions of parcels in Germany; Red Cross has only 50 trucks. We *may* get some in a fortnight or so. There is *no*

---

* His daughter.

chance of any more food from the Germans. They have no more. Four men died in the Revier* today, from weakness and starvation. Those German swine are murdering our men.

Sunday 25 March

Wonderful news this morning: Monty's armies – 1st Canadian and 2nd British with the 9th American and 1st Airborne Army, have advanced three miles without opposition. They are across the Rhine. Churchill says that Monty's action will long be remembered; the greatest air feat in history. Eisenhower says that complete victory will soon be ours. Everyone is very, very weak and the *unteroffizier* in charge of our tent is a most unmitigated bastard; he is quite insane and walks about talking to himself and then shouts at us. An air raid on Ziegenhain last night hit something big; it gave off heavy smoke till late. We are starting our blackouts again.

Monday 26 March

The news continues to be exciting: Monty's four bridgeheads over the Rhine have been joined up and form a single one 50 km in length. Gerry has no chance of driving him back. Churchill sailed down the Rhine and visited the armies. There is a drive NE of Remingen bridgehead (1st Army USA). We are approximately 80 km NE of it. The bridgehead at Mainz is now 12 miles wide and 9 miles deep. Things offered for sale: 1 bread ration (3 fags); marge ration (1 fag); loaf of bread (20 fags). Bread – whence? And fags? Mandalay fell some days ago and 14th Army is driving for Rangoon. I have been very difficult recently and have worried a lot. Sorry about it. Hunger and lack of smokes.

Wednesday 28 March

About 2.30 p.m. RSM Broderick has just been over to tell us that the German order was this: Camp has got to be vacated; we are going to Mülhausen – 5 or 6 days march at 15 to 20 km a day. The fit will walk; the sick will go by rail. We are to leave at 8 a.m. tomorrow. There is a check on now for rations, and we hear that there will be extra – don't believe it. There is an air raid in progress; strafing and bombing in and near Ziegenhain. *Later 6 p.m.* Rumour has it that Yank tanks are only 15 km away. We heard machine-gun fire and there is smoke on the horizon.

Thursday 29 March

About 3 p.m. I have been half afraid to write up my diary and am still a little afraid, having been through it once in Italy. This is what occurred

---

* Camp hospital.

about 1.30 p.m.: Broderick came into our tent and made the following remarks (before that we had been told that a large red cross and the words 'prisoners of war' had been placed on the football field). 1: He wanted a man to patrol the bread store, the potato dump and the kitchen. 2: He wants men to picket the roads. 3: He wanted a signaller in one of the sentry-boxes. 4: He wanted us all to stay inside the tents. 5. He wanted a strong WO and a man in the cookhouse. 6: He was in closest contact with the French, Russians, Yugoslavs, Serbs and Belgians. 7: We were now under military discipline and what he says goes. 8: He wanted a shorthand man to do the radio. 9: There are about 4 000 loaves of bread in the store. 10: He would be fetching between 6 000 and 9 000 parcels from the station today. 11: If the water supply failed, he wanted a water picket daily to a farm about 1 km from here, where there is a well which would supply us for about 4 days. 12: There are soup rations for 3 or 4 days. 13: Three Germans would be left in the camp; the 'Q', a *Sonderführer* and one in the kitchen. We were dumbfounded to hear it! One man asked if we were likely to stay here? He replied: "We will!" The gates would be opened when he decided it was advisable. If there is room, we will go into the barracks. We were not to fire the tents, as they may be needed when our forces arrive. He had a code with the Air Force for various needs – water, food etc. Yesterday he had put on the sign: IN DANGER. *Those are the facts.* WOs are meeting now. I will not write anything more until something really definite has come through. A RED CROSS FLAG WAS UNFURLED AND HOISTED IN THE CENTRE OF THE CAMP AT ABOUT 2.15 P.M. TODAY.

There are some ominous bangs – demolition? We have been warned that three German Officers are in the woods with spy glasses. We *must* stay in.

MONDAY 30 MARCH 1945

GOOD FRIDAY. Things are happening fast. There is tank fire going on outside. Our tanks on the west have opened fire on something, we don't know what; we are keeping down. Soup is being issued. All morning we have been waiting – waiting – waiting and now our own tanks are here. OUR TANKS ARE HERE!! Someone has just seen an Army Co-op plane land on the 'drome. THERE ARE WHITE FLAGS FLYING ALL OVER ZIEGENHAIN. We are very, very nearly FREE MEN!! Please God, let nothing go awry now!! No one has seen a Gerry in camp all day. *3.10 p.m.* I have just seen some Yank tanks and Jeeps going up the road, through the woods to the east. THANK GOD WE ARE NO LONGER PRISONERS OF WAR!!! A couple of Yank planes have been flying overhead too and they waggled their wings at us! I am still too dazed to realise what has happened, but the Yanks should be here any time now. The fellows are excited and how! Too weak to be hilarious. *Later, about 5.30 p.m.* We are still inside barbed wire, but we are no longer prisoners. The Yanks have been to our camp. Planes and tanks have been chasing about all over the place and everyone has been going mad. Too weak to jump about much. We are in a daze still and cannot realise our wonderful good fortune to be released. From now on the Yanks are tops with me!! ’

Herbert Cawood-Meaker was mentioned in despatches for the work he did in prisoner-of-war camps. He flew home with other prisoners of war. At 4.50 p.m. on Saturday, 26 May 1945 the aircraft crossed the Limpopo. At 5.50 p.m. it landed at Zwartkops outside Pretoria. He was back home on South African soil again.

Returning prisoners of war at Johannesburg Station. They were given an ecstatic reception by the people of Johannesburg. But for many it was a difficult time, adjusting themselves from the rigours of a long captivity to civilian life with their families. (Samler Gordon-Brown)

CHAPTER

71

'My Dad's back!'

Sally 'Suki' Simson and the return of Capt Philip Simson, 1945

In any other year, at any other time, the Death March would have been front-page news. It wasn't; indeed, it was never given much prominence, simply because there was so much else to write about.

The last months of the war saw a succession of victories, and they edged most other stories off the front pages. But from the beginning of 1945 little stories with headlines such as: First Square Meal Since 1942 informed the country that the men who had been taken prisoner at Sidi Rezegh, Tobruk, Gazala and hundreds of other places in the desert were coming home.

At first they came in dribs and drabs – fifty liberated by the Russians, a hundred by the British, and so on. That most of them were trudging through snow away from the advancing Allies was unknown. By April 1945 the men were coming home in large numbers. Some arriving *en masse* were met at Johannesburg Station by bands, bagpipes, crowds of radio reporters, a special lunch at the Wanderers, and of course by their families.

Few could grasp what the men had gone through, or how long it would take most of them to adjust themselves to civilian life again. They had, after all, been on their own for a long time under testing conditions.

One man who went to war in 1940 was Philip Simson. He left a wife and daughter behind, together with an extended family. Sally (he called her Suki) Simson was five when her father went off to war and eleven when he returned. This is how one little girl remembered the return of her father from the prison camps:

'It was a house full of women: my grandmother, my mother, two aunts, my one-legged grandfather and my great-grandfather. It was a big house, rather shabby, in lower Houghton. There were cottages in the garden. One aunt lived in one, another in a second, and my mother lived in her own little cottage. I stayed in the main house with Gan.

The Simson family: little Sally is in the front. With many of the men away during the war years families were matriarchal. When the men came home many difficult adjustments had to be made.

'Gan was a great gardener, and I loved gardening. I loved the flowers, the roses and the lavender. Every night I would do a special dance to get into bed: there was something terrible under it and the only way I could get into the bed was to take five steps forward and one step back and then jump on the bed. Whatever was there terrified me.

'The postcards from my father* had stopped coming a long time ago. I used to get one a week, all written around a chameleon. "The chameleon and I killed a snake," he would write, or "we both went for a drive in a tank". Something bad happened and I didn't hear from him again and the house was very quiet and very tense.

'One day I was in the sitting room when a telegram boy came up the drive. I went out onto the stoep and took the telegram he pulled out of a little pouch. I gave the telegram to my grandmother. She opened it and stood still for a minute and then she called for my mother. My mother came rushing in and read the telegram and she shouted for my aunt to come. And they were all standing there, hugging each other and crying.

'"What's happened?" I asked.

'"Your father is a prisoner of war," my Gan said. I was terribly upset. My father was a prisoner. I didn't know that they were laughing for joy because he was alive. All I really knew was that he was in a

* Mostly written from Tobruk, from which he escaped into the desert. After thirty days of privation he was captured by the Italians. He made three other attempts to escape while he was in Germany.

place called *Oflag 5A*.* My Uncle Ian and my Uncle Charles had also gone off to war. Then Uncle Charles disappeared. All we knew was that he had been injured. Then a long silence.

'One day I was sitting on the stoep playing with my budgerigar and my parakeet – they were climbing the wistaria – when I saw this man coming up the drive. He was in uniform, and he was limping badly and walking on sticks. It was Uncle Charles. I ran down to him and nearly knocked him off his feet. "Shh!" he said, and I burst into tears. "Shh, Suki; let it be a surprise for Gan." It was nearly supper-time and Gan came out on the stoep to call me in. She looked at Charles and froze. Then the tears.

'Then Ian came home. He had been taken prisoner of war in an Italian prison camp. He escaped and came back. It was wonderful while he was at home: he taught me Scottish dancing and we went for walks. Then he went back, to Italy, and he was killed there by a sniper. The house was very quiet in those days.

'Then one day, at the end of the war, we got another telegram. This time it was a really happy one: my father was in England, he was safe, and he was coming home. On the day when he was due home we drove to Pretoria to meet him. As we drove my mother was very still, very tense. She hadn't seen him for five years; and five years is a very long time to be separated from a husband. The rest of the family stayed at home.

'When we got to the airport there were barriers and we were told to stay behind them. I was hopping and fidgeting. I couldn't keep still. Then we heard the sound of a plane and there was a sort of murmur of people around us – the families of the other men on the plane. Then the plane landed, a door opened and these men in khaki stepped out. They were like skeletons, gaunt men with pale faces. They walked towards us. Then I recognised one of those men. It was my father.

'I jumped over the barrier and rushed across the tarmac, and then everyone else began running too. My father stood still. He caught me in his arms. "Hiya, Suki," was all he said. But oh, he was so thin. He and my mother sat in the back of the car, I sat in front with the driver, but I faced backwards the whole way. I just babbled. I told him that I had got A for English, that the dog had just had puppies, that the budgie was fine and that I could ride a bicycle. All the time my mother sat nervously beside him and he kept smiling at me.

'Cookie stood there with tears running down her face. My father picked her up and kissed her and said: "Cook, where's my mother?" And then everyone was there, everyone with tears in their eyes. Gan flung her arms around him, not saying anything. I don't think she could have spoken if she tried.

---

* Near Weinsberg near the Rhine and the French border. Prisoners from this camp were taken east to *Stalag VIIA* near Moosburg, north of Munich, as the Allies approached.

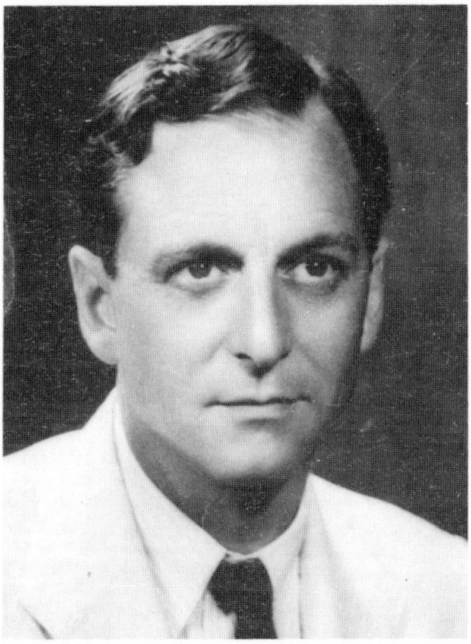

Philip Simson, father, husband, soldier and POW. When he arrived home he had been away for five years.

'I rushed past the grown ups to phone my best friend, Linda Gray. "My Dad's back!" I said. Her own father had been killed earlier in the war.

'At lunch I was able to look at my father properly. He was so thin his cheekbones stood out like steps on either side of his face. And his hands – he had lovely hands – were just skin and bone. He looked exhausted. We had overdone chicken and ice cream. Everyone was talking, but Dad was quiet. Then someone struck a chord on the piano. It sounded very loud. My father snatched up his table napkin, leapt to his feet and was halfway out through the door before he stopped. He didn't say anything. He sat down again as if nothing had happened. After lunch I took him for a walk in the garden. It was a big garden and very beautiful.

'He was very quiet. He took my hand in his and walked with me. "Look at this beautiful rose," I said. "Look at the lavender," and "The lilies are over but they'll grow again next year". He let go of my hand and felt the flowers. He kept touching them, feeling the petals.

'Gan had made a special dinner that night. By then he had huge dark circles under his eyes. And his eyes were so insecure, very blue in his thin, haunted face. After dinner he took me to bed. I did my usual five steps forward and one back and then jumped. "Why do you do that?" he asked.

'"Because there's something horrible under my bed."

'"Come," he said, "we'll face it together." And we lay on the floor and he lifted the bedspread. "See, there's nothing there."

'"It'll come back," I told him as he tucked me in.

'"I tell you what," he said. "I'll come back in five minutes and I'll check. And if you're still awake I'll come back in another five minutes. And by then you'll be asleep."

'"See you tomorrow, Dad," I said as he turned off the light.

'"See you tomorrow, Suki," he said. And I felt secure, so secure, because my dad was back home. '

• Interview 1991

CHAPTER

72

'The pandemonium of peace'

Huntley Stuart of the SABC reporting from Cape Town, VE Day

The men and the women were coming home. At the beginning of May 1945 Ouma Smuts's Gifts and Comforts Fund was informed that troops would be returned home by air at the rate of five thousand a month as well as by sea.

Dakotas carried twenty-four passengers, each man with sixty pounds of luggage; Venturas carried only thirteen. Former prisoners of war landing at Zwartkop were given cigarettes and fresh fruit by the Fund, and a telegram was sent to next of kin.

Part-time units were disbanding, plans for demobilisation were in preparation and everywhere, it seemed, there was a lightness in the air, although the war continued in both Europe and the Far East.

April was a momentous month. In the Pacific US troops landed on Okinawa; on 12 April Franklin D Roosevelt died and was succeeded by Harry Truman; the Russians occupied Vienna next day and in Italy the 6th SA Division took Monte Solo. It was virtually the South Africans' last battle. On 30 April, in his bunker in Berlin, which would soon be occupied by Russian soldiers, Adolf Hitler, the evil genius of Germany, committed suicide. On the same day the Allies opened Dachau.

Two days later the Russians occupied Berlin, and on 7 May 1945, after nearly six years of war, Field Marshal Jodl surrendered to Eisenhower. With the surrender next day by Field Marshal Keitel of the German forces in the east to Marshal Zhukov the war in Europe was over. It was 8 May 1945: Victory in Europe (VE) Day.

The celebrations were spontaneous. In grey and battered London, with spring breaking out on every tree, the crowds converged on Buckingham Palace where King George VI, Queen Elizabeth, Princess Elizabeth and Princess Margaret Rose and Winston Churchill stood smiling as the crowd cheered and roared in jubilation. The celebrations were no less spontaneous in South Africa.

In Cape Town, to a background of ships' salvoes, hooting tugs, bells, cars hooting and the cheers of a crowd which thronged the entire length of Adderley Street, Huntley Stuart of the SABC struggled to report the scene – the first broadcast of peace:

'Listen to the noise in Adderley Street. This is the noise, the voice of victory. This is the din, with the guns thrown in, of deliverance. It is the row, the racket, the rumble and the riot of relief. It is the pandemonium of peace.

'Now that you have heard the noise, let me try to describe what is going on. A warm clear sun beats down on this scene, Adderley Street, Cape Town, with buildings full of flags, flags of Britain, America, Soviet Russia, South Africa, Canada, New Zealand, Australia, India and every other nation of the Allied combine.

'There is bunting too, flying down from all the big buildings, the post office and all the big shops. There are crowds about, the Adderley Street flower people are waving their small flags and creating a din with ratchets. Even horses have feathers in their head gear and one very enterprising person has painted the flags of all nations on a large sheet. The town literally is littered with colour, the colour of all freedom-loving nations.

'Above all this, in the distance I can see old man mountain towering in his age-old solid way. There is no white mist on him today, it is a clear head, and he apparently understands as much as we do that there is freedom in the air. And now as I look up at the mountain and can see pigeons whirling and wheeling about. Even trees move in the breeze, flags flutter. Everything is agog with excitement, relief, of victory and peace.

'A few moments ago, Mr Churchill broadcast his speech to the world telling us of the final laying down of arms of an enemy. And the crowd has been reacting pretty strongly. There is excitement all over the place, high delight of the first water, people are literally delirious with joy – you can still hear the guns going off, you can still hear the people cheering. They are rushing about waving flags, the traffic has come to a standstill, there is movement everywhere indicative of freedom.

'Freedom and freedom again and then again. Brother clasps the hand of brother, sister kisses the cheek of sister and as far as I can see, occasionally a brother usurps the privilege of a sister and kisses her cheek as well. The bells are going, the sirens are going, the ratchets are going and the cheers are still going on. The salvoes are still being fired. And this mob, having listened to Mr Churchill's speech, is disintegrating and gradually dispersing.

'As a matter of fact, I can see a little dog running about, the little dog laughed to see such sport, and I wouldn't be surprised at any moment to see the other part of the nursery rhyme, to see the cow jump over the moon. But the moon is probably beaming its beams elsewhere. There is enough lunacy here without the effects of the lunar system on the Cape Town crowd today.

'It is, as I have said, the voice of victory, it is the relief, the racket, the riot and the rumble of relief. It is the pandemonium of peace.'

• SABC Archives

Epilogue

The cost of war is high. If the death of any man is worth while, then the cause for which he died should be a just one. If historians are more or less agreed that the 1914–18 war could have been avoided, they are also more or less agreed that the second could not have been avoided, that the menace of Hitler and all his fellow thugs was a pestilence that had to be tackled and destroyed.

South Africa alone lost 6 498 men.* The British Commonwealth and Empire, the USA, Russia, France and other European countries lost over fifteen million men in uniform (this figure does not include the three and a half million Chinese dead).

Russia alone lost nearly fourteen million soldiers, male and female. The British Empire and Commonwealth (in which figure South African casualties are included) lost 452 000 men. By comparison, the Allies in the 1914–18 war, including Russia, lost over five million.

In the First World War Germany and its allies lost three and a half million men; in the Second World War it lost fewer: three and a quarter million, but that was nearly half of the men under arms. Japan lost seventeen hundred thousand men.

But the numbers of civilian dead in the 1939–45 war are appalling. The bombing of Britain and Germany, the death camps, the invasions by the Germans and the Allies all caused the deaths of twenty-five and a half million civilian men, women and children between September 1939 and May 1945. Britain lost sixty thousand civilians, France three hundred and sixty thousand, Russia nearly eight million, Poland (whose combatant casualties came to 120 000), lost nearly five and a half million, and Yugoslavia thirteen hundred thousand.

---

* 4 307 were killed and died of wounds, 1 274 were accidentally killed, 381 died while prisoners of war, and 536 simply died. 5 917 were accidentally injured and 14 583 became prisoners of war.

The figure for South Africans in uniform was 334 324. The British and Commonwealth total was nearly nine million men and women. There were twelve and a half million Americans, twelve and a half million Russians, six million Japanese, and eleven million Germans.

For South Africa, untouched by bombings or invasions and free from the strict food rationing that prevailed all over Europe, the war brought one important benefit: industry.

So rapidly did the country begin production of war supplies that within a short time supplies were being exported to the Allies. South Africa made two and a half million mortar bombs; nearly four million shell cases; two million steel helmets; fourteen thousand GS waggons on three-and five-ton chassis; eleven hundred ambulances; thirty-seven hundred one-ton carriers fitted with hood bows; five hundred million .303 cartridges; over twelve million boots and five and a half million blankets.

The army was supplied with twelve tons of bacon and ham, a thousand tons of beans in tomato sauce, twenty-four hundred million cigarettes, a million gallons of beer, thirty-five thousand tons of jam, marmalade and syrup, twenty-six tons of lemon curd and two hundred thousand gallons of brandy. South African Railways, with no increase in locomotive power, moved over two and a half million tons of goods during the war, and carried a thousand million passengers. No one needed to march to Pretoria.

Epitaph

WAR

Yes, I have killed!
And I was wild with pride
And anger as they died.
High exultation filled
My heart and head like wine
With the sweet savage glory of success,
And surging thankfulness
The forfeit was their lives, not mine.

And when I soberly surveyed
The things of silent horror they became,
Dead in the sunshine, things that I had made,
No pity stirred in me, I felt no shame.
Coldly I looked at them and coldly thought
'This was the end to which their striving led.
'These were my enemies. We fought.
'I live, and they are dead.'

The conquered conquers, and brings low
The victor with him. We who marched and bled
To free the world from tyranny and woe
Have triumphed. But our hands are red. (Norman Clothier)

Through Kenya, the NFD, through Abyssinia, Somalia, the Western Desert and Italy, through rain and sand and flies, through heat and snow; in dugouts and tents, a young corporal with the 1st Transvaal Scottish (later a sergeant-major in the Royal Natal Carbineers), used his spare time to write poetry.

And there was lots of spare time for Norman Clothier, even when he was on duty. He composed the poems in his head when (for instance) he was on guard duty and later put them down on paper and revised them.

Some of his poems were bound in a book, published in the Union in 1943. It was an instant success, being snapped up by a public anxious to identify with their men Up North. *Libyan Winter* went into three wartime editions and, latterly, a fourth.

Norman Clothier, 1943

Bibliography

As We Were – South Africa 1939–1941, by Margot Bryant. Keartland Publishers. Johannesburg, 1974.

Avenge Tobruk, by Brig E P Hartshorn. Purnell & Sons. Cape Town and Johannesburg, 1960.

Caged Lion, The, by William Manchester. Sphere Books Ltd. Cardinal London, 1989.

Captivity Captive, by James B Chutter. Jonathan Cape. London, 1954.

Crisis in the Desert, by J A I Agar, Hamilton and L C F Turner. Oxford University Press. Cape Town, 1952.

Dancing in the Skies, by Carel Birkby, Howard Timmins. Cape Town, 1982.

Dictionary of South Africa: Biography. Editor in Chief: W J de Kock, Johannesburg, 1968.

Eagles Victorious – The SAAF in Italy and the Mediterranean, 1943/45.

East African and Abyssinian Campaigns, The, Vol 1 – South African Forces – World War II by Neil Orpen. Purnell & Sons. Cape Town, 1968.

End of the Beginning, The, compiled by Charles Eade. Cassel & Co. London, 1943.

Fighting Forces of Rhodesia, No 4 by H C P Anderson. Salisbury, 1977.

For Volk and Führer, by Hans Strydom, Jonathan Ball, Johannesburg, 1984.

General Dan Pienaar: His Life and His Battles, by Eric Rosenthal, Cape Town, 1943.

Greater South Africa – Plans for A Better World. The Speeches: General The Right Honourable J C Smuts, published by The Truth Legion. Johannesburg, 1940.

Gunners by 'Tort'. The Southern Rhodesian Artillery Association. Salisbury, 1947.

In The Bag, by Peter Ogilvie & Newman Robinson. Macmillan, South Africa. Johannesburg, 1975.

Lady In White, The, by Perla Siedle Gibson, Purnell & Sons. Cape Town.

My Herre en Strewe, by Gen Manie Maritz, Johannesburg, 1939.

OB: Traitors or Patriots, by George Cloete-Visser, Macmillan, Johannesburg, 1976.

One Man's War, by James Ambrose Brown, Howard Timmins. Cape Town, 1980.

Pienaar of Alamein, The, by A M Pollo, Union Bureau of Information. Cape Town, 1943.

Royal Air Force 1939–1941. Vol II: *The Flight Avails,* by Denis Richards and Hilary St G Saunders. H M Stationery Office. London, 1954.

Sailor-Women, Sea-Women, Swans, by Margaret P M Laver and others. Swans History Publication Fund, 1982, limited edition.

Salute the Sappers, by Neil Orpen with H J Martin, Sappers Association. Johannesburg, 1981.

Surgeon's Story, by Jack Penn. Private papers.

Sidi Rezegh and Its Call, by Field Marshal J C Smuts, Government Printer. Pretoria, 1942.

Sidi Rezegh Battles 1941, The, by J A I Agar, Hamilton & L C F Turner, Oxford University Press. Cape Town, 1957.

South Africa at War, Vol VII of South African Forces – WW II by H J Martin & Neil Orpen, Purnell. Johannesburg, 1979.

South African WAAF, by K Jameson & D Ashburner, Shuter & Shooter. Pietermaritzburg, 1948.

Springbok Record, SA Legion, British Empire Service League, compiled and edited by Harry Klein. Johannesburg, 1946.

Springbok Victory, by Carel Birkby, Libertas Publications. Johannesburg, 1941.

Standard Encyclopedia – Southern Africa, Vol II, Nason Ltd. Cape Town, 1975.

Strangers in our Midst, by Lucy Bean, Howard Timmins. Cape Town, 1970.

Strategy, The, by An Offensive Against Germany, 1939–1945, Vol I Preparation by Sir Charles Webster and Noble Frankland. H M Stationery Office. London, 1961.

Their Paths Crossed Mine, by Hans van Rensburg, CNA Ltd. Johannesburg, 1956.

Uncle George, The Boer Boyhood, Letters and Battles of Lieutenant-General George Edwin Brink by Carel Birkby, Jonathan Ball. Johannesburg, 1987.

Valley of the Mists, by Harry Klein, Howard Timmins Cape Town, 1972.

Vanguard of Victory, by Conrad Norton and Uys Krige, Bureau of Information. Pretoria, 1941.

Way Out, The, by Uys Krige, Unie-Volkspers Beperk. Cape Town, 1946.

With the 6th Division, by W L Fielding, Shuter & Shooter. Pietermaritzburg, 1946.

Womanhood at War – The Story of the SAWAS, by Gwen Hewitt, Gwen Hewitt, Johannesburg.

Women in Uniform, Pamson Low, Marston and Co Ltd. London, 1946.

World War II, The Stars, by John Pitts, ed Peter Joyce, Struik. Cape Town, 1989.

Index